We Do Not Have Borders

NEW AFRICAN HISTORIES

SERIES EDITORS: JEAN ALLMAN, ALLEN ISAACMAN,
AND DEREK R. PETERSON

*Books in this series are published with support
from the Ohio University Center for International Studies.*

David William Cohen and E. S. Atieno Odhiambo, *The Risks of Knowledge*

Belinda Bozzoli, *Theatres of Struggle and the End of Apartheid*

Gary Kynoch, *We Are Fighting the World*

Stephanie Newell, *The Forger's Tale*

Jacob A. Tropp, *Natures of Colonial Change*

Jan Bender Shetler, *Imagining Serengeti*

Cheikh Anta Babou, *Fighting the Greater Jihad*

Marc Epprecht, *Heterosexual Africa?*

Marissa J. Moorman, *Intonations*

Karen E. Flint, *Healing Traditions*

Derek R. Peterson and Giacomo Macola, editors, *Recasting the Past*

Moses E. Ochonu, *Colonial Meltdown*

Emily S. Burrill, Richard L. Roberts, and Elizabeth Thornberry, editors, *Domestic Violence and the Law in Colonial and Postcolonial Africa*

Daniel R. Magaziner, *The Law and the Prophets*

Emily Lynn Osborn, *Our New Husbands Are Here*

Robert Trent Vinson, *The Americans Are Coming!*

James R. Brennan, *Taifa*

Benjamin N. Lawrance and Richard L. Roberts, editors, *Trafficking in Slavery's Wake*

David M. Gordon, *Invisible Agents*

Allen F. Isaacman and Barbara S. Isaacman, *Dams, Displacement, and the Delusion of Development*

Stephanie Newell, *The Power to Name*

Gibril R. Cole, *The Krio of West Africa*

Matthew M. Heaton, *Black Skin, White Coats*

Meredith Terretta, *Nation of Outlaws, State of Violence*

Paolo Israel, *In Step with the Times*

Michelle R. Moyd, *Violent Intermediaries*

Abosede A. George, *Making Modern Girls*

Alicia C. Decker, *In Idi Amin's Shadow*

Rachel Jean-Baptiste, *Conjugal Rights*

Shobana Shankar, *Who Shall Enter Paradise?*

Emily S. Burrill, *States of Marriage*

Todd Cleveland, *Diamonds in the Rough*

Carina E. Ray, *Crossing the Color Line*

Sarah Van Beurden, *Authentically African*

Giacomo Macola, *The Gun in Central Africa*

Lynn Schler, *Nation on Board*

Julie MacArthur, *Cartography and the Political Imagination*

Abou B. Bamba, *African Miracle, African Mirage*

Daniel Magaziner, *The Art of Life in South Africa*

Paul Ocobock, *An Uncertain Age*

Keren Weitzberg, *We Do Not Have Borders*

We Do Not Have Borders

Greater Somalia and the Predicaments of Belonging in Kenya

Keren Weitzberg

OHIO UNIVERSITY PRESS ✆ ATHENS

Ohio University Press, Athens, Ohio 45701
ohioswallow.com
© 2017 by Ohio University Press
All rights reserved

To obtain permission to quote, reprint, or otherwise reproduce or
distribute material from Ohio University Press publications, please contact our
rights and permissions department at
(740) 593-1154 or (740) 593-4536 (fax).

Sections of this book have appeared in the *Journal of African History*, the *Journal
of Northeast African Studies*, and the book *Kenya after Fifty:
Reconfiguring Historical, Political, and Policy Milestones*.

All the maps in this book were made by Jacob Riley.

Printed in the United States of America
Ohio University Press books are printed on acid-free paper.♾ ™

27 25 24 23 22 21 20 19 18 17   5 4 3 2 1

Library of Congress Cataloging-in-Publication Data

Names: Weitzberg, Keren, author.
Title: We do not have borders : greater Somalia and the predicaments of
  belonging in Kenya / Keren Weitzberg.
Other titles: New African histories series.
Description: Athens : Ohio University Press, 2017. | Series: New African
  histories | Includes bibliographical references and index.
Identifiers: LCCN 2017018265 | ISBN 9780821422588 (hc : alk. paper) | ISBN
  9780821422595 (pb : alk. paper) | ISBN 9780821445952 (pdf)
Subjects: LCSH: Somali diaspora. | Somalis—Kenya. | Nationalism—Kenya. |
  Kenya–Ethnic relations—History.
Classification: LCC DT433.545.S75 W45 2017 | DDC 305.8935406762—dc23
LC record available at https://lccn.loc.gov/2017018265

Contents

Maps

Preface and Acknowledgments

THIS WORK DRAWS UPON MULTIPLE archives. Between 2008 and 2014, I carried out research at the British National Archives (TNA) in London, the Kenya National Archives (KNA) in Nairobi, and the Hoover Institution at Stanford. From all of these places, I collected a wide variety of colonial and postcolonial government documents. In addition, I have made use of non-archival written records, such as newspaper articles, traveler accounts, settler memoirs, and NGO reports. Between September 2010 and September 2011—shortly before the Kenyan invasion of Somalia—I also conducted over one hundred formal interviews in linguistically and culturally diverse sites in the Central and Rift Valley regions of Kenya and the Somalia/Kenya borderlands.

The staff at the Kenya National Archives greatly facilitated my research. Special thanks are due to Richard Ambani, who has generously supported many researchers and scholars over his years working at the KNA. My fieldwork would have been impossible without the help of multiple research assistants in different locations and at different stages of the project. Hassan Kochore and Hassan Ibrahim Hassan aided me during the initial, exploratory stages. Abdi Billow Ibrahim and Ibrahim Abdikarim were indispensable during the main phase of my fieldwork. Together, we conducted interviews during which we collected poetry, genealogies, oral "traditions," and life histories in Swahili, English, Somali, and occasionally Borana. Many of the poems recounted to me had not previously been put down in writing, to the best of my knowledge. I also had many informal conversations with Kenyan and Somali acquaintances and friends. These conversations informed my thinking in significant ways and left silent traces on my analyses that are difficult to cite or acknowledge directly.

I am deeply indebted to the many people who generously shared aspects of their lives with me, including very painful memories of warfare and state repression. I hope that I have done justice to their history. I also owe a debt of gratitude to the many people in Kenya who extended their hospitality to me and provided me with assistance during my research. They are too numerous to name, but special thanks are due to Hassan Ibrahim Hassan, Fatuma Ibrahim Ali, Ahmed Maalin Abdalle, Abdi Ahmed Ali, Amina Kinsi, Abdi Billow Ibrahim, and Mohamed Ibrahim.

While I interviewed a diverse sample of people, it goes without saying that I cannot tell all possible stories. John Jackson has suggested that rather than thinking in terms of mastery over the "other," of a complete archive, or of progressively accumulating knowledge, scholars should think in terms of "thin descriptions"—of multiple, sometimes incommensurable, narratives.[1] Not all of the people I interviewed would agree with my analyses. Nor, for that matter, did Kenyans always agree on a single interpretation of historical events. Some of my interlocutors would reflect upon the past differently today than at the time of our interviews. "Memories" were never unmediated recollections, and present concerns figured heavily in people's explanations of the past. While conducting interviews, I endeavored to collect a wide diversity of narratives and to remain attentive to marginal and heterodox voices. However, structures of power often constrained who could speak and be spoken to. One cannot smooth over the power dynamics involved in any kind of fieldwork. My race, comparative privilege, blind spots, ideological concerns, cultural misunderstandings, and missteps no doubt shaped the fieldwork experience in ways that were often invisible to me. My work is not a definitive or an objective version of Kenyan Somali history, nor is it a historical or ethnographic project intended to exhaust our understanding of "Somali society." However, my hope is that it will serve as a contribution to the field.

Many people too numerous to name helped me navigate and think through the complexities of the research and writing process. I am deeply thankful to Sean Hanretta, Richard Roberts, and Timothy Parsons for their mentorship. During my time at Stanford University, Siphiwe Ndlovu, Erin Pettigrew, Michelle Bourbonniere, and Donni Wang, among others, provided me with invaluable advice and read through early drafts of my manuscript. At the University of Pennsylvania, I benefited from help and intellectual inspiration provided by Lee Cassanelli, Cheikh Babou, Fred Dickinson, Tsitsi Jaji, Mauro Guillén, Amel Mili, Ali B. Ali-Dinar, Rasul Miller, and Jeremy Aaron Dell, among others. Writing workshops with

Alden Young, Amber Reed, Grace Sanders, Oliver Rollins, Clemmie L. Harris, and Dominick Rolle helped me to improve early drafts of my work. My undergraduate and graduate students at Stanford and Penn also deserve special thanks for their wonderful intellectual engagement. In addition, I am indebted to Abdul Adan, Wendell Hassan Marsh, Hassan Kochore, Natasha Shivji, Salah Abdi Sheikh, Mohamed Abdullahi, and Amil Shivji for many productive and invaluable conversations. Attending conferences and workshops with Tabea Scharrer, Neil Carrier, Mark Bradbury, Egle Cesnulyte, Alex Otieno, and Francesca Declich also shaped my thinking.

Writing this book has proved, in many ways, to be a collective project. Abdi Billow Ibrahim, Terje Østebø, Abdul Adan, Abdullahi Abdinoor, Abdullahi A. Shongolo, and Ali Jimale Ahmed all helped in some capacity with issues relating to orthography and translations. I owe an immense debt of gratitude to Ahmed Ismail Yusuf for his assistance with translating and transcribing the poems in chapters 3, 4, and 5. Jacob Riley produced all of the maps in the book. Richard Reid and Keith Breckenridge, two of the editors of the *Journal of African History*; James De Lorenzi and Lee Cassanelli, editors of the *Journal of Northeast African Studies*; and Michael Mwenda Kithinji, Mickie Mwanzia Korster, and Jerono P. Rotich, editors of the volume *Kenya after Fifty*, helped me refine many ideas contained in several of the chapters. In addition, I am grateful to the editorial team at Ohio University Press, including Derek Peterson, Jean Allman, Allen Isaacman, and Gillian Berchowitz, and the two anonymous readers of my manuscript. Special thanks also go to Cawo M. Abdi, Scott Reese, Pete Tridish, and Susan Alice Elizabeth Brown for providing feedback on drafts of my manuscript.

Over the course of my training, I have benefited from excellent Swahili and Somali teachers, including Regina Fupi, Sangai Mohochi, Jamal Gelle, Abdifatah Shafat Diis, Deo Ngonyani, and Abdi Ahmed Ali. In addition, my training, research, and completion of this text were generously supported by fellowships and financial support from Stanford University (including grants from the Center for African Studies, the Department of History, the Abbasi Program in Islamic Studies, and the School of Humanities and Sciences); the US Department of Education; the Andrew W. Mellon Foundation; and the Joseph H. Lauder Institute for Management and International Studies at the University of Pennsylvania.

Finally, thank you to Brenda, Moshe, and Oran Weitzberg for all their support over the many years leading up to the publication of this book. My family history also played an important role in drawing me to this topic. As a Jewish Israeli American and the granddaughter of four Holocaust survivors, I grew up with an awareness of the difficulties faced by minorities stretched across multiple countries, an understanding of the ease with which indigenous people can be rendered into foreigners, and a cognizance of the dangers of exclusionary nationalism and settler colonialism. While the experiences of Somalis in Kenya differ in many respects from those of European Jews or Palestinians, their histories refract shared twentieth- and twenty-first-century predicaments. With this in mind, I hope my book can contribute to broader conversations about the interrelationship between border crossing, reactionary nativism, and hatred of the internal stranger. While many people deserve credit for helping me to develop my ideas, any errors or omissions in this text are my fault alone.

Notes on Language

Kenya is an archetype of linguistic diversity, which to some extent reflects the historical absence of a concerted state project aimed at language standardization. It is not uncommon for people who identify as both Kenyan and Somali to speak at least three languages to varying degrees of fluency (including but not limited to Somali, Swahili, English, Borana—an Oromo dialect, Arabic, Kikuyu, and Luo). Many Somali speakers in Kenya were educated in Swahili and English (or, in the case of Qur'anic schools, Arabic). Having used Somali primarily as a spoken language, people will sometimes accept alternate or multiple spellings of Somali words and names. Moreover, there are multiple dialects of Somali, which itself can be written in more than one script. In order to facilitate reading and simplify this linguistic and orthographic complexity, orally recited poems in this book have been transcribed using the Somali Latin alphabet standardized by the Somali government in the 1970s. In addition, poems have been converted into the most commonly known dialects of Somali (and, in one case, Oromo), with the exception of a few words specific to northern Kenyan vernaculars. Since language is a political matter, opting to use the "standard" dialects of Somali and Oromo was not a neutral decision. Nor was determining the "correct" spelling and translation of certain words. I am indebted to the many people who brought their skills and expertise to bear on the transcriptions and translations. Special thanks go to Ahmed Ismail Yusuf for his help with the Somali poetry. I am resigned to the fact that all translations are ultimately mistranslations.

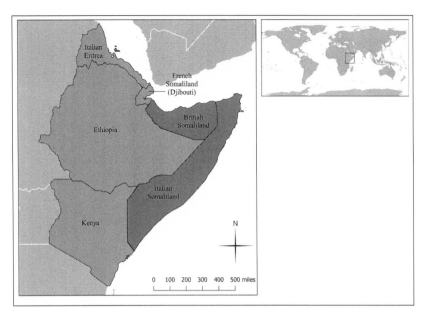

Map 1.1. Colonial Northeast Africa. (*Note:* All the maps in this book were made by Jacob Riley. Boundary lines and locations are approximate.)

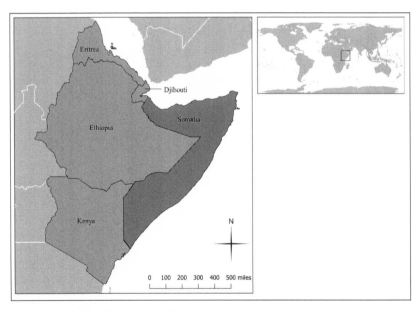

Map 1.2. Postcolonial Northeast Africa.

Introduction
"We Don't Unpack"

Wherever the camel goes, that is Somalia.

—Proverb from the era of Somali independence (late 1950s and early 1960s)[1]

THERE IS A POPULAR STORY IN WAJIR, a county in northern Kenya that was once part of the British colonial administrative region known as the Northern Frontier District (NFD) (see map 2.1).[2] It describes the arrival of the first European to the area. According to this story, the people living in Wajir were very welcoming toward their new guest. When the European visitor asked for accommodations for the night, they provided him with an animal hide on which to sleep. Much to their dismay, his hosts awoke the next morning to find that he had sliced the animal skin into a long rope, which he had used to encircle an area that he claimed as his territory.[3]

This evocative anecdote (which borrows tropes from oral narratives circulating in other parts of the Horn of Africa) depicts an item of hospitality transmuted overnight into a symbol of state sovereignty and land tenure.[4] As the story suggests, the legacy of colonial boundaries is the locus of much contention among the people of northern Kenya. In the late nineteenth century, the Ethiopian, British, and Italian governments divided Northeast Africa into five different territories: British Somaliland, Italian Somaliland, French Somaliland (Djibouti), Ethiopia, and Kenya. Over the subsequent decades, the Kenyan colonial officials attempted to further confine the populations of the NFD in an effort to impose their vision of order on the region. Fatima Jellow—a prominent resident of Wajir and wife of the NFD's first senator—explained that when her father, a member of the Somali Degodia lineage, refused to move to the "homeland" designated for his clan, he was jailed by British colonial authorities.[5] At various points over the last century, nomadic populations and their leaders have attempted to circumvent, redraw, or rethink the colonial borders that hindered their mobility and divided them from their kin and pasture. After World War II, Pan-Somali nationalist leaders advocated for unifying Somalis across Northeast Africa into a single nation-state. By the early 1960s, most of the nomadic inhabitants of Kenya's borderlands (including many people who were not normally considered "Somali") rallied around the idea of a Greater Somalia, which they hoped would dismantle the territorial borders that crisscrossed the arid north.

Alongside the largely nomadic population of the NFD, Kenya was also home to Somali-identifying people who had immigrated to the colony from coastal cities such as Berbera (in modern-day Somalia) and Aden (in modern-day Yemen) (see map 1.1).[6] Like their nomadic kin, they shared a history of skirting colonial boundaries. Mustafa (Mohamed) Osman Hirsi, a third-generation Kenyan, described his community as a people who were "not about boundaries," whose "umbilical cord was never cut." His grandfather, an *askari* (soldier) in the Somaliland Camel Corps, had come to Kenya after serving in the colonial military. Like many Somali veterans, he identified as a member of the Isaaq clan.[7] European settlers and British officials had recruited Isaaq men from cities and towns along the Gulf of Aden to serve as soldiers, porters, guides, and translators in East Africa. Under colonial rule, they had enjoyed many of the same privileges as South Asians living in Kenya, who had greater political rights and freedom of mobility than the vast majority of African subjects. Although born in Kenya, Hirsi had not lost touch with the land of his grandfather's birth. Despite being dispersed throughout East Africa and other parts of the former British Empire, members of the Isaaq diaspora continued to maintain connections to Somaliland. Upon arriving in a new country, Hirsi explained, "we don't unpack."[8]

Whether describing themselves as a people "without borders" or lamenting the colonial frontiers that divided them from their kin and grazing land, many of the people I spoke to invoked the negative effects of boundaries on their lives. This pervasive theme ran across dozens of interviews I conducted with Kenyan Somalis of diverse class, geographic, and clan backgrounds in 2010 and 2011.[9] Their shared frustration with borders provides a perfect lens through which to observe how the modern world is not, in fact, becoming increasingly "borderless" for many people.[10] Their experiences also show that there are ways of imagining borderlessness that are distinct from neoliberal rationality, which envisions people as market actors operating in a world in which capital and goods flow freely across national boundaries. As their histories indicate, narratives of transnationalism must account for both integration and disconnection, as well as reckon with ways of life and forms of belonging that predate the nation-state. Territorial borders are neither disappearing nor remaining intact; rather, they continue to be fought over, reimagined, and reconfigured.

Understanding this fraught relationship with borders is also key to addressing one of the central questions posed in this book: How did Somalis come to be thought of as only questionably indigenous to Kenya? Unlike studies that have looked at the Somali refugee community and their struggles as stateless people in Kenya, this work concentrates on a minority group whom many consider to be not fully "native" to a country where they have lived for generations.[11] Somali-identifying people dwelled in the area known today as Kenya long before it became a protectorate in the late nineteenth century. Nevertheless, they face widespread perceptions that they do not belong within the country. For many decades, scholars blamed their predicaments on the arbitrary or artificial nature of colonial boundaries.[12] Now frequently invoked by journalists and social scientists to explain virtually any ethnic conflict on the continent, this argument has become almost cliché. While it is certainly true that imperial powers imposed borders in the late nineteenth century with little regard for the nomadic people of the Horn of Africa, the concept of arbitrary borders does little to help us understand how ethnic territorialism came to be thought of as "natural" in the first place.[13]

The idea that groups naturally belong to homelands to which they are "native" became an increasingly dominant political logic as countries the world over transitioned from colonialism to independence. Mahmood Mamdani has persuasively argued that the colonial state constructed the distinction between native and non-native, politicized indigenousness, and reinforced these divides through spatial segregation and bifurcated legal codes. This had ongoing ramifications in the postcolonial era, when the state redefined citizenship as a right of natives, rather than of non-natives and settlers.[14] Yet Mamdani's work (and much of the academic scholarship that followed in its wake) has been limited by the assumption that the colonial state imposed these categories from above and that African subjects readily internalized them.[15] Instead, this book argues that older forms of cosmopolitanism, diaspora, and nomadic life came to coexist and compete with the modern territorial state.

The predicaments faced by generations of Somalis in Kenya (and their lack of a definitive status as an "indigenous" ethnic group) stand as an important challenge to the nativist, nationalist, and area studies frameworks that have long dominated the field of African studies. As Mamdani, Frederick

Cooper, and Jemima Pierre have pointed out, Africanist scholars have tended to focus on the construction of national and subnational identities at the expense of regional and extraterritorial forms of social and political affiliation.[16] The tendency to approach the continent in particularist terms has obscured the ways in which Africa has been historically integrated into the wider world. Historians have also marginalized the experiences of groups who did not fit into conventional nationalist and nativist histories, including those who actively benefited from the colonial racial order, supported rival nationalist, separatist, or irredentist movements, or identified as non-African or multiracial.[17] This has had the effect of reifying racialized boundaries, including the distinction between the "African" and the "Arab" worlds. For many of these reasons, historians of Kenya have, until recently, neglected the history of the Kenyan Somali population.[18]

Questioning methodological nationalism does not necessitate a wholesale rejection of the nation-state. Nor does recognizing the limitations of area studies entail a decentering of "Africa."[19] Such approaches do, however, call for a greater awareness of the importance of regional and global forms of solidarity in Africa, which went beyond the policed boundaries of empire and nation-state. Prior to European rule, Somali and other Cushitic speakers (as well as many people throughout the region) identified as members of Islamic, nomadic, and lineage communities that spanned Northeast Africa and Arabia.[20] The rich cultural and material residue left by centuries of nomadic travel, spiritual interaction, and trade enabled Somalis and other related groups in Kenya to participate in collective lives that stretched across colonial borders and to survive periods of economic downturn and ecological degradation.[21] In addition, collective histories and narratives about a past before the advent of immigration controls, border checks, and territorial boundaries have become fertile ground and rich symbolic terrain for envisioning new futures. Kenyan Somali political thinkers have creatively rethought citizenship by engaging both with models derived from Europe and with ideas of community that evolved out of the diverse worlds of Northeast Africa and the Western Indian Ocean. Since the early colonial period, people in the region have challenged dominant definitions of indigenousness and imagined supraterritorial alternatives to the Kenyan state. In the early 1960s, many Kenyan Somalis aligned around a rival form of pan-nationalism, which undermined the hegemony and exclusivity of the Kenyan nation-state. Today, they participate in transnational networks that do not always adhere to the demographic, territorial, and secular logics of the state.

These supraterritorial, pan-national, and transnational affiliations cast doubt on the notion that ethnicity is the overriding political logic in many parts of Africa, thus challenging the ethnic paradigm that has long dominated

Kenyan scholarship.[22] In the 1980s, Africanist scholars such as John Iliffe, Leroy Vail, and Terence Ranger argued that ethnic identities were neither timeless nor primordial, but rather inventions constructed by missionaries, colonial officials, and African elites.[23] In the 1990s, Kenyan historians such as John Lonsdale, Thomas Spear, and Richard Waller took the study of ethnogenesis in more nuanced directions by revealing the limits of colonial invention, the importance of precolonial institutions, and the internal moral debates around which ethnic communities constituted themselves.[24] More recently, East Africanists such as Laura Fair, Gabrielle Lynch, and Myles -Osborne have expanded our understanding of the gendered, generational, and class-ridden processes that led to ethnic invention.[25] While this body of literature has greatly advanced our understanding of ethnic formation (and provided an important corrective to the racist essentialism of colonial-era ethnography), it has also occluded other kinds of political imagination.[26] Moreover, while ethnicity has taken on political primacy of late, it is important to avoid the teleology that sees such an outcome as inevitable.

Rather than a study of a "people," this book analyzes Somaliness as a category and mode of thought, which has changed across time and place. At the risk of overemphasizing the importance of group belonging among Africans, such an approach provides an alternative to the scholarly focus on ethnonationalism. Examining how Kenyan Somalis imagined borderlessness from a position of marginality within the nation-state, *We Do Not Have Borders* offers new inroads into debates over African sovereignty, the "failed state," the "resurgence" of religion, and the meanings of being African. Drawing upon archival research and oral histories, it also analyzes how Somali and northern Kenyan political thinkers developed an oppositional politics that, at times, troubled the territorial, demographic, and secular politics of the state.

"SOMALINESS" AND ITS CHANGING MEANINGS

It is impossible to write about the history of Kenyan Somali people for an international audience without first addressing the place that Somalis occupy in the Western popular imagination. In the eyes of many analysts, Northeast Africa has come to embody many of the anxieties of the post–Cold War era. Since the early 1990s, the popular press has often treated Somalia as the emblematic failed state, and the Somali people have become associated with warlordism, piracy, and terrorism. Many commentators argue that these problems are now "spilling" into Kenya. After the Kenyan government under the regime of Mwai Kibaki invaded Somalia in 2011, al-Shabaab (a militant group that the United States designated a terrorist organization in 2008) launched a number of devastating attacks on civilian targets in Kenya. While the international community has rightly condemned al-Shabaab's brutal acts, many journalists, security analysts, and media pundits have sensationalized them, transforming tragedy into spectacle. Often these accounts reflect a fear not of violence per se, but of violence conducted by nonstate actors who operate outside the boundaries of the nation-state and the international norms of secularism.[27] At the same time, these popular media narratives mask the violence committed by other actors in the ongoing war in southern Somalia.

Ultimately, concepts such as warlordism, piracy, and terrorism provide a poor lens through which to analyze such complex phenomena.[28] As will be explained in later chapters, these paradigms tend to abstract events from their complex regional and transnational causes and reinforce the myopic ideological viewpoints of US policy makers who have drawn dubious connections between "failed" states and global security threats. Many of the popular ideas surrounding terrorism derive from a policy mind-set that consistently advocates military intervention over diplomacy.[29] Moreover, such concepts buttress racist tropes and popular prejudices about Africans and Muslims. These stereotypes affect Kenyan Somalis, even though few are directly involved in al-Shabaab's violent activities or profit from the hijacking of ships. They also serve, as Achille Mbembe argues, to define Africa in terms of "lack"—lack of order, lack of peace, and lack of governance.[30] In addition, according to Paul Zeleza, there is a tendency within the field of African studies to treat the continent as a whole as a "development problem."[31]

While Somali-identifying people in the region have built forms of community that circumvent state borders and challenge conventional notions of sovereignty, they should not be understood as an inherent threat to national and international security. Scholars on the right (such as Samuel Huntington) have tended to pathologize certain groups of people who operate outside the supposedly stabilizing forces of empire and nationalism.[32] Many on the left, however, have simply overlooked types of regional, continental, and global interaction that decenter the importance of Western phenomena, thus reducing what is "African" to mere "local color."[33] Both tendencies reflect ingrained ways of thinking that can be traced to the colonial era. The colonial state, as Talal Asad suggests, played a significant role in defining who and what was "local" and "universal" and classifying those who strayed from either norm as threatening and out of place.[34] Many of the transnational networks that emerged in the wake of the Somali civil war, which broke out in the early 1990s, can be understood as contemporary permutations of forms of organization that have much deeper roots in the region.[35] Despite their criminalization, they are not unusual when considered within a longer historical perspective.

Two other dominant concepts have shaped scholarship and journalism about the Horn of Africa. Since at least the 1940s, Somali nationalists have projected the idea that Somalis throughout the region were part of a homogeneous and ancient nation. For decades, Somalia was considered an exceptional case on a continent otherwise riddled by "tribal" attachments.[36] Revisionist scholars like Ali Jimale Ahmed have questioned the historicity of these narratives: "We cannot really demonstrate that all Somalis saw themselves as *one* people . . . before colonialism."[37] The outbreak of the Somali civil war in the early 1990s, on the other hand, gave credence to the idea that "clan" was paramount to Somali society. This was a notion popularized by the late pioneer of Somali studies, Ioan M. Lewis.[38] According to standard anthropological models, Somali society consists "of six patrilineal clan-families formed by the descendants of mythical Arabic ancestors who arrived in Somali twenty-five to thirty generations ago"; and each clan-family, in turn, encompasses "a set of patrilineally related clans, subclans, sub-subclans, and lineages."[39] Lidwien Kapteijns and Abdi Samatar argue that these anthropological concepts were implicated in the colonial construction of clannism, which became an influential epistemological category in the post–World War II era.[40]

While seemingly dissimilar, both frameworks are part of a common discursive field. Treating "clan" and "nation" as pre-political categories that preceded the imposition of the colonial state naturalizes an ethnoterritorial paradigm.[41] Clan affiliations have long been an important feature of Somali life, and many nomadic livestock-herding groups in the precolonial era organized themselves around kinship idioms. However, "clan" took on a profoundly new meaning in the twentieth century.[42] Moreover, Somali speakers have also lived in city-states and agriculturally based confederations, as well as Islamic settlements (typically known as *jama'a* or *zawiya*), where other forms of collective identification frequently took precedence.[43] "Somaliness" has also meant different things at different times, and its precolonial manifestations should not be seen as an inevitable precursor to the modern nation-state. Recent innovative research by scholars such as Abdi Kusow, for example, suggests that certain Somali clan names predated the usage of "Somali" as an overarching affiliation.[44] By the nineteenth century, many diverse populations in modern-day Yemen, Ethiopia, Djibouti, Kenya, and Somalia had come to see themselves as Somali—an identification that was often associated with being a pastoralist, a Muslim, and identifying with a clan or lineage that could trace its descent to a common ancestor (such as the eponymous Arab patriarch Samaale).[45]

This book focuses on the histories of two intertwined populations: nomadic Somali pastoralists, who have historically lived in northern Kenya on the borderlands abutting Ethiopia and Somalia; and the Somali diaspora community who came to the colony from British Somaliland, Aden, and Kismayo. (On the whole, it is less focused on the lives of more recent refugees who fled to Kenya to escape the violence and instability in neighboring Somalia beginning in the 1980s). Their histories cut across ethnic, national, racial, and continental borders. By the late nineteenth century, Somali immigrants from Berbera, Aden, and other coastal cities were in many respects already "globalized." This complicates conventional understandings of the Somali diaspora as being a product of the recent Somali civil war. Traveling through the circuits of informal and formal empire, Somali soldiers, seamen, traders, and porters settled in various parts of the British Empire, including Kenya. Most identified as members of the Isaaq or Harti clans.[46] Colonial officials in Kenya considered this small, privileged class to be legal immigrants to the colony and often referred to them as the "alien Somali." At the same time, Somali nomads living hundreds of miles farther south were making their way into what is now northern Kenya. They sought to escape the expanding Ethiopian Empire, gain access to new grazing land, and seize control over the expanding caravan trade. In some cases, newcomers assimilated with local residents whom they viewed as fellow Somali kin. In other cases, Somali nomadic groups enslaved or absorbed locals into subordinate relationships, or expelled those who resisted their encroachment. When imperial powers divided these nomadic populations between different territories in the late nineteenth century, many Somalis — including those who identified as members of the Ogaden, Garre, Ajuran, and Degodia lineages — found themselves living in Kenya.[47]

The term "Kenyan Somali" is commonly used to refer to these "indigenous" Somali populations. It is, however, an imperfect label. Qualifying Somalis as Kenyan (a convention rarely applied to other transnational ethnic groups in the country) has led some people to reject the moniker as discriminatory.[48] Critical theorists of US race relations have argued that dual and hyphenated identities can serve to normalize whiteness.[49] Though not an entirely analogous situation, some argue that marking Somalis as Kenyan marginalizes them from the imagined idea of the nation. Moreover, the term elides the fact that the line between an "authentic" Kenyan citizen of Somali descent and a Somali refugee or "alien" has always been blurry and contested. It is precisely this ambiguity and confusion that makes this case study so productive for examining questions of transnational belonging. In the face of long-term and successive patterns of dwelling, assimilation, conflict, and migration, the very concept of indigeneity becomes difficult to sustain.[50] While the book's narrative arc is intended to show the long-standing roots of Somalis in the country, one of its major goals is to reveal indigeneity itself as a categorical problem.[51]

Transnational conditions may arise when people cross borders or when borders cross people. A useful analogy for the Somali experience in Kenya can be found in the Mexican-American borderlands. Debates in the United

States over illegal immigration and citizenship frequently obscure the fact that "Latina/o" networks, in many cases, long predated the advent of the US/Mexican frontier.[52] Comparisons can also be drawn with the Kurdish community, many of whom feel themselves to be a nation divided between four countries.[53] In addition, one can draw parallels between Somali citizens of Kenya, who are often deeply connected to Somalia and who have been joined by more recent refugees, and the Jewish and African diasporas. Descendants of African slaves forcefully relocated to the Americas today interact socially and politically with members of the postcolonial African diaspora, who settled in the US and other countries more recently. Relations between both populations are sometimes fraught, but they share in a collective imaginary as "Africans." Many Jews in the United States and Europe see Israel as a kind of secondary homeland. Like Somalis in the "diaspora," they participate in a nationalist project from outside its borders.[54]

In different ways, both Somali pastoralists and urbanites in Kenya have struggled with the implications of living lives stretched across colonial and now national boundaries. Though often treated as aberrant, the Kenyan Somali condition mirrors that of many other populations within the country and continent more broadly.[55] Like other nomadic populations, such as the Tuareg of West Africa or the Maasai of Tanzania and Kenya, Somali pastoralists were divided into different territories in the late nineteenth century by imperial powers that disregarded their patterns of mobility and transhumance.[56] The experience of Somali urbanites also has parallels with that of the Nubian (Sudanese) and Indian diasporas in East and Southern Africa. Immigrants from South Asia and Sudan, like Isaaq and Harti intermediaries, were able to take advantage of imperial opportunities in order to travel and settle in different parts of the British Empire and were often exempt from the legal restrictions governing "native" subjects.[57] A number of Kenya's "indigenous" ethnic groups, such as the Luo, Luhya, Teso, Borana, Swahili, and Digo, to name only a few, also straddle international borders. By the same token, East Africa has experienced waves of migration over the nineteenth and twentieth centuries and is now home to many "diasporas." If such "borderless" conditions are indeed quite common, why are certain populations treated as alien and their lifestyles pathologized? Why have the Somali become the paradigmatic example of the internal stranger within Kenya (and beyond)?

OUTLINE OF THE BOOK

In order to answer such questions and contribute to alternatives to methodological nationalism and nativism, We Do Not Have Borders charts the history of a distinctive type of oppositional politics. Examining political alternatives put forward by Somali and Kenyan political thinkers is one means of writing a history of the present. Walter Benjamin famously stated: "To articulate the past historically does not mean to recognize it 'the way it really was.' It means to seize hold of a memory as it flashes up at a moment of danger."[58] Over the course of the twentieth and twenty-first centuries, Somali and northern Kenyan leaders and intellectuals envisioned diverse political futures, which were not always sovereign, territorial, or secular in scope or predicated on ethnic homogeneity. Some of these "past futures" may now appear obsolete, while others may seem to be brimming with unrealized potential.[59] Analyzing alternative futures and heterodox political models is a way of upending teleologies, of avoiding a narrative that leads inexorably toward the ultimate triumph of a nation-state built around colonial territorial and institutional structures. It allows one to explore overlooked possibilities and forgotten histories of interrelation that resonate with present-day concerns. Remaining attentive to these histories often requires different practices of reading, listening, and archiving (discussed in the next section).

The first chapter of this book shows that on the eve of colonial rule, conflicts in northern Kenya sharpened the boundary between Muslim and non-Muslim and contributed to a broader reconfiguration of what it meant to be "Somali." These notions of Somaliness were not predicated on territorial boundaries or structured by the binary racial distinction between "African" and "Arab." Chapter 2 describes how, in the early decades of British rule, Isaaq and Harti representatives imagined themselves as both imperial citizens and members of a wider Islamic world, developing a geographic and civilizational ethos derived from both colonial and Indian Ocean thought. In the 1930s, when the colonial administration tried to erode the special privileges of the "alien" Somali and treat them functionally as "natives," Isaaq representatives were able to mobilize through their kin in British Somaliland and the United Kingdom. They also reworked the racial vocabulary of empire by claiming to be a "race of Asiatic Origin."[60] Chapters 3, 4, and 5 examine the diverse nationalist imaginaries that emerged from these foundations after World War II. While Somali leaders frequently made claims within the dominant framework of the nation-state, their efforts also reflected the pull of extraterritorial affiliations.[61] Placing archival documents into dialogue with political poetry, chapter 4 analyzes the ways in which non-secular and nonterritorial affiliations were mobilized in the service of a territorial nationalist project. Political thinkers in the Northern Frontier District (NFD) found various ways to "domesticate" the nation-state and transform an elite nationalist project into a popular movement that appealed to many of the region's transhumant nomadic inhabitants. Finally, chapters 6 and 7 show how the defeat of the irredentist movement, the Somali civil war, and the attendant refugee crisis all sparked renewed debates over the meaning of the past and a profound reconfiguration of the idea of a "Greater Somalia." In the post–Cold War era, Somaliness has become more deterritorialized and less closely tied to claims on a normative, secular political order.

This book also analyzes how shifting practices of governance affected the ability of Somalis to participate in collectivities that stretched across territorial boundaries. While protectorate and colonial administrators generally sought to restrict African mobility, imperial structures were, by definition, supraterritorial. As chapters 1 and 2 show, colonial economies demanded flexibility for the movement of laborers, soldiers, traders, and capital across territorial borders. Many immigrant communities were able to form horizontal solidarities that stretched across colonial boundaries and to imagine themselves, as Thomas Metcalf notes, "not merely as colonial subjects but as imperial citizens."[62] In addition, nomads regularly crossed imperial frontiers and continued to see pastoralism as a viable strategy throughout much of British rule.

Nevertheless, the tensions of the imperial political economy heightened during the interwar period. Colonial and British officials came to think of Somali nomads and urbanites as a people "out of place" within the colony, who could not be confined to native reserves and who blurred the boundary between "native" and "non-native." The question of where they "belonged," already fraught during the early colonial era, became an ever more pressing and violent issue as Kenya transitioned to a developmentalist state (the focus of chapters 3 and 4). Developmental imperialism enabled the late colonial government to intervene much more extensively in the lives of Somali livestock traders and nomads in the 1940s and '50s.[63] Alongside development initiatives, postwar political projects also posed new challenges for Somalis in Kenya. Nationalist campaigns demanded loyalty to an exclusive territorial homeland, which forced states and subjects alike to determine where Somalis in Kenya belonged and to which nation they were "native." The rise of Pan-African nationalist movements proved problematic for a population that regularly traversed international borders and, at times, cast themselves as non-natives.[64]

Partha Chatterjee has suggested that nationalist models derived from European precedents never fully "colonized" the imaginations of colonized subjects.[65] Yet the universalization of the nation-state as the paradigmatic model of the post–World War II era placed a large number of restrictions on what could be formally implemented.[66] While African leaders imagined alternatives to the imperial configuration of territory, contests over the scope and nature of self-determination led to the hardening of colonial boundaries.[67] Chapters 4 and 5 examine sovereignty as an enduring problem for colonial subjects and postcolonial citizens. When Kenya achieved independence in 1963, the newly elected government took brutal measures to suppress the Pan-Somali campaign. By the late 1960s, Kenyan Somalis had effectively become foreigners on their own soil, their loyalty deemed suspect and their political activism delegitimized as a criminal revolt known by most Kenyans as the "Shifta War" (ca. 1963–1967).[68]

Looking back at colonialism and decolonization in the wake of the recent "structural transformations" that "unmade the postwar order," one gets a sense of vertigo, of history repeating itself.[69] From a certain vantage point, it appears that the crisis of the nation-state in Northeast Africa and the erosion of economic sovereignty that attended neoliberal restructuring led to a certain "rebirth" of decentralized networks that flourished prior to World War II. When Somalia became increasingly unstable in the late 1980s, people began to seek refuge in cities as dispersed as Nairobi, Dubai, Minneapolis, and London, creating a new, globalized Somali diaspora. Many drew on long-standing kinship ties with people in neighboring Kenya in an effort to avoid overcrowded and underfunded refugee camps. Chapters 6 and 7 examine how Nairobi developed into a site of asylum and a global hub for Somali business. Islamic and refugee networks also provided important economic and social alternatives for those pushed to the margins of the Kenyan political system.[70]

The arguments in this book are influenced by this recent turn of events and by a broader transnational turn that has reached across various disciplines. The rise of transnational studies (and the accompanying skepticism toward the nation-state) has taken the discipline of history in novel directions. Nevertheless, new paradigms can reproduce old mythologies.[71] Recent scholarly developments risk perpetuating older modernization theories and obscuring the highly unequal and unevenly connected nature of the "global" world.[72] The reemergence of deterritorialized networks in East and Northeast Africa thus should not be seen as simply the latest "stage" within the familiar, progressive narrative of postmodernity—a local analogue to multinational corporations, cosmopolitan elites, and global religious revivals.[73] Nor should these trends be interpreted as sounding the death knell for national sovereignty or citizenship.[74] In fact, the predicaments faced by nomads on the Kenyan/Somali borderlands, members of historic Somali diasporas, and refugees reveal just how much power state borders and notions of citizenship still have.[75] As chapters 6 and 7 show, while Kenyan Somalis have largely turned away from the idea of unifying under a Greater Somali nation-state, many are also trying to fight disenfranchisement and have their minority status fully recognized within the country.

Far from being parochial, the difficulties faced by Kenyan Somalis refract problems of global relevance. Debates over indigeneity have symbolically reordered the world, creating groups of people who do not "fit" into the nation-state. As Liisa Malkki has argued, minorities who do not fall neatly into received categories often become the targets of those who seek to naturalize and maintain established boundaries and classifications.[76] Whereas expatriates, aid workers, and international businessmen in Kenya (and across the Global South more broadly) tend to be thought of as worldly and cosmopolitan; nomads, immigrants, and refugees are often identified as "displaced, uprooted, [or] disoriented."[77]

Kenyan Somalis have been struggling for decades to find ways to be both "Kenyan" and "Somali" (or, in some cases, "Somalilanders" or "Ethiopians")—a goal that has been complicated by the Somali refugee crisis and the global "war on terror." To this day, traders, migrants, and nomads in Kenya cannot freely or easily participate in networks that stretch across territorial boundaries without furthering perceptions that they are alien to the country. Even those who are highly localist in their orientation, speak multiple Kenyan languages, and are considered to be culturally assimilated into Kenya are sometimes perceived as foreign. As Hussein Mohamed Haji complained, "I am 70. I was born in Kenya. I speak six Kenyan languages. But when other Kenyans see me they just make the assumption that I'm a Somali."[78] Kenyan Somalis have become the locus of anxious discussions over who is an "authentic" Kenyan citizen, who has rights to the city and a share in the "national cake," and what is the "proper" place of religion in political life.[79]

Contemporary efforts by activists, scholars, and theorists to envision a future politics less tethered to existing nation-state boundaries were, in many ways, anticipated by Somali and northern Kenyan political thinkers. For decades, Kenyan Somalis have looked beyond the horizons of the territorial state and toward alternative kinds of imagined communities (even though such strategies sometimes put them at odds with state authorities and made them vulnerable to political marginalization). As I argue most explicitly in the conclusion, it is possible to grasp the critical resonance between Somali tactics and the current conditions of those most affected by contemporary globalization, while guarding against simplistic revivals of the past. These transnational practices (and the political innovations that preceded and followed the universalization of the nation-state) can offer inspiration for future arrangements within the region and beyond.

METHODOLOGY

In many ways, studying Kenyan Somali networks both conforms to and requires certain departures from trends in African studies. In recent years, historians and anthropologists have begun to question the traditional focus of academic fieldwork: namely, the "local" ethnic group. Many scholars have abandoned this method in favor of multisited research projects.[80] At first glance, a study of Somalis living in Kenya may seem an example of the older model of "local" fieldwork. Yet my interviews, though largely (but not exclusively) confined to people who identified as both Kenyan and Somali, did not give rise to a picture of a bounded, local community situated within a delimited culture or territorial homeland. Rather, they revealed how individuals defined what it meant to be Somali in different ways and in dialogue and coordination with people living throughout the region—and, in some cases, across the globe.

Perhaps the greatest value of oral history is how it provides insights into forms of interpersonal connection that lie outside the state/subject and state/citizen relationship. Relying on state archives alone can reinforce what Nancy Rose Hunt refers to as the cliché of the colonial encounter—the tendency to reduce historical agency to an "epic-like meeting" between "colonizers and colonized."[81] Speaking to Kenyan citizens who identified as Somali revealed that loyalties and connections that took place outside the state's bureaucratic surveillance—connections to people in Somaliland, the wider diaspora, and the broader Muslim community—were of no less significance. It also brought to the fore dynamics that are otherwise occluded by state archives' reliance on the epistemologies of clan and ethnic belonging. It showed, for example, that many non-Somalis, including members of the Borana, Rendille, and Sakuye populations, had at times participated in the construction and development of Somaliness.

It is hard to disentangle the networks through which I traveled as a researcher—which were shaped by the forms of power inherent in my passport, my race, my institutional affiliations, and my comparative affluence—from the networks I was trying to study. These were shaped by some actors who were comparatively powerful, but many of whom were relatively powerless. I began my fieldwork in Nairobi, where I interviewed elders who could recall the late colonial and early postcolonial periods and met younger community leaders who put me in touch with many of my key interlocutors in other parts of the country. These social connections facilitated my movement across different regions. The checkpoints and miles of untarmacked road that I crossed moving between Nairobi and Northern Kenya were stark reminders of both my own privileged freedom of movement and the everyday barriers to mobility that many Somalis and northern Kenyans face. The very global structures of power that enabled me to move to Kenya to conduct research often inhibited the mobility of my Somali interlocutors and friends. Thus, my fieldwork became a means of meditating upon differential mobility and the policing of different transnational practices.

To conduct interviews, I traveled to various towns, including Nakuru, Isiolo, Naivasha, and Garissa. I also occasionally spoke with Kenyans who originated from other areas such as Mandera, Moyale, and Marsabit. However, most of my fieldwork was concentrated in two main sites. One was

Nairobi—Kenya's bustling, cosmopolitan capital and the country's largest city. The other was Wajir—a very marginalized (but in certain respects, no less cosmopolitan) rural area and one of the three districts (now counties) in the North Eastern Province (NEP), which had once been part of the Northern Frontier District (NFD). Examining Wajir and Nairobi together revealed the importance of multidirectional links between the country-side (often assumed to be the site of "traditional," "authentic" Africa) and the putatively modern city. It enabled me to see the ways in which people from different geographic, clan, occupational, and class backgrounds repro-duced and redefined what it meant to be Somali. Individuals and groups constituted themselves through "the continuous creation of the past."[82] By accumulating archives, sharing personal memorabilia, and drawing upon collective representations of the past, people were able to publicly define themselves as "the" Somali, "the" Isaaq, or as "Africans," "Arabs," and so on. The past weighed heavily on current generations, serving as both a resource for imagining new futures and a threatening reminder of dissident, outdated, or embarrassing subjectivities.

Moreover, carrying out interviews in different locations allowed me to let go of ideas that people naturally belong to specific "lands," that fieldwork gives a scholar privileged access to "local knowledge," or that one can simply enter or exit a defined "zone" of culture.[83] Moving to such diverse sites was challenging (each time I traveled to a new area, I had to gain people's trust anew and get accustomed to new cultural and linguistic norms). However, this productive disorientation also led to a heightened awareness of the mis-steps, misunderstandings, and negotiated power dynamics that color any research encounter.[84]

Michel-Rolph Trouillot argues that "lived inequalities yield uneven his-torical power."[85] One way this manifested itself was in the gendered nature of my interviews, which were skewed toward men. Despite my best efforts, I had a difficult time speaking to women. Unless they were recognized com-munity leaders, older women often directed me to elder men, who were widely seen to be the bearers of public history. Men also tended to have more experience with the performative aspects of history telling and more familiarity with the narrative expectations of being interviewed by a white foreigner. When I did speak to women, they sometimes told me stories that foregrounded the accomplishments of their male predecessors, thus rein-forcing the widespread notion that it is men that make history. To some ex-tent, such responses stemmed from the limitations of my own methodology and approach. Over time, I became much better at approaching women and asking questions that motivated them to talk about their experiences and understandings of the past. However, no feminist methodology can fully overcome the power imbalances that shape the interview encounter or the patriarchal dynamics that influence how women relate to narrative history (problems that are hardly exclusive to Africa or the Islamic world).[86] In order to reconstruct the lives and experiences of women, I often had to turn to texts written by Europeans or oral testimony by men, which I have analyzed with attention toward traces of female authorship.

While oral testimony plays an important role in my analysis, this book also draws upon extensive archival research at the British National Archives and the Kenya National Archives. The bulk of my source material came from a range of low- to high-ranking bureaucrats in the East Africa Protectorate and, later, the Colony and Protectorate of Kenya. I also relied upon records from officials in neighboring territories, such as the Protectorate of British Somaliland, and administrators in the Colonial, Foreign, and Home Offices in the United Kingdom. Africans wrought their influence on these archives in various ways, whether by writing letters and petitions directly to government officials or by affecting the knowledge and understanding of British administrators. Archival documents (and the scholarly work that draws upon them) also made their way into people's hands, shaping oral testimony. Thinking about distinct oral and written domains or distinct "African" and "European" spheres of knowledge (a dichotomy that becomes even less relevant for the postcolonial archive) obscures their mutual imbrication.[87] Treating sources (both oral and written) as situated performances (with different rules of inclusion and exclusion, privileged informants, and stylistic and rhetorical strategies) proved more analytically meaningful.[88]

Dispensing with the notion that there exists an authentic, objective, or unmediated voice, I instead focused on amassing a diversity of narratives.[89] Woven throughout this text are multiple archives comprising colonial documents, transcribed oral histories, poetry, memoirs, and other sources. For more recent decades (when government archival records were either closed or less substantial), I relied more heavily on newspaper articles and human rights and NGO reports. Using such varied materials brought important methodological and political questions to the fore. How do people invoke the past in everyday life to comment upon and intervene in the present? Whose narratives do you privilege when writing a scholarly historical account? How does one read sources for hidden silences and elisions? In what ways did my race, comparative privilege, and disciplinary training shape the production of knowledge? Each chapter grapples with these questions and others. The structure of this book thus follows a traditional narrative and builds up an argument about epistemology.

Many of the chapters serve as mediations on the limits of historicism. Chapter 4, for instance, draws upon oral poetry, showing that Pan-Somali nationalism was not merely an elite project, but rather one shaped by and oriented toward rank-and-file nomadic people. Such sources resist easy historicism, as it is sometimes difficult to determine their exact date of production and authorship. They thus challenge certain scholarly conventions, including the commitment to liberal agency and historical time. However, these poems and songs also provide very important insight into idioms, metaphors, and discursive practices that cannot be easily grasped through the archives alone. Communities record and transmit the past in ways that may unsettle scholarly epistemologies, which require that historians consider the disciplinary limitations under which they operate.[90] A number of chapters also examine the problems of politically irresponsible historicism. Acknowledging the dangers in authorizing a singular version of the past, this book points to different methods of analyzing politically sensitive topics (including through reference to divine intervention).

One of the greatest difficulties I encountered was carrying out research in a highly charged and politicized setting. Oral history is often endorsed as a means of democratizing history and giving "ordinary" people a voice.[91] Yet various Kenyan and Somali political thinkers have used history to incite ethnonationalist and religious divisions, which in turn shaped the way ordinary people came to view their neighbors. Some Kenyan citizens regarded Somalis with suspicion and resented their presence in the country. By the same token, some Somalis had internalized derogatory views of other Kenyan ethnic groups and perpetuated the chauvinistic idea that they were not fully "African." It is important, however, to recognize that such sentiments were far from universal. Since the start of the Somali civil war, Kenya has taken in hundreds of thousands of refugees—far more than any Western nation. While the country is not immune from anti-immigrant sentiments that plague nations throughout the world, it has also served as a refuge for people across the region and has often succeeded in accommodating very diverse ways of life.

Understanding these complex dynamics requires deconstructing the Manichaean division between colonizer and colonized. As Eve Troutt Powell reminds us, scholars must remain attentive to colonial forms of othering, while at the same time recognizing that colonized African subjects were also capable of excluding fellow Africans, reinforcing hierarchical forms of domination, and perpetuating colonial modes of racialization. African states like Egypt and Ethiopia have engaged in practices that have led some to label them as internal colonizers.[92] Members of the Somali community have, at times, harbored racist views toward other East Africans, promoted the idea that they themselves were not "African," and expressed religious chauvinism against Christians or other "inferior" Muslims. In the case of Kenya, however, discriminatory thinking has not always mapped onto political power. While some Somalis hold derogatory views of "Africans," they also face marginalization and are often subjected to discriminatory treatment by the Kenyan state. By showing the ways in which prejudiced thinking intersects with structures of power, this book reveals the sometimes-blurry line between victim and victimizer, while remaining attuned to important distinctions between institutionalized racism and bigotry.[93]

Conducting oral history was also challenging because the past was a highly emotive topic for many people. After independence in 1963, Somalis endured significant trauma at the hands of Kenyan officials, who often acted with the tacit and sometimes explicit support of the British and the US governments. Many were eager to speak to me about these painful memories of state violence and repression. Though some were suspicious of my intentions or simply unwilling to revive such painful memories, others saw me as a potential mouthpiece for highlighting their stories of suffering and marginalization, or an advocate who could connect their stories to an international human rights agenda. Rather than simply "compiling a record of horror, a kind of case for the prosecution," however, this book tries to uncover the logic that facilitated violence and made the relationship between Somalis and the Kenyan state so fraught and complicated.[94] It focuses not simply on the ways in which people imagined community, but also on moments and gestures of antimembership, rejection, and refusal. This study traces the reasons why Somalis have come to hold such an enigmatic, liminal status within Kenya, where they are often regarded as both locals and foreigners, citizens and strangers.

1 ∽ "Carrying the History of the Prophets"

About 800 or 900 years ago the Horn of Africa was politically and commercially more closely related to Arabia than it is at the present day, and it was at that date that the Somali race was first formed by numerous emigrants from Southern Arabia intermingling with, intermarrying with, and proselytizing the indigenous tribes, who were probably of Galla stock. Since then they have extended in all directions along the lines of least resistance.

— L. Aylmer, "The Country between the Juba River and Lake Rudolf," 1911[1]

FOR CENTURIES, GROUPS ACROSS Northeast Africa, the Red Sea, and the Indian Ocean had migrated, traded goods, exchanged cultural technologies, and intermarried. For Captain Aylmer, a British officer who policed the Northern Frontier District (NFD), this cultural mixing could be explained only through reference to the impact of a supposedly superior immigrant Arab race. Historical dynamism was tied to obliquely sexualized stories of a continent penetrated by foreign infiltration. British authorities came to believe that through conquest, they were hindering a seemingly inexorable invasion by Somalis, whose ancestors had emigrated from Arabia and slowly spread across Northeast Africa. Constructing a distinction between "indigenous" Africans and "foreigners," protectorate and colonial officials came to see the Somali as a racially ambiguous people who were neither fully African nor fully Arab.

Among Cushitic-speaking people at the turn of the century, however, different discursive formations governed talk and thought about what it meant to be "Somali." By the nineteenth century, Oromo- and Somali-speaking people had developed a range of social, intellectual, and cultural techniques well suited to the cosmopolitan Indian Ocean world and to the loose relationship with land that facilitated a pastoral economy in the Horn of Africa. On the eve of colonial conquest, many groups were engaged in complex arguments about the boundaries of who did and did not belong to the Islamic *umma* (community) and broader Somali lineages. In the nineteenth century, the stakes of these debates heightened as the region experienced an increase in foreign trade, an intensification of slavery, and the expansion of Ethiopian and European imperial power.

This chapter reconstructs the ways in which Somali and Oromo speakers in Kenya were redefining "Somaliness" on the eve of colonial conquest. It also examines how British protectorate and colonial officials in the late nineteenth and early twentieth centuries constructed the Somali as a quasi-foreign people whose movement into and within the East Africa Protectorate (later Kenya) needed to be carefully controlled. Doing so requires sifting through a historical record that is ineluctably incomplete, fragmented, and riddled by the effects of power. By bringing oral and documentary sources and African and colonial narratives into conversation, however, it is possible to generate richer and, in some cases, more subversive histories.

RACE AND COSMOPOLITANISM UNDER EMPIRE

Scholars have tended to conceptualize colonialism in Africa as the culmination of a long process of European expansion overseas. In the mid-nineteenth century, Western explorers began to travel deeper into the interior of the African continent, which shaped how they understood race and difference. European missionaries and surveyors who explored the East African interior often viewed themselves as pioneers "discovering" a new land. However, they frequently drew upon the knowledge and expertise of locals, many of whom were seasoned travelers in their own right. As David Northrup has shown, people from both sides of the Continental Divide traveled and came to "discover" the other.[2]

In 1854, Sir Richard Francis Burton arrived in Zeila, on the northeastern tip of the Horn, to embark on an ill-fated expedition to Harar, Ethiopia. Burton gained acclaim for his alluring travel memoirs. Often overlooked, however, are the African translators, soldiers, gun-bearers, and navigators who guided Burton and his companion, John Hanning Speke, through the Horn of Africa. One of Burton's recruits, Mohammed Mahmud (whom he referred to as *al-Hammal*, meaning "the porter"), was an experienced voyager who had begun his career as a coal trimmer aboard an Indian war steamer. According to Burton, Mahmud went on to rise up the "rank to the command of the crew" and "became servant and interpreter to travelers, visited distant lands—Egypt and Calcutta," before finally settling in Aden.[3] Prior to formal colonialism, people living in port cities along the Gulf of Aden had encountered European travelers and voyaged through mercantilist and capitalist circuits.

Burton was a prolific writer and linguist, whose translations and travel accounts became fodder for the Western appetite for the exotic. In one of his most famous memoirs, Burton described the Somali as one of the "half-castes in East Africa," who are "a slice of the great Gala nation Islamized and Semiticized by repeated immigrations from Arabia."[4] He painted the Somali as an admixture of two distinct racial types, which he assumed to be meaningful sociological identities. His writing helped to entrench a belief in the Somalis' ambiguity: a population that Europeans came to see as neither quite Arab nor quite African.

That Burton saw features of the "Arab" world among the Somali speakers he encountered is hardly surprising. For centuries, people living around the Gulf of Aden and the Red Sea had intermarried and traded extensively with one another. It was also common among people living in East Africa to claim descent from putatively more civilized, foreign ancestors. Swahili-speaking people in the coastal city-states of East Africa had inherited a long-standing political tradition, which was widespread among Bantu speakers throughout Central and Southern Africa, of basing rights to rule on origins from exogenous conquerors. With the gradual spread of Islam and the Omani occupation of the coast, it became commonplace for East Africans to assert foreign ancestry in Arabia or Persia. While Swahili speakers on the East African coast often claimed *Shirazi* (Persian) descent, Somalis living in the Horn of Africa and Aden tended to trace their roots to Arabia. Many groups in Northeast Africa also took pride in reciting patrilineal genealogies to the prophet.[5]

Groups thus coalesced around a common belief that they were descendants of spiritually empowered sheikhs from the Arab world who had intermarried with local women. The Isaaq lineage, for example, derives its name from the eponymous founding father, Sheikh Ishaq ibn Ahmed al-Hashimi, whose tomb in northern Somalia remains to this day an important site of pilgrimage. According to one of my interlocutors, Sheikh Ishaq originated from Arabia and immigrated to northern Somalia, where he married two local women of Oromo and Amharic descent.[6] Hagiographies have been and continue to be important ways through which East African Muslims maintain an orientation toward the wider Islamic world. This is not to suggest that genealogies are part of an unbroken or timeless tradition, but simply that precolonial intellectual and cultural practices continue to have relevance into the present.[7]

The formalistic nature of oral and written genealogies and hagiographies can easily obscure the manifold ways in which people have interpreted, reworked, and subverted claims of foreign descent at different moments in time. It is, nevertheless, heuristically useful to contrast an idealized model of "European" and "Somali" notions of descent. For European explorers, Muslim genealogies were evidence that the coastal towns of North and East Africa were "products of a Persian and Arabian diaspora that had spread around the Indian Ocean."[8] Combining new forms of scientific racism with an older Christian metaphysics, European thinkers in the mid-nineteenth century reinterpreted the biblical story of Ham. The myth of Ham, as Mamdani explains, posited the existence of a superior alien race and "explained away every sign of civilization in tropical Africa as a foreign import."[9] Somalis, in the eyes of many European explorers, were a product of intermarriage between a foreign people (posited to be either Hamitic or Semitic) and the indigenous populations of Northeast Africa. Somalis in the nineteenth century, however, did not conceptualize descent through the same racial and geographic categories. For many people in Northeast Africa, being "Somali" very likely meant participating in the theologically defined space of the wider Islamic *umma*.[10] Descent was not conceptualized through a continental understanding of geography, a secular conception of historical time, or an essentialized "racial binary" between indigenous Africans on one hand, and nonindigenous foreigners on the other.[11]

Though Burton constructed racial barriers between himself and the inhabitants of the Horn, he was much celebrated for his intimate and often controversial appreciation of the cultures of the "Orient." The philosopher Anthony Appiah paints Burton as an unusual combination of cosmopolitan and racist misanthrope who was often nihilistic in orientation. Adventurous and linguistically adept, he successfully passed as a Pathan from India's North-West Frontier in order to attend the hajj in Mecca.[12] Few others possessed the linguistic skills and the recklessness to flit so easily between various cultural milieus. However, many of Burton's hagiographers have overlooked the fact that he conducted most of his travels within an international Islamic space.[13] The Indian Ocean was a well-traveled region in which populations mixed and where foreigners, as Engseng Ho elegantly notes, "settled and sojourned in towns big and small and entered into relations with locals that were more intimate, sticky, and prolonged than the Europeans could countenance."[14] Immigrants were by no means an unusual presence, and this climate no doubt facilitated his ability to assimilate. Appiah traces the genealogy of cosmopolitanism back "to the Cynics of the fourth century."[15] However, this lineage neglects forms of cosmopolitanism that derive from neither Hellenic nor imperial origins.

If being "cosmopolitan" is understood as a kind of stance aimed at navigating across cultural, religious, and linguistic differences and finding ways to "belong" to multiple worlds, then it is clear that the Horn of Africa had

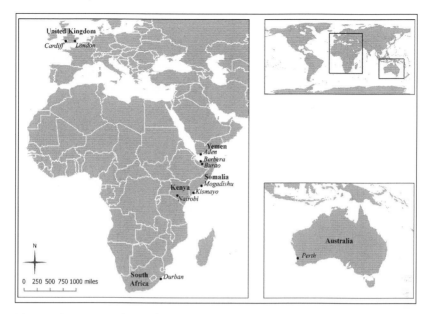

Map 1.1. Some sites of Somali residence in the late nineteenth and early twentieth centuries. (*Note:* This map shows modern political boundaries.)

its own traditions of cosmopolitanism. Coastal cities such as Berbera and Mogadishu were major ports of call for the region as well as centers for cultivating these cosmopolitan sensibilities. Monsoons brought dhows (lateen-rigged ships) across the Indian Ocean, which enabled locals to take advantage of long-distance trade and forced foreigners to stay until the winds reversed. Somali speakers developed social technologies to incorporate these strangers and bridge the parochial divides of language, culture, and geographic origin. Unlike European traditions, which were predicated on overcoming the narrow limitations of citizenship, Somali forms of cosmopolitanism were aimed at assimilating migrants, forging ties of kinship to neighbors, and making claims to spiritual universality.[16]

Kinship and prophetic genealogies, which were typically traced through the paternal line, provided a powerful language for incorporating strangers, neighbors, and migrants. However, they were also social tools that could be used to exclude. There is no pure form of cosmopolitanism unencumbered by exclusionary dynamics. By asserting membership in Islamic lineages, Somali speakers could define themselves as superior in relation to those perceived to live beyond the civilized world of the *Dar al-Islam* and, thus, legitimize the subordination of slaves. Some groups also distinguished themselves from "casted" lineages, who occupied a stigmatized status that, while distinct from slaves, marked them as socially marginalized from the free-born.[17] In addition, descent was sometimes invoked to claim superiority over nonpastoral lineages, whose members farmed along the Juba and Shebelle Rivers.[18] Livestock ownership is yet another distinction that has long underpinned hierarchical relations in the region.[19]

European encroachment further complicated this cosmopolitan, if unequal, world and facilitated the spread of a Somali diaspora. After the opening of the Suez Canal in 1869, European merchant ships regularly stopped off at the coastal cities bordering the Gulf of Aden (see map 1.1). Berbera was a bustling commercial center at the time, and Aden soon developed into a major port of call—as Faisal Devji notes, in many ways "the Dubai of its time."[20] Due to the accidents of geography, Isaaq and Harti Somalis who lived along the Gulf of Aden were particularly well placed to take advantage of these new opportunities. Somali seamen and stokers recruited from Aden and the surrounding littoral (including regions incorporated into the Aden Protectorate and the Protectorate of British Somaliland in the 1800s) voyaged and settled abroad. Some established small communities in dispersed port cities, such as Cape Town, Cardiff, and Perth. Others served as soldiers for British imperial regiments or as navigators and porters for European explorers. Somalis guided Lord Delamere, who in 1897 launched his now infamous expedition into Kenya. Kenya's fertile soils and rich economic opportunities attracted many of these male recruits, who came to the colony over the next half century through various waves of emigration from Aden, British Somaliland, and, to a lesser extent, Kismayo (a port city in southern Somalia).[21] Sometimes they married local women; in other cases, they were joined by women from Somaliland and Aden. Even as protectorate authorities began to hem their subjects into new racial and ethnic categories, many Somali migrants continued to identify with their kin in Aden, Somaliland, and the wider region. They were able to draw upon precolonial cosmopolitan practices, resist the full effects of deracination, and reorient themselves toward the Gulf of Aden and the wider Islamic world in new ways.

BECOMING SOMALI IN THE NORTHERN FRONTIER
DISTRICT OF KENYA

Farther to the south, another emigration was taking place. Impelled by a number of economic and political pressures, Somali-speaking nomads who identified as Ogaden and Degodia moved out of the southern regions of what is today Ethiopia and Somalia. By the turn of the century, they had established themselves in what is now northern Kenya (see map 2.1). Not only did shared discourses circulate between the coastal city-states of Northeast Africa and the pastoral interior, but nomadic groups also possessed their own cosmopolitan praxis. As they traveled, they came into conflict with Oromo speakers living north of the Tana River, brought with them new understandings of "Somaliness," and helped to reconfigure the boundaries of belonging in the north.

In the mid-nineteenth century, members of the Ogaden and Harti lineages began to move into what is today Jubaland (in modern-day southern Somalia). The caravan trade, which wound from the interior and converged upon the coast, attracted many Somali migrants to the region. Economic gain, however, was not the only driver impelling migration southward. Groups also sought to escape internal conflicts as well as the expanding Ethiopian Empire, which by 1906 had extended its state almost to its present-day contours. Many Degodia fled to what is today northern Kenya and, shortly thereafter, other Somali clans followed in their wake.[22]

When approaching this history of migration, there is an inherent risk of reifying clan and ethnic labels. Archival documents construct particular objects of knowledge. In the late nineteenth and early twentieth centuries, protectorate administrators were quite fixated on determining the "tribal essence" of East African society and often described people exclusively in ethnic terms, conflating communal categories with collectivities. Other kinds of affiliations were obscured, as was the individuality of people in the region. Oral testimony, on the other hand, risks projecting modern communal identifications onto the past. As Michel-Rolph Trouillot writes, "The collective subjects who supposedly remember did not exist as such at the time of the events they claim to remember. Rather, their constitution as subjects goes hand in hand with the continuous creation of the past."[23] A careful reading must attend to the ways in which oral and archival sources give rise to an image of bounded, relatively timeless, and internally homogeneous groups.

In addition, histories of migration often dredge up complex stories about intermarriage, assimilation, and expulsion. In the case of northern Kenya, recent conflicts over land, grazing, and political constituencies have reignited debates over the so-called Somali conquest of the region.[24] Studying these narratives poses certain problems for historians due to the stakes involved in their interpretation. Without acknowledging the limits of their own authorial power, scholars risk validating a certain representation of history that may reinforce contemporary nativist claims.

While people from the north often provided divergent accounts of this era, their narratives tended to converge upon several common themes that had become fixtures within collective memory.[25] As Rogers Brubaker notes, people cannot freely invent history. Certain kinds of pasts, he argues, are "made 'available' for present-day use not only by the events themselves . . . but also by their subsequent incorporation into commemorative traditions."[26] What virtually all the sources from this era—whether archival, oral, or scholarly—agree upon is that Somali migrants came into an area where the Oromo had been in some way dominant.

Günther Schlee and Abdullahi A. Shongolo (who have done pioneering work on northern Kenya) describe the period prior to this phase of Somali immigration as one of relative peace and security.[27] According to their account, from the sixteenth to the nineteenth century, the Borana, an Oromo-speaking group, had adopted a number of diverse people under an alliance that became known as the Worr Libin, or the People of Libin. Over the centuries, various Somali-speaking groups had gained a foothold in the region by becoming *sheegat* (which can be roughly translated as "clients") to these established Borana residents.[28] Through *sheegat*, newcomers could adopt the name and assimilate into another clan or lineage. According to Schlee and Shongolo, this period of "Borana hegemony" led to "a multiethnic political system that was the major unifying factor in the region before the introduction of modern statehood."[29]

The Pax Borana, however, came undone in the late nineteenth century. Ogaden and other Somali lineages began fighting ex-slaves for control of the Juba riverbank and pushing farther westward and southward, displacing Oromo speakers. Population pressure, opportunities to monopolize the southern leg of the caravan trade, and internal conflicts likely spurred this move southward. By the 1870s, Somalis had taken control over much of lower Juba and had begun to press farther south into northern Kenya.[30] Wajir was one of the major sites of conflict in the first few decades of the twentieth century. This was most likely due to the importance of its water resources and its location along the caravan routes.[31] When they reached Wajir in 1906, the Ogaden and their various *sheegat* met other lineages living under the Pax Borana. They encountered the Ajuran, who spoke Oromo and were almost indistinguishable from the Borana (perhaps because they were, to all extents and purposes, "Borana"). Living among the Ajuran were also more recent Somali immigrants, such as the Degodia, who had fled earlier Ethiopian incursions.[32]

As Somalis gained control over the area, they displaced many established residents. They also supplanted the importance of the Borana name, instead cementing "Somali" as an overarching affiliation. How exactly this occurred is the main source of disagreement within oral testimony and written accounts. Different sources provide different interpretations of this era. Did established residents forcefully or willingly assimilate into broader Somali ways of life? Did locals "invent" or simply "rediscover" their Somali roots? Was this a liberating foray or an oppressive invasion?

Historical events are overdetermined, riddled by silences in the historical record, and obscured by the retrospective significance conferred on them. It is misleading to imagine that we, as scholars, can peel away the bias in these various accounts or simply triangulate between them to get at a singular, unmediated truth. Events, as Bruno Latour argues, are best understood outside the fact/fiction binary; rather, they are "matters of concern" that inspire a "gathering" of people in debate.[33] For Latour, this is not recourse to blunt deconstructionism disinvested from empiricism, but rather a call for a productive and renewed realism that accounts for the ways in which issues become arenas for debate.[34]

Local political thinkers give rise to new stories, elaborate upon old ones, and keep them in circulation, which in turn helps to reinforce collective representations. Many chroniclers of these stories in northern Kenya were older men, often charged with projecting the public face of the community's history. This also meant that the history of the region was frequently told with an emphasis on patriarchal and masculine features. One such orator was Ahmed Maalin Abdalle of Habasweyn, who was also one of my main interlocutors. Fluent in multiple languages, Abdalle, a former teacher as well as a community peace builder, was well known for his humor, erudition, and knowledge of local history. Abdalle recounted a narrative about the new Somali immigrants, whom he argued had "liberated" the Ajuran from a state of semislavery to the Borana. According to his account, the Ajuran were forced to distinguish their residences from those of the Borana by inverting the animal hides covering their *aqal* (huts) and exposing the sides with fur. The Borana were allowed to approach any *aqal* with exposed fur during the night and rouse the sleeping husband, who was obliged to exit to give the visitor access to his wife. To add insult to injury, the husband was also expected to offer milk, the classic gesture of hospitality, to his guest the following morning.[35] Rights to sexual access to women often emerged as a central and overriding trope—especially within stories told by men.

Abdalle did not necessarily tell this story with the intention of condemning any particular group of people. However, this provocative narrative could easily enable one to paint a territorial incursion as a liberating activity and claim the Ajuran, who had long-standing roots in the region, as oppressed kin. The allegation that the Borana had reduced the Ajuran to a state of virtual slavery is particularly ironic given that British officials of the era, as a means of justifying their own conquest, leveled similar accusations against the Somali.[36] While one cannot immediately take Abdalle's account at face value, his story calls into question the assumptions of scholars, such as Günther Schlee, who have described the Pax Borana as a relatively peaceful era. What to Schlee and Shongolo was a nonviolent relationship of clientship, Ahmed Maalin Abdalle described as an oppressive, gendered form of domination.

Others recounted the history of this period in ways that reinforced Somali chauvinism and racial and religious exclusion. A resident of Habasweyn, who was in his early eighties at the time of our interview, also provided an account of this early "conquest" period. "The land," he explained, "was inhabited by black, ignorant Gallas, who were naked and black." He described the Somalis as "a people with religion, of the book, carrying the history of the prophets."[37] In his eyes, the Somali were a superior people who helped bring civilization to the "backwards" non-Muslim populations who had been living in the region. For at least some people, these stories helped justify their rights to the land, assert their supremacy over non-Somali and non-Muslim groups, and reinforce the conceptual boundaries between Somali and "other."

Not everyone from northern Kenya, however, would agree with such a chauvinist depiction of Somali conquest. Adan Ibrahim Ali, for example, argued that the Somali had distant kin in areas as far away as Chad, Egypt, Israel, and Rwanda. He also maintained that other Kenyan groups, including the Maasai and Luo, had hidden Somali roots.[38] Ali claimed affinity with a variety of people both within and outside the Kenyan nation-state and appealed to a highly inclusive idea of kinship.[39] While one man's interpretations of the past helped to buttress the conceptual and moral boundaries between Somali and *gaal* (the non-Muslim "other"), the other incorporated diverse people (including "black" and predominantly non-Muslim groups) into the Somali lineage system.

Trying to tease out the factual elements in any of these accounts strips them of much of their meaning.[40] As John Jackson argues, storytelling is often a way for people to cultivate community, not circulate facts.[41] In addition, it is important to position oneself (the "scholar") not as the ultimate authority, but as one of many storytellers. Dwelling upon the constructed nature of oral sources and no less tendentious and partial written records can also be a productive means of gesturing toward a certain unknowability regarding the past and thus avoiding the dangers of a "politically irresponsible historicism."[42]

At the same time, oral testimony should not be treated merely as a form of historical memory irreconcilable with the work of guild historians.[43] Doing so would deny its utility as a source of factual information about the past. Bracketing certain prosecutorial questions of who is to blame for past conflicts, these stories have much to tell us. They suggest that new immigrants and more established residents were engaged in a reconceptualization of belonging, which enabled "Somaliness" to become an encompassing affiliation for diverse people throughout the region. At the turn of the century, conflicts between Borana and Somalis led to realliances and redefinitions of "us" and "them"—whose effects continue to have reverberations into the present.

Until the twentieth century, identification as Somali was likely neither as widespread nor particularly contentious. Far more significant was one's status as a Muslim. As one interviewee told the scholar Virginia Luling: "People in those days did not talk of Somali but of Muslims and *gaalo* (infidels)."[44] Throughout the nineteenth century, southern Somalia underwent rapid economic transformation. The European demand for cash crops fueled agricultural production on the plantations along the Juba and Shebelle river valleys of southern Somalia and the island of Zanzibar. This, in turn, fed the market for domestic slavery and transformed the city-states on the southern Somali coast into hubs of international trade.[45] The expansion of the slave trade made debates over one's Islamic status (and, by the same token, one's ability to be enslaved) more pressing.

In the late nineteenth and early twentieth centuries, groups throughout southern Somalia and northern Kenya came to equate being Muslim with being "Somali," and collapsed the distinction between a prophetic and an agnatic genealogy.[46] Lee Cassanelli describes this process as the "fusion of Islamic and Somali identities."[47] Those who seized control of the land, asserted their Somali origins, or claimed a status as an independent lineage likely had to draw a strict, and perhaps violent, distinction between people who, only a few years earlier, would have been considered members of shared groups. Certain people, including many Oromo speakers, were able to successfully claim the name Somali. Rather than be absorbed into subordinate relationships, they were incorporated as long-lost kin. Other groups were enslaved or integrated into dominant Somali lineages as unequal clients. Still others were violently expelled. Casting certain people as "*gaal*" (a derogatory term for a non-Muslim) no doubt helped to limn the boundaries of groups that had a long history of interaction.[48]

The binary distinction between Somali and *gaal* became a key conceptual boundary throughout the region—one that has been reanimated over the course of subsequent decades. After new Somali immigrants entered the region, groups in what is today Wajir District, who had once lived under the protection of the Borana, began to rework notions of lineage. For example, oral histories suggest that many Degodia acquired an independent status at this time. This was accomplished when Degodia migrants broke off from the Ogaden, unified with their kin who had been living under the Ajuran, and declared themselves no longer *sheegat*.[49] Oral histories also indicate that many Ajuran, on the other hand, avoided eviction by "reawakening" their Somali Hawiye roots.[50] As the historian Richard Waller aptly notes: "What 'clan' means in any given context is itself a puzzle."[51] The long history of interaction between "Somalis" and "Borana" was, nevertheless, not so easily effaced. During the colonial period and into today, the question of who was and is a Somali is not nearly as straightforward as many social scientists have assumed.

It is worth noting that the above description of northern Kenya runs counter to certain Somali nationalist versions of history. Nationalisms in general often lay claim to an ancient past or, in some cases, invoke a timeless national identity. In contrast, I have suggested that Somaliness was a product of recent historical and political struggle, rather than a natural or transhistorical category.[52] In so doing, I have built upon the scholarship of Ali Jimale Ahmed and others who have examined the "invention of Somalia."[53] Nevertheless, it is also imperative to consider why mythico-histories of Somalia (which continue to provide a basis of unity and an anti-imperialist language) remain so salient for many people.

MYTHS OF CONQUEST

After gaining a foothold in the area, many nomadic groups came into violent conflict with imperial representatives. Archival records from this era provide clues to the escalation of conflicts between Somali leaders in the Jubaland region (which was until 1925 part of the East Africa Protectorate/Kenya) and officials from the Imperial British East Africa Company (IBEAC). Like any collection of written records, documents from this period enable certain kinds of historical readings and disable others. The stories they do offer historians, however, were obscured by later generations of colonial officials, who discarded the history of the IBEAC as they produced their own narratives of conquest. Reexamining this history, which was later buried under newer colonial mythologies, provides a means of questioning standard narratives about the isolation of the region.

In the late nineteenth century, the IBEAC tried to seize control over Somali caravan routes, whose outlets converged on the Benadir coast. Historical trade routes crisscrossed the region, which at various points in time had been connected to Arabia, India, and even distant China and Indonesia. After declaring a protectorate over the sultan of Zanzibar in 1890, the company claimed much of the East African interior (including Jubaland) to be under its sphere of influence. However, company rule remained largely nominal. Many of the surviving archival records from this period provide glimpses into the enormous strategic and tactical obstacles that the IBEAC faced to making profits in the region.

T. S. Thomas's seminal 1917 work, *Jubaland and the Northern Frontier District*, offers one of the few in-depth, retrospective accounts of the failed attempts by company authorities to capture the profitable trade. Thomas, who served as senior assistant secretary to the protectorate government, drew upon official records to compile an administrative history of the region. According to his account, the company tried, through the use of a river steamer, to redirect the caravan trade away from Barawa and Merca and farther south toward "its natural outlet at Kismayu," although this enterprise proved a "complete failure."[54] Officials also attempted to appropriate title deeds to land around the port city of Kismayo in Jubaland. When the company representative, H. R. Todd, tried to negotiate this transfer with Kismayo residents, the meeting quickly devolved into an open rebellion during which local Somali populations teamed up with the company's mutinying Hyderabad troops.[55] In 1895, the Foreign Office took over the administration of the country from the bankrupt company.

Thomas's detailed report diverges greatly from the accounts that colonial officials produced only a decade later. Reading them together reveals the working memory of colonial power. By the late 1920s, colonial officials were creating new founding myths, which elided the ignoble failures of the IBEAC to capture the caravan trade. By the beginning of formal colonial rule in 1920, officials in the north had come to internalize a belief in the "civilizing" effects of British rule on an otherwise "barbaric" and anarchic people. As colonial officials came to conceptualize themselves as rulers of a backward and isolated region, they effaced the history of these once-extensive caravan routes. Rather than a conscious or intentional suppression, this elision reflects the ways in which certain kinds of logic became sedimented in colonial thinking.

By the 1940s, Pan-Somali nationalists had developed their own history of the region. In the eyes of many Somali irredentists, the late nineteenth century was a lamentable period during which four colonial powers—France, Italy, Britain, and Ethiopia—divided the historical Somali nation into five territories. While protectorate and colonial accounts paint a picture of disorderly tribes in need of colonial order, Somali nationalists portray inhabitants of the Northern Frontier District (NFD) as a homogeneous people divided by arbitrary borders. Although Somali nationalist discourse provided an important critique of colonial power, it also did not give much heed to the internal dynamics of the region. Rather, both Somali nationalist elites and colonial officials crafted an image of the NFD that reflected a certain vision of state power.

While the inhabitants of the Horn may not have been the homogeneous nation that Pan-Somali supporters retrospectively imagined, there is little doubt that imperial powers drew boundaries with little regard for nomadic populations. By the late 1890s, the protectorate regime had claimed a vast territory beyond its coastal garrisons.[56] In the hope of checking Ethiopian and Italian expansion, the Foreign Office hastily secured its rights to the poorly surveyed terrain stretching west of the Juba River and south of the Ethiopian Empire. The art of cartography was a key technique through which British authorities created a semblance of sovereignty over the interior of the East Africa Protectorate, where they largely lacked effective control. Most of these frontiers were nominal artifacts of imperial diplomacy that cut through communities and partitioned nomadic populations for whom these colonial conventions were largely meaningless.[57] Labeling these borders "arbitrary," however, is misleading. It suggests as a corollary the possibility of a "natural" border, which assumes that people innately belong to fixed territories.[58] Transhumant groups, however, have not always imagined community in ways predicated on territorial boundaries (which is not to say that nomads did not have links to certain lands and geographies).

In the late nineteenth century, imperial representatives had recognized that northern Kenya and southern Somalia were interconnected to a much broader regional and global economy. By the turn of the century, however, British officials had turned their attention to the construction of the Uganda-Mombasa railway farther south, which was completed in 1901. The IBEAC's experience in Jubaland revealed the inviability of capturing pastoral trade networks as well as the challenges of seizing control over nomadic regions. Rather than attempt the task of redirecting capital flows or securing effective administration over the sparsely populated, arid northern expanse, the thinly staffed protectorate regime concentrated instead on halting the southward migration of the area's armed, nomadic people into the fertile central highlands and Rift Valley, which soon became the focus of the government's commercial interests.[59]

By the early twentieth century, the East Africa Protectorate regime had come to see the region as an extremely challenging area to govern best thought of as a buffer zone, analogous to the North-West Frontier of India. To hinder Somali migration into Central Kenya, in 1902 the administration applied the Outlying District Ordinance to the north, which effectively made the region a closed area; movement in and out was restricted to holders of a special pass.[60] In 1910, the protectorate government appointed the first "officer in charge" of the newly formed Northern Frontier District (NFD) (see map 2.1). It would take another decade, however, before the protectorate regime could claim effective control over the area.[61]

In 1913, the explorer Ignatius N. Dracopoli encapsulated colonial sentiments when he described the region as "the outskirt of civilization, on the frontier, as it were, of a fertile and well-watered land, beyond which lie the arid and sun-scorched wastes of a great desert."[62] More than two decades of periodic combat with Somali groups only nourished this image.[63] The concept of the frontier enabled officials to incorporate the area into the protectorate, while simultaneously emptying it of its own "cultural significance" and obscuring the alternative geographies of its inhabitants.[64] Although colonial officials naturalized the north's status as a buffer zone, which marked the outer limits of imperial control, its isolation and marginalization were neither natural nor inevitable. Rather, they were the by-product of shifting imperial strategies as well as decades of struggle between Somali nomads, company representatives, and protectorate officials.

Officials and officers charged with securing the frontier, as George Simpson notes, often "imagined themselves impartial arbitrators who were bringing a more enlightened system of governance to a people so caught up in narrow and parochial disputes that they could not recognize the blessings that were being bestowed upon them."[65] The protectorate regime lauded itself on the suppression of slavery and claimed to be safeguarding weaker populations from southward Somali aggression. They also attributed the causes of conflicts in the north to a "tribal" culture left unchecked and suggested that solutions lay in the civilizing effects of British rule.

This attitude surfaced in the way protectorate officials treated a series of disputes between subclans of the Ogaden. While protectorate authorities tried to contain Somalis and limit their migration southward, Ogaden leaders fought one another for hegemony over the eastern portion of the NFD. This conflict culminated in the killing of Ahmed Magan, the sultan of the Muhammad Zubeir, in 1914. People in Garissa District often refer to this series of conflicts as the Kalaluud, which can be roughly translated as "stalemate." For the British, however, the Kalaluud was not a historical moment to be named, but simply one of many administrative headaches. In official correspondence, this complex political struggle was treated as a timeless cultural aspect of nomadic life, which highlighted the ungovernability of the Somalis: "The fighting between these two tribes was throughout of the most savage description. . . . It was impossible for the Government, engaged as it was with the Marehan Expedition, to take any steps to induce or compel the tribes to come to terms. . . . The combatants were left to themselves."[66] Local accounts, however, inflect the Kalaluud with far different significance. Unlike the colonial archives, oral histories attend to the political motivations of these struggles.

While oral accounts of the Kalaluud are hardly straightforward reports, they are nevertheless useful as a means of destabilizing dominant, and no less straightforward, colonial narratives. They do not offer "corrections" to colonial texts, but rather an entirely different framework for understanding the past.[67] Ahmed Maalin Abdalle told one of the most evocative versions of the events that triggered the Kalaluud. The conflict began, he explained, when a Muhammad Zubeir woman, who was married to a man from the Abdalla lineage, left home one day to graze her goats. While she was out in the field, the hooves of one of her animals dug into the soil, exposing an elephant tusk. This discovery precipitated a dispute between leaders of the Muhammad Zubeir and the Abdalla, both subclans of the Ogaden. Citing the fact that the woman was their daughter, the Muhammad Zubeir claimed ownership of the tusk. Members of the Abdalla, however, contended that they were the rightful owners, as she was the wife of one of their sons.[68]

One way to interpret this story is as an allegory for a historical conflict over control of the ivory trade. Such an interpretation is not without historical justification. As the scholar Scott Reese notes, by the second half of the nineteenth century, "population movements, sedentarization and continued hunting" had depleted animals from the coast, which forced merchants and hunters to move farther into the interior.[69] If, in fact, the Kalaluud began as a contest over the changing orientation of the ivory trade, then stories of this conflict may have traveled down the generations in the form of a metaphor about a woman, her goats, and the fortuitous discovery of a tusk.

The problem with such methods of interpretation, however, is that they demand that historians differentiate between the "metaphorical" and the "historical" aspects of any given oral testimony. In the absence of some other, more "valid," corroborating historical source, oral histories tend to be treated as mere metaphor, their historical reliability rendered dubious by the lack of confirmatory evidence.

This has particularly pernicious consequences for the study of women and gender, where evidence outside of oral testimony is often fragmented or entirely nonexistent. Ahmed Maalin Abdalle provides rich insights into the gendered debates surrounding patrilineal inheritance. To resolve the dispute over the tusk, he recounted, the elders of the Muhammad Zubeir and the Abdalla subclans summoned the woman. When asked about how she had come across the ivory, the woman explained that she was walking and had spotted the tusk between her legs. "Anything between her legs is ours," happily concluded the Abdalla leaders, who claimed ownership over the ivory.

Oral histories of this nature often enable elder men to reinscribe patriarchal norms over the past. By equating the ivory to an offspring, who "belonged" to the father's lineage, this story plays upon ideas of patrilineal inheritance. In this account, the woman is simply the ground for a larger debate between men over proprietorship (even though Somalis, like many East Africans, have long subscribed to ideas of female property rights).[70] While hardly a clear-cut reflection on the way gender relations "really" worked in the precolonial period, this story provides insight into the ways in which gender was animated—often in humorous and provocative ways—to make sense of the past.

There are other ways of interpreting Maalin Abdalle's creatively ambiguous and polysemic story that are more subversive of patriarchal norms. While the maintenance of lineage ties has frequently turned on the control of female reproduction and sexuality, it would be a mistake, as Christine Choi Ahmed suggests, to assume that Somali women were little more than chattel. To do so would be to reproduce an androcentric and Eurocentric vision.[71] Similarly, David W. Cohen argues that historians and anthropologists often miss the important role played by women, because they attend "to the form and play of 'larger,' and in a sense 'masculine' structures and segmentary processes."[72] He notes that "the ideology of patrilineal segmentation" may not be the "overarching system defining identity and constituency as has been thought," but simply "one means of conceptualizing and animating complex social activity over time."[73] Another possible reading of Abdalle's account is to see the conflict emerging not from differing interpretations of patrilineal inheritance, but rather due to the breakdown of ties of *xidid* (matrilateral relations). Via marriage, women have often played a central role in bringing together families of different clans.

In addition, Ahmed Maalin Abdalle's story shows how quickly mobilizations of clan could change. After claiming the ivory, the husband went to the market in Bardera to purchase a large bull. He had the misfortune, however, of returning to Habasweyn after a period of drought. According to Abdalle's account, members of the Muhammad Zubeir clan stole the man's newly purchased bull to replenish the herds killed off by the drought. Members of the Abd Wak lineage, who claimed a common descent with the Abdalla in this era, retaliated for the theft. This triggered the series of battles known today as the Kalaluud.[74] After the struggles between the Ogaden subclans subsided, such a way of conceptualizing kinship fell out of favor.[75] This story serves as a reminder to contemporary observers of Somalia, who have tended to view recent mobilizations of clan as ancient and natural, that one cannot accept the present as traditional or given.

As the Kalaluud conflict indicates, the early twentieth century was a tumultuous time for nomadic groups living in the NFD, who struggled over control of land and resources. British accounts depoliticize the Kalaluud and paint it as an unexceptional "tribal" conflict against which the supposedly stabilizing, neutral colonial state could be deployed. Ahmed Maalin Abdalle, on the other hand, embedded this conflict within regional dynamics, local power struggles, and control over pastoral resources and trade routes. Relying on oral histories of this nature thus helps to counteract the depoliticizing effects of the archives and recenters Somali knowledge production.

Correspondence suggests that many lower-ranking officials were aware of the complex struggles and thorny reconfigurations of lineage ties, but simply found the complexity overwhelming. Actionable administrative discourse required officials to cut through this intricacy. Gradually, many protectorate and colonial administrators came to accept the myth of southward Somali expansion and perpetuated the idea that they were hindering a timeless conquest by a Muslim race of foreign extraction.[76] This view of history eventually became ingrained in administrative logic. By 1963, R. G. Turnbull, provincial commissioner (PC) of the NFD, argued: "There can be no doubt that had it not been for European intervention the Somalis, pushing before them the Galla and the remnants of other displaced tribes, would, by now, have swept through Kenya; the local Bantu and Nilotes could scarcely have held them for a day."[77]

This narrative of conquest painted Somali nomads as foreign encroachers whose movement needed to be closely contained. By the early twentieth century, protectorate officials had come to see the Somali nomad as an administrative problem as well as a threat to the safety of white settlers and the functioning of the colonial economy. Rarely could protectorate or colonial administrators fully control nomadic movement. However, in transforming migration into a legible problem of governance, protectorate officials stigmatized long-standing patterns of transhumance and equated the "Somali" with unregulated and dangerous mobility.

2 ↶ "Kenya Is Regarded by the Somali as an El Dorado"

*I am not an anthropologist, but I believe that I am correct in say-
ing that Somalis have been in Africa hundreds of years or even
thousands of years, and I am not at all sure how far one has to
be back in order to determine the origin of a race. Surely if an
Imperial Act were to refer to a person of British origins it would
not be competent for that person to allege that he came from
Normandy in 1066.*

—Attorney General of Kenya, 31 May 1934[1]

IN 1934, THE ATTORNEY GENERAL of Kenya intervened in a much wider
debate over the legal classification of the Somali population. Construing of
race and nation as natural categories and approaching the issue through
a positivist epistemology, he suggested that careful anthropological investigation could ultimately resolve the matter of Somali origins. He nonetheless speculated that the foreign roots of the Somali people were vestiges
of a distant past, drawing an analogy with British people who could claim
"Norman" ancestry. His comments prefigured a broader crisis in the late
1930s, when the status of the Somali came under increased scrutiny.[2]

For decades, historians neglected the history of Somali subjects.
Nationalist historians overlooked their experiences because they did not fit
into conventional definitions of indigeneity and seemed to embody a tragic
liminality.[3] Scholars have only just begun to explore the subjectivities of
those who were not governed so explicitly as "natives." Labor historians also

tended to elide the histories of Somali traders and nomadic pastoralists, who did not fall within the category of "workers."[4] Yet the lives of Somalis in Kenya have much to teach us about the range of colonial subjectivities as well as the social and political horizons beyond the territorial confines of the state. This chapter examines how empire facilitated certain kinds of diasporic and regional engagement, and how these possibilities began to unravel in the years leading up to World War II.

Throughout early colonial rule, Somalis in Kenya maintained a loose affiliation with territory that sustained models of membership that did not conform to colonial or juridical logics. Despite being confined to the north, northerners continued to see pastoralism as a viable, sustainable strategy; avoided becoming deeply incorporated into the colonial labor economy; and frequently crossed the porous boundaries between Ethiopia, Italian Somaliland, and Kenya with little regard for their authority. Unwilling to invest significant funds or manpower in the NFD, authorities regularly yielded to these forms of transhumance. By enlisting Somalis from Aden and British Somaliland in the imperial project, colonial authorities also enabled them to form horizontal solidarities that stretched across colonial boundaries. Members of the Isaaq and Harti community often claimed non-native status and saw themselves both as imperial citizens and as dispersed members of a wider Islamic and genealogical community.

Bringing the metropole and colonies into a single framework, this chapter analyzes some of the fundamental tensions at the heart of the imperial political economy. Colonial economies demanded flexibility for the movement of laborers, soldiers, traders, and capital between continents and across territorial borders. However, colonial and British authorities also sought to restrict the mobility of colonized subjects, including Somali nomads, traders, and seamen. While British and colonial administrators at times imagined Britishness in terms of a global imperial subjecthood, they also remained committed to an ethnic and racial understanding of African identity. As these tensions heightened in the interwar period, British officials began to erode the legal status of the Somali people.

IMPERIAL CITIZENSHIP

Although they left various kinds of "ethnographic" traces, Somali travelers who arrived in Kenya in the late nineteenth and early twentieth centuries produced few written records themselves. Archival records contain Somali "voices," but are often mediated through colonial discourses, which defined a limited terrain of communication. Postcolonial nationalism has so shaped contemporary testimony that it is also difficult to reconstruct the thinking of early generations of Somali immigrants through oral history alone. Many of my Isaaq and Harti interlocutors described their patriarchs as Kenya's pioneers. Through proud, patriarchal narratives, second-, third-, and fourth-generation Somalis emphasized their long-standing roots in the country, highlighted their community's contributions to Kenyan history, and countered widespread perceptions that they were "alien" to the country.

Given the fragmented nature of the historical record, it is difficult to determine how newly arrived Somali migrants conceptualized their relationship to British power and the locals living in East Africa. Studies of other immigrant communities nevertheless enable some tentative conclusions to be drawn. Throughout the nineteenth century, Indian traders, moneylenders, and laborers had flocked to East Africa—creating economic and political inroads for British colonialists.[5] In addition, British officials initially toyed with the prospect that East Africa would become an "America for the Hindu."[6] In the late nineteenth century, it was not yet obvious that white settlers would come to occupy such a privileged place in Kenyan society.

Somalis from Kismayo, Aden, and British Somaliland (much like their Indian counterparts) may have seen the East African interior as a land of opportunity and themselves as purveyors of "civilization." Over the course of the twentieth century, through various waves of immigration, vibrant Somali communities formed in towns and urban centers throughout the colony. Some assisted the British administration in "pacifying" the interior to make way for the Uganda-Mombasa railway. Others were veterans of early colonial military campaigns who relocated to Kenya after their service. Their numbers were later augmented by Somali veterans of the two World Wars. Protectorate officials relied on Somalis to serve as translators, while many white settlers recruited them to assist in establishing ranches and farms in the Rift Valley and fertile highlands of Kenya. Members of the Somali merchant class of Kismayo also migrated into the Northern Frontier District (NFD) as traders. Isaaq and Harti immigrants established small settlements along the railway and livestock routes.[7]

Somalis arrived in East Africa as a racial hierarchy was still taking shape. Bonds of intimacy with white settlers blurred the divide between colonizer and colonized, while never fully effacing the distinction. Lord Delamere and Karen Blixen cultivated close, personal relationships with members of their Somali staff, whom they allowed to reside on their farms along with their extended families and livestock. On several occasions, Delamere served as an advocate for Somali migrants from British Somaliland and Aden and petitioned colonial authorities on their behalf.[8] Although Blixen viewed Europeans as the superior race, she also saw her Somali staff as relatively "civilized" people, noting their shared Abrahamic religious traditions.[9]

Settlers like Blixen fabricated ideas of civilization and whiteness through interaction with Somali employees, traders, and shopkeepers. Racial hierarchies did not simply emerge through legal fiat, but rather were constructed via the mundane, daily micropolitics of colonial life. According to some of my interlocutors, white settlers relied on Somali butchers because they considered the halal slaughtering process more hygienic than other local butchering practices.[10] After the outbreak of the plague in the early 1900s, protectorate authorities began to enforce a system of racial segregation in Nairobi—at which point disease became intimately tied to "blackness" in the eyes of many Europeans.[11] Somali migrants, many of whom had taken up the role of livestock traders, tried to distance themselves from such associations. They continued to supply cattle to white ranchers in the Rift Valley and sold milk, meat, and other animal products to Indian and European clients.[12]

Proximity to whiteness generated an aspirational politics. Some Isaaq and Harti proudly referenced their relationships to now-famous figures like Blixen, which they also cited as evidence of their long-standing roots and contributions to the country. Hussein Nur suggested that I read Elspeth Huxley's book about Lord Delamere in order to learn more about "their" history. His father was among the Somalis who had helped guide Delamere into the interior of East Africa.[13] Speaking to me (a white foreigner), it is quite possible that people were more inclined to portray Europeans in a positive light. However, there was also a tacit acknowledgment that rapport with white settlers, though asymmetric, afforded Somali employees a certain elite status. The relationship between these two immigrant communities, nevertheless, grew increasingly tense as racial lines hardened over the early twentieth century and contests over land intensified. One man in Nanyuki recounted a story of a Somali man who, while out herding his cattle, killed a white farmer. The settler had brandished a gun and shot his animals, which had wandered onto the settler's farm. A colonial judge gave the Somali herder a relatively lenient sentence on the basis of self-defense. This story conjures up a moment when power was briefly reversed and some measure of equality under British law was possible. It speaks to both a desire for British justice and a recognition of white settler violence and land expropriation.[14]

By the second decade of British rule, the protectorate administration had begun to work out a system of spatial and racial segregation in concert with white settlers and in consultation with the Colonial Office. Efforts to codify race and restrict African control over land spurred petitioning from many groups. This included Muslim populations, such as Swahili speakers on the coast, who did not want to lose political or economic ground by being consigned to the status of "natives."[15] Under threat of being removed from Nairobi ostensibly on the grounds of health and sanitation, Somali leaders began negotiations with the Colonial Office and protectorate authorities.[16] They also petitioned against legislation that would classify them as natives.[17]

Having fulfilled many of the crucial economic and political demands of empire, Somalis who had served as guides, soldiers, translators, and porters were well positioned to make claims on the state and mobilize for a higher status within the emerging racial hierarchy.

Eventually, protectorate officials relented to their grievances. In 1919, the governor enacted special legislation exempting certified Somalis from the definition of "native" under certain ordinances.[18] Technically, the exemption ordinance had strict qualifications. It required that recipients demonstrate the ability to read and write in either English or Arabic and verify that no fewer than three generations had lived in Asia.[19] In practice, administrators were fairly liberal in applying this ordinance to the small minority of Somalis who were urban, comparatively wealthy, and could prove a history of government service. In addition, as one Somali elder humorously pointed out, the law applied to "anybody who looked like Somalis, who could pretend he is a Somali."[20] The ordinance effectively gave the Isaaq and Harti many of the privileges of non-natives. Like the Asian community of Kenya, they could legally reside in the urban centers of the colony, access the special wards of hospitals, and enjoy greater rights to mobility. In addition, they paid higher non-native taxation rates. The Isaaq and Harti (and other similarly positioned Somali urbanites and veterans) were not only exempt from carrying a *kipande* (a pass card that restricted African movement), but some also possessed British passports for international travel.[21]

As Carina Ray argues, the color line was not static, but was "transgressed, contested and revised over time."[22] Many Somali migrants in the late nineteenth and early twentieth centuries aspired for political equality with white settlers, Indians, and other African elites—members of the fairly narrow segment of Kenyan society who could access what Mamdani refers to as the civil side of the "bifurcated" colonial state.[23] The entrenchment of white privilege in Kenya, however, undercut more liberal models of imperial membership, which were less explicitly predicated on notions of racial purity. Somali urbanites and town dwellers navigated the construction of racial difference in a variety of ways, but often found the color line difficult to cross.

BETWEEN NATIVE AND NON-NATIVE

The distinction between "native" and "non-native," which assumed an isomorphism between people, culture, and territory, became central to British colonial thought. Mahmood Mamdani has persuasively argued that protectorate and colonial authorities imagined most Africans as part of "tribes" who could be consigned to defined territories, represented through "native" institutions with limited jurisdictions, and whose spiritual and cultural practices could be confined to the sphere of "customary law."[24] Historians such as James Brennan have qualified these arguments by noting that colonial administrators could not fully police the boundary between "native" and "non-native." In practice, they used racial and ethnic ideas as convenient abstractions rather than rigid categories, for reasons of both bureaucratic expediency and economic necessity. Colonial racial thought was also internally contradictory (officials, for example, debated whether legal categories, such as non-native status, should be based on cultural or biological difference). Moreover, African subjects selectively appropriated and retooled colonial classifications.[25] While one must acknowledge the limits of colonial power, Mamdani's thesis remains particularly relevant at the level of discourse. Legal debates over the status of the Somali population were increasingly structured through the binary distinction between native and non-native.

Although Isaaq and Harti Somalis were able to secure non-native privileges for themselves, their status was highly tenuous and provisional.[26] In 1920, the acting Crown counsel for the attorney general attempted to clarify some of the confusion surrounding the Somali Exemption Ordinance, whose implementation was subject to the discretion of local authorities. Noting that while Nairobi Township Rules had "no definition of the term 'Native' in connection with the issue of bicycle tickets," it was "the practice of the municipal authorities to issue a differently shaped ticket for European, Asiatic, and African."[27] Consequently, Somalis clamored for the "coveted diamond shaped ticket instead of the despised circular one."[28] He joked: "This bicycle dispute is reminiscent of the old Court of Versailles where questions of precedence assumed such an importance that the Duke of St. Simon on coming into power, tells us the first important matter he dealt with was the question of the right of the dukes to wear their hats at a 'Lit de justice'!"[29]

This sardonic image of mimicry ignored the possible reasons for placing such weight on so seemingly trivial an issue. Colonialism encouraged a kind of fetishism of paperwork, which often granted its bearers important legal rights. In March 1920, the PC of Nyeri wrote of Somalis who had come into his office, thrown their Non-Native Poll Tax receipts on his office table, and complained "that the government had deceived them by issuing them Receipts marked" in pencil, as though the ease with which one could rub out pencil marks was analogous to the potential erasure of their status.[30] The 1920s and 1930s were marked by an enduring debate over paperwork, taxation, and other markers of legal status. Anxiety over losing these symbols illustrates how fragile Somalis perceived their position within Kenya to be, and shows that Somali subjects both participated in and subverted racial hierarchies.

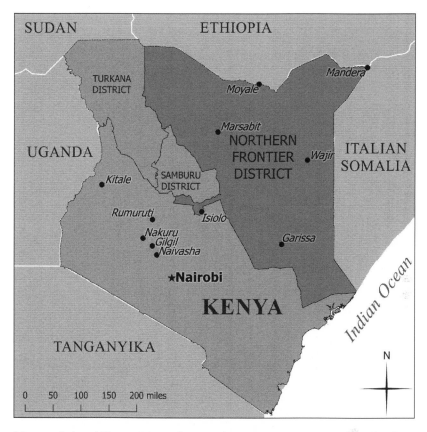

Map 2.1. Colonial Kenya. (*Note:* This map shows Kenya's international borders from 1926 to 1963. Though widely known as the Northern Frontier District [NFD] throughout the entirety of British rule, the region was formally renamed the Northern Province [NP] in 1925. Samburu District was separated from the NFD in 1934, and Turkana District was added in 1947 [after which the NP was technically known as the Northern Frontier Province].)

Although the Exemption Ordinance was a temporary provision, the administration never concretized the legal status of the Somali people. Benedict Anderson argues that state officials were notoriously intolerant "of multiple, politically 'transvestite,' blurred, or changing identifications."[31] Similarly, Homi Bhabha asserts that colonized subjects with hybrid identities threatened colonial power by destabilizing the line between ruler and ruled.[32] Yet ambiguity could also be conducive to colonial power. As Talal Asad contends, radical critics are mistaken to assume "that power always abhors ambiguity"; rather, state authority "has depended on its exploiting the dangers and opportunities contained in ambiguous situations."[33] Officials in Kenya appear to have ruled their "alien" Somali subjects in part by keeping their status undefined, ambiguous, and contestable. They could then selectively reward Somali soldiers and intermediaries without calling into question the broader logic of the color bar or creating a legal precedent that might hold implications for other colonies, regions, or other "ambiguous" populations, such as the Swahili.[34]

NEW FORMS OF DIASPORA UNDER EMPIRE

Jonathon Glassman has recently argued that racism in Africa was a coproduction between Africans and European officials and has cautioned against underestimating "the role African thinkers played in the construction of race."[35] While Isaaq and Harti political thinkers helped to perpetuate exclusionary politics by bringing their own notions of descent into dialogue with colonial conceptions of race and ethnicity, one must always be attentive to the power dynamics that shaped such claims. Colonial rule frequently set the terms of political debate, which encouraged African subjects to frame their demands for greater rights within a racialized language. Moreover, Somali articulations of their origins did not always align with colonial racial ideas. Common vocabularies could also eclipse diverse and often contrary meanings. What Somali leaders espoused was sometimes closer to a cultural chauvinism (similar to the beliefs of the more liberal contingent of British officials) than racism in the strictly biological sense.[36] In addition, their notions of descent and civilization often turned on understandings of culture and patrilineality that prized proximity to the wider Islamic world.

White settler memoirs are an important source of information on the racialized experiences of Somali town dwellers and urbanites. One of the most detailed windows comes from the writing of Karen Blixen, who arrived in Kenya in 1913 to establish a coffee plantation. Her famous memoir, *Out of Africa*, is replete with references to Farah Aden, a Somali employee whom she met in Aden. Farah Aden helped her establish her coffee plantation outside Nairobi and served as the steward of her household. Several passages of her book are also devoted to Farah Aden's wife, who traveled from Somaliland escorted by family members after relatives arranged for their marriage.[37] According to oral testimony, this was common practice among Kenyan Somalis. Many left deposits with Indian moneylenders when they traveled back to British Somaliland, who then provided short-term loans to other Somalis. Some returned with wives whose unions had been facilitated by relatives abroad.[38] The circulation of marriageable women and money set the foundation for a diaspora. Alongside his wife and her relatives, who created a domestic sphere, Farah Aden was able to cultivate a home in a foreign place.

Blixen's work exemplifies many of the racist assumptions of her contemporaries, but is also unique in that she cultivated a close relationship with elite women from Somaliland and gained a rare insight into their interior, domestic lives. Though her work is deeply exoticized, it would be a mistake to dismiss it offhand.[39] Carolyn Hamilton explains that the texts of white settlers and colonial officials often contain traces of indigenous discourses.[40] Blixen interpreted her findings through the cultural constructs of her era, but nevertheless drew upon the information provided by her Somali employees, some of whom she knew well. Fieldwork is a useful metaphor in this case. The result was a kind of contingent truth shaped by racialized power dynamics, but also influenced by close "participant-observation" and interactive discussions with her "informants."

A woman who defied many of the gendered norms of white settler society, Blixen took a particular interest in the lives of Aden's female relatives and occasionally recoded their voices into her own words. She notes, for instance, how Farah's relatives confided in her their shock to learn "that some nations in Europe gave away their maidens to their husbands for nothing," which they deemed profoundly disrespectful of women and their virginity.[41] Denying the coevality of Africans, Blixen equated their "maidenly prudery" with an earlier phase of European development.[42] This act of distancing also enabled Blixen to define herself as an ostensibly liberated white subject. Her description of this inverted ethnographic encounter, however, also suggests that women could exercise considerable authority, even within the constraints of patriarchy. Some elite Somali women may have seen marital monetary transactions not as an exchange that rendered them into "property," but as a means of actualizing their worth, labor, and contributions to the household (a topic I will address in greater depth in chapter 6).

Blixen's description of differing gendered restrictions regarding marriage also touches on an important aspect of Muslim life in East Africa.[43] Throughout the Indian Ocean region, groups privileged the idea of patrilineal descent and consanguinity with the prophet's family. This tended to afford men greater sexual freedom than women. Engseng Ho, writing about the Hadrami diaspora, argues that genealogy frequently "turned on the control of the community's women, especially daughters, and their marriage choices."[44] Because lineage as well as an Islamic identification were typically traced through the paternal line, Somali men could take a non-Muslim East African wife with some guarantee that ideas of Somaliness would be reproduced in the subsequent generation and their children considered full-fledged members of the Somali (and Muslim) world. Genealogy allowed Somali men to become "locals" in Kenya, Tanganyika, and Uganda, yet remain cosmopolitan in their outlook and connected to their Muslim kin elsewhere.[45]

Such gendered norms, however, did not go uncontested. There is little doubt that Somalis debated the boundaries of exogamy and endogamy in the colonial era and that there were differences of opinion over marriage that likely fractured around gender and differing theological persuasions, among other issues. In *Out of Africa*, Blixen noted that some women flouted social restrictions on their behavior. She wrote that while "the honest Somali women were not seen in town," there were at least "a few beautiful young Somali women, of whom all the town knew their names, who went and lived in the Bazaar and led the Nairobi Police a great dance."[46] How these women positioned themselves within debates about purity, mobility, and miscegenation is unclear. Such issues were rarely discussed by my interlocutors, who tended to describe "immoral" female behavior as a modern vice caused by poverty and the erosion of traditional culture. (And perhaps also chose to avoid such sensitive topics with an outsider like myself.) Blixen's brief, tantalizing comment gives us only the barest glimpse into these lifeworlds.

Despite their different ways of conceptualizing descent, Somalis, white settlers, and colonial officials shared many overlapping ideas. Both European and Somali women of this era, for example, faced added limitations on their sexuality, while men were more likely to be seen as entitled to sexual access to the "other." At the same time, Indian Ocean Islamic discourses also differed from Western understandings of race in several key respects. Colonial authorities and settlers tended to think of descent as an inheritable, biological condition and race as a specifically scientific category. Western eugenicists had developed several diverse and often mutually incompatible ideas of race. One was the "pure race model," in which the world's populations were imagined to be descendants of three "original" racial strains (a theory derived from the pre-Darwinian biblical story of Noah).[47] Given the broad acceptance of men marrying non-Somali and non-Muslim African women, it is unlikely that Somalis subscribed to anything analogous to a biological notion of race or that they imagined themselves as "admixtures" of two or more "pure" racial types.

This is not to say that Somalis were unoccupied with fears of cultural loss through intermarriage (or that Somali men, like their European counterparts, were not anxious about female sexuality). During one interview, I was told about an incident in which several Isaaq subclans in Nairobi fought over women who had recently arrived from British Somaliland.[48] Public conversations about descent also became increasingly mediated through the racialized discourses of colonial rule. On more than one occasion, I was told that during a colonial trial to determine their legal status, Somali leaders brought forth the lightest-skinned members of their group in order to "prove" their foreign origins. In the 1940s, Somali leaders in Uganda professed to colonial authorities that they had not intermarried with local women and thus should not be relegated to the status of "natives."[49] Ann Laura Stoler argues that racial difference in the colonial era was constituted through the management of intimate sexual relations.[50] By denying the practice of exogamy, which was clearly widespread, Somali leaders tried to better approximate colonial ideas of racial purity.

The ways that Somalis understood their descent did not quite map onto European racial categories. Yet Somali intermediaries and European settlers were able to form a mutually beneficial, if asymmetric, relationship around a set of similar ideas. These working misunderstandings enabled settlers and colonial officials to cultivate a new notion of Somaliness, which painted Somalis as a more civilized "race" within an imperial theater of territories.

To this day, intermarriage is a contentious topic of discussion. Although several elder Somali women explained that girls today have far more choice over whom they will marry, those who choose to wed "African" men continue to face stigma. Many people also debated the degree to which past generations had intermarried with East Africans, and often my interviewees provided me with contradictory information. Some argued that the Isaaq preserved their cultural distinctiveness by not intermarrying with locals, instead bringing marriageable women from British Somaliland.[51] Others emphasized that the Isaaq were more "flexible" and open to other Kenyans precisely because they had intermarried with locals over the years. These debates refract contemporary anxieties over assimilation and belonging and reveal how the specter of colonial-era racism continues to haunt social relations in East Africa.

One of the unintended consequences of British rule was to enable Isaaq and Harti voyagers to travel, expand their diaspora, and establish a range of fidelities to communities across the region. Endogamy enforced through restrictions on female sexuality very likely provided (and continues to provide) one of the most important countermeasures against deracination. Robin Cohen points out that diasporic consciousness is not a natural outcome of migration or cultural difference. Rather, diasporas unfold over time and require "a strong attachment to the past, or a block to assimilation in the present and future."[52] A much romanticized watchword of the late modern era, the term "diaspora" risks normalizing the idea of a fixed territorial homeland and, for this reason, may not be entirely fitting for Somali migrants in the early twentieth century. Nevertheless, emigrants from British Somaliland, Aden, and Kismayo were able to develop a consciousness as a dispersed and translocal people. This was in no small measure due to the racially enforced colonial order. Attaining the privileges of non-native status allowed them to travel and maintain links to their kin abroad. Like white settlers and British colonialists, Somali urbanites also retained a public identity distinct from that of other African populations. British passports from the colonial era, which many children and grandchildren proudly held on to as memorabilia, were testament to this status and freedom of movement.[53]

In 1920, Somali leaders formed the Ishakia Association, which also facilitated the reproduction of this group identity.[54] Oral testimony suggests that the Ishakia Association probably began as a welfare society. According to Duthi Jama, the women's branch required monthly contributions from its members and provided a fund in cases of emergency or death.[55] Ege Musa, one of the few Kenyan Somalis literate in English, became its president in the 1930s.[56] According to one of my interlocutors who knew him well, Ege Musa was a well-traveled and worldly individual. Born in British Somaliland and raised in Aden, he took a position on a ship in 1889. After traveling the world, he settled in Durban and worked at a hotel run by two European women, through which he acquired an education in English. Musa parlayed this experience into a position serving as an English-Somali translator for the Kenya colonial government. Once settled in Kenya, he married a woman from British Somaliland.[57] By traveling throughout the empire, becoming proficient in English, and joining the Somali community in Kenya, Musa embodied a unique cosmopolitanism that owed itself to both British colonialism and the regional practices of Northeast Africa.

Had he stayed in South Africa, his children may not have retained the same relationship with the wider Somali community. Many Isaaq and Harti people juxtaposed themselves with the Somalis who had settled in South Africa, whom they claimed did not "maintain their culture."[58] There is reason to be somewhat skeptical of assertions of this nature. Claims to have resisted assimilation were often ways for my interlocutors, as James Clifford puts it, to "stage authenticity *in opposition to* external, often dominating alternatives."[59] In addition, I was unable to speak to those who had assimilated into Kenya and had lost their identity as "Somalis"—thus becoming invisible to my methods of identifying "representative" members of the community.

While many colonial officials and settlers saw Isaaq and Harti subjects as a "hybrid" people—who disturbed the line between settler and native—it is much harder to unearth how Somalis of this era conceptualized ideas of "localness," "mixture," and cosmopolitanism. Did Somali immigrants to Kenya understand themselves as people somehow in between cultures? Through what vernacular terms did they debate who was local and foreign, who was uprooted and worldly, and who had lost and who had retained their "culture"? Not all pasts are recoverable, and some questions cannot be answered through a fragmented historical record. What is clear, however, is that claiming non-native status was about more than positioning oneself in a vertical racial hierarchy. It also allowed members of the Somali community to maintain horizontal solidarities that cut across colonial boundaries.

Economic circuits had brought the Isaaq and the Harti to far-flung territories, where they fell under the jurisdiction of different legal orders. Perceived to be "out of place" in the various territories in which they settled, Somalis were often the locus of contention over racial boundaries. Battles over racial definitions in the colonies also held implications for the meaning of Britishness in the metropole. The very racialized structures that enabled Somali migrants to occupy a comparatively privileged status in East Africa relegated them to the margins of British society. Race was at the center of the making of metropolitan Britain and the capitalist structures that sustained it.

Somali sailors had been living in London, Bristol, Cardiff, Liverpool, and other English port cities since the nineteenth century, when they had first arrived on European merchant ships.[60] Ostensibly, as emigrants from territories under the sovereignty of the British Crown, they enjoyed formal equality with all other British subjects.[61] In practice, the British government created a tiered citizenship based upon the perceived "whiteness" of their imperial subjects. Moreover, many Somalis were considered protected persons rather than British subjects, since British Somaliland was technically a protectorate, not a colony. While this distinction was often negligible in practice, emigrants from protectorates enjoyed fewer rights and were subject to stricter labor and deportation laws than those from other parts of the empire. Inhabitants of Somaliland who lawfully immigrated to the United Kingdom were defined as aliens.

World War I drew European nations and their colonial subjects ever closer, even as it tested the limits of imperial promises of equality. During the interwar period, the British state took steps to restrict further emigration from the colonies, and deported many of the seamen and munitions workers who had come to England and Wales during the war. After race riots broke out in 1919, the Home Office enacted several pieces of racially discriminatory legislation, including the Aliens Order (1920) and the Coloured Alien Seamen Order (1925). The latter was used, as Kathleen Paul argues, "to harass all 'coloured seamen,' 'aliens and British subjects mixed,' and to prevent as many as possible from settling in the United Kingdom."[62] Such legislation was motivated by fear that uncontrolled migration would entrench a black, urbanized underclass in the heart of European cities, who could claim unemployment benefits, jobs occupied by the white working class, and blur the boundary between black and white. Many colonial subjects, including those who had worked and sacrificed on behalf of the Crown, were denied hospitality within the country.

There has been much theorizing as to why internal difference has so often become the locus of intolerance within otherwise liberal nation-states.[63] Part of the answer may lie in the fact that many European nation-states made themselves and their sense of national identity through their expansion and colonization overseas.[64] Discovering the "other" at home eroded the ability to maintain the separation between colonizer and colonized. Alien Somalis were, to reappropriate Mae Ngai's elegant expression, a kind of "impossible subject," "at once welcome and unwelcome."[65] They personified many of the key tensions within the imperial political economy, which depended upon colonial labor in various forms.[66]

Government officials in the United Kingdom frequently worked out ideas of race at home, in close collaboration with the Colonial and Foreign Offices. Racial difference was also fashioned through dialogue across different colonial territories. Although the color bar was global in scope, protectorate and colonial regimes often defined and enforced legal hierarchies differently, which was sometimes a cause for concern. In 1926, Sir Harold Kittermaster, governor of British Somaliland (and formerly officer in charge of the NFD), informed locals at a meeting at Burao in British Somaliland that "it is to Swahilis that" the Somalis "are properly comparable," not Indians or Arabs.[67] Kittermaster warned his colleagues: "There is frequent interchange of Somali residents in Nairobi with their homes here, and they maintain their roots here even after years of absence. To give them a status in Kenya so different from what they must have here would tend greatly to embarrass the administration of this Protectorate."[68] The Swahili occupied a similar "awkward position" as the Somali, "having neither a recognized African 'tribal' identity nor the higher legal status of Non-Native."[69] Irrevocably "impure," they, too, were part of a cosmopolitan Indian Ocean world whose elements did not conform to the cultural "wholes" to which colonial authorities imagined their subjects belonged.

Although the Isaaq and the Harti had managed to attain many of the rights of Asians within Kenya, colonial authorities were wary of creating any legal precedents that might have empire-wide ramifications. Consequently, officials in Kenya lacked a consistent vocabulary for classifying the Isaaq and the Harti, whom they alternatively labeled "Natives," "Arabs," and, in some cases, "Asiatics."[70] The label "Asiatic" was especially fraught, and in many ways reflected the fundamental ambiguities of colonial racial thought. Before World War II, European cartographers often lumped the Arabian Peninsula with "Western Asia"—a geographic concept eventually displaced by the term "Middle East."[71] While it was typically "used to describe people from South Asia," as James Brennan notes, the terms "Asian" and "Asiatic" "were also shifting legal and political terms that sometimes, but not always, joined Arabs and Indians together, and sometimes Chinese as well."[72] In addition, many Isaaq had originated from Aden, whose inhabitants were subjects of British India until 1937.[73] Competing definitions of indigenousness further complicated their legal status.[74] However, it also opened the door for Somalis to self-fashion by stretching the boundaries and definitions of what it meant to be native.[75]

PASTORAL MODES OF TERRITORIAL GOVERNANCE

Though in ways quite distinct from Somali town dwellers, nomadic populations in the north of Kenya also challenged a certain colonial imagination of indigenousness. For the first two decades of protectorate rule, authorities did not so much administer the north as attempt to suppress the southward migration of nomadic peoples. After ceding Jubaland to Italy in 1925 in exchange for its participation in World War I, the colonial government placed the NFD under civilian control and declared it a closed district—movement in and out of which was restricted to holders of a special pass (see map 2.1).[76] Protectorate and colonial officials came to see northern nomads as part of a physical and metaphorical frontier, situated on the margins of "civilization." One of the ways in which the colonial government cultivated an image of British "order" was by projecting an idea of anarchy onto the north.[77]

The nature of British rule in the NFD can be examined through the colonial archives, which provide selective vestiges of the working operations of power, as well as the ways in which colonial authorities authorized and rationalized that power. There are significant limits to how creatively or subversively these written records can be read.[78] Archival records homogenize the passing of time during the colonial era—transforming the history of the north into a recurring, self-fulfilling debate over borders, administrative control, and registration efforts.

Using the archives alone, it is very difficult to reconstruct the practices and beliefs that we anachronistically call "religion."[79] To come to "know" and govern their subjects, authorities had to parse which streams of "local" knowledge were serviceable to empire.[80] Many important aspects of Somali and northern life, including Islamic spiritual practices, were often ignored. In 1929, the district commissioner (DC) of Bura District, M. R. Mahony, wrote a report in which he dismissively described the Somali as "a fanatical Mohamedan though ignorant of the true tenets of Islam."[81] In his mind, Somalis were both more fervent and less orthodox than their Muslim counterparts on the coast. The "majority are illiterate," he noted, and the "bush Sheiks and Sheriffs have only learnt to recite, read, and laboriously write a few of the better known texts from the Koran."[82] Like many Orientalist thinkers of his era, he treated literate Muslims and "Arab" Islam as more authentic and narrowly defined Islamic orthodoxy as textual. In general, colonial officials delved into Somali spiritual practices only when they believed a particular religious thinker or practice might cause discord or held some kind of threatening potential.[83] Religious practices largely escaped the colonial gaze and, as a consequence, assemblage within the archives. These silences, however, should not be equated with irrelevancy.[84]

Historians will, however, find no shortage of sophisticated clan charts or intricate genealogical histories in the archives. Officials took an almost obsessive interest in clans and produced a veritable corpus of anthropological material.[85] Preferring to govern through "chiefly" leaders, most colonial officials did not interfere in the religious life of northerners—a policy that also facilitated the broader depoliticization of Islamic thought and practice. In the eyes of most colonial officials, Islam was a belief system that should be confined to the sphere of "customary law."

Nevertheless, local administrators could never fully disregard Islamic identification or patterns of conversion. In 1929, Mahony complained that the "bar to peaceful intermixture between Galla and Somali is only religion," and they otherwise "intermarry freely," and "no gazetting or delimiting of grazing areas will prevent" this.[86] As the previous chapter has shown, *gaal* was not an "ethnic" designation, but rather a derogatory label in local vernaculars for a non-Muslim.[87] Nevertheless, colonial officials recoded the distinction between *gaal* and Somali into ethnoterritorial terms. They also created and loosely enforced a border that cut across the NFD, known as the Somali-Galla line, which each group was ostensibly prohibited from crossing.[88] Reading local categories through the epistemology of clan, colonial officials often overlooked the links that cut across collectivities.

Throughout the colony, officials struggled to police mobility and give their subjects singular and unambiguous ethnic labels.[89] These difficulties were nevertheless compounded on the borderlands of the NFD. Islamic claims to universality and practices of conversion challenged colonial efforts to neatly demarcate clan and ethnic boundaries. In addition, nomadic populations defied what Liisa Malkki refers to as the sedentarist metaphysics of the modern state.[90] Local administrators were beset by the anxiety of indeterminacy—the fear that the Somali were "really" Borana, that one lineage comprised *sheegat* who "originally" belonged to a different clan, or that Italian or Ethiopian subjects might be "passing" as British. Groups traversed international and regional frontiers in order to use dry season wells, return to their historic grazing lands, visit leaders and kin, or evade government requirements such as taxation and military recruitment.[91] Northerners also crossed borders for spiritual reasons—whether to attend the hajj or make pilgrimages to spiritually significant gravesites, join a *zawiya* (Islamic settlement), or pursue a religious education.[92] In addition, the differential price regimes of the Italian, British, and Ethiopian governments allowed a vibrant cross-border economy in livestock, guns, and ivory to thrive.[93]

Unable to control movement across the porous international frontiers, the administration resigned hope of rendering northerners into countable "populations," issuing identity cards, or drawing up definitive maps of ethnic "homelands." In 1930, F. G. Jennings, the DC of Wajir, argued that a census would be both unpopular and expensive to complete, and, "further it would serve no useful purpose so long as the Somali adopts the attitude of moving over the boundary into Italian territory at will."[94] Colonial officials were frequently far more concerned with enforcing some semblance of state control than with rendering their subjects "legible."[95] In Wajir, local authorities were unable to create ethnic homelands and instead divided the wells in the district between the major clans. This approach, as Schlee notes, was a precolonial governance strategy common among the Borana.[96] Capitulating to nomadic patterns of transhumance, beleaguered administrators developed techniques that had far more continuity with precolonial practices of governance than with Weberian ideals of bureaucracy.

Throughout the 1920s and 1930s, the administration worked out a hybrid form of sovereignty that blended territorial governance with nomadic forms of mobility.[97] One might be tempted to portray colonial power as weak, incapable (as Jeffrey Herbst suggests) of broadcasting its power across this arid, northern expanse.[98] Yet conceding to nomadic practices and cultivating an image of the north as "ungovernable" proved to be commensurate with broader colonial goals. Eschewing assumptions that governments seek only to inhibit their subjects' movement, Darshan Vigneswaran and Joel Quirk argue that "mobility makes states."[99] In defining certain kinds of movement as a problem, colonial officials worked out ideas concerning the reach and scope of their own authority. Administrators often recoded their failures as new strategies of governance—reframing Somali and Borana initiatives in terms decipherable to administrative logic. Such an approach enabled officials to justify the financial and administrative neglect of the region, naturalize its isolation from the rest of the colony, and keep governance in the NFD as cost-effective as possible. It also allowed for overlapping notions of sovereignty, space, and authority to flourish on the borderlands of the state.

THE SOMALI "EL DORADO"

The British Empire brought Somalis from diverse lineages and lands together under a single territory. Mobile and spatially dispersed, both the nomadic populations in the NFD and the "detribalized" urban traders living in Nairobi disrupted colonial efforts to police spatial and racial boundaries. Segregationist policies, however, always existed in tension with the needs of the colonial economy, which was dependent upon the mobility of Africans, including Somali traders.[100] Managing this tension was key to the colonial project.

By the early 1920s, a tenuous project of racial segregation was taking shape in Kenya's capital. In 1921, the colonial government gazetted the township of Eastleigh. Though technically reserved exclusively for Indian residence, Eastleigh incorporated several neighborhoods already inhabited by Somalis. Failure to invest funds in maintaining the area deterred wealthier and higher-caste Indians from settling there. Somalis from Ngara (and, later, veterans of World War II) also moved into the neighborhood, where they lived alongside Goans, Indians, and Seychelloise.[101] The creation of Eastleigh was part of a much larger, colony-wide process of land alienation and racial segregation, which developed in tandem with the commercial economy.

Eastleigh embodied many of the contradictions of the migrant labor system. Colonial authorities enforced racial segregation by, in part, naturalizing the idea that Africans belonged in rural areas. The urban economy, however, was predicated upon the exploitation of African laborers, many of whom had been forced onto their supposedly "traditional" homelands.[102] Soon after its establishment, Africans from the countryside took up residency in Eastleigh, since (unlike squatter residences that lacked legitimacy) the police "did not enter houses" in the neighborhood "searching for illegal residents."[103] Somali traders in Nairobi also troubled colonial ideas of spatial and racial order by maintaining a circulation of livestock between rural areas and the city. Elder Somalis wistfully recalled that Eastleigh and the Nairobi Commonage had once had ample grazing land, on which their community used to pasture their animals.[104]

Many of the tensions of the migrant labor system were mirrored in the colonial livestock economy, which also unsettled the line between urban and rural (a distinction central to colonial projects of segregation and visions of modernization). Recognizing their skills as livestock brokers, colonial administrators had given Somali and Arab traders special permits to enter the NFD, move across tribal grazing boundaries, and bring restricted numbers of livestock from the north into the rest of the colony. Unlike nomadic inhabitants, who were largely barred from settling in town, these "alien" traders were allowed to own commercial plots in the townships of the north.[105] Somali traders provided pastoralists with cash to pay colonial taxes and enabled animals from the north to be circulated into the commercial livestock economy. These policies ensured that nomadic populations were confined to the north, excluded from southern grazing land, and barred from competing with white ranchers.[106] Livestock smuggled in by Somali traders also served as foundation stock for white ranchers, and were essential to African squatters, who provided inexpensive labor on white commercial farms.[107]

Gradually, Somali traders began to accumulate animals along the stock routes in towns as dispersed as Rumuruti, Naivasha, Gilgil, and Kitale, where they came into conflict with white settlers (see map 2.1). Their trading and residence privileges also enabled them to take advantage of the illegal poaching and game trade, transgress quarantine regulations, and covertly bring animals into African native reserves.[108] By moving onto land speculated by white farmers and ranchers and amassing "so great an accumulation of stock," Somali traders became a threat to white interests and supremacy.[109] Conceptual and political categories were also at stake.

This issue reached a head in the mid-1920s, when settlers demanded the forced removal of Somalis living and grazing animals on white farms and Crown land in Laikipia.[110] In 1924, the resident commissioner of Rumuruti complained of former Somali traders:

> who have settled down by permission of the farmers themselves on payment of grazing fees, and are now beginning to breed stock in competition with Europeans. . . . They are responsible for cattle running, they are continually in trouble with their Kikuyu herdsmen, and the danger of infecting the District with cattle diseases is great.[111]

Portraying Somalis as encroachers and parasites on the land ignored the pivotal role they had played in establishing the white farms and townships of Central Kenya and the Rift Valley.

Officials found a solution in the underutilized livestock quarantine of Isiolo, which had been created when the government envisioned a large livestock trade from the NFD. Throughout the 1920s, the administration compelled Somalis in many of the townships, including Rumuruti, to sell their cattle or move onto the Isiolo quarantine.[112] Although the quarantine had once been home to the Samburu, who had been removed by the colonial state, administrators redefined the area as the primary, if not official, homeland of the "alien" Somali.[113] Notions of who was "native" were continually unmade and remade. Even as they alienated land, however, colonial officials could not fully efface memories of prior occupancy—memories that would later generate an array of competing land claims.[114]

In moving Isaaq and Harti traders and their families onto the Isiolo leasehold, the colonial regime hoped to govern them more effectively as a "tribe." This desire for administrative order, however, was undercut by paranoia about the dispersed and unregulated nature of Somali kinship networks. Fearful of encouraging overpopulation and overgrazing, the administration decided to reserve Isiolo solely for those who had a long history of military or colonial service.[115] They also stopped short of creating a formal native reserve. In its 1934 report, the Kenya Land Commission (KLC) cited an ominous warning from the district commissioner of Isiolo. A few years earlier, he had cautioned that "Kenya is regarded by the Northern Somali as an El Dorado" and that if "infiltration from Northern Somaliland" was not controlled, "the area set apart for the Somalis would" prove "insufficient, and the Somalis, having obtained political rights and power, would then again demand consideration of their claims."[116] For the next thirty years, as colonial officials debated the status of the Isiolo leasehold, they constantly cited this passage—projecting fears that any attempt to codify Somali rights to the land would open a floodgate of immigration into this "El Dorado."[117] Colonial authorities worked to ensure that tenure rights in Isiolo remained tenuous and that no legal precedent would be set that could grant Somalis permanent rights to the area.

To restrict migration onto the Isiolo leasehold, officials kept a register of legal residents and required that visitors carry passes. Abdullahi Elmi and Hassan Good, two Somali residents of Isiolo, explained that Isaaq and Harti residents would occasionally skirt these measures, especially when it came to hiring Turkana herdsmen.[118] Nevertheless, Isiolo inhabitants were often complicit in the enforcement of segregation. Some of the people I spoke to recalled the colonial period as a time when they were ensured access to land, and "outsiders" were kept at bay by colonial powers. What emerged was a fairly workable compromise among Somali veterans, their kin, and colonial officials, who had shared desires to keep the land exclusive. The fact that colonial administrators and Somali town dwellers conceptualized the idea of the "stranger" differently did not preclude the possibility for negotiation and agreement.

Colonial policies in Isiolo had deep implications as they established legal and historical precedents for rights to land. Today, people from five major groups share and are making claims to Isiolo District. According to Saafo Roba Boye and Randi Kaarhus, "These claims seek legitimacy through reference to historical processes, to first-comer status and to former governments' decisions, to citizenship dues, as well as to 'tribal' group rights."[119] Many Somali residents argued that the colonial government had given them the area as a reward for their military service.[120] At the same time, residents often obscured the participation of their predecessors in colonial policies of segregation.

CIVIL RIGHTS AND THE COLOR BAR UNDER EMPIRE

Denied definitive non-native status as well as full recognition as "natives," Isaaq and Harti Somalis had only provisional access to legal rights. By the 1930s, their legal status was coming into crisis. To some extent, this was the result of fundamental tensions within the imperial political economy. On one hand, the British Empire created globally interconnected economies, disseminated a universalizing vision of "civilization," and provided a language of civil rights linked to British subject status. On the other, colonial regimes remained committed to the belief in a racial and ethnic core to group identity, both by extrapolation from Englishness and as a practical consequence of indirect rule.[121]

In the early 1930s, British authorities throughout the empire began to debate how best to shore up the racial order and define the limits of civil rights. A relatively obscure court case in 1929, which involved a "half-caste" in Nyasaland, triggered a much larger debate between the Colonial Office and colonial regimes throughout Africa over the definition of the term "native" and the legal rights of Westernized Africans and "mixed-race" subjects.[122] British authorities may have been working out ideas of race in the colonies in order to allay anxieties and resolve similar questions at home. The Great Depression heightened debates over the color bar, which was already destabilized by the spread of Western education and the recruitment of soldiers from the colonies during World War I. In 1930, the National Union of Seamen in the United Kingdom, in collaboration with the Shipping Federation, instituted a rota system that restricted the employment of Muslim seamen, most of whom came from Yemen and Somaliland.[123] As competition for working-class jobs in the UK intensified, many of the racially charged issues of the past were reignited.

Empire had facilitated the spread of Muslim communities, which offered colonial subjects an alternative form of global membership and a means of mobilizing outside the narrow confines of the color bar. An example can be found in the figure of Lt. Abdullah Cardell-Ryan, a Muslim convert of Irish origin. Having served in Africa and the Red Sea, the lieutenant had taken a personal interest in the welfare of veterans from British Somaliland. Hailing from a land that had also been subject to English colonization, perhaps he felt a special affinity for the plight of his fellow Muslims. Somali veterans likely turned to him in the hope of gaining the ear of the British administration. In response to the discriminatory measures of the Shipping Federation, Cardell-Ryan petitioned the secretary of state for the colonies. In his letter, he protested against the boycott of loyal Somali stokers who had fought in World War I and dismissed the economic rationale for the rota system.[124] He also complained that the distinction between protectorate and colony was so dubious that few Somalis anticipated being labeled "protected Subjects (whatever that may mean)" upon arrival in England.[125] Oral and written testimony suggests that many Somali sailors and soldiers considered the distinction between "subject" and "protected person" irrelevant. Having fought on behalf of the Crown, Somali veterans became wedded to the idea of being British subjects and often referred to themselves as "British Somalis."[126]

Rather than privilege a narrower racialist view that entitled only Europeans to work and reside in the United Kingdom, colonized subjects living and working in the UK argued that the British government should hold true to the tenets of imperial citizenship. Somalis faced an imperial power that, under varying circumstances, favored two incompatible ideas of citizenship: one founded on ideas of racial difference; and another based upon service and loyalty to the Crown. To forestall deportation, many Muslim activists in the UK appealed to the latter concept, highlighting the sacrifice involved in military service. In September 1934, Abdul Majid, who had founded the Islamic Society, wrote to the undersecretary of state for the colonies to protest the proposed deportation of three Somalis, saying: "A great many of such 'Aliens' both from India and African Crown Colonies served with great loyalty to the British Crown in the Great War. . . . They wish to be treated in exactly the same way as British born subjects."[127] Figures such as Majid, an Indian barrister, and Cardell-Ryan reveal the possibilities for multiracial and cross-class alliances among Muslims.[128] Despite their efforts, however, the British government implemented few reforms to anti-immigrant legislation during the interwar period.

While Somalis in the United Kingdom sought to diminish the significance of the color bar, those living in the colonies often took actions that reinforced its importance. Panracial and Islamic solidarity existed in tandem with discourses of racial difference. In the colonies, where promises of a universalizing imperial citizenship rang especially hollow, Somali leaders often highlighted their putative foreign descent.

In the 1930s, Somali and Arab representatives fought against colonial efforts to erode their legal status.[129] In 1930, leaders of the "Ishaak Shariff Community" wrote to King George V with a list of grievances, among which was the denial of access to the special Asian wards of Nairobi's hospitals, inequitable treatment in regard to the livestock trade, and lack of political representation. The authors of the petition described themselves as a community "of Asiatic origin and extraction" who were "emigrants of Aden and Southern Arabia" and "Ishaakian Arabs Shariff."[130] In 1932, Isaaq leaders—referring to themselves as "Arabs"—once again petitioned the Kenyan government after being barred from entry into the Asian wards of hospitals.[131]

These demands took on greater urgency by the end of the decade. In 1937, in an effort to increase the revenue stream, the Kenyan governor implemented a new ordinance that revised the existing taxation system for non-natives. The Non-Native Poll Tax Ordinance introduced a sliding scale for Europeans, Asians, and "other" non-natives. "Others" were defined as Arabs, Swahilis, and Somalis. Presumably, the division between Swahili, Arab, and Somali was too tenuous for the colonial regime to maintain on a legal register. This new legislation also reduced Somali tax obligations from thirty to twenty shillings.[132]

Out of fear that tendering a lowered tax would lessen their privileges, many Isaaq and Harti Somalis began petitioning the colonial government and—in an unusual reversal of typical forms of tax resistance—demanded to pay the higher, Asian rate of thirty shillings. The community also mobilized around the Ishakia Association, contending that their community was distinct from other "native" Somalis. Due to their comparative wealth, their history of colonial service, their discrete genealogy, and their long-standing connections with the Arab world, the Isaaq were uniquely positioned to protest against the new tax ordinance. In 1937, the secretary of the British Ishak community wrote to the secretary of state for the colonies to explain:

> While the definition of a "Native" might appropriately be applied to a majority of the Somalis who have migrated into this Colony from Italian or French Somaliland or other territories, the British Ishak Community is unquestionably distinct from all such Somalis. They are no more Somalis by reason of their long residence in Aden or other parts of British Somaliland than Indians or Europeans could be called Africans because they have lived for generations in various parts of Africa.[133]

The secretary of the Ishakia community glossed over more complex questions of intermarriage and cultural assimilation and portrayed the Isaaq as foreign migrants on the continent. He also rehearsed the common Western stereotype that saw Africans as rooted in their "native" soil and "civilized" people as more capacious and rootless.

Despite their relatively small numbers (there were no more than a few thousand Isaaq in the colony as a whole), administrators refused to concede to their demands.[134] They feared that granting the Isaaq Asiatic status would open the door for all Somalis throughout Kenya and other colonies to claim similar rights. In 1939, Reece cautioned: "There is some evidence that they have already tried to interfere with the Samburu destocking scheme, and to encourage Ogaden Somalis in the Northern Frontier to start a demand for their own non-native status."[135] Richard G. Turnbull, the DC of Isiolo, noted that "the Darod Somalis are watching the situation with interest and would, I consider, join the Ishaak agitation provided they could find a strong leader."[136]

It goes without saying that the distinction between "Isaaq" and other Somalis was tenuous at best. Much like race, the abstractness of lineage also made it "effective"—"it is not easily susceptible to empirical disproof, and it can coexist with social relations that belie the premises of different" models of kinship.[137] Moreover, it could be traced in multiple ways. The Isaaq had intermarried with fellow Harti immigrants, members of local communities, and Somalis living in the NFD—rendering the line between one lineage and another (as well as between "native" and "non-native") dubious.[138] Yet it is often when social and cultural boundaries are the most ambiguous that leaders mobilize to defend them.[139] In order to better position themselves within the racial binaries of colonial thought, Isaaq leaders mobilized around a particular genealogical imaginary.

The poll-tax campaign led to various shifts in rhetorical strategies. Not only did Isaaq representatives (at least within colonial petitions) distance themselves from the term "Somali"; they also began to shed the label "Arab," which no longer offered them elevated privileges under the new tax legislation. In 1938, in a petition to the colonial secretary, the "Elders of the British Shariff Ishak Community of Kenya Colony" maintained that they "can neither be classified as Arabs or Somalis. Your Petitioners' Community are a race of Asiatic Origin."[140] Isaaq leaders toyed with the ambiguity of the term "Asiatic," which colonial authorities had used, often inconsistently, as a legal, geographic, and racial category. Such tactics, as Christopher Lee notes, represented "a kind of folk racism that only oppression could conceive."[141] They also suggest that African subjects did not always internalize the continental theory of race introduced by colonial rule.

In the 1980s, Africanist historians began to interpret cases of this nature as "inventions of tribalism."[142] More recently, scholars have highlighted the "agency" of Africans engaged in a kind of "auto-ethnography"—capable of appropriating the colonizer's terms for their own purposes.[143] These paradigms helped to dismantle rigid, primordialist views of ethnicity. However, they also tended to overstate the reach of colonial power and the centrality of colonial categories, while collapsing the arguments that African elites made about race with underlying social structures and "identities."[144] Moreover, the term "invention" can appear derogative from the point of view of those struggling to prove the validity of their origins and entitlements. The officer in charge of the NFD, Gerald Reece, for example, dismissed the name Ishakia as a mere fabrication: "They have decided to abandon their name of Somali and to call themselves Ishakia—a word which I presume they have themselves invented."[145] Seeking to naturalize and legitimize categories of identity, political thinkers have often treated changes in identification as discoveries rather than inventions.[146]

The ways that groups reorient themselves toward the past (and future), as Talal Asad argues, is "more complex than the notion of 'invented tradition' allows."[147] First, one must consider the role of the archive in shaping the kinds of knowledge available for historical reconstruction. James Clifford notes that while colonial subjects wrote to European authorities, "their voices were adapted to an imposed context" aimed at addressing "white authorities and legal structures."[148] For this reason, it is difficult to determine whether labels such as "Asiatic" ever became popular or folk categories. Second, the efforts of Somali leaders should not be seen as full-fledged appropriations of colonial racial thought. In the case of the Isaaq, newer vocabularies, like "race" and "civilization," were linked to older concepts, such as *qabiil* and *shariif*. As Muslims and imperial subjects, many Somali elites conceived of themselves as members of a "civilized" world linked to both imperial geographies and Islamic notions of the *Dar al-Islam*. In addition, it would be reductive to see petitions of this nature as simply rational pursuits of greater social and economic gain, as some scholars have suggested.[149] Rather, these strategies reflected broader discursive shifts as well as a desire for the constellation of rights and concepts that had come to be associated with "non-native" status.

That Isaaq leaders would reject both their indigenous roots is an uncomfortable reminder that many Africans participated in the segregated colonial order. However, it also shows that empire provided a powerful language for demanding greater civil rights.[150] As oppressive as the color bar undoubtedly was, it made global inequalities explicit and political.[151] If properly connected, racialized discourses could also become a powerful tool of redress. Unlike the majority of "native" subjects, Somali leaders could acquire the items of bourgeois political legitimacy and access what Mamdani refers to as the civil side of the bifurcated colonial state. This was the face of the state that "governed a racially defined citizenry" and "was bounded by the rule of law and associated regime of rights."[152] They were able to hire British lawyers, who sent letters on their behalf directly to the secretary of state for the colonies and King George VI.[153] Isaaq representatives in Kenya were also able to turn to their kin abroad in order to bypass lower-ranking officials and "internationalize their struggle for Asian status and rights."[154] They appointed Haji Farah Omar, a prominent anticolonial nationalist, to serve as their representative in British Somaliland and petitioned the Duke of Gloucester through a local agent during his visit to the protectorate. In addition, they selected Abby Farah as their representative in London and requested that he hire a solicitor to represent their interests before the Colonial Office.[155]

The goals of alien Somali leaders in Kenya converged, as E. R. Turton notes, "with the interests of their brethren in British Somaliland."[156] At the same time as the poll-tax campaign in Kenya, religious and political leaders in Somaliland were resisting British attempts to implement a school curriculum that would include Somali written in the Roman, rather than Arabic, script. Opponents of the curriculum—which included Haji Omar and several Qadiriyya sheikhs—feared that rendering their language decipherable to European powers would reduce them to a "Bantu" people and enable the protectorate government to implement a system of registration and direct taxation. They were also concerned that the new curriculum would undermine the authority of religious leaders and hasten Christian proselytizing by allowing for the translation of the Bible into the vernacular. Rumors circulated that the director of education was a priest in disguise.[157]

To some extent, the campaign against a Latin script can be understood within an instrumentalist framework—as an effort to avoid taxation, registration, and a reduction in status. Nevertheless, this conflict also reflected differing understandings of education, language, and religion. Influenced by a nineteenth-century view of nationalism, colonial and protectorate authorities saw language as largely coterminous with "culture." They operated along the premise that their subjects could be similarly subdivided into members of delimited "tribes," each with a distinct territory and dialect. Many Muslims, however, did not conceptualize Arabic as an "ethnic" language that belonged exclusively to Arabs. Rather, it was a divine medium of instruction.[158]

British officials and their Somali subjects also held differing understandings of what constituted proper education. Most Somalis in this era viewed Western schooling as akin to Christian evangelism (not an unwarranted conclusion given how many schools were run by missionaries). One Somali elder, who had been sent to Hargeisa by his parents to be educated, described enduring taunts from his peers in British Somaliland, who called him a Christian.[159] Ali Bule of Garissa explained that people did not want to study in colonial schools because they thought they would become Christian.[160] These sentiments did not reflect a wholesale rejection of education, but rather a repudiation of colonial and secular approaches to schooling. Many Somalis attended *dugsi* (Qur'anic school) and some furthered their education at Islamic universities or under the guidance of religious sheikhs.[161] Moreover, those who did see the value of British schooling often demanded instruction in Arabic and English, a language that offered them obvious benefits within the structures of colonial power. Haji Farah Omar, who was educated in India, where he fell under the influence of Gandhian philosophy, shunned the new curriculum not because it was Western or un-Islamic, but because it was based on an inferior "adapted" curriculum.[162]

Like the Isaaq leaders of Kenya, Somali leaders in British Somaliland fought a reduction in status by asserting their foreign origins and making reference to a broader geographic horizon beyond the colonial state. According to R. E. Ellison, the superintendent of education, the *qadi* (judge) of Hargeisa informed the administration: "We Somalis are Arabs by origin and we like to consider ourselves as still being of the Arabic race. We can never consent to our being considered as Africans. We are afraid that if our sons are taught to write Somali they will . . . forget that they are really Arabs."[163] Omar also argued that Somalis were "Arabs" and that Arabic, the language of religious instruction and legal contracts, could not be considered a "foreign language."[164] In July 1938, an article appeared in the Arabic newspaper *Al Shabaab*, which was published in Cairo. According to a government translation, the author (whom protectorate officials posited to be Haji Farah Omar) decried British attempts "to suppress the Arabic language . . . to build an iron wall between the Somalis, the Arab nations and the Moslems, in order that there should not be any connection between them."[165] The British protectorate administration feared they had inadvertently fostered a Pan-Arab and Pan-Islamic nationalism.

Mobilizing through the juridical categories of empire led to a confusing patchwork of different legal identities. Isaaq and Somali leaders in different territories adopted their own localized strategies, which points to the contingent, situated, and strategic nature of identity politics. Yet their tactics also reflected broader discursive changes afoot across the Empire and the Muslim world. The strategies of leaders in Somaliland foreshadow epistemic shifts in Islamic education and reveal the links between colonial racialization and emergent forms of Pan-Arab nationalism. As Talal Asad argues, the idea of an Arab nation represented "a major conceptual transformation by which" the notion of an *umma* was "cut off from the theological predicates that gave it its universalizing power" and "made to stand for an imagined community that is equivalent to a total political society, limited and sovereign."[166] These moments thus highlight powerful new ways of mapping one's place across the region and the globe.

NON-NATIVE STATUS COMING UNDONE

The poll-tax campaign and the quest for Asiatic status escalated colonial fears about the fragility of the racial order. In response, the colonial administration scrambled to find a way to render the Isaaq into visible, traceable subjects. In April 1938, the colonial secretary urged officials to refuse the higher tax rendered by Somalis and demanded that a census be prepared to identify the number of alien Somalis resident in each district.[167] Anxious because they could determine neither their location nor their exact numbers, the colonial administration also devised plans for a Somali Registration Bill. Colonial authorities complained that the Isaaq "refused to acknowledge the authority or leadership of their own Headmen lest . . . they should be regarded as behaving as natives."[168] They were also concerned that "there is at present no adequate means of ascertaining the numbers and whereabouts of Somalis in the Colony. In the majority of cases it is not even possible to identify a Somali or to trace his past history."[169] Reece noted that "a Somali tribesman at Wajir might sometimes be mistaken by some people for an 'alien,' but any other Somali could easily tell from his voice and dialect (if not from his appearance) whether the man was a Hawia, Darod or Isaak."[170] He attempted to inscribe in dialect and physiognomy some kind of meaningful identification system.

The untraceable Somali—unconfined to a fixed territory, without an obvious leader to co-opt, lacking easily identifiable markers—became a source of colonial vexation. World War II renewed these anxieties, stigmatized

Somali political demands, and threw the alien category into further disarray. As Harti and Isaaq leaders divided over the poll-tax issue, they began to accuse one another of being Italian agents disloyal to the British Crown. Such accusations fed into colonial fears of Somalis as potential "spies and sedition mongers."[171] The colonial government imprisoned several agitators, considered tighter immigration and deportation laws (which the attorney general felt could be "justified as a war measure"), and implemented registration efforts in the NFD that targeted alien residents.[172] Plans for a Somali Registration Bill were, nevertheless, abandoned out of concerns of wartime embarrassment and accusations of racial discrimination. Kenya was under pressure from the Colonial Office, which feared that members of the Somali diaspora in Cardiff—who had contacts with British MPs—would raise Somali grievances in Parliament.[173]

The poll-tax agitation finally wore down in the early 1940s amid the global militarization of World War II and a changing imperial political climate. In 1940, the Kenyan colonial regime decided to implement a personal taxation system that based non-native tax on income rather than race, which disaggregated taxation from the thorny question of political rights.[174] With the rise of Fascism, explicit racism was becoming less acceptable within the international community. Nationalist and Pan-African movements were also heightening their demands for greater rights for indigenous communities. In such a context, claiming Asiatic status no longer made political sense. Burdened by postwar economic constraints and ever-higher taxes, the Isaaq leadership eventually abandoned their campaign.

As older ideas of empire gave way to a new model of imperial development and Africanization, Somalis discovered that claiming to be non-natives, far from ensuring them greater autonomy and rights, was now leaving them vulnerable to political marginalization. The changing language of citizenship rights did not always lead to more inclusive forms of politics. Nationalism complicated questions of belonging and precipitated new dilemmas for many groups, especially transterritorial populations such as the Kenyan Somali people. The question of where Somalis belonged and to which country they were "native" became an increasingly divisive issue in the years after World War II.

3 ∽ "The Goodness of the Past Is Gone"

The intention is that eventually the whole territory will be divided up into tribal areas. . . . I realize very fully how difficult it is to organize the many portions of tribes which inhabit the N.F.D., and nearly all of which belong to bigger units on the other side of the frontiers, and I know that the difficulty is greatly increased by constant movement, for political or other reasons, across the international borders.

— Gerald Reece, officer in charge of the
Northern Frontier District[1]

BY 1940, A NEW ECONOMIC and social vision of empire was sweeping through the continent, enabling the state to intervene far more radically in the lives of subjects. Frederick Cooper argues: "The ideological context in which Great Britain and France turned to development—the need to find a progressive basis for continued colonial rule in an era when major powers had made 'self-determination' a slogan of international politics—coincided with the heightened needs both had for their empires."[2] Ostensibly, "development" was meant to increase economic output, fuel the war effort, mitigate African demands for greater rights, and improve social welfare through the implementation of a set of technical projects.[3]

As the previous chapter has shown, many colonial officials viewed the Somali as a people "out of place" (both temporally and spatially) within the colony. Postwar governance projects magnified these sentiments and enabled colonial administrators to intervene more extensively in the lives of nomads and livestock brokers. Many officials came to see pastoralists as inherently irrational, damaging to the rangelands, and in need of reform. Influenced by new ecological models, the administration tried to better regulate their movement, implement clan-grazing zones, and confine them to ethnic "homelands." The colonial state also took greater control over the livestock trade, which impinged on the lives of Somali stockbrokers, who saw their privileges waning. Nomadic pastoralists and Somali urbanites were painted as "detribalized" subjects whose lifestyles did not align with the prospects of development.

Although the Colonial Office tried to forestall decolonization by implementing new development schemes, African leaders across the continent only heightened their demands for expanded rights and independence. Like many development schemes, nationalist projects were predicated on a certain ethnoterritorial logic. Nationalist and Pan-African campaigns portrayed citizenship as a right of natives, rather than a right of settlers and non-natives. Competing nationalist projects also claimed the Somali population (and the territory upon which they lived) as part of their future nations. The rise of nationalist movements thus further intensified questions of where Somalis in Kenya belonged. As leaders debated how the boundaries of the nation would be drawn (and who would be defined as "native"), Somalis in Kenya found themselves in a progressively more precarious position.

The postwar era gave birth to the contemporary development paradigm and ushered in new debates over the contours of citizenship. Faced with an erosion of their rights to mobility and obstacles to accessing livestock markets and pasture, Somalis across the colony struggled to navigate the economic and political changes wrought by development initiatives. They also moved to position themselves within a new political climate defined increasingly by nationalist movements. As this chapter shows, they were hemmed in by new conceptions of progress and changing notions of indigeneity, which undermined the fragile compromises worked out in the early phases of empire.

CONSPICUOUS TIN ROOFS

In 1940, Parliament passed the Colonial Development and Welfare Act, which pledged to invest more funding and manpower in the African colonies.[4] The newly elected Labour government also began to advocate for the reorganization and "modernization" of rural societies in colonial Africa. The postwar years ushered in interventions from a host of ecological experts, who brought new technorationalist views about population growth, ecology, and the environment to the colonies.[5]

In northern Kenya, administrators became increasingly anxious about population pressure, overgrazing, and erosion, which shaped policy toward the Somali population. As described in the previous chapter, the Kenyan government had embarked on a series of efforts to move "detribalized" Somalis to Isiolo. At the outbreak of World War II, the administration renewed these efforts to relocate Somalis from the Nairobi Commonage and other townships in accordance with the recommendations of the Kenya Land Commission (KLC).[6] However, this settlement scheme quickly ran afoul of the new ecological mind-set. Fears soon permeated colonial correspondence that Isiolo, if opened up to all "alien" Somalis, would be swarmed with untraceable, unbranded stock. In 1939, Gerald Reece, the officer in charge of the Northern Frontier District (NFD), wrote that "alien Somalis have dumped here many thousand head of cattle and many tens of thousands of sheep and goats. The owners often live at Moyale or Mombasa or Nakuru."[7] According to Reece, Somalis were relying on extended kin, particularly women and children, to retain herds of animals on the leasehold.

As Reece's comments suggest, male mobility was often predicated upon female immobility. Wives, mothers, and extended kin allowed Somali traders to maintain roots and distribute wealth across different locations.[8] According to several of my interlocutors, unless they had an influential male intermediary who could win them a pass, unattached women in the NFD were prevented from residing or legally engaging in trade in the townships of the north. As elsewhere in the colony, those who went to work in town were often cast as prostitutes.[9] Labor historians have noted that freedom of movement during the colonial era was highly gendered, as colonial officials naturalized African women's place in the rural household (and African men often reinforced such claims). Nevertheless, it is easy to underestimate the extent of female mobility, which often went unrecorded.[10] S. I. Ellis, the district commissioner (DC) of Isiolo, complained that because women did not have to carry Outlying District passes, ejected men could continue keeping stock in the leasehold with their wives.[11] As legal minors, African women were largely treated as an extension of the male-dominated rural household, and not as potential laborers worthy of being surveilled. This sometimes enabled them to circumvent colonial authorities. Having left fewer archival traces, their movement can be more difficult to historicize.

Concerns with unregulated African mobility and reproduction heightened as "'surplus' population" became "the specter—and planning and state agency the panacea—of colonial advisers and policy makers in London."[12] Harping on their supposedly "irrational" nomadic mentality, Reece argued that "alien" Somalis would welcome their seemingly limitless kin from the Somalilands onto Isiolo, and "after a short time we will be embarrassed with an even more serious shortage of land."[13] By the early 1940s, the Somali settlement scheme had been sidelined out of fear of environmental degradation and concerns that Isiolo was already far past its stock-carrying capacity.[14]

These anxieties were not the outcome of careful empirical investigation; rather, they were products of broader shifts in the colonial imagination. In 1942, Thomas G. Askwith became district commissioner of Isiolo. Development-minded and more liberal in orientation, he appeared, unlike his predecessors, to be far more optimistic about the capacity of the alien Somali population to be "modernized." Yet his most iconoclastic position was his dismissal of former officials' fears of overgrazing: "We appear to be ignorant of the real factors governing the holding capacity of the land, and although the area is supposed to have room for about a third of the stock existing at present, the grazing still appears to survive."[15] In 1943, after conducting a census of non-natives in the north, Askwith noted, to his own surprise, that—in spite of colonial concerns with Somali overpopulation—the number of houses in Isiolo appeared to have decreased, rather than increased: "It will thus be seen that the number of houses at Isiolo far from increasing since 1939 has actually decreased by about 40. The settlements appear to have increased by reason of the fact that the new tin roofs render them more conspicuous than previously."[16] One can imagine these conspicuous tin roofs, catching the light and the eye of colonial officials as they monitored the vast, pastoral terrain in airplanes. By questioning the reliability of colonial surveillance techniques (and the emphasis on the visible), Askwith challenged the preoccupation with overgrazing and overpopulation and interrupted the illusion of colonial oversight and knowledge.

Askwith's observations went largely overlooked by colonial administrators, whose anxieties soon became "commonsense." By the end of the war, officials had become more concerned with the ecological impact of unregulated Somali mobility and population growth. In 1943, D. C. Edwards, the senior agricultural officer, published an influential study on ecological deterioration in the rangelands of the north. In it, he connected land degradation to the breakdown of "tribal" authority.[17] Reece echoed Edwards's suggestions, arguing that "the damage that is taking place . . . was due to the failure of the Government to maintain the old tribal organizations" and advocating for the formation of clan grazing reserves.[18]

By portraying these schemes as a return to a "traditional" way of life, the colonial administration obscured the novelty of this new vision of the rangeland. James E. Ellis and David M. Swift refer to this as the "equilibrium myth." Experts who have studied pastoral ecosystems, they argue, have often operated from the assumption that they "are potentially stable" and "become destabilized by overstocking and overgrazing."[19] However, "equilibrium" conditions are rarely attainable in nature. While colonial officials held pastoralists responsible for ecological degradation, the quality of the rangeland, as Ellis and Swift show, is frequently dictated by "external forces" such as rainfall, rather than "internal biotic factors" such as population or livestock numbers.[20] Moreover, Edwards's suggestions represented a profound misunderstanding of "traditional" methods of conservation, which involved grazing camels and cattle separately and moving long distances in combination with the rains so as not to exhaust the pasture.

Edwards's dubious conclusions nevertheless became accepted administrative logic. Unaware of the true causes of damage to the rangeland, colonial officials presented borders as the solution to improving the pastoral sector. This presupposed that one could contain adequate wet and dry season grazing, salt licks, water supplies, and a regulated population on a single territory. In 1943, R. Frank Dixey, an expert staff member in the northern Rhodesian government, undertook a survey of the NFD and proposed the improvement and construction of pans, dams, tanks, surface catchments, and other water resources.[21] The government hoped that by implementing Dixey's and Edwards's technical suggestions, they could overcome the geographical and ecological constraints to reserves.

While most of Dixey's proposals were too expensive to put into effect, the entry of experts enabled the colonial regime to become far more interventionist in the north. In Isiolo, officials embarked on a series of more concerted attempts to cull stock, remove undesirable residents, gain a monopoly on stock trading, and gazette the boundaries of the Isiolo leasehold and township. Such measures had been sidelined in the past out of fears of engendering Somali resistance. These new ecological studies, however, allowed officials to reframe efforts to control and remove Somali veterans and their families, who could invoke the powerful language of human and indigenous rights, in terms of environmental preservation.

IMPERIAL DEBT AND RECIPROCITY

Colonial schemes aimed at reforming the livestock sector through central planning ran up against an older model of imperial citizenship. Dixey, Edwards, and other specialists hired by the colonial state deployed the ostensibly neutral language of expertise. Somali veterans, on the other hand, pointed to an ongoing relationship of imperial debt and obligation, which challenged the evolutionary assumptions of development experts. By highlighting their loyalty and service to the Crown, Somali representatives countered the logic and ethics of "development."

The language of imperial subjecthood was especially powerful for those who had completed military service. As they contemplated the viability of a Somali settlement scheme in Isiolo and the possibility of Somali veterans remaining in what would later become the Nairobi National Park, colonial officials made reference to the precedent set by the Nairobi neighborhood of Kibera.[22] The protectorate administration had originally designed Kibera to house Sudanese soldiers, but the area quickly grew into a site of land squatting and illegal liquor brewing. The Sudanese presence prevented the government from razing the neighborhood.[23] Concerned that areas like the Nairobi Commonage would follow the example of this now-infamous Nairobi "slum," the colonial regime delimited Somali landrights throughout the 1940s. In 1943, ex-*askaris* (ex-soldiers) from the NFD—citing their government service, regular payment of taxes, and loyalty to the Crown—petitioned the government about their rights to Isiolo.[24] Disenfranchising a population that had fought on behalf of the Crown was a political liability for the Colonial Office, particularly at a time when many Somali soldiers were fighting abroad in the war against Fascism.

Gregory Mann argues persuasively that a "blood debt" developed between colonial officials and West African veterans "composed primarily of claims, demands, and contestation."[25] In many cases, African soldiers developed affective ties to empire and internalized notions of imperial loyalty. Isaaq and Harti families often described their community's connection to the British government in terms of duty, mutual obligation, and reciprocity. Citing the service of their forebears was an important rhetorical claim for current generations, as they sought to reenvision their relationship with Britain and counter the abdication of responsibility entailed by decolonization. "They were brave men," Amina Kinsi explained, describing her forefathers, who "looked after the safety of the British."[26] Protesting the lack of recognition for their service, Hussein Nur quipped: "The soldiers do all the fighting and the generals get all the credit."[27] This relationship was animated not only by a sense of obligation, but also by fear and mutual suspicion. Adan Ibrahim Ali described how Somalis, after fighting abroad in World War II, refused to return alone. Convinced that British army officials would take their lives on their voyage home, they demanded to sit next to British soldiers on the planes and ships that carried them back to East Africa.[28] Having fought in "Europe's" war, African soldiers had become familiar with both Western technologies of violence and the fragility of white power. Military service had conferred on them certain skills and forms of power that made them both an asset and a threat to colonial regimes.

This sense of imperial debt was, nevertheless, gradually undercut by a growing belief among Kenyan authorities that urban Somalis were detribalized and inassimilable, vestiges of an earlier phase of empire who were no longer necessary to the functioning of the colony: "Even the good type of Somali, as opposed to the scalawags who preponderate, will probably never be assimilated into the life and structure of the Colony."[29] In 1941, the DC of Isiolo described the Harti and Isaaq as town dwellers who broke pass restrictions by smuggling in Turkana herd boys to care for their stock, as they "prefer[red] to congregate in the Isiolo coffee shops weaving their perpetual intrigues, drugging themselves with miraa and generally making themselves a nuisance with their endless intersectional disputes."[30] In addition, many colonial officials eyed them suspiciously as potential Italian spies.[31] Increasingly inclined to see Somalis as an obstacle to "progress," the colonial administration attempted to reserve special privileges solely to older veterans, while casting their families, nonveterans, and younger generations as undeserving of such rights.[32]

The war years proved to be a decisive time that reconfigured the meaning and contours of imperial citizenship. Nazi Germany had subjected the Western world to colonial methods previously reserved for nonwhite populations. The devastation of World War II forced many Western powers to rethink their commitments to formal imperialism and explicit racism. After the war, the Kenyan government tried to salvage empire by casting it as less racially discriminatory. Mounting demands by Africans for greater civil rights meant that colonial regimes could no longer exclusively privilege a small minority who had acquired non-native status.

As development needs shifted and colonial governments sought to make their territories more lucrative, Somali urbanites were increasingly seen as inimical to the prospects of state-led development and as barriers to Africanization. For decades, Somali traders had exported limited numbers of sheep, goats, and hides from the NFD, which the colonial government had kept under a nearly perpetual cattle quarantine. In so doing, they had helped to maintain the segregated livestock economy that was so essential to white ranchers. The colonial administration, however, began to intervene much more extensively in the marketing of livestock during the war years. In the early 1940s, the colonial state lifted quarantine regulations in the north to supply meat for the war effort. In 1937, the government had allowed 768 cattle to be legally exported from the NFD; in 1942, this number reached roughly 20,000.[33] In the same year, the Meat Control Board began to compete against private traders at livestock auctions.[34] The Livestock Control Board (which was eventually replaced by the Meat Marketing Board) also attempted to establish an official monopoly on the purchase of livestock in Isiolo.[35] These moves threatened to formally usurp the role of alien Somali brokers. When Somali traders complained, colonial officials maintained that there was "no longer any scope in East Africa for this particular kind of person."[36] In 1945, the colonial secretary described this in terms of the "natural" evolution of modernization:

> Now that the natives of East Africa have become more sophisticated, it has been found that they function satisfactorily as "askaris" and servants and that they are cheaper and easier to handle than

Somalis. Moreover all the tribes in Kenya have now learnt to trade for themselves and the day is past when as Isaak Somali can go to Turkana with a ten shilling bag of tobacco and return with a hundred pounds worth of goats. It should also be borne in mind that while most of the Indians who come to Kenya, and also many Africans, are now literate or skilled as artisans, very few Somalis indeed have had any education whatever.[37]

The colonial secretary portrayed East Africa as traditional and untouched prior to being "opened up" by British forces with the help of a few "advanced" tribes. While the reform of the pastoral sector had been long considered part of the natural sweep of modernization, the late colonial regime began to envision the state (rather than Somali intermediaries) as the main agents of that transformation.

Modernization theory has become a seductively powerful narrative for Westerners and Africans alike. One former trader explained that when the Isaaq had first arrived in Kenya, the locals were backward, ignorant of even the basics of trade. The Isaaq, he argued, helped to draw the locals out of their state of primitiveness and taught them to sell their cattle.[38] Despite the popularity of such narratives, trade was by no means new to the nomadic populations of the north. Somali, Borana, and various other groups had engaged in a caravan trade with the Benadir coast that probably dates back to the late seventeenth century.[39] In many respects, northerners had been far more connected to the global economy in the nineteenth century, before the effects of colonialism had undermined their caravan routes and dramatically transformed the regional political economy.[40] Throughout the colonial period, Somali traders had facilitated an extensive legal and illegal stock trade between the NFD; the Meru, Embu, and Kikuyu Reserves; and the white settler ranches of the Rift Valley. The colonial government was seeking to monopolize a portion of these trade routes and further their commodification, but it was not exposing "unenlightened" pastoralists to the virtues of commerce.

Despite the colonial secretary's prolific use of free trade rhetoric, it soon became apparent that government parastatals could not always compete with private traders. Due in part to increased government overhead, the fixed prices offered by colonial marketing boards were rarely comparable to those of private traders. In 1944, as Kitching explains, to avoid paying the prices demanded by the free market, the Livestock Control Board began to restrict sales to a limited number of official auctions, where they could serve as a monopoly buyer. This led to a rapid expansion of the "black market," which cast Somali traders into roles of illegality. When supplies dried up, the government was forced to once again allow Kikuyu, Somali, and other African livestock brokers to operate at the auctions.[41]

Although the government further integrated the north into the commercial livestock market after the war, it did little to reverse the larger trends isolating the NFD.[42] The colonial regime was also unwilling to commit more than minimal resources to developing the region. In 1945, Reece—perhaps obliquely referring to himself—recommended that administrators serving in the northern frontier be allowed to spend time in other parts of East Africa lest they "fossilize."[43] This image of the north as fossilized in the putative prehistoric past governed halfhearted colonial development measures.

RECONFIGURATIONS OF SOVEREIGNTY

Scholars argue that postwar development initiatives, rather than remedying the problems of land degradation and landlessness, only nourished African nationalists' calls for independence (and contributed to the tensions that eventually erupted in the fratricidal war known as Mau Mau).[44] Buoyed by the ostensible ideological commitment of Western Europe and the United States to the idea of self-determination, Western-educated nationalist leaders throughout the continent heightened their demands for greater African participation in government in the midst of the imperial push for development. Most of these leaders accepted the basic premises of development, including the role of the state in bringing about improved social and economic welfare, but believed that "development that would serve African interests required African rule."[45]

By the close of World War II, "self-determination" had also become a sacrosanct term within global political discourse, which led many African leaders to affix their hopes for greater rights on independence and territorial nationalism. While colonized elites were not exclusively committed to the idea of a nation-state, "the discursive availability of the imagined geography of the nation," as Akhil Gupta notes, gave it a great deal of "political legitimacy."[46] Many African elites had internalized liberal ideas linking progress to constitutional reform. By the mid-1940s, political leaders in Kenya and Somalia had created formal political parties, such as the Kenya African Study Union (later renamed the Kenya African Union) and the Somali Youth Club (later renamed the Somali Youth League), through which they advocated for greater political rights for "native" subjects and, in some cases, national independence.

Walter Benjamin argues that origins are a historical category. Distinct from the empirical genesis of a phenomenon, they are constituted through the relation between past, present, and imagined future.[47] Unsurprisingly, scholars who have studied the origins of Somali nationalism have emerged with widely varying dates. There is also a tendency to assume that Somaliness has been an important political identity for centuries. Some trace its advent back to the famous sixteenth-century Somali leader nicknamed Ahmed Gurey. Others, as Abdi Kusow notes, simply treat the Somali nation as *"sui-generis, a priori."*[48] Conventional scholarship has also tended to privilege southern Somalia, and (like most nationalist histories) obscured the contributions of minorities and women. Since the start of the Somali civil war, a revisionist historiography has challenged many of these dominant assumptions.[49] Always in the process of becoming, Pan-Somali nationalism will undoubtedly be rehistoricized in coming decades as the future of the global Somali diaspora and the federalist Somali nation-state unfold.

While other kinds of political identification had taken precedence in previous centuries, many diverse people in southern Somalia and northern Kenya had coalesced around a common Somali affiliation by the late nineteenth century. As explained in chapter 1, these groups came to see Somaliness as an overarching affiliation that signaled membership in the wider Muslim *umma* (community). In the early twentieth century, Pan-Somali sentiments also captured the imaginations of merchants, traders, sailors, interpreters, and others living in Aden and port cities farther afield, such as Cardiff, Liverpool, London, and New York. According to Ahmed Samatar, members of this diaspora were panclan and Pan-Islamic in their orientation, as evidenced by the creation of the Somali Islamic Association in the 1920s. They imagined Pan-Somaliness through international circuits and, much like people in southern Somalia and northern Kenya, were inspired by the dervish struggle of Sayyid Muhammad Abdullah Hassan. Their ideas traveled back to residents of Berbera, Hargeisa, and Burao, who set up various social welfare clubs in the 1930s. This interwar mobilization, argues Samatar, eventually led to the formation of the Somaliland National Society (later the Somali National League), often described as the country's first nationalist party.[50] It was through such organizations that Somali leaders were able to see themselves as a political constituency and imagine Somaliness through the epistemological contours of territorial nationalism.

In general, European officials were wary of anticolonial movements that sought to form larger panethnic political units. In the case of Somalia, however, the aspirations of Pan-Somali thinkers converged with the imperial ambitions of the British and Italian governments. When the Fascist Italian regime invaded Ethiopia in 1935, it envisioned the creation of *la Grande Somalia*. After Italian defeat on the African front, all contiguous Somali territories, with the exception of Djibouti, fell under a single British administration. Seizing the opportunity to assert its hegemony over what appeared to be a "natural" geographic and cultural unit, the British government began to promote the Pan-Somali vision. According to Timothy Mitchell, the idea of self-determination was born out of colonialism and served as a means for European and American powers to reframe the nature of imperial control and tame calls for democracy in the wake of World War I.[51] Though appropriated by African nationalist leaders, the concept remained a technology of imperial rule and a means by which colonial powers were able to adapt to a shifting international climate. British officials encouraged Somali leaders to form the Somali Youth Club in 1943. In 1946, the British foreign secretary, Ernest Bevin, went before the international community to advocate for amalgamating British and Italian Somaliland and the adjacent section of Ethiopia into a single trust territory.

Pan-Somali sentiment conformed neatly to the idealized myth of ethnonational unity, even though what emerged was not necessarily nationalism in the Andersonian sense (founded on such concepts as secular, homogeneous time).[52] Proponents of a "Greater Somalia" called for the union of all Somalis across the region into a single nation-state. This envisioned nation was to include British Somaliland, Italian Somaliland, French Somaliland (Djibouti), the Ogaden area of Ethiopia, and the NFD in Kenya (see map 3.1). Much like advocates of a Greater Syria, Pan-Somali proponents envisioned a polity larger than the existing system of colonial territories.

In various ways, African nationalism was imbricated in the colonial project. Colonial legal precedents (and the dictates of imperial powers) frequently determined the terms through which nationalism could be legitimated and made legible. Bevin's proposal was fiercely opposed by Haile Selassie, the emperor of Ethiopia, who had gained renown through his impassioned speech at the League of Nations against Fascist aggression. The emperor claimed that the British government was bound by the terms of the 1897 Anglo-Ethiopian treaty, which gave the Ethiopian Empire control over the Ogaden and Haud.[53] These debates were the product, not of "arbitrary" borders dividing supposedly natural communities, but rather of competing ideas of sovereignty and territoriality (which derived in part from older models of authority and belonging).[54] Ultimately, the Ethiopian Empire was able to garner support from the United States, which sought to protect American interests in newly discovered oil in the region and stem communist influence. Compelled by the remainder of the Four Powers Commission—composed of France, the United States, and the Soviet Union—which accused the British of empire building, the British government abandoned its plan. By 1954, it had turned over the Ogaden, Haud, and Reserved Area to Ethiopia.[55]

The contest over Somali territories precipitated by World War II foreshadowed some of the central debates of decolonization. What constituted the difference between a claim to self-determination and an act of territorial annexation? Which territorial claims had greater legitimacy and what political bodies were entitled to make such a determination? By the 1940s, Kenyan, Ethiopian, and Somali nationalist leaders were beginning to construct different, and sometimes competing, models of a future nation-state.

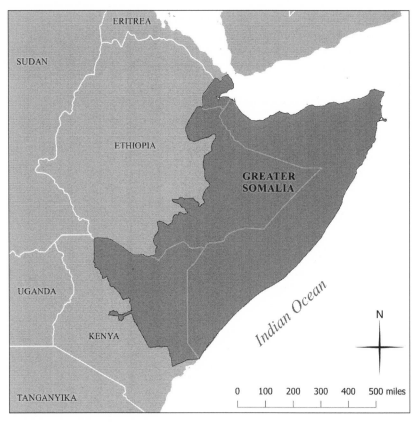

Map 3.1. The vision of Greater Somalia (at its most expansive). (*Note:* Borders are approximate.)

These disputes do not bespeak the problematic nature of sovereignty in the region; rather, as Yarimar Bonilla suggests, they signify that "sovereignty itself" was "a categorical problem."[56] One of the most pressing issues for Somalis in Kenya was determining how to respond to these indeterminate and nascent ideas of nationalism.

FROM "ASIATICS" TO "AFRICANS"

Nationalist campaigns—with their emphasis on territoriality and indigenous rights—changed the conversation about citizenship and posed new dilemmas for Somalis living in Kenya. These movements had particularly ambiguous implications for Somalis residing outside the NFD, in regions that went unclaimed by proponents of Greater Somalia. Some Somalis who lived in Kenya "proper" lent support to the Pan-Somali movement, while others aligned themselves with Pan-African nationalist campaigns (and some did both). Regardless of the strategies they adopted, however, urban Somalis tended to find themselves consigned to the margins of dominant nationalist imaginaries.

By the early 1940s, Isaaq spokesmen faced internal disputes over who could represent their community to the colonial government. In 1943, several leaders claiming to speak on behalf of members of the Isaaq community wrote to the government discrediting the British Ishakia Association and suggesting that its leader did not represent all the subclans.[57] They demanded that he "be prohibited to act on behalf of the community and be ordered to surrender all documents, seals, rubber stamps, papers and other articles to the Government."[58] A contest over leadership thus centered on control and monopoly over the items of political legitimacy—stamps, stationery, documents. These writing tools enabled a political association to engage with the colonial government (and also archive their activities, thus making them legible to subsequent scholars). Reece painted the British Ishakia Association as a group of corrupt, elite political agitators and emphasized their distance from and lack of support among the inhabitants of Isiolo, from whom they exhorted monetary support.[59] One must be skeptical of a depiction by a colonial official, especially one who was generally dismissive of Somali political activity. Nevertheless, Reece's derisive aside suggests that Somalis, who were under greater financial pressure by the early 1940s, may have begun to question the efficacy of their contributions.

Ultimately, archival sources can provide only tantalizing glimpses into the contours of such intersectional disputes. Colonial officials often treated "native informants" as representative of their respective "tribes." Colonialism required that leaders petition the government as collectives, which could hardly encapsulate the class, gender, clan, and other internal divides that cut across communities. Legal conventions held in suspension divisions within populations that "were always made up of people who were 'different and unequal' and divided by 'infinite incommensurabilities.'"[60] Nor are disputes of this nature part of the proud, orchestrated public face of contemporary oral testimony. In this case, oral and written sources tended to conspire to present a highly homogeneous picture of Somali society.

These sources also suggest that older strategies of claims making were becoming less effective. Demanding the rights of Asians and refusing the label "Somali" no longer made political sense. African nationalists were demanding greater rights for "native" populations, while colonial authorities, in an effort to mollify them, were beginning to elevate a small number of Africans into positions previously reserved for "non-natives." At the same time, Somali leaders were espousing a panclan ideology. By the mid-1940s, the Isaaq campaign for Asiatic status had begun to look like a vestige from a bygone era.

Although many Isaaq and Harti supported the Greater Somali project, they also began to integrate themselves into Kenyan nationalist movements.[61] As early as World War II, leaders representing the Isaaq and Harti populations established bonds with political elites in Kenya. One of the founding members of the Kenya African Union, for example, was a Somali. Mohamed Hassan Ismail was a close friend to Kenyatta and his daughter Margaret (in addition to being the father-in-law of the future Somali ambassador to Kenya).[62] In 1946, he and other Somali leaders held a tea party in honor of Jomo Kenyatta upon his return from London. Henry Muoria, editor for the Kikuyu-language nationalist newspaper *Mumenyereri*, captured the details of this meeting in a political pamphlet aimed at promoting Kenyatta's populist appeal. In attendance were representatives of the Kenyan Somali community, who referred to themselves as "British Somalis," as well as other famous Kikuyu leaders, including E. W. Mathu and Harry Thuku.

According to Muoria's account, several prominent Somali leaders made speeches in Kenyatta's honor and proclaimed the unity between Somalis and other Africans. Mohamed Hassan Ismail "went on to say that, these days, the Somali are together with other Africans in all things. Their fathers had made a great mistake when they declared themselves not to be Africans but Asians like the Indians."[63] Another Somali elder echoed these sentiments: "The Somalis who came to Kenya long ago were misled when they declared themselves not to be Africans but white-skinned Asians. If we look at a map of Africa, we can see that the Somali Country is close to Kenya, and that Somalis are not white but black people like ourselves."[64] These remarks diverged sharply from strategies of a decade earlier. Exegetes of Muoria's work note that he later edited out Hassan Ismail's "admission that Somalis had to be shown how to be African."[65] Muoria no doubt feared that the Somali leader's appeal would be interpreted as either illegitimate or opportunistic, and perhaps sought to portray African nationalism as a natural, rather than pedagogical project. Muoria's omission shows that there were fundamental ambiguities surrounding the meaning and definition of the term "African." It also reveals tensions at the heart of Pan-Africanism between, as Kwame Anthony Appiah explains, "the project of a continental fraternity and sorority" and "the project of a racialized" nationalism.[66]

So many diverse groups on the continent have come to identify as African that it is easy to forget that the concept itself is a product of relatively recent history. The emergence of Pan-Africanism in East Africa has been woefully understudied, due in part to the lack of dialogue between scholars in African studies and Africana studies (previously black studies).[67] Born largely in the diaspora out of a shared experience with racism, slavery, and colonialism, Pan-African nationalism had gained widespread currency in East Africa by the early 1940s.[68] Many groups were coming to see themselves as African during this period, and, thus, it would be a mistake to see Somalis as somehow anomalous. Since race marks a relationship to power, this transition was nonetheless especially challenging for those who were classified as nonnatives and enjoyed special privileges under colonialism.

Muoria's political pamphlet indicates that some Somali leaders were testing out new rhetorical strategies and "rediscovering" their African origins as the campaign for Pan-Africanism gained force. Representatives of other communities deemed racially "ambiguous" under colonial law pursued similar moves.[69] More and more, political rights hinged on the ability to prove one's autochthony. It is difficult to ascertain how widespread these changing sentiments were. They may have remained confined to the urban centers of East Africa. Just two years prior to the tea party held in Kenyatta's honor, soldiers in the Somaliland Camel Corps in British Somaliland mutinied over a proposed move to Kenya for training. Fearing "East Africanization," they demanded Asian uniforms, rations, special accommodations, and promotions.[70] Pan-Africanism did not circulate evenly throughout the diaspora, and ideas of belonging to a wider Pan-African community continued to coexist with notions of foreign, Arab descent. Moreover, for many, "African" and "Arab" were not mutually exclusive categories.

Within the towns and urban centers of Kenya, many members of the Somali diaspora embraced a Pan-Africanism in the years after World War II. One of my regular interlocutors, Mohamed Ibrahim, expressed this sentiment with a story about his childhood. Ibrahim was a well-traveled, multilingual, and cosmopolitan Isaaq elder who promoted the idea of a pluralist Kenya. During one of our interviews, he shared an anecdote about the Asian primary school he had attended as a child in his hometown of Nyeri. According to Ibrahim, the teacher once asked the class: "Who discovered Mount Kilimanjaro?"—to which the young Ibrahim had responded: "the natives living there." Hoping to elicit the name of a European explorer, the teacher struck him for his defiant answer. The next day, his father went to the school, confronted the teacher, and returned the injury. From then on, he sent his son to a local African school.[71] Through this narrative, Ibrahim was able to align himself with broader currents of anticolonial and Pan-African thought.

Unlike Somalis of the NFD, whom the colonial administration had isolated from the rest of the colony, the Isaaq and the Harti had intermarried, learned local vernaculars, and adopted the Swahili language. These memories could be woven together to create a shared past—one that, as Gabrielle Lynch notes, did not necessarily "have to be historically accurate," but had to "hold resonance with cultural traditions."[72] By the late 1950s, as many Somali leaders were promoting the idea that Somalis were distinct from other "African" nations, a small group of Kenyan Somalis were instead aligning themselves with Kenyan nationalist thought. This urban, cosmopolitan mind-set was certainly rife with its own exclusions, but it furnishes evidence of Somali contributions to Pan-African nationalism.

GREATER SOMALIA AND THE NFD

As earlier imperial models of economic progress gave way to notions of statist development, new geographic imaginaries emerged. Somalis whom colonial officials had labeled legal "aliens" started to abandon older notions of imperial citizenship and, in some cases, reconceptualized themselves as members of a Pan-African nation. Postwar development schemes also shaped the political subjectivities of nomadic populations in the north. The colonial government, buoyed by an array of ecological and agricultural experts, began to enforce tribal grazing zones in the north. By confining different clans to different grazing lands, officials hoped to rein in populations whose boundaries, numbers, and property were far too indistinguishable, indeterminate, and interchangeable (in their eyes) for comfort.[73] Locating solutions on ethnically homogeneous lands also relocalized the problem of poverty. These visions of "tribal" order encouraged many northerners to align around the alternative political geography put forward by Pan-Somali nationalists.

To enforce these new "tribal" areas, the local administration relied heavily on the help of "chiefly" authorities, whom they co-opted into the structures of the colonial administration. Colonial officials glossed the various Somali terms for authority (*boqor, suldaan, ugaas*) by translating them all as "chief." Colonial authorities also recruited grazing guards, who policed the new boundaries and fined trespassers by confiscating a portion of their livestock.[74] These borders were often coterminous with the region's network of unpaved roads, which suggests that border making was primarily a bureaucratic measure, rather than an ecological endeavor aimed at ensuring adequate grazing. Skirting these boundaries was risky, as many people explained.[75] Mohammed Sheikh Abdullahi complained that if caught crossing into the territory of another community, one had to watch with indignity as grazing guards removed their helmets to collect milk from the confiscated livestock.[76] Oral testimony suggests that, to a certain extent, locals internalized the idea of collective land tenure, which may have held some resonance with older clan-based geographies.[77] According to Abdisalat Abdille, northerners began to self-police—under colonial constraints, but perhaps also in order to maintain control over water and pasture.[78]

While the colonial regime was able to loosely enforce the idea of ethnic territory, the territorialization of ethnicity was a fragile accomplishment that had to be continually sustained through strategic compromises with

Somali leaders. In 1948, during a meeting with chiefs and headmen, the local administration in Wajir responded to a request by the Ajuran chief to extend his community's tribal boundaries. The chairman explained: "Any consideration to extend boundaries would entirely depend on tangible evidence of an increase in population. This could most effectively be shown by an increase in tax collection."[79] In many cases, territory and population figures were, in essence, negotiable, and the size of a community was often a nominal fiction of bureaucratic arrangements.[80] Colonial administrators and Somali representatives also continually negotiated temporary and permanent border adjustments. In 1951, the administration made a "slight amendment" to the borders in order to give the Degodia access to salt grazing, which, the administration admitted, was probably "indispensable to the well-being of their beasts."[81]

Two stories from Wajir District speak to the coexistence of multiple spatial logics in the north. Both narratives revolve around Ahmed Liban, the senior chief of the Degodia. Liban, who came to power in the 1930s and died in 1967, was among the leaders who helped the colonial state enforce their new tribal borders.[82] He was also the subject of many anecdotes in Wajir. Birik Mohamed, a resident of the small town of Kotula, told me one particularly provocative tale. According to Mohamed, the DC once consulted Liban when the Asharaaf sought to cross over into Ogaden territory. In order to maintain administrative order, the DC wanted them to accept *sheegat* status and, in effect, "become" Ogaden. Liban, however, refused. The Asharaaf, according to many Muslims, are direct descendants of the prophet. They would become clients, Liban said, when the sun no longer rose in the sky.[83] As a religious lineage, they were meant to remain independent, unaffiliated with any particular clan. Although the DC viewed them as one of many smaller subclans that needed to "fit in" to the larger tribal schema, Liban insisted that the Asharaaf occupied a different ontological and social place, as Islam was meant to transcend clan distinctions.

On a separate occasion, Mohammed Sheikh Abdullahi shared a different story about a meal that was once served to Ahmed Liban by members of his subclan. Liban had become accustomed to being served the prized fatty meat from the camel's hump. On this particular visit, however, Liban was handed a plate of lean meat. When he inquired as to the cause of this breach of hospitality, his hosts began to complain that the grazing land reserved for them was inadequate. As a result, their animals were lean and undernourished. Refusing to relent to their grievances, the chief said that he would rather eat lean meat than allow his people to trespass onto another clan's land.[84]

There are many ways to interpret these creatively ambiguous stories. One narrator described how Liban defended the right of the Asharaaf to circumvent tribal boundaries. The other suggested that he aided the administration in preventing lineages from moving outside their designated borders. Side by side, these stories show that colonial policies only partially inhibited the mobility of pastoralists. As Godwin Rapando Murunga explains: "The endogenous conception of space among the Somali . . . came to co-exist with the colonial idea of demarcating territorial limits and served the Somali in unpredictable ways."[85] Clan boundaries overlaid, but never fully displaced, the saliency of alternative forms of belonging, including membership in a deterritorialized Islamic *umma*.[86]

Colonial borders were often the subject of anecdotes and poems, as well as the topic of general political debate in the north. In the town of Wajir, I was told the following poem:

> *Likoley iyo Laq Boqol*
> *Laanta Carabley iyo Libiga*
> *Lurkoodaa seeraha xuduud*
> *Ladantii horaad la waa*
> *Meel aan lagu lumi ahayn*
> *Lafaley waa kuu diyaar*
> *Ee lalamada iga yaree*
> *Lugtaada lorriga ku luut*

> Likoley and Laq Boqol
> Lanta Carabley and Libiga[87]
> All their problems of the border
> The goodness of the past is gone
> A place where one does not get lost
> Lafaley is ready for you
> (So) don't let your limbs tremble
> Follow the tire tracks of the lorry.[88]

According to the man who recited it, this poem was composed in the colonial era by a Degodia pastoralist, who performed it for his camel while attempting to hide in neighboring territory. At the poem's end, the pastoralist decides to return to Lafaley, which was located on the land designated for his clan. The piece expresses a deep nostalgia for a past before the creation of borders. While most likely an artifact from the colonial period whose message continues to resonate in the present day, the poem may also be a recent production that evokes the past in order to comment on contemporary conflicts in Wajir over colonial-era borders. A historicist model of homogeneous, linear time does not help us understand the articulations between past and present encapsulated in the performance of such a piece. Alongside other oral and written sources, this poem shows that northerners have been and continue to be engaged in a long-term discursive debate over the legacy and legitimacy of colonial boundaries.

Others recalled British policies in more positive terms, describing the colonial era as a time of relative peace and prosperity. During this period, the government closed off portions of grazing land around the Wajir wells and circulated its usage in order to ensure the regeneration of pastures. Some praised this method, which they saw as an effective state intervention and a means of conserving grass, preventing overgrazing, and discouraging conflict. Contrary to popular belief, pastoralists are not inherently at odds with all the state's "modernizing" initiatives.[89] In recent years, with the scope for pastoralism much reduced, northerners are also reflecting upon older policies in new ways.

In the late 1940s, however, the range of thinkable options available to northern residents was quite different. By advocating for a "Greater Somalia," the Somali Youth League (SYL) offered an alternative to this rapidly expanding vision of tightly segmented borders. In 1947, the provincial commissioner (PC) complained:

> The people now appreciate the fact that there must be properly observed boundaries between tribes. . . . They do not however like the closing of large areas when it actually comes to be done, and the Somali Youth League has made political capital out of this by propaganda to the effect that as soon as it comes into power there will be no inter-tribal boundaries but all Somalis will live together happily and wander at will throughout the Horn of Africa.[90]

At least initially, the SYL was an urban phenomenon. Its supporters in the NFD were mostly Harti traders with ties to the political milieu in southern Somalia.[91] Its members paid dues and wore badges, all of which gave the organization an urban and elite veneer.[92] In 1948, fearful of the party gaining traction in the north, the Kenyan colonial government banned the organization and arrested seven of its leaders in Garissa.[93] Officials were concerned that outside British supervision, the SYL would become an anticolonial, Pan-Islamic movement. Its prohibition, however, did little to abate the party's growing popularity.

Today, some people from the north argue that local pastoralists were "duped" into joining the movement by "foreigners" and Somali elites, whom they claim spearheaded the campaign.[94] By playing into widely held stereotypes of pastoralists as uninformed and credulous, they have tried to retrospectively deny their community's involvement in a movement that

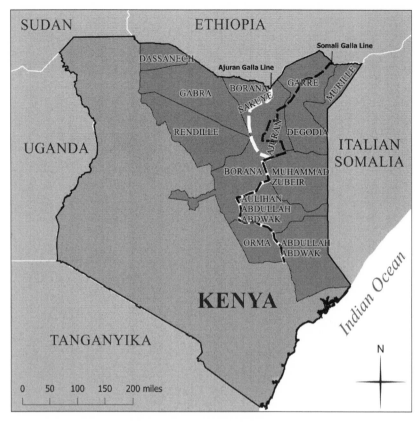

Map 3.2. The Northern Frontier District of Kenya (showing colonial clan boundaries). (*Note*: Based on Kenya, *Report of the Northern Frontier District Commission, Presented to Parliament by the Secretary of State for the Colonies by Command of Her Majesty* [London: Her Majesty's Stationery Office, 1962], 36.)

ultimately turned tragic for most inhabitants of the NFD. Rejecting the agency of nomads, however, hardly provides an adequate explanation for the SYL's popularity.

Why were pastoralists gradually drawn to the party's vision of breaking down borders and creating a united Somali terrain? One partial explanation is that postwar development initiatives, which placed greater pressure and constraints on nomads, enhanced the appeal of "Greater Somalia."[95] As Christopher Clapham argues, "Though a territorial state was, within the conventions of modern diplomacy, what the Somalis were technically seeking, it would be truer to say that what they really sought was not the creation of boundaries but their removal."[96] For some, Pan-Somaliness offered a territorial nationalism predicated on nonterritoriality.

Despite the prohibition on the SYL, opposition to new registration, branding, taxation, and grazing control measures did not subside. In 1951, Desmond O'Hagan cautioned his successor about the Borana on Mount Marsabit, who "have stated all sorts of absurd reasons for their objection to branding."[97] "No doubt the real reason," he maintained, "is that they fear they will no longer be permitted to move their cattle backwards and forwards between Ethiopia and Marsabit and that the number of cattle they may subsequently be allowed to hold on the mountain may be controlled."[98] In the same year, the DC of Wajir warned the incoming administrator against over-collecting taxes, since tax receipts served as a "certificate of residency" for Ethiopian or Somali inhabitants seeking entry into Kenya.[99] Nomadic ways of life defied bureaucratic codification and were deemed "fugitive" by many colonial officials. By framing these new controls as "development"—natural elements on the inevitable path toward progress—the administration left unexamined the transformation of a very narrow and parochial set of sedentary practices into the bureaucratic norm.

New clan boundaries were also incapable of accommodating changing climatic conditions. After a period of abundant rainfall in 1951, the Uaso Nyiro River, which fed the Lorian Swamp, almost changed its course. The concerned PC remarked: "Unless the river can be persuaded to resume its old channel, or can cut itself a new way to the Lorian Swamp . . . a redistribution of the grazing areas of the whole of the central N.F.D. may be necessary."[100] Another pressing issue was drought. Evidence indicates that the permanent part of the Lorian Swamp shrank from 150 square kilometers in 1913 to 39 square kilometers in 1960 (and had reduced by another 31 sq. km in the early 1990s).[101] While the government implemented the Dixey scheme in order to prevent just such a problem, the scheme faltered due to lack of funding and because, as Mohamed Farah writes, "no clan boundary, no matter how well-adjudged, could be said to contain all that was necessary for the needs of the livestock."[102]

Technocratic solutions frequently failed to resonate with people in the region, who dealt with the vagaries of climatic change differently. Pastoralists in Northeast Africa often interspersed materialist explanations for declining rain and pasture with moral and spiritual reasoning. Colonial authorities were sometimes eclipsed by "traditional" leaders who remained outside their orbit and beyond British sovereignty.[103] Many Degodia recognized the authority of a *suldaan* (ruler) who operated in Ethiopia. According to Ali Hassan, in order to rise to his position, the Degodia suldaan had to display certain signs of spiritual power, such as the ability to foretell with great precision the coming of the rains.[104] Such beliefs (the realm of the "irrational," in the eyes of colonial authorities) signified a different means of legitimizing authority and approaching the problem of environmental uncertainty.

Colonial administrators believed climatic change was knowable, quantifiable, and governed by a set of rational principles. Yet their proposed solutions often served only to further exacerbate ecological degradation.

Suggesting that northerners turned to the Pan-Somali project in reaction to postwar development initiatives risks reinforcing what Nancy Rose Hunt refers to as the cliché of the "colonial encounter"—the scholarly tendency to fetishize the colonial era and assume that the most significant historical engagements occurred between European officials and African subjects.[105] The SYL's mission gained popularity in the NFD for reasons that were complex, overdetermined, and irreducible to colonial policies. However, there is little doubt that the misguided colonial initiatives of the postwar era lent further legitimacy to the Pan-Somali vision, which became popular in the heady years leading up to decolonization.

THE VAGARIES OF DEVELOPMENT

While the term "development" implies a linear process toward greater integration with the capitalist economy, postwar colonial projects often had disintegrative effects, causing African subjects to experience disconnection and displacement. In the early 1950s, in an effort to more closely regulate the livestock economy, the colonial administration established two new government parastatals: the Kenya Meat Commission (KMC) and the African Livestock Marketing Organization (ALMO). ALMO funneled cattle from the pastoral areas to the KMC, which supplied them to a canning factory that exported corned beef.[106] The government takeover of the livestock trade and the entryway of other African middlemen (a result of colonial efforts to gradually deracialize commercial markets) further eroded the profits of Somali traders, even as it provided new economic outlets for pastoralists.[107]

During the same period, colonial officials worked to remove animals from Nairobi and other townships in the colony.[108] By creating national parks and banning animals from urban centers, the colonial regime sought to separate "wilderness" from "civilized" urban life—a spatial logic that is so often the hallmark of modernizing projects.[109] These efforts created new patterns of spatial segregation less explicitly predicated on race. It also caused many Somali traders to turn away from the livestock sector. Mohamed Ege Musa, whose father had been president of the Ishakia Association, associated the start of the modern era with the development of Nairobi: "After 1945, Kenya became what it is now." Somalis had been permitted to graze on (what is today) South C, Embakasi, and the Nairobi National Park when "there was nothing but wild animals." An influx of soldiers, Indian traders, and European officials, however, spurred economic and infrastructural expansion, compelling former livestock traders to adapt to new economic circumstances. "Somalis were so well-known in keeping cattle, because this is how we used to live. We had nothing else. We used to keep cattle; sell milk every morning. And of course a little bit of business," Musa added, "like selling secondhand clothes from auction, like opening a butcher here and there, but the main thing sustaining us in Nairobi here was selling milk in the morning." After the war, they were forced to sell their cattle at government auction, though at very generous prices.[110]

Faced with a changing colonial economy, some Somali urbanites and townspeople strove to take advantage of postwar educational initiatives. As Sana Aiyar notes: "The colonial state in Kenya tried to strike a delicate balance between maintaining its racial pyramid to keep Europeans at the top and facilitating African civilizational progress through carefully formulated structural policies in employment and education."[111] In an effort to reform imperialism after the war, colonial authorities gradually expanded educational services for Africans. After several requests for funding, the colonial government agreed to establish a few institutions, including a boarding school in Naivasha, in order to accommodate the new generation of Somalis.[112] During the inauguration ceremony for a new primary school in Nairobi, Bille Issa, speaking on behalf of the Somali Parents Association, described the school as "the realization of a much cherished need . . . to keep pace with the march of time in Kenya."[113] Concerns that their children would be left behind on the march toward "modernity" colored the perceptions of Somali parents. In addition to creating new spatial constructs, development schemes also gave birth to new temporal logics.

The few resources devoted to African "uplift" were typically reserved for young men. One woman I interviewed explained that her father had wanted her to attend Wajir Primary School, one of the first colonial schools in the NFD, which was opened in 1948. However, the colonial administration refused to register girls.[114] Enrollment in the intermediate boarding school in Naivasha was also reserved exclusively for boys.[115] Many Somali elders and colonial officials imagined potential agents of modernization as male. Women tended to be associated with rural life and with a past that (according to many practitioners of development) was slowly receding.

Modernity is probably best understood not as a stage, but as a predicament, rhetorical trope, and conceptual tool.[116] In comparison to northern pastoralists, Somali urbanites were better positioned to adapt to the conditions dictated by changing imperial visions of modernity. In various ways, Somali representatives wove themselves into narratives about the colony's changing future, hoping to position themselves as adept participants in the making of a developmentalist state.

Development initiatives failed to resolve, and in many cases exacerbated, the problems of growing inequality and social stratification in the African reserves and the urban centers of Kenya. The postwar push for development was also one of the contributing factors behind the outbreak of "Mau Mau" in 1952. A fratricidal civil war and anticolonial rebellion in Central Province, Mau Mau is popularly and somewhat erroneously perceived to be a purely "Kikuyu" affair. It has also become a key site around which Kenyans have constructed a nationalist imaginary.

The majority of fighters who took part in the rebellion were Kikuyu, Meru, and Embu, but Somalis living in Naivasha, Nyeri, Thika, and other towns actively aided Mau Mau insurgents. Using their access to markets in Ethiopia, Somalis sold guns and ammunition to fighters. In his memoirs, Waruhiu Itote described purchasing a pistol and bullets "from a Somali for Shs. 200."[117] In his powerful book on the Wagalla Massacre, Salah Abdi Sheikh attributed to the late general Mwariama the following testimony: "You could be betrayed by your brothers but never by the Somali. Somali traders fed, clothed and smuggled guns and ammunition to us."[118] In addition, several of my Somali interlocutors argued that their community hid and offered refuge to fighters.[119] Some pointed me toward Mohamed Ali (popularly known as Ali Kabati), a well-respected former councillor and deputy mayor in Thika (a town outside Nairobi), and somewhat of a local legend. Kabati was a close confidant to Jomo Kenyatta and a member of his regime after independence. In the 1950s, he owned a *duka* (a shop or store) in Juja, where he unlawfully sold beer to the future president and aided Mau Mau operations. His son-in-law proudly recounted how Kabati's late wife once distracted colonial officials with her beauty, while Dedan Kimathi hid in their home.[120] Such testimony suggests that some Somalis not only abetted Kenya Land and Freedom Army (KLFA) fighters, but were also ideologically aligned with the movement.

Bethwell Ogot has cautioned scholars that conducting oral history on the Mau Mau civil war is a highly political endeavor.[121] Not only is Mau Mau a fraught and sensitive subject for many residents of Central Kenya, but some people highlight (or aggrandize) their role in the war as a means of staking claims to reparations and participating in the larger nationalist imaginary. While the boundary between what happened and what is said to have happened is inherently ambiguous, this distinction, as Michel-Rolph Trouillot argues, cannot be entirely collapsed.[122] Those involved in political and legal disputes often search for actionable and verifiable "proof" about past deeds, a fact that constructivist historians cannot overlook. Through reference to their support for KLFA fighters, members of the Somali community could counter accusations of colonial collaboration, rebuff charges that they were "alien" to the country, and portray their community as defenders of the nation. Despite the tactical and political nature of such narratives, it is quite possible that the role of Somali accomplices, as well as members of other Kenyan groups, was far more extensive than scholars have previously assumed.

The participation of Isaaq and Harti in Mau Mau has also been cited as evidence of their assimilation into "Kenyan" life. All too often, the concept of assimilation is deployed either to model ideas of cultural purity or to imply that groups can move only in unilinear directions. Many colonial officials had internalized a belief that societies moved predictably from the "traditional" to the "modern" and that the rural was the preserve of authentic culture. "Tradition" was seen as bound to native lands and immigration as triggering cultural loss and displacement. Over the last half century, however, Isaaq, Harti, and other Somali urbanites and migrants had reinvented cultural pasts, retained links to their kin abroad, and imagined new futures in Kenya. They adopted a range of strategies, which cannot be reduced to a binary choice between "assimilation" and "separatism."

As Pan-African nationalism and state-led development gained ground, new pressures to fit into dominant and evolving visions of the Kenyan nation loomed large. For those Somalis living in Central Kenya, the postwar era ushered in a very complex set of opportunities and constraints, which tested the limits to which they could incorporate themselves as minorities into a future Kenyan nation-state. Tensions surrounding assimilation came to the fore during a conflict over the newly established Intermediate Somali Boarding School in Naivasha. Schools have often played an important role in the production of national subjects and the creation of national culture. Designed for Somali boys, the boarding school was the outcome of years of petitioning by several Somali parents, who realized the necessity of education to gain the tools associated with "modernity." As several people recalled, the Naivasha school provided a high-quality education to its students.[123] However, it was closed down shortly before Kenya achieved independence and eventually reopened to students of all backgrounds.

As a Western researcher to whom the community sought to project a positive public face, I was rarely made privy to the causes of the school's closure. A few people nevertheless implied that the school was shut down due to student incitement.[124] Mohamed Ibrahim—who had proudly recounted how his father had rejected the racist revisionism of his primary school teacher—attended the school and provided me with the clearest explanation. According to his account, students protested when a new headmaster, an Arab from Wajir, tried to replace their diet. In lieu of *injera*, a typical Somali food, he forced the students to eat *ugali* and *maharagwe*, "African" staple foods eaten throughout the region. When the students refused the new diet, the headmaster struck one of the boys, who fought back. Police arrived, only to be chased away by the rioting students. Soon after, the Education Office in Nakuru shut the school down.[125]

We can only surmise what divisive politics lay behind the student protest. Was the student protest an example of opposition to "Africanization," a form of resistance to Arab chauvinism, or a protest against forced assimilation? These various explanations need not be mutually exclusive. What is clear is that a celebratory Pan-Africanism could not neatly efface the racialized divides and power dynamics inherited from the colonial period. African nationalist leaders sought to counter the denigration of black African culture but, in doing so, sometimes devalued the "cultures" of people deemed to be foreign to the nation (though Europeans typically remained the silent referent for the modern and universal).

Andrew Arsan, drawing upon the work of Sunil Amrith, has argued that the transition away from colonial rule "closed off certain routes for circulation, and curtailed certain patterns of movement and ways of thinking about the world," even as it expanded opportunities in other ways.[126] As the colonial racial order gave way in the late 1950s, Somalis living in Kenya were forced to alter their strategies in order to situate themselves within a nationalist political discourse that favored indigeneity and promoted modernist futures. They also found their privileges and autonomy waning. State-led development offered new visions of progress that not only marginalized Somali livestock brokers and keepers alike, but marked them as temporally "behind."

Development initiatives as well as nationalist campaigns were often grounded in an ethnoterritorial logic, which linked African populations to specific territories. For people who had enjoyed special privileges under the colonial racial order, regularly crossed colonial borders, and saw themselves as part of communities that reached across international boundaries, this proved to be a difficult political transition. However, as the next chapter illuminates, Somali political thinkers found various ways of weaving themselves into the new nationalist projects taking shape.

4 ～ "The Fattened She-Camel Has Been Snatched by the Hyena"

They are not Arabs. . . . They are just non-negro types who occupy the whole of the area of the horn of Ethiopia and the right bank of the Nile. How they got there and whether they are of European stock or came from the Caucasus, we do not yet know. But they are non-negro . . . and the dividing line in East Africa between non-negroes and others is the Northern Frontier District, which is a most convenient boundary.

— Excerpt from a pamphlet published by the Somali Ministry of Information, May 1963[1]

DRAWING UPON THE COLONIAL HAMITIC MYTH, the Somali Ministry of Information claimed the Northern Frontier District (NFD) as part and parcel of "Greater Somalia"—a nation, it argued, that was distinct from both the Pan-Arab and the Pan-African movements gaining traction in this era. By reframing colonial-era racial ideas, the Republic of Somalia was able to broadcast the idea that the Somalis were a homogeneous nation. After British and Italian Somaliland formally unified in July 1960, many Pan-Somali nationalists hoped that French Somaliland (Djibouti), the Ogaden in Ethiopia, and the NFD in Kenya would soon follow. On the eve of Kenyan independence, Somali government officials continued to advocate for the unification of majority-Somali regions into a single nation-state. Nonetheless, this vision of a Greater Somalia troubled Kenyan formulations of multiethnic nationalism. Kenya's mainstream political leaders viewed the internal Somali population as simply one of many ethnic groups in a multiethnic nation and, like their Ethiopian counterparts, rejected any movements that threatened the territorial integrity of the country.[2]

Taking recourse to the idea of the arbitrary nature of colonial boundaries, scholars have often contrasted the supposed naturalness of Pan-Somali nationalism with the putative artificiality of Kenya. However, as this chapter will show, nationalist leaders in Kenya and in Somalia shared many overlapping ideas about race, territory, and sovereignty, even as they advocated for competing nationalist projects. By the late 1950s, the territorial nation-state had become the paradigmatic model upon which leaders throughout the colonized world based their claims.[3] For all their ideological and political differences, Kenyan and Somali elites worked within a common discursive framework and grappled with similar issues stemming from the institutional legacy of colonialism.

Nationalism, however, was never purely an elite project. Nor did ideas derivative of Europe fully saturate the imaginations of colonial subjects. This chapter moves beyond formal political discourse by turning to oral histories, songs and poems from the era, and archival files that give insight into discourses that circulated outside the realm of meeting halls and official conferences. As these sources indicate, Pan-Somali advocates throughout Northeast Africa, though constrained by its normalizing project, found various ways to domesticate the nation-state. To make Pan-Somali nationalism resonate with the fears, hopes, and expectations of the diverse inhabitants of the Horn of Africa, political thinkers emphasized a common pastoral lifestyle, highlighted ties of Muslim brotherhood, and invoked a common, overarching lineage. In the NFD, local leaders drew upon the most inclusive aspects of their shared history in order to reject incorporation into Kenya as disempowered minorities. Pan-Somali proponents mobilized an array of nonterritorial, nonsecular affiliations in the service of a secular, territorial nationalist project.[4]

Engseng Ho has described the transition toward nationalism "in prison terminology" as "the equivalent of a universal lock-down" for diasporic groups.[5] In contrast, this chapter argues that there was capacious potential to the nation-state and the ideas that circulated around it. Kenyan Somali political thinkers found various ways of reconciling their nomadic and diasporic connections with the new nationalist framework. In addition, some viewed "Greater Somalia" not as a project aimed at territorial unification, but as an overarching form of political identification, and attempted to cultivate transnational sensibilities. Some Kenyan Somalis "rediscovered" their African origins, aligned with Kenyan nationalist projects, and believed they could live as minorities within the country. Nevertheless, the pressures of decolonization and the constraints of international law created a polarized political environment. This resulted in the hardening of colonial boundaries, limiting what could be formally enacted.

Kwame Anthony Appiah argues that conflicts often arise over shared, rather than opposing values.[6] In spite of their differences, ideological influences, and choices of how to align within Cold War international politics, virtually every mainstream political party in Northeast and East Africa struggled with a similar set of issues in the late 1950s and early 1960s. These parties attempted to gain a place in what Liisa Malkii refers to as "the national order of things — an order which, despite its historical recency, presents itself as ancient and natural."[7] Just as Africans negotiated spaces for themselves within the colonial system of indirect rule, so did various constituencies struggle to situate themselves within a new taxonomic order mediated through the postwar international state system in the 1960s. This was an order that, as Talal Asad argues, perpetuated "its vision of a universe of national *societies*" and subnational ethnicities with "the state being thought of as necessary to their full articulation."[8]

Until 1963, the picture of postcolonial Kenya remained ambiguous. By the late 1950s, the British government was facing mounting pressure to fully withdraw from its African territories. The independence of India in 1947, the Suez crisis of 1956, and the independence of Ghana in 1957 were among the various independence movements that gave decolonization the air of an inexorable watershed. Having fought a costly war against the "Mau Mau," the beleaguered British government was also eager to disentangle itself from the responsibilities of governance.

Disillusionment with the nation-state is reflective of the zeitgeist of the contemporary (post–Cold War) era.[9] It is important, however, to recognize that the adoption of the nation-state model was not simply a concession to the postwar world order, but also an outcome of struggles over how to decolonize the state.[10] Understanding the rise of African nationalism entails considering what could have been its alternatives. In Kenya, one alternative was entrenched white minority rule.

The British government delayed formal independence in Kenya, a settler colony recovering from the divisive Mau Mau civil war out of concern for the white settler community, an influential minority at home and abroad. Officials attempted to contain the growing demand for African majority rule by implementing what was euphemistically called "multiracialism." The creation of a "multiracial" society in Kenya was an effort by the Colonial Office to reframe white minority rule within a new democratic model. This system gave rights to racial communities, rather than individuals, based on ratios skewed toward whites and Asians. This ensured the political and economic supremacy of the white settler community, who had a powerful voice in the Legislative Council. Widely decried by most populist African politicians, it opened only a very small space for greater African representation.[11]

The prospect of entrenched nonblack minority rule gave further urgency to the call to Africanize state institutions. By 1960, the colonial government had abandoned multiracialism in the face of widespread opposition from African members of the Legislative Council, who had displaced the more conservative Kenyan politicians in the elections of 1957. The newly elected prime minister, Harold MacMillan, advocated for accepting the reality of African majority rule. Under his leadership, the government adopted a new goal: transfer power to "moderate" African rulers amenable to British strategic and economic interests. The new secretary of state for the colonies, Ian Macleod, began to dismantle the emergency security apparatus in Kenya, hasten the transition toward decolonization, and ensure the marginalization of the more "radical" segments of Mau Mau.[12]

According to Siba N'Zatioula Grovogui, this transfer of power was constrained by international law, which offered African states only a limited degree of sovereignty.[13] Decolonization in Kenya was undoubtedly a conservative process, but the legal fiction of formal equality did more than simply paper over a neocolonial relationship.[14] It also enabled African leaders to deracialize the state and secure a place within the postwar international order.

In 1960, Kenyan nationalist leaders attended the first of three Lancaster House Constitutional Conferences, during which the terms of Kenya's future constitution were negotiated. They drew upon models of governance derivative of Europe—even though adopting those models, as Partha Chatterjee notes, did not completely dominate their imaginations.[15] After the conference, Kenya leaders splintered into two main political parties: the Kenya African National Union (KANU) and the Kenya African Democratic Union (KADU). Constrained by a choice between different, "modular" forms of European nationalism, Kenyan leaders with differing agendas, coalitions, and hopes for independence divided around two competing models of the nation-state. This split was couched in a dispute over whether the postcolonial nation should be highly centralized or united along a decentralized, federalist system.

While African members of the Legislative Council ultimately succeeded in defeating the "multiracial" model proposed by departing British authorities, they did not fully break with many colonial institutions of statecraft.[16] Older colonial divides were instead translated into new forms of nationalist difference. Those who aligned around KADU, for example, were bound together by a fear of becoming minorities under the new system of electoral politics, and thus sought to preserve certain aspects of indirect rule. Espousing concerns about the dominance of a Kikuyu/Luo majority, leaders of smaller African populations (including the Maasai, Mijikenda, and Kalenjin) forged an alliance with representatives from the minority Asian and settler communities. Coalescing around KADU, they pushed for a federalist system. Under their plan, power, resources, and control over land would be distributed across regions, known as *majimbo* (Swahili for "states"), and be governed by a relatively weak central state.[17] The colonial government initially backed KADU, which they deemed a more "moderate" party that would ensure settler privilege as a minority "tribe."

Rejecting KADU's proposal and its alliance with the departing colonial government, KANU sought instead a strong, centralized state and eschewed all claims that they were a party of majority tribes.[18] Steeped in the discourse of ethnicity, colonial officials did not anticipate the reach of KANU's panethnic support. In the eyes of many British officials in the Colonial Office and Kenyan government of this era, the split between the two parties was "tribal rather than ideological in origin."[19] Most colonial authorities saw tribes as rigid, sociological facts. They also attributed conflict to the "divisive" forces of ethnicity, rather than recognizing the role that colonialism and electoral politics played in reifying race and politicizing ethnicity. Upon his release from prison in August 1961, Kenyatta established his control over a party that proved to be remarkably diverse in its ideological and ethnic makeup. As the elections of 1961 and 1963 ultimately proved, KANU garnered widespread support even outside its putative ethnic bases.[20] Nevertheless, in spite of KANU's promises to engender national unity, overcoming a colonial legacy that had institutionalized ethnicity within the very structures of representational politics proved far from simple.

The first generation of nationalist historians tended to see KANU as "nationalist" and KADU as "tribalist."[21] Politics in this era, however, cannot be encapsulated through any simplistic explanatory binary—whether moderate/radical, collaborator/resister, loyalist/rebel, modernist/traditionalist, or tribalist/nationalist. A less polarizing interpretation is to see KADU and KANU as two parties that advocated for different and, in some respects, competing nationalist visions with differing views on how to accommodate Kenya's diversity and translate the institutional legacy of indirect rule into an independent nation-state.

COMMONALITIES ACROSS BORDERS

Neither party, however, was able to gain significant ground in the north of Kenya, where people were drawn to the prospect of unifying with Somalia. As explained in the previous chapter, Pan-Somali nationalism became increasingly popular over the course of the 1950s. By the early 1960s, most Somalis and northerners in Kenya preferred to speak the language of national unity rather than that of minority and ethnic rights.

Many northerners ultimately sided with the Pan-Somali movement due, in large part, to concerns that they would face political and economic marginalization within Kenya. Constitutional debates created a fiction of legal inclusion, but left serious questions of structural inequality unaddressed. Belated measures—such as the creation of African District Councils in the NFD eleven years after other Kenyan districts had obtained such rights—did little to offset a half century of political and economic isolation.[22] In addition, by using the Somali-Galla line to mark out electoral jurisdiction in preparation for Kenya's elections, the colonial government legitimized a colonial conception of ethnicity that effectively transformed northerners into political minorities.[23] The independence of British and Italian Somaliland, which had merged to form the independent Somali Republic in July 1960, only lent further legitimacy to the Pan-Somali cause.

At the normative, ideological level, the idea of Greater Somalia seemed directly at odds with KADU's and KANU's differing visions of a multiethnic state. Upon achieving independence in 1960, the Somali government portrayed its envisioned nation as natural, historical, and authentic—to be contrasted with the supposed "inauthenticity" of other African states, such as Kenya. There are a number of significant problems with interpretations that juxtapose the supposed naturalness of Somalia against the artificiality of Kenya.[24] Neither Kenyan nor Somali nationalism was wholly "traditional" or wholly "invented." Rather, African leaders in both countries folded older intellectual traditions into the new "modular" frameworks of the nation-state—thus blurring the "distinction between 'derivative' and indigenous."[25] Like their Kenyan counterparts, Somali nationalist elites also drew upon and were constrained by the formal limitations of the post–World War II political order. Moreover, a close examination of Somali political mobilization reveals that the strict dichotomy between "civic" and "ethnic" nationalism is dubious.[26]

Political parties in Somalia imagined diverse futures, which reflected both the pull of extraterritorial loyalties and the influence of localized forms of community. David Laitin persuasively argues that there were many possible configurations of the nation, "with 'Somali' being only one of them." This included "the possibility of a breakup into clan families" as well as a "supra-Somali Cushitic nationality."[27] In 1947, leaders of the predominantly agricultural Rahanweyn formed the Hizbiya Digil-Mirifle (HDM), which also included Arabs and other minority groups who were excluded from dominant definitions of Somaliness. By 1958, the HDM was pushing for a federalist system out of fear of domination by an alliance of two major groups—a campaign that bore remarkable resemblance to that proposed by KADU in Kenya.[28] Jean Allman argues that labeling such movements "tribalist" or "ethnic" (as opposed to "nationalist") perpetuates the narratives of the winning side.[29] The emergence of opposition parties, like the HDM, exposes the diversity of imaginaries and opinions on the nature of the Somali state and nation.

African leaders built upon the vestiges of the colonial state, fashioning nations partly out of the institutions of representation codified under colonial rule.[30] There was, nevertheless, much that was new to the nationalist moment. The stakes were greater, as were the hopes and the uncertainties. Constitutional debates introduced a new kind of demographic politics to the region, which Amitav Ghosh refers to as the profoundly modern (and incendiary) "language of quantity, of number."[31] Under this system, rights depended not only on the ways in which constituencies were drawn and ethnicities defined; they depended also on a group's numerical size as well as the legal definition and franchise entitled to minorities and majorities. In addition, decolonization triggered new debates over who would be deemed an outsider or an insider, the meaning of equality and development, and how best to preserve diverse ways of life after independence.

DOMESTICATING THE NATION-STATE

Terms such as "secessionism," "separatism," and "irredentism" all imply a certain acceptance of a national lens. Although I use such terms to describe the movement in the north of Kenya, it is important to recognize that, despite their ubiquity, these labels are of limited analytic value. Characterizing the campaign as an irredentist movement risks reinforcing the putative naturalness of the Somali nation. By the same token, it is unclear whether a people can be described as "separating" from a country into which they were never truly integrated. Thinking about the northern campaign as a separatist movement naturalizes its place within Kenya, obscures the extent of the north's isolation, and projects an idea of indivisible territorial sovereignty.

Continuing to think within terms and debates that became hegemonic during the divisive years of independence can also inhibit one from envisioning the nation in new and more inclusive ways. For this reason, it is important to look beyond the horizons of official political discourse. To engage with the colonial government, African leaders had to articulate their demands within the ethnic and the nationalist taxonomies privileged by the state. Shared discourses often circulated between locals in the NFD and the nationalist elites who represented them. However, outside these elite domains, Kenyan Somalis tended to debate nationalism through different sets of idioms.

Many northerners were able to recall poems, plays, and other slogans that they remembered hearing or reciting during the heyday of Pan-Somali nationalism. Some poems and plays were authored locally, while others were disseminated throughout the Horn of Africa through vehicles such as Radio Mogadishu. These sources are difficult to historicize in the traditional manner. Determining their authorship, the original location in which they were produced, or the specific individuals who recited or listened to them is sometimes difficult. Moreover, it is hard to evaluate just how popular and representative their views really were. The desire for some of these details also reflects the democratic assumptions of liberal scholars concerned with questions of individual agency.[32]

Nevertheless, sources of this nature are very important. Clifford argues that "oral societies—or more accurately oral domains within a dominant literacy—leave only sporadic and misleading traces. Most of what is central to their existence is never written."[33] Elements of oral culture enable us to move beyond formal political discourse, which was largely framed around debates over self-determination and different models of the constitutional nation-state. By the end of World War II, ideas such as citizenship were part of a globally intelligible political language, but were nevertheless elite concepts that may have had little traction among the majority of northerners.

When contextualized with archival documents from the era, these oral sources provide important insight into the internal logic of the NFD separatist campaign and demonstrate the significant role of Somali, Oromo, and northern Kenyan intellectuals. Political thinkers used songs, poetry, and plays to make the Pan-Somali nationalist rhetoric resonate with nomadic inhabitants throughout the various territories claimed by irredentist proponents. They also transformed an urban, elite phenomenon into a widely popular movement by rearticulating the meaning of the nation within terms relevant to the lives of northerners.

PAN-CUSHITIC AND PAN-ISLAMIC ALLIANCES

Although the Somali Youth League (SYL) had been banned in the NFD, several parties evolved within the region in the late 1950s, sometimes with the explicit support of the local administration.[34] Most of these smaller political parties eventually aligned with the popular Northern Province People's Progressive Party (NPPPP), which served as the main advocate for union with Somalia. To the outside world, the NPPPP espoused Pan-Somali unity (stressing the "naturalness" of Greater Somalia). Nevertheless, the party was remarkably diverse, drawing support from a panethnic constituency that included Sakuye, Rendille, and Borana people, and incorporating chiefs and educated elites into its fold.

While masking internal heterogeneity was intrinsic to the party's strategy, the actual expanse of its envisioned nation included many people who were not (at least by normative definitions) considered Somali. According to a provisional census in 1962, the NFD had a population of 388,000, approximately 240,000 of whom were Somali.[35] This meant that over a third of the population (at least in the eyes of the colonial government) belonged to other groups. To represent its members, the NPPPP intentionally chose a panclan and multiethnic leadership, which included the Rendille leader Alex Kholkholle and the Borana leader Wako Hapi.[36] This diversity eluded most government officials and outside observers, who portrayed the NPPPP as a distinctly Somali party.

As previous chapters have shown, the line between "Somali" and "non-Somali" had always been blurry. Nationalism gave new stakes to older debates and briefly opened a window for non-Somalis to renegotiate their claims to parity with dominant lineages. The following poem, which was composed in the Borana language, encourages people to join the movement:

> *Kootaa waliin yanaa* (x 2)
> *Waan duri lakkifna*
> *Aaddaa waliin yanaa*
> *NPPP qorannaa*

> Come together (x 2)
> Leave behind (forget) the past
> Brothers and sisters, join together
> Join (enlist in) the NPPP[37]

The suggestion that people "forget about the past" likely alludes to previous conflicts over political power and control of land and pasture, which members of the NPPPP were undoubtedly trying to put behind them.

Irredentist proponents also began to collapse the distinctions between Somalis and non-Somalis of the region, whom they suggested shared a common descent.[38] These ideas are still alive within some circles. Gadudow Garad Alasow, a former leader of the NPPPP, argued:

> Borana, Sakuye, Gabbra, Rendille: all these are one people who are united. . . . We had the same symbol, a symbol of unity. . . . The Gabbras are related to the Garre. . . . All of these are [part of] the Somali culture that has changed.[39]

The separatist movement was able to incorporate groups of varying backgrounds, including non-Muslims, by drawing upon these expansive ideas of lineage.[40] Local intellectuals stressed that people of the north shared an overarching kinship with Somalia, as expressed in the title of one song: "The Two Brothers Share Things in Common."[41] The notion of Somaliness was, at times, submerged and other forms of kinship highlighted. Many of the supporters of the NPPPP, for instance, emphasized that they were part of a common Cushitic family.[42] The idea of a Pan-Cushitic nation was more inclusive and undoubtedly more appealing to many non-Somalis in the region, who lived not only in the NFD, but also in neighboring Ethiopia and Somalia.[43]

In addition, northern political thinkers brought together their diverse supporters by highlighting their unity as Muslims.[44] The following poem draws upon an explicitly Islamic idiom:

> *Kulub waa kulanow*
> *Wada kitaab*
> *Kacbada aan u jeednaa*
> *Karinkow na kalmey*

> The Club that gathered
> Followers of the book [students of Qur'anic (*dugsi*) school]
> We face the Ka'ba
> Oh God, help us[45]

This poem promotes a shared Islamic bond, reinforced through Islamic education and a set of ritual prescriptions, such as facing Mecca during prayers. The party's appeal to Muslim solidarity and Islamic universalism enabled it to attract non-Somali populations who identified as Muslims or converted during the heyday of Somali nationalism.

Not all northerners were convinced by the NPPPP's gestures of inclusivity. Faced with historical barriers to their equality, some Borana leaders argued that they would become a *nyaap* (enemy) in Somalia, and would experience less discrimination as a minority within Kenya.[46] The most popular opposition party was the Northern Province United Association (NPUA), which was dominated by non-Muslim Borana. At least initially, KADU gained inroads among these opponents of secession.[47] On the whole, regionalism gained a following among groups who had experienced historical discrimination (such as members of farming communities on the Tana River, non-Muslim Oromo speakers living in Marsabit and Moyale Districts, and subjugated Somali clients).[48]

A more cynical observer might argue that the appeal to Muslim solidarity and the forging of a common, overarching lineage was simply a pragmatic move to portray the NFD as a viable political player and to convince non-Somalis living in the NFD, without whom separatism could be derailed, to join the movement. It is also possible that many minority groups, believing that the NFD would be handed over to Somalia, hastily attempted to align themselves as much as possible with what they perceived would be the winning side. On the other hand, the fact that so many diverse groups were able to unify, at least temporarily, under the rubric of a Cushitic and Muslim identity points to the extent to which northerners, in spite of their differences, imagined a commonality between themselves, feared marginalization under an independent Kenya, and sought to eliminate the barriers restricting their movement and separating them from their neighboring kin to the north.

A PASTORAL NATION-STATE?

Many non-Somalis were also drawn to the irredentist cause because Pan-Somali nationalists were able to articulate a nationalist vision that did not tie modernity to urban or sedentary life. Nomadic livestock herding was a defining feature of life in the north, which cut across linguistic, religious, and ethnic distinctions. Livestock ownership was more than simply a lifestyle and survival strategy; it was also a key conceptual category that defined the boundary between "we" and "they." Under colonial rule, and particularly after World War II, nomadic populations had experienced unprecedented restrictions to their mobility. By the 1960s, there were growing concerns that the Kenyan government would be equally unaccommodating to nomads.

In many ways, local intellectuals brought the diverse supporters of the NPPPP together around a desire to safeguard the nomadic way of life. This sentiment was expressed by leaders of the United Ogaden Somali Association (UOSA), who sent a petition to the metropolitan government in 1961. Although the UOSA was a relatively small party, these ideas were widely felt among northerners and were in no way exclusive to any particular lineage or faction:

> Just as Europeans are justly proud of being Europeans, so we Somalis are proud of being Somalis and have no intention of changing our customs and our outlook to approximate to those of certain African tribes. We should consider it not only a backward step to do so, but something quite wrong as judged by our standards of religion and ethics. . . .
>
> Our life is so different from that of the settled agricultural communities who constitute the majority of Kenya's population that it is quite impossible for them to understand our desires and our needs, even if they were willing to make the attempt, which we have no reason to think they will be.[49]

The author of this petition refuted the association between civilization and a sedentary lifestyle. He fashioned instead a heterodox vision of progress in which adopting an agricultural lifestyle was considered a "step backwards." He also explained the importance of grazing and water rights and suggested that "African" leaders could not appreciate the needs of the northern inhabitants given their vision of development:

To take a simple example, these people (the Africans), and particularly their leaders, consider that education is all important. While not belittling the value of education, water and grazing are to us of infinitely greater importance. They are matters of life and death to us, our cattle and our camels in our thirsty country. Our people can, if they must, live without schools. They cannot live without water and grass.[50]

The president of the UOSA minimized the importance of Western education and focused instead on what he perceived to be more pressing needs facing nomadic pastoralists. Northern elites, who did not always share the same interests as their rural constituents, often decried the lack of schools and other infrastructure in the north and demanded greater investment in the educational system.[51] However, not everyone shared these concerns. Only gradually did much wider changes within the global and regional political economy cause many people in the north to reexamine the effects of empire, at which point their lack of education came to be perceived as a process of marginalization in which they were "left behind."

From today's perspective, it may appear radical that the separatist movement would attempt to accommodate nomadic livestock herding within a territorial nation-state, as expressed in the quip "Wherever the camel goes, that is Somalia."[52] Yet being nomadic is not, by definition, irreconcilable with a modern state. Northerners sought a form of nationalism that was more accepting of pastoralism, less likely to render them political and cultural minorities at independence, and that would allow them to maintain control over water resources and grazing land.

Poems and songs from this era exhibit how Somali nationalists appropriated the idioms of pastoralism and developed a political language derived from nomadic terms.[53] For example, Idhoy Ibrahim recalled poems that women in Wajir used to publicly chant to drum up support for the Pan-Somali cause, such as the following:

> *Hayeey bal eega*
> *Hasheyda naaxday (NFD)*
> *Dhurwaaga haysta*
> *Dhiiga baa ka hoow leh*
>
> Woe is me, would you look around
> The fattened she-camel (NFD)
> Has been snatched by a hyena
> And the blood is pouring forth[54]

By referring to Kenya as a pack of hungry hyenas and the NFD as a prized camel, this song utilized core imagery from the Somali nationalist campaign, which equated the country to a *Maandeeq*, a she-camel that gives abundant milk.[55] Several of the poems that Ibrahim was able to recall used this she-camel metaphor:

> *Adduunyo hal baan lahayn*
> *Hashiina horor bay iga cunay*
> *Haruub maran baan sitaa*
> *Hoogayeey ba'ayeey ma hadhay*
>
> In this world, a she-camel is all we own
> (But) she was eaten by a beast
> (So) I am carrying an empty vessel
> Oh misfortune has ruined us all[56]

This poem was among several that were familiar to Ahmed Ismail Yusuf, a poet and scholar based in Minnesota who helped me with their translations.[57] Moved by reading verses that he had not heard in many years, he identified this poem as the work of the famous intellectual Ali Sugule Egal. Yusuf was born and raised in northern Somalia (often referred to today as the Republic of Somaliland).[58] The fact that he recognized a poem collected and recorded miles away in northern Kenya (and carried across the Atlantic) speaks to the extent to which ideas and words can travel. It also shows that we cannot underestimate the epistemologies and technologies of transmission in African societies. Treating both the content and the genre of the poem as a historical artifact, one can gain insight into the diverse modes by which nationalist imaginaries were forged. The rhythm and alliterative qualities of the poem facilitated its memorization and diffusion, while enabling locals to make slight alterations or rework its meaning by reciting the poem in new contexts. For example, when she initially recalled the poem transcribed on page 102, Idhoy Ibrahim replaced the word *hayeey* with *hooyo* (mother), rendering it "Mother, would you look around," or "Mother, behold." She thus adapted a well-known poem to specifically appeal to and address women.

This pastoral imagery is also mirrored in other famous poems that were played during the war over Radio Mogadishu, one of the greatest tools for the dissemination of the vision of Greater Somalia.[59] The following is an excerpt from a poem recited by residents of Wajir:

> *Ka soo hoyo hororka iyo waraabaha*
> *Hubkana qaato oo harsada geed*
> *Huriya baaruudda holacda leh*

Come in (for safety's sake) from the wild animals and the hyenas
Take up arms and take shelter in the shade of a tree
Ignite the gunpowder (and fan its) flames[60]

Subsumed yet not suppressed within the normalizing nationalist project was a desire to make space for the nomadic way of life, which many leaders hoped to reconcile with new and emerging visions of "modernity." The fears of northerners were not unwarranted. Many Kenyan leaders had internalized colonial attitudes toward nomads and some even spoke in denigrating terms about the arid and pastoral areas of the country.[61] To many Kenyan leaders, nomads were a backward people stuck in an atavistic way of life. In 1961, L. G. Sagini, a KANU member, tried to discredit Maasai leaders before the Legislative Council. Alluding to the Russo-American space race and the rapid technological advancement of the twentieth century, he warned that if the Maasai stayed pastoral, "somebody will invade them in an aeroplane and shoot them from overhead."[62] Inverting a colonial technique for surveying vast pastoral expanses, he invoked the threat of state power.

Local intellectuals activated many different forms of fidelity in order to tie a diverse constituency together and challenge the legitimacy of down-country Kenyans to represent them. The idea of a nation built around pastoralism, rather than hostile or indifferent to it, was perhaps one of the most compelling aspects of the movement.

THE LIMITS OF INCLUSION

Scholars and journalists who study northern Kenya have tended to focus on materialist explanations for the irredentist movement. To explain why northerners advocated for union with Somalia, they have pointed to a long history of isolation from the rest of Kenya, a lack of infrastructural and educational development, and a fear of political disempowerment and economic marginalization under an independent Kenyan state.[63] The ideational aspects of the campaign, however, have been less extensively examined. Consequently, scholars have avoided tackling more politically sensitive topics.

To ignore the chauvinism and xenophobia that motivated the irredentist movement would be to cede an uncomfortable issue to those who invoke Somali racism as an excuse to deny them a share in Kenya's history.[64] Like any other nationalist movement, local intellectuals defined the boundaries of membership by identifying those who did not belong. One of the plays produced by the Sunlight Club, a cultural group that rallied around the NPPPP, was titled "The Monkeys Don't Have Elders. Who Will You Complain To?"[65] This spurious claim that Kenyans had no elders and thus, like monkeys, lacked the qualities of civilization inherent to meaningful justice revealed the extent of Somali prejudice and intolerance. By casting downcountry Kenyans as inferior "Bantu" others, irredentist supporters also undermined efforts to incorporate non-Somali minorities into the movement.

Racial discrimination is still prevalent within Somalia and in the diaspora, although there are those who seek to combat this problem internally.[66] Some people I spoke to glossed over the chauvinistic aspects of the irredentist movement by focusing on the north's economic and political isolation. Others were more explicit about the role of racial thinking. One former Kenyan soldier in Garissa explained: "We wanted to join Somalia because we were the same race."[67] Another Garissa resident made comments I took to be intentionally provocative, including the following: "Somalis are one people from here until Djibouti. There were no borders. Somalis are the same. They wanted to be under the same borders. We didn't want our girls marrying the slaves."[68]

Among Somalis, derogatory labels such as *addoon* (slave) or *jareer* (hard-haired) are still used to refer to "downcountry" Kenyans. The etymology of these terms suggests that certain forms of discrimination predate colonialism. At the very least, modern racist prejudices are entangled in a much longer intellectual tradition linked to the precolonial slave trade.[69] Despite the prevalence of these ideas, however, they are not universally accepted. Some Somalis rejected these highly gendered and racialized forms of discrimination, which they deemed to be un-Islamic.

Recently, historians such as Bruce Hall and Chouki El Hamel have argued that racism in Africa predates colonialism.[70] These arguments have had salutary effects by helping to expose problems of discrimination and exclusion within the Islamic world. At the same time, these authors risk transforming racism into a transhistorical phenomenon, collapsing various phenomena under a common rubric, and potentially obscuring the notable differences between precolonial modes of othering and modern institutions of racism. Attentiveness to the politics of translation and a consideration for the work of critical race theory is necessary when examining issues of race in a non–Atlantic World context.[71]

Nationalist thinking in Northeast Africa was sometimes racialized, but this did not always equate to an antiblackness. Some Pan-Somali proponents coalesced around an anti-Arab nativism in the years after World War II. In both the NFD and Somalia, Arabs were among a small class who resided almost exclusively in townships and cities and owned many of the retail stores in the region. Like other "non-natives," they enjoyed special commercial and legal privileges under colonial rule. Decolonization and the attendant demands for redistribution and more equitable representation often took on a nativist dimension, which opened the door for discrimination against Arabs and Indians.[72] When the colonial government chose

Sherif Kullatein, a Kenyan of Arab descent and head of the Wajir primary school, to be representative of the Northern Province in the Legislative Council, they were faced with protests from the local population. Officials were eventually forced to replace him with a Somali politician.[73] In 1948, anti-Arab riots broke out in Mogadishu, and, after independence, Somali legislators considered implementing policies that would restrict Arab businesses. According to David Laitin, when the war finally broke out in the NFD, Somali nationalists took "the opportunity to loot Arab shops."[74] There is also evidence that irredentist supporters in northern Kenya inverted racialized thinking to mark Arabs as "other."[75]

Local intellectuals were reworking the meanings of race, genealogy, and descent on the eve of independence. As with all forms of nationalism, dynamics of inclusion coexisted with exclusionary rhetoric. Chauvinism was at play both in attempts by Pan-Somali nationalists to subsume the Oromo into their envisioned nation and in efforts to exclude Arabs and Africans. At the same time, Pan-Somali proponents were often quite inclusive of the diverse array of people living in Northeast Africa, and at times stood in solidarity with Pan-African and Pan-Arab nationalists.[76] Thus, one cannot speak of a singular Somali nationalism, but rather of multiple nationalisms that drew the boundaries of belonging in different and sometimes incommensurable ways.

THE MULTIPLE VISIONS OF GREATER SOMALIA

Canonical histories of Kenya tend to paint a portrait of a singular Pan-Somali movement, which is often described as antithetical to Kenyan nationalism. In actuality, "Greater Somalia" captured the imaginations of people from diverse backgrounds and persuasions. It meant a variety of things to those living in Kenya, ranging from an abstract and deterritorialized form of affiliation to an irredentist vision. If one of the goals of scholarly writing is to uncover how the seeming inevitabilities and linearities of "history came to appear as such," then it is important to recognize that Somalis and northerners in Kenya imagined a number of possible configurations of the nation on the eve of independence.[77]

Historical traces suggest that Pan-Somali ideology had become a promising new political avenue for many urban residents in the years after World War II. Sifting through the archives from the 1950s, one finds far fewer petitions signed by the Ishakia Association or the Darot Welfare Society. More and more documents were instead composed on the formal stationery of Nairobi-based groups such as the United Somali Association (USA) and the Somali Independent Union (SIU)—names that invoked a Pan-Somali ideology.

Historical understandings of this era cannot be entirely divorced from fraught contemporary testimony. Eager to leave the divisive history of the 1960s behind them, many of the people I spoke to elided their community's contribution to the Greater Somalia vision. For example, some members of the Isaaq and Harti population argued that the irredentist movement was "not our fight."[78] There is ample evidence, however, that some Somalis living outside the NFD supported the separatist campaign and even joined pro-irredentist parties.[79] The Nairobi-based SIU openly advocated for the union of the NFD with Somalia. The SIU was eventually sidelined by leaders of the NPPPP, who painted its leadership as "alien" interlopers meddling in the affairs of pastoral populations.[80] The wide economic and cultural rifts that had formed between the Isaaq and Harti trading class and the rural people of the north posed challenges for the vision of a Greater Somalia, especially as it evolved from a predominantly urban and elite phenomenon to a popular movement with strong support among its rural and pastoral constituents.

Identifying and sympathizing with Pan-Somali nationalism, however, did not always preclude a desire for political integration within Kenya. In March 1957, under the multiracial Lyttleton constitution, the Kenyan regime held elections for eight African members of the Legislative Council (Legco) under a limited franchise.[81] After the elections, the United Somali Association (USA) petitioned the government to give those "Somalis in Kenya (outside NFP)" their own member in Legco. They nevertheless emphasized, "We feel that a Somali is a Somali, whether he is an Ajuran, Dugudia, Issak, Darod, Gare or Hawiya."[82] Eliding clan distinctions and identifying as Pan-Somali nationalists, the USA nevertheless sought rights and representation for their constituents as a distinct minority group within Kenya.

Some Somali leaders advocated for incorporating the north into Kenya—a position that should not be seen as inherently antithetical to Pan-Somali nationalism. Abdi Haji Abdulla recalled how his father had exhorted a *baraza* (public meeting) by asking: "Why, if we can see Mount Kenya from Isiolo, would we want to be ruled from Mogadishu?"[83] Others believed that union between the NFD and Somalia could be achieved through political mediation with Kenyan leaders. Colonial intelligence reports from the late 1950s and early 1960s provide insight into these arguably more "moderate" strategies, which the polarizing effects of decolonization eventually forced off the table. For obvious reasons, relying on British surveillance reports is problematic. They are riddled with exaggerated fears of Soviet interference and hyperbolic reports of Pan-Islamic mobilization, as well as the standard ethnic clichés. In the absence of other sources, however, they provide an important window into some of the lesser-known political opinions of this era, which—because they are politically fraught and more easily forgotten—are rarely discussed in contemporary oral testimony.

In 1958, the director of Intelligence and Security reported on the formation of the Somali National Association (SNA), which he described as "an amalgamation of the United Somali Association (Darod) and the Central East African Ishaakia Association (Isaak)."[84] Though most of the elected leaders of the SNA were listed as Isaaq or Harti, the surveillance report notes that the leadership committee included a Garre elder from Nairobi. This hints at the diversity that always underlies seemingly homogeneous groups. The president of the SNA was Ali Guleid, a member of the Somali Youth League, who was born in Rumuruti and whose family had come to Kenya from British Somaliland. The director of Intelligence and Security noted that Guleid believed in negotiating with Kenyan leaders: "He favours Somali co-operation with African politicians and has been in contact with TOM MBOYA."[85] In addition, the leadership committee received advice from an Isaaq judge in the subordinate court in Hargeisa, who had "long advocated cooperation between tribes."[86] Pro-secessionist and Pan-Somali in orientation, members of the SNA, according to the director of Intelligence and Security, were grappling with how best to navigate the transition toward African majority rule.[87]

The SNA attended the inaugural meeting of KADU in June 1960, which formed around an aspiration for a federalist model.[88] During a two-day conference in September 1961, the founding members of KADU decided that Maasailand, the Kericho region, the Rift Valley, and the NFD would each acquire a separate regional government.[89] Initially, KADU's vision for majimboism kept the NFD intact and endowed it with a degree of power and autonomy as a federalist region. Scholars have largely ignored the influence of the SNA on KADU, which speaks to a broader erasure of Somali political thought. Until recently, scholars have also overlooked the history of KADU (a party often derided as tribalist). Kenya's recent transition to a devolved political system, however, has reinvigorated interest in older models of decentralized power. While it is impossible to know whether the original federalist system proposed by KADU could have provided a viable alternative to separatism, such counterfactual history allows for a productive reengagement with the past and its imagined futures.

Minority positions also show that political stances did not neatly map onto clan or regional lines. Leaders in the north (where irredentism had far more pressing implications) also toyed with different strategies and political futures. In many cases, smaller parties left only vague and fragmented traces on the historical record. However, their existence shows that Somali nationalism was far more heterogeneous than orthodox nationalist histories have often acknowledged.

Some of these parties considered alternatives to joining either Kenya or Somalia. There is a scarcity of written sources on these minority positions, so it is difficult to assess their popularity. However, their calls for a third path show that political debates in the north were irreducible to bilateral politics. Over the course of the 1960s, the UOSA espoused multiple, often conflicting political agendas.[90] Its leaders briefly flirted with the idea of regional independence apart from Somalia and Kenya, as well as the prospect of a united Ogadenia comprising the Ogaden-inhabited regions of Kenya, Somalia, and Ethiopia.[91] The Northern Frontier Democratic Party (NFDP) also initially supported regional independence for the NFD without union with Somalia, although the party eventually opted to support the NPPPP.[92]

Several people I spoke to invoked these positions in a positive light. Political stances that once appeared to be dead ends may become prescient, as James Clifford writes, since "the direction or meaning of the historical 'record' always depends on present possibilities."[93] Over the last few years, the idea of regional autonomy and possibly independence from both Kenya and Somalia has gained a following among a small number of northern inhabitants, who have been influenced by the federalist models gaining ground in Somalia.

Magnified by the ensuing war, the polarizing effects of decolonization have obscured the many paths that were not taken. A Somali veteran of the King's African Rifles (KAR), who was living in Garissa at the time of our interview, shared an anecdote that illustrates a certain ambivalence toward the Kenyan nationalist project. As a whole, he spoke positively of the Pan-Somali nationalist campaign and quite critically of Jomo Kenyatta's treatment of the Somali people. However, he also explained that he had once been an admirer of the man who became Kenya's first president. As a soldier, he and his commanding officer had visited Kenyatta prior to his release from prison where, in defiance of his officer's warning, he had saluted the imprisoned nationalist leader. Kenyatta, according to the veteran's account, promised to personally reenlist him, were he to be discharged for disobedience, once he became head of state.[94] By the late 1950s, deep divisions had formed between Kenyan and Somali nationalists. The colonial state's reliance on Somali soldiers in its fight against Mau Mau had only exacerbated these divides. Nevertheless, the veteran's story provides a trace of the kind of alliances that might have formed under different historical circumstances. It also betrays complex sympathies upon which new nationalist scripts could be inscribed.

The fabled dilemma between separatism and integration obscures the manifold ways in which minority groups relate to a dominant ethnos. Somalis and northerners felt loyalty to a variety of overlapping and, at times, competing nationalist visions, some of which may have been capable of reconciling the Pan-Somali and Kenyan nationalist projects. Nevertheless, decolonization provided little space for flexible notions of citizenship that might have allowed people to come to see themselves as transnational or dual citizens.

THE CREATION OF HOMELAND

Throughout the late 1950s and early 1960s, Pan-Somali nationalism offered an expansive vision onto which people of varying backgrounds could project their hopes and expectations. Northerners sang such patriotic songs as: "Let the Five [Somali Regions] Unite," "Let the Five Follow One Another," and "We Are the League's Successors."[95] In the 1960s, Ahmed Maalin Abdalle explained that people thought "to see a Somali flag was something wonderful. . . . Everyone was wearing blue things." His brother, a tailor, "used to get money from sewing blue things."[96] Although he now regrets the separatist movement, Yusuf Yasin of Isiolo expressed nostalgia about a time when people were under "*kiti moja*" (one seat), unlike the "tribalism" of today.[97]

A minority of Kenyans remains committed to the prospect of a Pan-Somali territorial nation-state. Alongside his father, Deghow Maalim Stamboul was one of the main heads of the northern separatist movement. He was detained by the Kenyan government before the start of the war and has only recently returned to Kenya to take up his position as chief in Garissa after more than twenty years in exile in Somalia. Decades later, he remains an unapologetic advocate for Greater Somalia. When I tried to point out the similarities between the Somalis and the Maasai, who also move and have kin across a national border, he readily dismissed such a comparison. Somalis, he argued, were a nation, whereas the Maasai are "an endangered species" and a threatened minority at risk of dying.[98] Perhaps unwittingly, Stamboul echoed the logic of British protectionism, which likened the Maasai to animals and their reserve to a zoo. Embedded in such rhetoric was "the idea that the Maasai face extinction, a vision rooted in the Hindes' 1901 classic *The Last of the Masai*."[99] He refused to portray his people as a powerless minority consigned to the putative past.

Stamboul's reasoning mirrored the standard language of Somali nationalism. In 1963, the Somalia Ministry of Information published a pamphlet emphasizing: "Everywhere else if you ask a man who he is he does not say, 'I am A Kenyan' or 'I am A Galla'; he says, 'I am an Orma' or, 'I am a Turkana' or some such tribal name. The Somalis have one name for all their clans. And one language is broadcast to the whole of these people from this country from Moscow and from Cairo."[100] Pan-Somali nationalists perpetuated the idea of Somali exceptionalism—the notion that they were a unique nation on a continent of "tribes." "Tribe" and "nation" are best understood as idioms that allowed various groups, who were struggling over the stakes of independence, to build coalitions, bolster their credentials to be an entitled majority or a disempowered minority, or (in this case) discredit rival nationalist campaigns. Within the context of decolonization and an institutional setting that linked resources, territory, and political rights to ethnic taxonomies, invoking such an image was rhetorically persuasive. Retooled by political thinkers from the region, Somaliness was both a claim to belong to a mythic and unified nation and a means of rejecting the alternative: disempowered minority status.

The idea that people can be ordered into natural cultural units tied to specific lands has come under increasing question in the past few decades.[101] Many scholars, however, still tend to understand separatist conflicts on the African continent through reference to the peculiarity of African borders. For decades prior to the Somali civil war, scholars tended to see Somalia as an authentic nation divided arbitrarily by colonial borders. Kenya, on the other hand, was largely perceived as a colonial invention that united a diverse array of ethnic groups. Recourse to the idea of arbitrary borders, as Anatole Ayissi argues, makes little sense in a world "where borders of every sovereign entity are man-made."[102] Although unacknowledged by Somali leaders, the area claimed by Somalia, including the NFD, was also based around colonial territories.

NFD nationalists engaged in a highly creative endeavor: one that fused a territorial nation-state with an array of nonterritorial affiliations. As nationalist movements began to "naturalize people's connection to their territory," many Somalis in Kenya crystallized around the idea of a homeland. As irredentism became less feasible, they started to see themselves as a people cut off from their "historic" nation.[103] If we see nationalism not as an inevitable or natural stage, but rather as a dominant political moment, it becomes possible to see how Somali political thinkers continued to carve out spaces for deterritorialized, cross-border networks even within the constraints of a territorial nationalist project.

5 ∾ "If We Were Brothers, We Would Have Met Long Ago"

It was a land of silence, scorching sun and hyena laughter
And what is freedom to win that way, morals decline
A volley of riflemen revenge on our women and children
Who is guilty and who is innocent, there is no definition.

—Abdinoor Ali Khansoy (excerpt from a collection of poems
written in Mandera between 2002 and 2003)[1]

MICHEL-ROLPH TROUILLOT ARGUES: "Any historical narrative is a particular bundle of silences."[2] This chapter concerns a series of silences concerning the "separatist" conflict, which is popularly and derogatively known as the Shifta War. The British and colonial governments tried to silence the fact that they had abrogated their own constitutional procedures—a process through which separatist supporters had peacefully articulated their aims before taking recourse to violence. The newly independent Kenyan government attempted to elide the nationalist claims of the Northern Frontier District (NFD) population in order to paint separatist fighters as *shifta*, or bandits. Today, Somalis and northerners struggle to bury ambivalent and divisive memories of war, which may threaten or complicate their work to gain full citizenship rights within the Kenyan nation.[3]

This chapter also addresses the silencing of alternative nationalisms. To attach oneself to one vision of the nation-state entails that other, equally feasible alternatives be subsumed, suppressed, or entirely silenced. The violence of the Shifta War reinforced the cultural identity of the Kenyan nation, but at the cost of excluding Pan-Somali advocates, who proposed a competing, yet equally viable nationalist vision, which has yet to be fully effaced from people's imaginations.

Finally, this chapter concerns that which is "under erasure." The literary critical meaning of *sous rature*, or "under erasure," refers to a concept that is inadequate yet indispensable.[4] Nationalism is one such concept. Pan-Somali irredentism was a product of the postwar order, a historical moment when African leaders gravitated toward the powerful language of self-determination, national homogeneity, and state sovereignty. While Kenyan and Ethiopian representatives portrayed the Pan-Somali project as an imperialist incursion and a tribalist ideology, delegates from the north insisted that they were asserting their natural right to self-determination. While it is important to treat the Pan-Somali project as a legitimate form of nationalism (especially in light of its brutal suppression by the Kenyan government), one must also move beyond normative framings that hinge on whether the NFD movement truly was or was not an authentic nationalist campaign. This demands attentiveness toward forms of belonging and difference that exceed the grasp of juridical politics and resist being easily assimilated into nationalist scripts.

ELISIONS OF RACE

While nationalist thinkers throughout East and Northeast Africa often imagined nonracial and multiracial futures, the racial hierarchies of the colonial era did not simply dissipate with decolonization. Broader systems of global white supremacy shaped the transition to independence. Moreover, nationalist movements bred their own kinds of exclusions.[5] For all its liberatory ends, Pan-Africanism risked alienating populations who were not considered (or did not consider themselves) "black" or "native." Rather than take recourse to ideas of false consciousness, we should consider why certain groups did not fully identify as "African."[6]

Many northern leaders felt pressure to make demands within the dominant discursive framework of Pan-Africanism. This was evident at a meeting that took place in early September 1961. Several representatives of the NFD took part in this preliminary meeting, which was held in the Government House in Nairobi, a few months before the second Lancaster Conference. Before Kenya's major nationalist leaders, who had come together to discuss the constitution, the NFD delegates each gave a short speech to express their grievances and their reasons for wanting to secede. The presence of Kenya's future leaders shaped their rhetorical strategies. One of the delegates was Guyo Jattani, a Sakuye chief from Isiolo. He explained that although he lived his whole life in the NFD:

I have never before met African leaders. We are all the same colour but if we were brothers we would have met long ago. We have always considered the Northern Frontier District as an area by itself. There was trouble in Kenya a few years ago but not in the N.F.D. We want to secede and join the Somalia Republic.[7]

Disaggregating race from brotherhood, Jattani underscored the distance between the people of the north and what he referred to as "Kenya." He also implied that the NFD had played no role in Mau Mau, which had become a major fixture around which a nationalist imaginary was forming.

Yusuf Haji Abdi, one of the delegates representing Garissa, was careful to avoid blaming Kenya's future leaders: "We are never troubled by our African brothers—they never come to fight us."[8] Instead, he argued, responsibility lay with the British:

> We are in the hands of the British Government. When the British Government came they found the Kikuyu and the Masai and they found us in the Northern Province. For generations we have been Islam. Before the Europeans came to Kenya there were no religious people here. Now in Kenya the people are human beings and we are like animals. The Government did that to us. This matter may cause bloodshed between us. We support our African brothers in having their rights but we beg them to support us to have our rights. We are in darkness, with no schools or hospitals. We are like a people thrown away, like a people in a big closed cupboard. This has been done by the British Government.[9]

Expressing little regard for precolonial, non-Abrahamic traditions, Abdi lamented the remarkable reversal of status that Somalis had endured under colonial rule. By the 1960s, many northern leaders were increasingly aware of the wide gap that lay between them and the more "developed" regions of Kenya. Abdi's laments reflected the growing importance of being able to gain access to what James Ferguson refers to as the "political and economic conditions of life that are normally characterized as 'modern.'"[10]

No doubt anticipating a cold reception from Kenyan leaders, northern leaders instead focused on the moral obligations of the departing colonial regime. The delegates' tactics were powerful rhetorical gestures, which painted decolonization as an abdication of responsibility. This language had purchase, as the British government, recovering from an international scandal over its conduct during Mau Mau, was concerned about engendering yet another public relations crisis.

Throughout their impassioned appeals, the delegates delicately approached the issue of race. By the early 1960s, explicit racism had become illegitimate within many formal political discussions. Northern leaders used either the nonracial language of self-determination or the more inclusive language of Pan-Africanism. Jattani, for example, emphasized: "We are all the same colour," while several of the delegates, including Yusuf Haji Abdi, referred to Kenyans as their "African brothers." When they finished their appeal, Julius Kiano, one of the founding members of the Kenyan African National Union (KANU), bluntly addressed the issue that the delegates had tried to avoid. Kiano made reference to a statement that had been issued earlier by Ali Aden Lord, the representative for the Northern Province in the Legislative Council, which had declared that the people of southern Kenya were of a different race.[11] He confronted the delegates with this matter: "Most leaders in Africa prefer the concept of pan-Africanism to tribalism. How do we understand pan-Somali policy?"[12] Wako Hapi, the president of the Northern Province People's Progressive Party (NPPPP), reframed Lord's statement: "We do not dispute we are Africans. But we have different religions and customs; we have stock—you cultivate. We are Islam. That is why we say we are different although still being Africans."[13] Hapi thus shifted the discussion from an issue of racial to one of cultural difference. He suggested that the people of the NFD and those of "Kenya" had incompatible lifestyles, which were ultimately too dissimilar to be easily reconciled.

On one hand, Hapi's statement could be interpreted as an attempt to gloss over the exclusionary aspects of the irredentist campaign. On the other hand, his response also suggests that behind the chauvinism of the secessionist campaign lay a claim for the recognition of difference. Kenyan leaders had promised a multiethnic state that would be inclusive toward all minorities. However, many northerners were unable to find a place for themselves within KANU's and KADU's definitions of the nation, which implicitly privileged sedentary ways of life over pastoral ones and rendered Muslims into a minority.[14] In addition, wide material disparities hindered the development of political alliances between the north and the rest of the country.

The racist thinking of the economically and politically powerful, such as colonial officials and white settlers, demands unequivocal condemnation. Addressing prejudice within African societies and among politically and economically marginalized groups, however, raises questions that can be challenging and uncomfortable.[15] Some critical race theorists have argued that in the absence of political and social privilege, those who hold chauvinistic beliefs do not exercise "racism," which implies a structural position of power.[16] As a dominant majority within Somalia and the NFD and a marginalized minority in the context of Kenya more broadly, Somalis had an ambiguous relationship to structures of power.[17] Regardless of how one chooses to define the scope and meaning of racism, there were clearly "oppressive potentialities" to even the nationalism of the "dominated."[18] One can remain critical of the chauvinistic and exclusionary aspects of the irredentist campaign while still recognizing the fears underpinning the prospect of integration and assimilation into Kenya.

SUPPRESSING ALTERNATIVE CONCEPTIONS OF SOVEREIGNTY

As the previous chapter showed, local politicians drew together the diverse people of the north in the early 1960s. By invoking an Islamic bond, a shared genealogy, and a common pastoral lifestyle, these political entrepreneurs were able to build widespread support for their movement. Yet it was not enough for Somali and northern leaders to mobilize a broad coalition within the NFD. They also had to articulate their demands within the domain of elite politics and convince British elites to support their claim to self-determination.

After their relatively cold reception at the Government House in Nairobi, northern leaders sent a formal delegation to the Second Lancaster House Constitutional Conference in February 1962.[19] The conference revealed, as John D. Kelly and Martha Kaplan note, how "alternative conceptions of sovereignty sometimes died hard in the decolonization process."[20] During the conference, the Kenyan African National Union (KANU) and the Kenyan African Democratic Union (KADU) put forth competing models of a multi-ethnic nation-state.[21] Representatives of the two parties worked out the details of the constitution, debated whether to adopt a bicameral, unicameral, federal, or centralized system, and discussed how best to distribute power and define political units within these various options. As they came to a set of tense and tenuous compromises, northern leaders continued to push for territorial union with Somalia and petition through the lingering structures of imperial citizenship.[22] Under empire, northerners were not a minority easily overruled by the more powerful factions within KADU and KANU. Rather, they could envision themselves as citizen-subjects capable of making demands on an imperial power, which was increasingly subject to international scrutiny.

Debates over the future of the region unearthed fundamental paradoxes surrounding the nature and scope of state sovereignty.[23] As Luise White and Douglas Howland argue: "International law maintains a pair of often incompatible ideas: self-determination, on the one hand, and a state's right to sovereignty and territorial integrity on the other."[24] NFD representatives insisted that their right to self-determination be recognized by the departing colonial power. They were rightly concerned that at the much fetishized moment of independence, the Kenyan state would be able to claim the right of territorial sovereignty and noninterference. Self-determination was, in many respects, a condition of empire—a right that had to be conferred upon northerners by a polity already recognized as sovereign.

Self-determination had also become a sacrosanct concept that had resonance internationally. That high-ranking officials in the British government felt pressure to respond to the NFD delegation's demands was evidenced by a conciliatory letter written to the Ethiopian government by a representative in the Foreign Office shortly after the conference. In the letter, the official explained that the British government could not ignore the delegates because they had been popularly elected. Thus, they "had to investigate their claims further, if only because to accept them or to reject them outright would have unacceptable consequences internationally."[25] Officials in the Foreign and Colonial Office remained committed to the performative aspects of constitutional procedures, even as they engaged in profoundly unconstitutional political negotiations.

As a result, the NFD delegation walked away from the Lancaster House Conference with a significant concession. In response to verbal petitions from the delegation, the secretary of state for the colonies agreed to send a commission to investigate secessionist claims and assess the desires of northern inhabitants.[26] The British government also agreed that "a decision" based upon the commission's findings would be "taken by Her Majesty's Government, before the new constitution for Kenya was brought into operation."[27] This position was discordant with the public stance taken by Kenyatta, who in subsequent months became more intransigent about the prospect of any kind of territorial dismemberment and rejected any moves that would shift the country further away from becoming a centralized state.[28] The statements published in the Colonial Office's official report on the conference would eventually become an embarrassing echo of the promises made at Lancaster.

British officials and Kenyan leaders toyed with the possibility of brokering a resolution to the NFD matter through alternative models of governance and territoriality (including the possibility of a UN-administered region or an East Africa Federation).[29] However, such layered forms of sovereignty were ultimately trumped by the singular sovereignty of the territorial nation-state. The decision to send a commission to assess the desires of northern inhabitants kept the region in political limbo, while at the same time framing the matter as a choice between two mutually exclusive states. Self-determination was a powerful language, but one that had to be increasingly articulated through a highly constrained model of territorial nationalism.

As Kenyan leaders worked out the details of the constitutional arrangement agreed upon at Lancaster, northerners awaited the arrival of the NFD Commission. Led by two independent officials from Nigeria and Canada, the commission began its tour of the NFD in October 1962, where it received delegations from various parties and conducted a series of *baraza* (public meetings).[30] The commissioners also evaluated the range of positions, divided them into "Kenyan" or "Somali" opinions, and conducted what was essentially an ethnographic report of the region. The commissioners' notes and final report provide insight into the internal logic of northern parties. Although the voices of northerners were recoded and reinterpreted by the commissioners, these written records—much like the poems and songs discussed in the previous chapter—provide fragmentary traces of non-elite discourses and debates.

The commissioners appeared to be searching for a fundamental cultural logic that would allow them to give northern inhabitants what Liisa Malkki refers to as "a fixed and identifiable position" in an imagined world in which the boundaries of ethnic and religious groups were orderly and clear-cut.[31] They adopted many of the ethnic clichés of the colonial government, including the propensity to differentiate between "Somali" and "half-Somali." However, the commissioners ultimately found an ethnic reading of the campaign unsatisfactory. In their final report, they argued for an underlying religious cause: "We noted that the division of opinion almost exactly corresponds to the division between Moslem and non-Moslem."[32] The logical extension of this argument was to rebuff the desires of members of the Gelubba and the Rendille who sought to join Somalia. Unable to understand why these predominantly non-Muslim groups would seek union with Somalia, the commissioners concluded that the Christian and Muslim leaders were misrepresenting their largely "pagan" constituency.[33]

The commissioners' thinking was also shaped by colonial-era ethnography, which tended to group the Rendille and the Maa speakers together. They marshaled ethnographic data; in "their dress and customs," the Rendille "have in fact more in common with those of the Samburu and Masai."[34] James Ferguson cautions against conflating a set of surface features with a "total way of life" or "way of thought" or converting "particular stylistic practices into badges of underlying and essential identities."[35] Culturalist paradigms not only tend to flatten the internal heterogeneity of movements, but they also fail to recognize that "culture" itself is constituted through economic, social, and political relations.[36] Although the Rendille could claim various kinds of connections to the Samburu, in this era, many were positioning themselves with Pan-Somali supporters. Moreover, as "folk" etymologies and vernacular discourses attest, non-Muslim groups were sometimes included in Somali kinship networks. Several people I interviewed recounted how the Rendille had once rejected Islam during the reign of the Ajuran Dynasty—thus earning the name *"reer diidey"* (the family that refused).[37] This popular etymology points to a means of conceptualizing belonging that is not easily captured by standard nationalist narratives.

Despite their misunderstandings, the commissioners left in their wake a variety of materials that give us insight into the internal tensions and composition of the irredentist movement. They also received several letters from groups anxious about becoming subordinate citizens, who rejected union with Somalia. One of the petitions was from a self-professed group of "Boran, Sakuye, and Watta tribesmen" in Isiolo District, who expressed fears of being subjected to discriminatory treatment and dispossessed of their land and livestock if forced to join Somalia.[38] They wrote that joining Somalia "will only make us shegats and slaves. . . . Somalis will steal our land and cattles [*sic*]."[39] While it is difficult to assess the popularity of these petitions, they shed some light on opinions otherwise obscured by the NPPPP's rhetoric of ethnic homogeneity. Some minority groups remained unconvinced by the promise of equality within the Somali Union—due, most likely, to remembered histories of being driven off land or forced into oppressive relations of clientship.

At stake was the very question of who belonged. Some opponents of Pan-Somali nationalism adopted an explicitly nativist rhetoric. One letter described the NPPPP's supporters as "secession demanding immigrant races."[40] In another petition, a leader from Moyale District portrayed the Borana as the true autochthons of the region: "Before the British came to the N.F.D., I would like to make it known to you that we people of the Galla Community owned the whole district. The very first time Somalis penetrated into our country is when the British came to the N.F.D. . . . they are altogether foreigners."[41] Antisecessionists cast Somalis as aliens to the area and, in so doing, appropriated the colonial myth that saw Somalis as an "expansionist" people. Through the creation of these new narratives, opponents could efface the shared histories that wove the diverse groups of the north together and tie old histories of land dispossession to new ideas of citizenship. Such rhetorical tactics reveal the influence of colonial nativist discourses on local political thought. At the same time, these petitions point to an alternative geography of a land and to the concerns of those who had been displaced by Somali movements into the area.

In its final report, which was published in December 1962, the commission stated that inhabitants "almost unanimously favour the secession from Kenya of the N.F.D."[42] The report also made clear that people of wide-ranging backgrounds supported irredentism.[43] By carrying out the commission so near to formal independence, the British government not only emboldened supporters of union with Somalia, but also gave legal weight to their claims.[44] Moreover, the commission helped to constitute northerners as a "people," situated in a discrete geographic region, expressing a collective will, and thus capable of exercising self-determination.

Without discounting the results of this report, one must also resist the tendency to reaffirm majoritarianism. Groups are always heterogeneous, bound together by differences that are as likely to be suppressed by nationalist projects as represented by them. The petitions of minority groups, however numerically small, reveal some of the diversity, tensions, and inequalities shaping politics in the NFD, which many Pan-Somali advocates were attempting to submerge within a project of national unity.

SUPPRESSING ALTERNATIVE NATIONALISMS

By the time the commissioners had completed their tour of the NFD, the political climate had begun to change. Benedict Anderson may be correct to suggest that nationalism is inherently "modular," easily capable of being pirated and transferred to radically different contexts.[45] However, its flexibility also made it dangerous and thus limited its scope. The question of how to resolve the status of the north was never an internal affair capable of being addressed solely at the level of Kenyan constitutional processes. Rather, it took on meaning within a much broader set of debates occurring on the continent and the international arena.

The NFD irredentist campaign coincided with a continent-wide debate over the legitimacy of colonial borders. Most issues of self-determination had interregional and international implications, since independence movements defined themselves in relation to potential or existing forms of nationalism. In Kenya as elsewhere on the continent, boundaries—whether in the form of the KADU's decentralized regions, Somalia's national frontiers, or the internal borders of the NFD—became one of the major points of contention. Boundaries "bounded" ethnic groups for the purposes of political representation, determined how power would be distributed within a federal or centralized state, distinguished the mutually exclusive reach of neighboring states, and defined who would be considered "native" and who "foreign."

In the 1950s, when African leaders had seriously contemplated the possibility of a Pan-African federalist state, Somali nationalists were able to internationalize their claims for self-determination.[46] The first two All-African People's Conferences (held in Accra in 1958 and Tunis in 1960) adopted resolutions that explicitly endorsed Somali unification, which was consonant with broader efforts at the time to rethink colonial boundaries.[47] The scope of Pan-African politics, however, narrowed significantly during the early 1960s. Gradually, many African leaders—especially those dealing with the threat of secessionist movements within their own territories—came to a common consensus over the need to protect the sanctity of colonial borders.[48]

Although many of the political negotiations of this era likely took place "offstage" (and outside the archival record), there is some evidence that Kenyatta initially vacillated over the NFD issue. According to official reports from the Colonial Office, just months after an unofficial visit to the emperor of Ethiopia, Kenyatta held private negotiations with the Somali prime minister. During this meeting, he expressed a willingness to consider separatist demands for territorial union with Somalia if confined to Wajir, Mandera, and Garissa Districts.[49] The emergence of other movements for autonomy and secession, however, precluded such a settlement.[50] Outside the NFD, Kenyatta faced opposition from the Mwambao United Front, which sought independence for the coastal strip of Kenya and union with Zanzibar; and the Masai United Front, which threatened to declare an independent state in concert with the Maasai of Tanganyika.[51] If successful, the Somali irredentist campaign could legitimize similar campaigns elsewhere on the continent, posing a threat to many multiethnic states, most notably Ethiopia.[52]

Decolonization in East Africa was a process not simply of building nations from colonies, but also of subordinating competing nationalisms into their fold. Northern Kenya became one of the major sites on which Western and African leaders displaced broader anxieties about national independence. Although the NFD was an arid, sparsely populated, and (in the eyes of many leaders) economically invaluable piece of land, it became a threatening reminder to African elites that there existed no singular, uncontested definition of the elusive concept of the "nation."

Guarding the integrity of national borders also enabled African elites to resolve anxieties over internal minorities. The NFD question not only threatened the Kenyatta regime by potentially legitimizing other separatist movements, but it also affected the distribution of power between Somalia's various politically defined constituencies. Much like Kenya, the Somali Union was facing pressure due to regional disparities. In June 1961, Somalia had conducted a referendum to formalize the new constitution. Political leaders in the former British Somaliland, unhappy with the distribution of power in the union and their exclusion from major positions within the civil service and the military, encouraged a boycott of the referendum. A few months later, military officers in northern Somalia attempted a coup. Although Pan-Somali nationalism was first given formal political expression by political leaders in British Somaliland, by the early

1960s, many elites there had come to see the quest to "reclaim" the NFD as a "southern" project that would only further disenfranchise the north (as well as jeopardize the possibility of an East African Federation).[53] In a similar fashion, postcolonial leaders in Somalia eventually pared down their support for foreign Somali fighters in the Ogaden and NFD due to fear of shifting the distribution of power within the country and arming people outside their direct control.[54]

It would be misleading to read these conflicts as products of primordialist ethnic or clan rivalries. Rather, they reflected tensions inherent to the liberal nation-state, which has historically fostered anxiety among groups who perceive their demographic predominance to be waning.[55] One former irredentist fighter in northern Kenya argued that authorities in Somalia did not provide them with automatic weapons, as they felt threatened by the widely dispersed Ogaden clan. The Ogaden "carried three twenty-shilling notes in their pocket," he explained, alluding to the three different types of currency used in Somalia, Kenya, and Ethiopia.[56] The former fighter's interpretation touches on the paranoia exhibited by a state unable to discipline a widely dispersed nomadic community with the threatening potential to become a "majority."

A number of political theorists, such as Hannah Arendt, have pointed to the structural problems with the nation-state. Arendt suggests that statelessness is constitutive of all processes of nation building, which inevitably privileges certain dominant ethnos.[57] The tendency for political leaders to jealously guard territorial sovereignty, however, can be just as dangerous as their propensity to equate the demos with an ethnos. African states' commitment to territoriality (which was often laden with ethnonationalist undertones) marginalized the Somali population, effectively rendering them stateless. The outcome of decolonization in Kenya suggests that regardless of its civic character, the nation-state is not an inherently stabilizing force threatened by the destabilizing forces of "ethnicity." Nor is it a transcendent form of identification capable of subsuming other forms of difference to itself.

BURIED PROMISES AND HIDDEN TRACES

Government archives construct certain objects of knowledge and privilege certain types of logic and causality. They also evince the state's fetishism of paperwork. As British correspondence from this period shows, archives can also reveal the fraught process by which official narratives are constructed.

One of the first public indications that the British government might turn against the possibility of secession came in August 1962. Against the protests of NPPPP leaders, the Regional Boundaries Commission—which was charged with determining the regional (later provincial) boundaries to be enshrined in the new constitution—visited the NFD.[58] By the end of the year, high-ranking officials in the Colonial Office were altering their blueprint for decolonization. A growing contingent within the British government believed that guaranteeing the territorial integrity of Kenya and Ethiopia was the best means to protect white settler interests, curb Soviet influence in the region, and contain militant elements from gaining ground. Aware of Kenyatta's widespread popularity, the new Conservative secretary of state for the colonies, Duncan Sandys, argued that refusing to mollify the majority would enflame the radical and leftist elements of KANU. The Colonial Office also realized that they could not continue to bolster KADU, which was unable to garner majority support. Conceding to politics on the ground, the Conservative government decided to strategically hand over power to KANU.[59]

Even as they retreated on their position toward secession for the NFD, however, the British government was careful to maintain a fiction of justice. The idea of self-determination was too central to the modernist conceits of European governance to be so blatantly disregarded. In the final weeks of 1962, the Colonial Office patched together a new story line in an effort to reinscribe an alternative interpretation over the constitutional process. The Report of the Second Lancaster Conference included a written trace of the government's promise to reach an advance decision based upon the findings of the NFD Commission—a commitment upon which the government was now retreating. In November 1962, F. D. Webber from the Colonial Office sent a telegram to acting governor E. N. Griffith-Jones. The secretary of state, he informed Griffith-Jones, "was very anxious that reports of the [Regional Boundaries and NFD] Commissions did not, in so far as they covered the same ground, reveal conflicting conclusions."[60] The governor of Kenya therefore organized drinks and a buffet lunch to ensure that the commissioners were "able to 'compare notes' so that should there be any danger of conflict, Commissions could consider together how this might be avoided."[61] By arranging for notes to be "compared" over a buffet lunch, the Colonial Office gave a few bureaucrats the power to sustain an appearance of a fair and orderly constitutional process.

The reports of the Regional Boundaries Commission and the NFD Commission were both published in December. To preserve the territorial integrity of Kenya and silence threats of secession, KANU and KADU included the NFD in its blueprint for the postcolonial nation. In its final report, the Regional Boundaries Commission advocated for dividing the Northern Province into three sections, each of which would be incorporated into the larger Eastern, North Western, and Coast Regions.[62] For obvious reasons, those who advocated for union with Somalia perceived this as a betrayal. However, even many of the anti-irredentist parties were unhappy with this settlement. Just as they resisted inclusion in a Somali state, the anti-secessionist factions also opposed incorporation into Kenya as disempowered minorities.[63] Northerners of all political persuasions thus found themselves sidelined from what was now simply a matter of finalizing a constitution in which their leaders had played little role.

A small inaccuracy in the NFD Commission's final report nevertheless enabled the Colonial Office to maintain the aura of a rational, orderly constitutional process. In the summary at the end of its report, the commissioners stated that "the Somali Opinion as expressed to us verbally" is "based on the premise that there can be no question of secession before Kenya gets independence."[64] This directly contradicted a memorandum that a coalition of party elites and chiefs had submitted to the commissioners during their tour of the NFD. The authors of this memorandum had stated that they could not "accept the argument, advanced by some Europeans, that our freedom to unite with the country of our choice must be delayed."[65] No doubt anticipating a challenge from its signatories, the commissioners' report dismissed the petition on the grounds that it was "obviously prepared by some central authority."[66]

Archival documents are often elusive testaments to the complex ways in which powerful and unacknowledged forces reshape the historical record.[67] The final report created the semblance of a democratic process by invoking the "voice" of the people of the NFD. Yet this act of ventriloquism only affirmed the authority and finality of official documentation. By reframing the results in these terms, describing the memorandum as a "foreign" intervention, and forestalling secession, the NFD Commission retrospectively imposed legitimacy on a decision to ignore the popular opinion of the north. Delaying the NFD question until after Kenyan leaders took over the reins of power also fetishized the moment of independence, masking and displacing colonial responsibility for the outcome of decolonization.

Somalis often remember this moment as an unanticipated and unjust deception. One former councillor in Wajir explained that after encouraging secession and telling Somalis to join their brothers, the British surrendered the NFD to the Kenyan government in exchange for the security of the settler community.[68] Many people I spoke to suggested that the British deliberately derailed separatism to protect white settlers within the country. Others argued that Western powers refused secession because they were interested in the NFD's potential oil reserves, for which BP Shell was prospecting in the 1960s.[69] Attributing responsibility for the breakdown of negotiations solely to the British government is misleading, as the outcome of decolonization frequently surpassed the intentions or expectations of any single actor. Nor can decolonization be reduced to simple, unicausal explanations. Yet these narratives speak in powerful ways to the deep sense of betrayal that many northerners experienced. In addition, they challenge the British self-image as "neutral" arbiters within the context of decolonization.

By breaching its own constitutional process, retracting on its promise at Lancaster House, and deferring the decision until after independence, the Colonial Office had planted the seeds of fear and suspicion, which largely precluded the possibility for a peaceful solution. In March, shortly after Duncan Sandys announced the creation of the North Eastern Region, rioting broke out in Isiolo (see map 6.1). Britain's disregard for the popular opinion of the NFD, gauged by its own 1962 referendum, caused the Somali Republic to sever diplomatic relations. Over the course of 1963, chiefs and officials in the north resigned from government posts, residents boycotted the elections, and fighting against government forces intensified.[70]

FORGOTTEN MARTYRS: THE DEATH OF WABERA

Shahid Amin points out that the "master saga of nationalist struggles is built around the retelling of certain well-known and memorable events," which are often used to distinguish "popular protest from 'crime.'"[71] In the NFD, one of the most controversial events occurred in the wake of the Isiolo riots, shortly before the start of the war. On 28 June 1962, two Somali fighters shot Daudi Dabasso Wabera and Haji Galma Dido. Wabera was the first African DC of Isiolo. He had been appointed by the colonial government as it was Africanizing the civil service. Haji Galma was the Borana paramount chief. They were on their way to a cattle auction when the assassins ambushed their car and shot Wabera. Haji Galma, who had wrapped himself around Wabera in an effort to protect him, was also killed by the assassins' bullets. Afterward, the fighters fled to Somalia, which refused extradition.[72] Wabera's death—which is widely perceived to have been a crime rather than a political assassination—has since been memorialized by many of the parties in the conflict, who deem it tragic for differing reasons.

Although Wabera was not a well-known figure outside the NFD, a central road in downtown Nairobi still bears his name. Nearby streets are dedicated to famous political figures from the 1960s, including Ronald Ngala, Dedan Kimathi, and Mama Ngina. By including him in the litany of better-known nationalist heroes, the Kenyan government no doubt attempted to discipline his murder within the nationalist memory. Through his memorialization, the state also obscured his inscription into other kinds of nationalist and communal narratives.

Even if many Kenyan citizens no longer remember Wabera, his death is a fixture within northerners' popular memory. Many Borana cited the murder of these two respected Muslim leaders as a sign that they would have never been fully included within the Somali nation.[73] Nationalist sentiments in northern Kenya today are very different from those that dominated in the 1960s. Several conflicts in the intervening years have shifted the views of non-Somali groups in the north. Persistent racism against minorities within Somalia, land and political conflicts in Eastern Province, and the rise of Oromo nationalism in Ethiopia are just some of the reasons why so many Borana and Gabra today express regret for having participated in the irredentist campaign. For many, Wabera is symbolic of these feelings of betrayal.

However, Wabera is not only a tragic figure for members of the Borana and the Gabra communities. Many Somalis also decried these fratricidal murders. Ali Hassan, an elder from Wajir, expressed grief over the death of Haji Galma, whom he described as a deeply pious man whom fighters had killed without cause.[74] Abdi Haji Abdulla, an elder from Isiolo, explained that his father had helped convert Wabera to Islam. He lamented his killing quite passionately.[75] For many, his death is emblematic of the barriers preventing Muslims from achieving unity. Wabera's murder has become a central event around which northerners discuss the moral ambiguities surrounding the war. By labeling his death a "crime," many northerners seek not to delegitimize protest, but to give voice to suffering. Oftentimes, these ethical debates aspire toward a universalism capable of transcending differences of ethnicity, race, and nation.

ECLIPSING INTERNATIONAL HORIZONS

As Wabera's murder shows, by the end of 1963, the hope of a diplomatic solution was waning. Increasingly unable to gain traction on the national or imperial level, Somali leaders turned instead to international organizations. British officials and African leaders in Kenya and other neighboring countries, on the other hand, cast the NFD problem as either a diplomatic question between independent states or an internal security matter. These debates, which relocalized the conflict, narrowed the possibilities for envisioning sovereignty, diplomacy, and justice.

The future of the NFD held implications for a set of contentious global debates over the terms of national sovereignty, the moral obligations of departing colonial powers, and the purview of postwar international bodies. Was the NFD issue a colonial problem for which the departing British government bore responsibility? Was it a matter to be worked out between sovereign and independent African nations after independence? Or was it a question of self-determination to be brought before the Organization of African Unity or the United Nations (UN)? Defined differently, the NFD issue could be considered a concern of relevant African regimes, the British government, the OAU, or the UN.

In May 1963, the Somali government brought the separatist issue before the inaugural conference of the OAU. The summit became a forum for African leaders to reaffirm the sanctity of colonial borders. Already drawn into the evolving civil war in the Congo, the beleaguered organization was unwilling to legitimize any other separatist movement.[76] In a memorandum submitted to the conference, the Kenyan delegation described the Somali government's petition as a "tribalistic doctrine" and "expansionist plot" and accused Somalis of having succumbed to the "mental colonisation," "pseudo-anthropology," and divide-and-rule tactics of the colonial state.[77] By casting territorial challenges as an affront to Pan-Africanism, Kenyan leaders elided an older model of Pan-African thought that was far less committed to indivisible and *uti possidetis* conceptions of sovereignty. The Kenyan delegation also quoted a statement from Kenyatta, who had announced in 1962 that those who refused to integrate could "pack up [their] camels and go to Somalia."[78] Such fiery rhetoric, which used nomadic mobility as a distancing technique and placed territorial integrity above fidelity to one's fellow citizens, only served to further alienate the people of the NFD.

British mediation attempts also divorced the NFD question from the international arena, which further impeded the possibility of a layered sovereignty emerging in the region. In a final attempt to peacefully resolve the conflict and disentangle itself from a politically charged, embarrassing, and rapidly escalating political impasse, the Foreign Office brokered a conference in Rome between representatives from the Kenyan and the Somali governments. Amid the preparations for the conference, some British officials briefly entertained the possibility of an interim administration managed by the British government, the UN, or a joint Somali/Kenyan dispensation. Ultimately, however, the future of the NFD was framed as a bilateral or multilateral affair between African states.[79] During the conference and later before the UN General Assembly, the British government maintained that a solution should be wrought by the "African governments concerned" and within an "African framework."[80] Kenyan leaders, for their part, used the talks to preclude any efforts to bring the issue before the UN.[81] British and Kenyan representatives narrowly defined the terms of acceptable international diplomacy, which reaffirmed the norms of noninterference and territorial integrity made paramount by the OAU. This approach turned a colonial predicament into an "African problem," muted the popular opinion of northerners, and obscured the power differentials between nominally equal nation-states.

The separatist issue quickly moved from the purview of international diplomacy to the realm of military operations. After the August conference in Rome proved unsuccessful, the Kenyatta regime imprisoned the main heads of the NPPPP.[82] Gadudow Garad Alasow, who was tipped off by a British intelligence official and managed to escape arrest, fled to Somalia, where he helped found the Northern Frontier District Liberation Front (NFDLF), the armed wing of the NPPPP.[83] On 25 December 1963, just weeks after formal independence, the Kenyan government declared a state of emergency in the NFD.[84] In an effort to deny the irredentist fighters a claim to self-determination and avoid a direct war with Somalia, the Kenyan government recast the irredentist struggle as a criminal insurgency. This not only contributed to the ensuing violence, but also marginalized the NFD from any kind of constitutional or judicial process.

Efforts by British and Kenyan leaders to relocalize the NFD issue also obscured the geopolitical dimensions of the conflict.[85] The NFD soon became a militarized front in a war for which the causes extended far beyond its borders. The British government gave Kenyan officials logistical and financial support for a number of military operations in the north.[86] Despite public denials, Somali state officials surreptitiously armed the fighters, who fled into their territory and acquired weapons at training camps near the border with Kenya. The Somali government, though the recipient of Soviet military aid, was nevertheless fearful of triggering a war with neighboring states and arming factions outside its direct control.[87] In 1964, Kenyatta and Haile Selassie signed a mutual defense pact, which exacerbated Somalia's strategically weak position.[88] This fostered an asymmetric war between a relatively powerful military and small groups of armed fighters who received intermittent aid from Somalia.[89] It also led to the widespread displacement of violence onto local inhabitants of the north.

MASKING VIOLENCE IN THE NORTH

A number of critical theorists have noted that the suspension of the rule of law is, in fact, central to the very project of governance.[90] By meting out violence against northerners and asserting control over the NFD through emergency law (even when actualizing that control was difficult), Kenyan leaders were able to perform sovereignty, construct an enemy, and transmute the memory of Mau Mau into a bid for national order and unity. The war in the north became an opportune moment for the Kenyan government to restore the credibility of its military. At the start of 1964, a mutiny had spread throughout the national armies of Tanganyika, Uganda, and Kenya by African KAR troops disappointed by the lack of gains from independence.[91] As it was fighting northern separatists, the Kenyatta regime was also struggling to tame the divisive legacy of the 1950s. While memories of Mau Mau were being suppressed or, at times, quietly memorialized, the insurrection in the north was being cast as a criminal insurgency.

Echoes of Mau Mau resonated in the ways in which the Kenyan government suppressed the conflict. The postcolonial regime borrowed extensively from the counterinsurgency tactics that their former colonial rulers had deployed against Mau Mau. They imposed curfews on towns in the NFD and implemented expanded emergency law. Under these parameters, security forces could detain people without trial, confiscate the property of entire communities as retribution for guerrilla activities, and restrict freedom of assembly. The death penalty was made mandatory for those caught with firearms. The Kenyan government also deployed the General Service Unit (GSU), a specially trained paramilitary force that had fought against the Kenya Land and Freedom Army (the guerrilla fighters often referred to as "Mau Mau"). Charged with securing a vast region—which many considered to be not only on the frontier of territorial "Kenya," but also on the fringes of the legal system—security forces frequently operated outside even these expanded legal parameters. Oral testimony from inhabitants of the north points to the widespread use of illegal forms of communal punishment. Many people witnessed or had been the victims of rape, torture, shootings, beatings, and castration.[92]

In 1965, after separatist fighters began planting land mines on the roads carrying troops to the north, the Kenyan regime forced northern inhabitants into enclosed villages—a counterinsurgency tactic that the colonial regime had used against Mau Mau to cut off support for the forest fighters.[93] Villagization was the culmination of what Alex De Waal refers to as a "military onslaught on the entire pastoral way of life."[94] Faced with an elusive and decentralized body of fighters who adopted hit-and-run tactics, security forces increasingly conflated nomads with *shifta* (bandits), thus criminalizing the northern population as a whole.[95] Many pastoralists, especially those moving outside designated zones, were killed during the war. Government forces also gunned down camel herds, which they associated with elusive and unregulated mobility. According to Richard Hogg, between 1963 and 1970, the camel population of Isiolo District "declined by over 95 per cent."[96] The Sakuye, who were herded into concentration camps, were almost decimated by the war.[97] Many Oromo speakers remember this era as the "*gaf Daba*, or 'the period when time [and people] stopped.'"[98] In the early 1980s, anthropologist Paul Baxter returned to Isiolo District only to discover that "people who some thirty years ago were probably the wealthiest and most productive pastoralists of the Horn are now among the poorest"—a reversal he attributed directly to the Shifta War.[99] By greatly inhibiting movement, occupying wells, and targeting nomads moving outside designated zones, the government, in essence, criminalized pastoralism itself.[100]

The Kenyan regime repeatedly denied that "Nazi tactics were being used against the people" of the north or that emergency law prevented the exposure of these crimes.[101] While many of these abuses went undocumented, it is noteworthy that the Kenyan National Archives contain an entire file of unrequited compensation claims from Isiolo District. These letters blame government soldiers for destroying property and shooting and stealing cattle. One letter was written by the widow of the local *qadi* (judge), who was one of several unarmed civilians gunned down by soldiers in the Isiolo mosque in 1967.[102] Today, demands by victims of the Shifta War for some kind of recompense remain, like these letters, unanswered.

Alongside its military assault, the Kenyatta regime also embarked on a propaganda campaign.[103] As mentioned above, the fighters were labeled as *shifta*, an Amharic term for "bandit" that had been adopted by the colonial government. Among even top government officials, *shifta* became a blanket term for all Somalis.[104] Hannah Whittaker persuasively argues that "the notion of shifta veiled various forms of violence in the NFD."[105] Like the name "Mau Mau," this label enabled officials to empty the movement of political meaning.

Repression of the movement also went hand in hand with promises of development. In late 1964, the Kenyatta government offered amnesty to fighters who surrendered and assured that government aid would be made available once fighters relinquished their weapons. In a letter appealing to two chiefs who had defected to the Somali cause, one Kenyan senator dangled the "carrot" of development. He explained that "the Kenya Government has allocated hundreds of pounds for development of your Region including water resources, education, adult literacy and health service. . . . I appeal to you once more on behalf of our President, to come out and compromise."[106] One only has to travel through the northeast today (where you will rarely find paved roads, running water, electricity, or significant infrastructure outside the main towns) to realize that these promises of development never came to much effect. The Kenyatta regime proposed governance as the sole solution to the problems of the NFD, even while the promise of national integration remained elusive.

SILENCING FEMALE NARRATIVES

Like so many other conflicts, the war was often played out on the bodies of women.[107] One resident of Kotulo recounted a story about a female villager who was approached by Kenyan soldiers during the war. She began to cry out to her deceased male relatives for protection. The soldiers, believing that she was calling to armed fighters hiding in the bush, fled the scene. The woman was thus spared.[108] This story not only reflects the susceptibility of women to sexual violence, but it also points to the ways in which people of the north perceive the presence of God in their daily lives.

Stories like this shed important light on the serious issue of sexual assault. However, they also tend to perpetuate an image of women as exclusively victims of war and men as primarily protectors or aggressors.[109] Conventional histories frequently bypass the roles and perspectives of women by focusing on conflicts and deliberations between largely male political elites. Female narratives are less readily attended to, partly because they often occurred outside the domain of elite politics.

In some cases, poems can provide insight into the buried and overlooked experiences of women. Several of the people I interviewed in the village of Kotulo recited the work of a popular local poet who had lived through the Shifta War. The following are extracts from her oeuvre, which speak to the dilemma of pastoralists caught between government forces and separatist fighters. Her poetry offers a more complex picture than that of mere female victimhood. It also reveals the often-invisible role of women's labor:

Affey iyo Jeeley ka joog
Duuqowdaa jilib baa ku culus
Jamhuriyad noqosho jirkeed ha sugin
Ma jebin karin John Keniyaat
Ariga jiray la jihaadayaan

Affey and Jeeley, stay away
Elders with the heavy knees
The Republic will never be attained
John[110] Kenyatta will never be broken
These (two) are fighting with our goats

* * * *

Karrarid ku xaabsadow
Karayaad soo marudsadow
Sagaal kurus diirayow
Kabaha geel dubanayow
Kadeed anigaa arkee
Kanina kii kale ka daran
Koofida weyn soo kamkami
Koob biyo ahi koron kuugu daaq
Jeebkaygu kordhiimo ma leh

Kalkaa ana layga raacay
Kulayl fuudkaan ku nacay

He who scoops up the bag[111]
He who licks out the pot
He who devours nine camel's humps
And roasts the hooves of the camel
Hardships I have seen
But this is worse than any that came before
Big hat that is so smelly
A cup from which a castrated camel could drink and be satisfied
My pockets are empty [of money]
Yet they want more of mine
I hate you for the hot soup you take

* * * *

Ileen Affey waa abtigey
Afkey kuma caayi karo
Addo iyo Liban waa abaar
Ayda ay dhehaan Wajeer
Iridkastoo ay aadayaan
Ee'aad baa ay soo maqlaan
Indhaha lama saari karo
Ee Affeyow edeb lahow
Abolaha celi erga ah.

Affey is my uncle
I can't bear to malign him
Addo and Liban are in a drought[112]
The bush that is called Wajir
At every door they approach
A bleating goat is heard
One can't bear to look
So, Uncle Affey, behave yourself
Stop your soldiers and send back the envoy[113]

The nuances and humor of these poems, which are rich in descriptions of the soldiers' gluttony (and made many of my interlocutors laugh), defy easy translation. As Abdi Billow Ibrahim, my research assistant, explained, the poems paint the fighters as abusive and exploitative, their demands far overreaching normal expectations of assistance and hospitality. The war did not simply pit government forces against civilians. Internal divides and patriarchal power relations, which existed outside the state/citizen relationship, also shaped the conflict. Poorly armed in comparison to Kenyan troops, irredentist fighters sometimes sought out arms and supplies by raiding civilians.[114] Fellow Somalis were not immune from such raids. Pastoralists often experienced looting at the hands of the underfunded fighters claiming to liberate them, although former fighters frequently denied such accusations. Women, who were frequently left to take care of homesteads and provide much of the unofficial and unacknowledged support for the guerrilla fighters, were particularly vulnerable to such abuse. Nevertheless, as this poem attests, they could exercise power by publicly shaming separatist fighters. This poem also shows how geopolitical contests often manifested as violence upon the most marginalized members of society. As will be discussed in the next chapter, the war normalized the use of armed violence against civilians. Public shaming, however, remained a powerful tool of dissent, especially for women.

BURYING THE PAST

To avoid reproducing conservative versions of history, historians often look for buried or hidden histories.[115] Richard Kearney cautions scholars to be discerning toward "*when* it is right to remember and *when* it is better to forget. Or, indeed, *how much* we should remember or forget."[116] The war left significant traces on northern inhabitants—not the least of which are the physical scars of bullets. Forgetting is unlikely to be a reasonable political or personal option. However, sentimentalizing remembrance or celebrating historical reconstruction was also problematic in this context.[117]

Formal peace negotiations obscured the fact that patterns of state violence continued long after the end of the "Shifta War" and have yet to fully diminish. In October 1967, the Somali and Kenyan governments ended the conflict by signing the Arusha Memorandum of Understanding.[118] Faced with growing economic and political isolation, the newly elected Somali government, headed by Abdirashid Ali Shermarke and Mohamed Haji Ibrahim Egal, pursued a policy of forging détente with neighboring states.[119] Egal and Kenyatta attended the talks, which were mediated by Kenneth Kaunda of Zambia.[120] The detained NPPPP leaders were absent from the conference, which enabled the Kenyan and Somali governments to bypass the separatist leadership and work toward normalizing relations. This also reflected the Kenyan government's ambivalence toward naming the war. On one hand, the Kenyatta regime treated the issue as an internal security matter. On the other, it resolved the conflict through a formal agreement with a neighboring foreign power. It was precisely this indeterminacy that enabled the Kenyan state to publicly declare peace, while maintaining emergency regulations in North Eastern Province (NEP) until 1992.[121] The persistent and often unacknowledged use of collective punishment was a lasting legacy of the "Shifta War."

Many northerners were understandably desirous to tell their stories about the war. Some were looking to counter dominant perceptions of the war as a criminal insurgency and saw me as a vehicle through which to construct a history of the movement's legitimacy. By highlighting the role of the major political elites such as Wako Hapi and Abdirashid Khalif, northerners tried to counter the label of banditry and prove that they, too, had their cast of "respectable" nationalist heroes. Frequently mentioned was the 1962 commission, which was a way for people to show that northern leaders had used civic and democratic channels of redress before turning to militant means. Others were insistent on detailing the abuses committed during the war and politicizing the rape and murder of unarmed civilians. In 1970, the Kenyan parliament passed the Indemnity Act, which shielded government officials and soldiers from civil or criminal liability for any human rights violation committed in the course of security operations between 25 December 1963 and 1 December 1967.[122] Many northerners—in search of reparations and recognition—were keen to bring the abuses of the war to an international public and connect them to a global human rights agenda, where they might have greater traction.

Other people were eager to put this period behind them. For some, it was not worth reviving such contentious and divisive memories, which continued to hold implications for present-day conflicts. Several people, including former NPPPP leaders and NFDLF fighters, lamented their involvement in the irredentist campaign. There was enormous regret for a movement that had turned tragic, divisive, and that most people no longer considered a politically viable option.

This collective ambivalence came across in various divergent opinions about the late leader Abdirashid Khalif. Once a vocal supporter of separatism, Khalif had defected from the NPPPP and by September 1963 had formed the Frontier Independent Party, through which he tried to rally support for joining Kenya.[123] In November, just before the outbreak of the war, members of his clan kidnapped him and brought him to Somalia, where he remained until the end of the conflict.[124] Some northerners viewed the late Khalif as a traitor who had "sold" the land. One story alleges that when offered a bag of sand and a bag of money, Khalif chose the latter. Others admired Khalif's pragmatic commitment to peace. One inhabitant of Wajir praised Khalif for helping to institute a cease-fire and encouraging the surrender of armed fighters.[125] He was celebrated not for his "collaboration," but for his "foresight."[126] Some also portrayed him as a champion of human rights and defender of the north. Zeinab Abdi Ali described how Abdirashid Khalif once threatened Oginga Odinga for suggesting the government poison wells in order to quash the separatist movement. According to this popular story, Khalif allegedly brandished a knife and warned Odinga (a Luo, who are traditionally uncircumcised) that he could still be circumcised.[127] Some Somalis had come to memorialize Khalif as a hero—capable of emasculating (literally) the enemy.

Abdirashid Khalif is representative of the constrained, yet heterogeneous political choices available to educated leaders of his era. Although he chose to work within the Kenyan regime, he remained a vocal critic of government policy toward the north throughout his life.[128] As Khalif's career indicates, we cannot reduce complex and diverse historical possibilities to a set of binary nationalist classifications (like collaboration versus resistance).[129]

Nationalism nonetheless creates various kinds of demands on memory. Some people engaged in revisionist interpretations of the past in order to reframe their membership position within the nation-state. My interlocutors, for instance, sometimes suggested that their own clans were less involved in the movement out of fear of minority status within Somalia. Others deliberately played on widely held stereotypes of pastoralists as uneducated and unenlightened in an effort to exculpate themselves. They blamed the Somali government and the supposedly worldlier, town-dwelling Harti and Isaaq for manipulating the fighters into joining the movement. Still others claimed that the majority of northerners sought not integration with Somalia, but rather independence as a region.

"False" stories, as scholars of oral history have noted, often speak to important truths.[130] Alessandro Portelli argues that victims of violence sometimes draw dubious causal connections as "a way of averting the gaze, of exorcising the massacre or at least attenuating its impact, to rationalize it or explain it away."[131] Long denied a space in the nationalist imaginary, many northerners sought to create new histories that could reconcile memories of the war with their bids for national inclusion.

Perhaps the most powerful narrative device was spiritual. Attributing agency to the divine is commonplace in the north, where people often interpret the presence of God in everyday events whose underlying significance may be opaque. Many people alluded to being spared due to divine intervention. Some argued that losing the Shifta War was simply part of God's design, as northerners were subsequently able to provide refuge for those displaced from the civil war in Somalia. One resident of Wajir town praised God for having kept them in Kenya. Had things gone differently and had it not been for the British, she argued, Kenyan Somalis would have been a minority in Somalia and among the refugees scattered all over the world.[132] Such arguments enabled northerners to give meaning to a war whose tragic outcome few anticipated. They also reflect the diverse temporalities and intellectual traditions through which northerners make sense of the past—not all of which can be easily assimilated into a linear, secular historical narrative.

These patterns of interpretation, in many cases, reflect a changing orientation toward the Kenyan nation-state. To understand these contemporary elisions and strategies and the reasons why so many northerners struggle to tame memories of the separatist movement, we must look not toward the past, but rather at the decades that have passed since the end of the war.

6 ⤚ "Their People Came Here to Seek Asylum"

The saga between the Supreme Council of Kenya Muslims and the Members of Parliament from North-Eastern Province on the screening of the Somali community resident in Kenya, which the Government says is being done to flush out aliens, is not a laughing matter. . . . If what is happening to the Somalis in Kenya is out of the fear of some leaders in the province to be politically outdone, then let them ponder the story of Moses and the Pharaoh and who emerged victorious.

—A. Mirimo Wandati, chairman of the Muslim Youth Forum, in an article in the *Daily Nation*, 29 November 1989[1]

INVOKING BIBLICAL IMAGERY, A. Mirimo Wandati, chairman of the Muslim Youth Forum, protested the screening and deportation of Somalis living in Kenya. Implemented in 1989 in reaction to the escalating Somali refugee crisis, the screening process was aimed at "sorting out" and deporting illegal aliens. In Kenya, as in many parts of the world, the recent growth in transborder migration has been accompanied by a proliferation of border controls.[2]

After independence, the categories through which the Kenyan state ruled and repressed the Somali population became increasingly discordant with the survival strategies of many Somali migrants, nomads, and refugees. The postindependence system of electoral politics reinforced the colonial legacy of ethnic "homelands." Various state policies underlined the idea that representation as a "minority clan" would be the only acceptable political option for Somalis in Kenya. During the 1980s, the Moi and Barre regimes actively incited and organized ethnic violence through nativist politics and clan cleansing campaigns.

As the Kenyan state tried to reterritorialize clan affiliations and suppress Pan-Somali nationalism, the Somali civil war gave birth to a new "global Somalia." Asylum seekers (deemed refugees according to the norms of international law) moved to cities as dispersed as Minneapolis, London, Nairobi, and Dubai. During the 1980s and early 1990s, Nairobi developed into a hub within a global Somali trade network, which largely functioned outside state surveillance, legal channels of movement, and official banking, tax collection, and identification systems. Globalized Islamic and refugee networks, which were not routed so exclusively through the nation-state, provided an alternative locus of economic and social opportunities for many Somalis pushed to the margins of the Kenyan political system.

The exclusion of "strangers," though intrinsic to all forms of national citizenship, was particularly punishing for Somalis in Kenya. By continuing the colonial policy of politicizing clan, the Kenyan government effectively criminalized many of the "informal" transnational networks that people relied upon to navigate a challenging political and economic climate. As a result, the stigma of the Shifta War never fully faded. By the 1990s, many Kenyan state elites and ordinary citizens had come to see Somalis as a dangerous and alien presence in the country—who unsettled the tenuous and ambiguous lines between citizen and foreigner, nation and ethnicity, and minority and majority. As this chapter argues, the policing of Somali networks became a theatrical means of managing anxieties about the shifting contours of national sovereignty, the constraints of ethnoterritorialism, and the unraveling of the developmentalist state.

THE DEMOGRAPHIC AND CADASTRAL POLITICS OF CLAN

The politicization of clan was an overdetermined process. Various forces gave the idea of clan its political currency. Numerous socioeconomic factors—stemming from poverty, crime, and climate change—encouraged inhabitants of the north to stake claims to state resources by mobilizing through ethnic patronage networks and aligning defensively around the idea of clan "homelands." The system of electoral politics implemented during the transition toward independence also reinforced the colonial logic of ethnicity, entrenching the epistemology of clan within the postcolonial political order. Moreover, postcolonial elites played an important role in instrumentalizing ethnic affiliations and subsidizing violence.

More than any modernizing initiative by the colonial state, the Shifta War probably had the greatest impact in turning northern residents toward permanent settlement. After the war, impoverished northern pastoralists became increasingly dependent on wage labor and foreign aid.[3] This was especially true for those living in Isiolo District, which had suffered the brunt of the government's military assault. By 1971, Elliot Fratkin notes, the Borana of Isiolo District "were in a state of genuine starvation, surviving only by means of the massive famine relief of the Catholic Relief Services."[4] To gain access to these services, northerners had to settle into more permanent locations, furthering a process of sedentarization initiated by Kenyatta's forced villagization policies.

Having lost much of their livestock in the war, northerners also experienced worsening and, in some cases, permanent conditions of poverty. The hardship induced after independence cannot be productively understood as a "local" problem divorced from international events. Nor can their impoverishment and isolation be attributed to being "untouched" by the global economy. Despite its seeming remoteness, the north was affected by various global processes, including climate change engendered miles away in industrial centers. The Sahelian droughts of the 1970s marked the beginning of a long decline in rainfall.[5] Worsening ecological conditions were yet another factor that led people away from nomadic livestock rearing.

Northerners also faced greater insecurity after the war, as violent crime became a much more regular feature of life in the region. Many people I spoke to differentiated between the "political" phase of armed guerrilla fighting in the 1960s and the forms of criminality that arose in its aftermath, which they often referred to as "economic banditry." One resident of Habasweyn described this new phase of banditry as "tribal" and "economical." He also argued that chiefs and political elites were often responsible for inciting ethnic violence and promoting illegal activities, such as poaching and arms dealing.[6] The Kenyan press and government officials, however, continued to deploy the term *shifta* (bandit) to describe virtually any criminal incident in the region.[7] Invoking the elusive yet ubiquitous *shifta* became a substitute for more meaningful political discussions on the causes and consequences of crime in the north. It also normalized the use of government violence and gave the Kenyan public the widespread impression that insecurity was a habitual part of life in the region—an idea that remains prevalent to this day.

Poverty, elevated crime rates, and climate change exacerbated contests over land and political rights, which became increasingly tied to the issue of autochthony. As Hussein A. Mahmoud explains: "The European colonial administrators demarcated territories in northern Kenya on the basis of ethnicity and clan affiliations, thus setting the scene for people to perceive themselves as belonging to different ethnic groups and locations."[8] By implementing an electoral system without deinstitutionalizing the colonial legacy of ethnic boundaries, the Kenyatta regime tied political and economic entitlements to ethnicity.[9]

In various ways, clan became the privileged mode for engaging with the state. Postcolonial censuses, for instance, divided people by the major "indigenous" lineages and consigned all others to the ambiguous category "Other Somali."[10] Such techniques gave birth to a new form of subjectivity: institutional representation as a minority. Salah Abdi Sheikh notes that "clans were registered as tribes. Degodia, Ogaden, Murule, Ajuran, and Garreh each became a tribe equal to the large ethnic communities like Kikuyu, Kamba, Luo or Luhya."[11] This elided the fact that lineage ties cut across international borders and Somalis could trace their genealogy in multiple, incommensurate ways.

Throughout the north, groups also grew wary about engaging in grazing arrangements with neighboring lineages or assimilating kin. Older forms of transhumance and migration became especially problematic in the context of electoral races, in which a community's numerical predominance determined seats in local and central government. Fearful of losing demographic control over constituencies now thought of as ethnic "homelands," many groups (in northern Kenya as well as other parts of the country) came to think of international and internal migrants as outsiders on their land.[12] At the same time, protracted droughts and amplified competition for pasture also forced families to relocate to areas where they were increasingly conceptualized as strangers. The instability ushered in by decolonization had discordant effects—causing some to draw upon their dispersed kinship ties in order to migrate into safer and more ecologically robust territories; and others to mobilize around highly territorialized ideas of clan rights in order to secure access to state channels of resource distribution.

One woman explained the challenges she faced as a displaced person in the decades over independence. Compelled to move from her birthplace due to *abaar* (drought), she first tried to establish herself in Garissa District. Unable to attain an ID card, access water, or safeguard her animals due to discrimination against her clan (the Garre), she was eventually forced to move to Wajir District. When locals with police connections began to burn down the houses of members of her clan, she hid herself among her Ogaden friends in the district. Later, she migrated to a neighboring town in a predominantly Degodia area.[13] As a minority in Wajir, she continued to face various forms of prejudice, even though she had many Degodia relatives, several of whom were sitting in her compound during our interview.

Ken Menkhaus and Cedric Barnes show that people throughout southern Somalia and northern Kenya debated ideas of citizenship through a variety of idioms after independence. In Kenya and the trans-Juba area of Somalia, it became more common for people to differentiate between *galti* (newcomer) and *guri* (indigenous). Nevertheless, many people living along the Kenya/Somali borderlands also distinguished between ideas of *u dha-shay* (born for a region) and *ku dhashay* (born in a region)—a discursive distinction that roughly maps onto the Western concepts of jus sanguinis and jus soli.[14] Still others promoted the concept of *ku dhaqmay*, which, as Menkhaus suggests, rejects the primacy of genealogy or birthplace and instead "holds that Somalis may naturalize in any region and enjoy full rights there."[15] Among the population, there was no clear consensus as to who could claim full citizenship rights and whether those entitlements belonged to anyone with genealogical ties to a given territory, regardless of their place of birth; anyone born in a region, regardless of their clan background; or anyone who came to settle in an area. These debates show that there has never been a single uncontested definition of Kenyan citizenship. While the discourse of autochthony has shaped the lives of northern inhabitants, it is by no means the overriding political logic in Kenya.[16]

ETHNIC POLITICS . . . AND ITS LIMITS

The centrality of ethnicity to African politics is often seen as evidence of the "undeveloped" character of democracy or the corruption that is supposedly endemic to African societies.[17] In actuality, ethnicity is part and parcel of a political rationality that is far more ambivalent and multivalent than many commentators have assumed. The moral ambiguities at play are captured by Jean-François Bayart's expression, the "politics of the belly," a concept conveyed by the Kenyan phrase "It's our turn to eat."[18] In contrast to the social scientific discourse of corruption, the idiom of eating is more neutral. While eating to excess while others go hungry may be corrupt and immoral, everyone must eat to survive. For many Kenyans, having one's "own" in power ensures that a certain amount of wealth (whether through "licit" or "illicit" channels) will flow down to ordinary people through social relations of kinship and clientage. These lines of patronage can be essential to people's basic survival and cannot be readily dismissed as "holdovers" from the past or as evidence of "stunted" development.[19] Moreover, as Moradewun Adejunmobi argues, the turn toward nativist politics often reflects a deep insecurity about home tied to the instability brought on by crime, drought, and state violence.[20]

This is not, however, to minimize the pernicious effects of ethnic politics.[21] By the late 1970s, political elites were using a rhetoric that othered members of certain ethnic groups as a tool to suppress political opposition. The year 1978 proved to be pivotal: Daniel arap Moi came to power in Kenya; and Mohamed Siad Barre, the president of Somalia, lost the Ogaden War. Both regimes held on to power by further institutionalizing a mode of thought that transformed individuals into synecdotes for their "clan," who could then be equated with the "enemy."

Mohamed Haji Ingiriis argues that Barre created a "clanocracy—the domination of state power by certain clans."[22] He thus primed the political climate for much of the communal violence that occurred in the early phases of the Somali civil war.[23] After waging an ill-fated war against Ethiopia in an effort to "liberate" the Ogaden, the Barre regime began to stifle dissent by targeting citizens who shared a common clan background with opposition leaders. In the late 1970s, the Somali government resettled refugees from the Ogaden War in the area once known as British Somaliland. This further alienated inhabitants of northern Somalia who already felt marginalized within the Somali Union. When leaders in exile from northern Somalia formed a resistance movement (the Somali National Movement), Barre retaliated by deploying counterinsurgency measures against civilians in the region. At the height of this operation, the government bombed northern cities by air, killing countless civilians.[24]

By inflicting communal punishment on lineages associated with the enemy, Barre and his political entourage encouraged groups within Somalia to mobilize around clan idioms. Many Isaaq and Harti in Kenya deeply internalized Barre's persecution of their kin. Even those who were only indirectly affected by the Barre regime's brutal policies often interpreted these actions as a perceived hurt on all members of "the Isaaq." The tactics of the Somali government also helped to reify a set of highly abstract genealogical constructs, around which Somalis later polarized during the civil war of the 1990s. Rather than an ancient rivalry, these disputes engendered new understandings and configurations of lineage. As one former separatist fighter in northern Kenya pointed out, in the 1960s, "there was nothing called Hawiye and Darod."[25]

Like Barre in Somalia, the Moi regime in Kenya implemented various policies aimed at fracturing citizens along ethnic lines. Under Moi's rule, election seasons often became sites of interethnic violence, as politicians generated hatred against those deemed to be living outside their "native" territory. Many people I spoke to emphasized that these were not merely "tribal" clashes over grazing land or incidents of "cattle rustling," but rather political conflicts in which state politicians played an intimate role.[26] In Wajir District, Degodia, Ajuran, and other neighboring lineages became embroiled in violent contests over land. These conflicts were largely centered on Wajir West, a political constituency that was coterminous with colonial "tribal" boundaries and widely perceived to be the Ajuran homeland. In 1979, when Ahmed Khalif, a Degodia, defeated two Ajuran candidates to be elected as MP of the area, fighting intensified. Khalif's victory was tainted by accusations that he had illegally issued Kenyan ID cards to "alien" Degodia who had come into the country from Ethiopia.[27]

Electoral contests affected the distribution of power and resources, and, ultimately, the question of who truly "belonged" in the country. Yusuf Ibrahim Kulow gave expression to two competing sentiments: on one hand, the desire to give asylum to one's kin; and on the other, the need to protect one's land (and, by the same token, one's rights to political representation):

> The Ajuran have been robbed of their land. . . . This happened for many reasons. The Somali tribes who live in Nairobi, who are Somali and who live in North Eastern [Province], for example the Ogaden, Degodia, Garre, and Murille, the other half of their people live on the other side of the border in Somalia and Ethiopia. The people of Somalia and Ethiopia were not living in a state of stability. . . . Their people came here to seek asylum amongst their kin. . . . When they increased in numbers they moved here [onto our land]. The land we live in is the best in Kenya, Ethiopia, and Somalia.[28]

Independence had created a confusing and unclear context in which older models of assimilation, migration, and exclusion came to coexist and contend with newer ideas of territory and representational politics. While the constitution allowed for freedom of movement within the country, electoral politics stigmatized many of the basic strategies by which people in the region survived drought, conflict, and fluctuating grazing conditions. Elections also exposed the tension between an individualized conception of citizenship and a model based on membership in legally entitled ethnic groups. The conflict in Wajir District thus refracted broader tensions inherent to the postcolonial system of representation.

THE WAGALLA MASSACRE

Writing about ethnic violence, as Lidwien Kapteijns argues, poses special problems for scholars, who risk "reproducing the definitions, concepts and categories of identity that result from violence" and "reading these back into the past as if they were the causes."[29] One can easily become a voyeuristic witness to brutality, while contributing little to deconstructing the logic that made such violence possible. Many popular explanations for the conflicts in the north risk validating the idea that certain "clans" are the victims of violence, while others are to blame for it. Attributing causality in this way can naturalize ethnicity and obscure the factors that made clan such a potent idiom in the first place.[30]

This is important to consider when seeking to explain incidents of ethnic cleansing, such as the Wagalla Massacre. The massacre began on February 10, 1984, when Kenyan security forces arrived in Wajir, ostensibly in an effort to collect illegal arms and put an end to the ongoing clashes between the Degodia and surrounding lineages. Kenyan forces beat and raped civilians and, in a transparent act of ethnic profiling, sorted out and exclusively detained Degodia men. The subsequent events, which unraveled over the

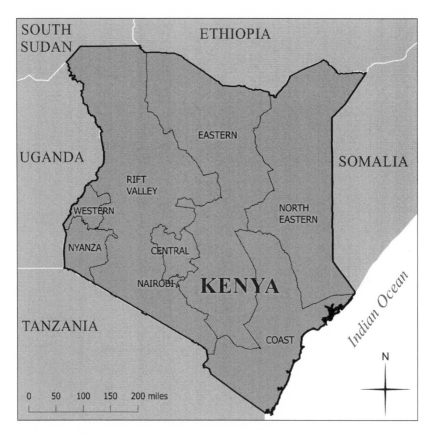

Map 6.1. Postcolonial Kenya. (*Note:* This map shows the administrative boundaries prior to the implementation of the 2010 constitution, which replaced the eight provinces with forty-seven counties.)

course of several days, are a matter of ongoing emotional and litigious dispute. The punitive operation ended on a decommissioned airstrip in the village of Wagalla, where members of the Kenyan military tortured and murdered a still-contested and perhaps unverifiable number of civilians.[31]

In the wake of the massacre, scholars, journalists, activists, filmmakers, and victims have searched for ways to make sense of the violence. The killings have been attributed to a number of factors: the government sanctioning of communal punishment and extrajudicial killing, the dehumanization of the Somali population, political competition between elites in Somalia and Kenya, and clan chauvinism. In a recent article in the *Daily Nation*, journalist David Njagi gave expression to some of these explanations. He reported that Wagalla was an attempt to "muzzle the populous Degodia clan so that" they would "not shape NEP politics." He also argued that Barre "colluded with some powerful officers in Kenya to punish the Degodia because of their leaders' alleged involvement in Somalia's internal affairs."[32]

Many people connected the Wagalla Massacre to the rise of "the Ogaden" into positions of power. In 1982, members of the Kenya Air Force had launched a coup against President Moi. Major General Mahmood Mohamed, a Somali who hailed from Garissa, played an instrumental role in thwarting the uprising. To reward his loyalty, President Moi promoted him to commander of the Air Force (and later chief of general staff) and elevated a small entourage of Garissa elites into power.[33] According to one person I spoke to, Wagalla was connived by Ogaden politicians in Kenya and Somalia who feared the rise of the "Hawiye" into positions of dominance and convinced Moi that a shift in the balance of power could reignite the question of secession. Another person maintained that Wagalla was an excuse to lower the number of Degodia in the country.[34]

Due to testimonial from the Truth, Justice, and Reconciliation Commission of Kenya as well as work by activists and scholars, such as Salah Abdi Sheikh and David Anderson, we now have a much more detailed account of the events that led up to the massacre and who might be responsible.[35] Both popular stories and investigative reports surrounding the incident make visible the complicity of state officials. They show that episodes of violence were not localized skirmishes, but rather political conflicts in which politicians on both sides of the border played an intimate and often central role.[36] The Wagalla Massacre thus cannot be reductively portrayed as a military operation gone awry; rather, it was part of a systematic pattern of government abuse.[37] In holding whole communities responsible for acts of lawbreaking, the state not only criminalized Somali populations writ large, but also obscured the forces that generated insecurity in the north, many of which were tied to regional and geopolitical dynamics.

Addressing the "Whodunit?" question is imperative. However, it is also important to consider the range of narratives surrounding the massacre (including those that do not lend themselves easily to a courtroom setting).[38] Some victims and their family members have veered away from explicitly political explanations for the Wagalla Massacre and have turned instead to accounts that reference divine agency. When I sat down with three northern residents, at least one of whom had been a victim of Wagalla, they gave me an account imbued with spiritual meaning. According to one man, an imam killed in Wagalla had a premonition prior to the massacre. A few days before military forces arrived, he had encouraged the people to slaughter a camel and read a sura from the Qur'an, but they had failed to heed his warning. Another described how, after a few days on the airstrip, a *shaykh* (leader) had encouraged the cordoned men to grab sand in their right hands and run toward the barbed-wire fence enclosing them. By a miracle, the bullets did not reach them as they fled. I was also told that a

Somali informant who had helped military forces locate and sort out Degodia men later died from a curse. He became afflicted with throat cancer (a common disease of corrupt men who "eat" too much).[39]

While these modes of explanation may appear irrational according to most accepted scholarly standards of evidence, I am reluctant to label them fictive.[40] Luise White notes: "The labeling of one thing as 'true' and other as 'fictive' or 'metaphorical'—all the usual polite academic terms for false—may eclipse all the intricate ways in which people use social truths to talk about the past."[41] People understand the past through diverse imaginaries, temporalities, and epistemologies, not all of which can be easily assimilated into a linear, secular historical narrative. Not all forms of knowledge are ultimately accessible to historians, who are bounded by a fragmented written and oral record, limited by the scope of scholarly rationality, and constrained by the need to tell a progressively unfolding story. Moreover, explanations that cite divine agency (which point to alternative loci of authority and legitimation) are not easy to reconcile with juridical understandings of agency, justice, and guilt.

Making sense of tragedy through reference to the miraculous was often a way of making moral and political claims and taming memories of suffering. Islamic discourses have long "provided a continual thread of social commentary, an alternative voice on governance and public morality."[42] Narratives that attribute agency to divine intervention move beyond narrow nativist discourses, opening up different kinds of space for public debate over how to assign guilt, determine the terms of justice, and define the path toward reconciliation.

SCREENING AND DEPORTATION

During certain moments of crisis, northerners have aligned (often defensively) around state-mediated understandings of clan. However, they have also continued to conceptualize descent, lineage, and kinship in ways that challenge the very logic of political ethnicity. During the 1980s and 1990s, as the country became increasingly unstable, over a million citizens of Somalia sought asylum abroad. Many escaped the deteriorating political and economic conditions by relying upon kin living across state borders. The importance of kinship bonds belied the "dominant, Weberian prophecy about modernity," which predicted that "earlier, intimate social forms would dissolve."[43] As a number of scholars have noted, Weber's predictions have proved to be more naive than prescient.

The arrival of Somali refugees into the country coincided with internationally backed efforts to liberalize Kenya's economy and implement multiparty democracy. In the 1980s, lending agencies, such as the International Monetary Fund (IMF) and the World Bank, attached new conditionalities to their loans that called for radical privatization, currency devaluation, and the reduction of government expenditure. By the start of the Somali refugee crisis, the Kenyan government had also begun to buckle under international and domestic pressure to allow multiparty elections. With the Cold War coming to a close, American and British officials were far less willing to prop up antidemocratic rulers on the basis of their anticommunist credentials.

As pressure to institute constitutional reforms mounted, the Moi regime also faced international criticism over the hunting of endangered species. With the transition toward neoliberal economic policies, illegal wildlife poaching had developed into a profitable business. Facing financial constraints from the IMF and the World Bank, state officials throughout the region were forced to reduce government expenditures and downsize the civil service, which caused them to turn to new sources of private accumulation.[44] In the nineteenth century, an extensive ivory trade had connected Somali caravans with the wider world. Now channeled through the criminalized circuits of the black market, poaching provided bureaucrats, politicians, and their friends and family with a substitute for older channels of resource distribution. Their activities soon came under the scrutiny of international conservation movements, which took a negative toll on the tourist industry.

In April 1989, after poachers attacked two tourist buses, Moi acceded to international demands and created a new government parastatal: the Kenya Wildlife Service (KWS). The KWS, which received substantial international funding, was authorized with wide-reaching powers to fight illegal game hunting. Those charged with enforcing environmental regulations often took enormous liberties with whom they defined as "poachers." Somali nomads were sometimes killed, beaten, and castrated by KWS units, who conducted raids that frequently resembled paramilitary operations. The involvement of Somali poachers, many of whom were former or current soldiers in the Barre military, encouraged the KWS to escalate its use of force and focus its operations on northern Kenya.[45] Targeting those who operated at the lowest level of the poaching business also allowed Kenyan officials to obscure the ongoing participation of state elites in illegal commodity chains. Unable and no doubt unwilling to address the systematic factors fueling the international poaching trade, they instead shifted blame onto anyone seen as potentially "alien."[46]

The unregistered and unprocessed entry of Somali immigrants—who were sometimes indistinguishable from citizens—also posed significant implications for a country reeling from structural adjustment programs and poised to become a multiparty democracy. As Francis Nyamnjoh and Peter Geschiere write: "A striking aspect of recent developments in Africa is that democratization seems to trigger" xenophobic reactions "against all those who 'do not really belong.'"[47] Immigrants, who may be able to gain access to the entitlements of citizenship and shift the outcome of a future election, often become the locus of these concerns.

Around this nexus of political events, antipoaching exercises quickly became entangled in ethnic profiling, which led to an odd marriage between seemingly laudable environmental causes and discriminatory forms of nativist politics. In 1989, on the eve of the transition to multiparty democracy, the Moi regime implemented a screening process for all Somalis living in Kenya. To avoid deportation, "authentic" Kenyan Somalis had to prove the legitimacy of their citizenship and acquire identity cards, which listed their clan and *jilib* (subclan).[48] These highly visible, pink-colored screening cards were reminiscent of the colonial-era *kipande* pass—giving many the impression that national independence, rather than displacing the imperial racial order, had simply created new forms of exclusion and segregation. Screening cards allowed the state to bluntly cut through the complex ways that Somalis engaged in lineage networks and to expediently differentiate between the "indigenous" and the "alien."

Sovereignty was reenacted by targeting those whose presence in the country was a salient reminder of the government's inability to regulate its borders. Criminalizing Somali mobility became a means for the Kenyan government to project—if not necessarily to realize—a sense of order and control over the territorial and metaphorical boundaries of the nation. The concurrence of democratization and structural adjustment had fueled debates over who "belonged" to the country (and who had rights to the diminishing entitlements of citizenship). Leveling blame on "aliens" in the name of protecting the country's natural (read national) resources allowed the state to both mollify and redirect these public anxieties.

Ostensibly an antipoaching and antibanditry effort intended to "flush out aliens," the screening process quickly became a means for state elites to confiscate property, break the political threat posed by more recent Somali refugees and immigrants, and target their economic and political competitors regardless of the authenticity of their citizenship.[49] While screening is often remembered as a Moi-era abuse perpetrated against the Somali population, Kenyan Somali leaders were among those who used the process to secure their political base and prevent rivals from seeking office in Kenya.[50] Emma Lochery argues that screening reinforced ethnic territorialism by associating certain lineages with old colonial ethnic blocs and demanding that "outsiders" return to their "native" district.[51] Rather than curbing crime or poaching, screening further institutionalized ethnic politics.

Serena Parekh persuasively argues that states overwhelmed by mass migrations often respond "not by attempting more naturalizations, but rather by denaturalizing citizens of the same origins as the refugee."[52] Thus, the presence of newer refugees and migrants can taint "the status of all people from that country."[53] The screening procedure also exposed the fragility behind the very idea of a coherent national identity. In his impassioned appeal in the *Daily Nation*, Mirimo Wandati called on Muslims to oppose the discriminatory legislation and drew a comparison between Somalis and other Kenyan communities that traversed national borders. He cited the "Maasais on the Kenya-Tanzania border," who "are nomads"; the "Tesos on the Kenya-Uganda border," who "intermarry and interact"; and the "Samiras on the Kenya-Uganda border," who "share a common cultural background."[54] His article provoked questions that proved difficult to answer. What were the essential features of the Kenyan national identity? Could one easily identify a Kenyan citizen? He thus normalized the Somali condition, which was not significantly different from that of many other "indigenous" communities in Kenya.

THE REVIVAL OF A GLOBAL SOMALI DIASPORA

By leveling blame at Somali asylum seekers for myriad societal ills, the Kenyan government obscured a much broader crisis of citizenship in the region. The delinking of economic entitlements and citizenship, a result of broader neoliberal reconfigurations, fueled new kinds of insecurity among those who were politically included, but economically excluded. It also galvanized hatred against noncitizens and migrants perceived to be benefiting at the expense of locals. The development of a deterritorialized "global Somalia" revealed the extent to which states could no longer guarantee protections to citizens and refugees alike.

The breakdown of the Somali state exposed the glaring inadequacies of the formal refugee system. Beginning in the 1980s, Western countries had attempted, as Cindy Horst explains, "to close their borders and use the refugee regime to contain refugees in developing countries"—a decision that was nevertheless accompanied "by a reduction in funds" for the Office of the United Nations High Commissioner for Refugees (UNHCR).[55] By the early 1990s, the refugee crisis had overwhelmed the Kenyan government, the UNHCR, and other development agencies. Although Kenya instituted an encampment policy, Somalis often turned away from overcrowded refugee camps on the frontier, preferring instead to rely on "informal" kinship ties with Kenyan citizens and integrate themselves into the country's major urban centers.[56]

Kinship and lineage networks provided refuge where state and international institutions failed. Ethiopia, Yemen, and Kenya—places of historical Somali residence and migration—absorbed the vast majority of refugees. According to recent UNHCR estimates, these three countries took in almost 95 percent of the over one million refugees who were estimated to be living abroad by 2012.[57]

In Kenya, most refugees fled to the North Eastern Province and to Eastleigh, which already had established Somali communities. As Ioan M. Lewis argues, many of these uprooted "war victims" were, in essence, "refugees 'at home.'"[58]

Due to the arrival of hundreds of thousands of people from Somalia, Ethiopia, and other neighboring countries during the 1980s and 1990s, Nairobi experienced a kind of "globalization from below."[59] In Eastleigh, around the edifice of deteriorating roads and open sewer lines, Somali refugees helped to build imposing shopping malls, hotels, restaurants, and money transfer operations. Garissa Lodge, once a hotel for migrant guests, developed into the neighborhood's first major shopping mall. Remittances from refugees in Europe, America, and the Middle East (estimated at over $2 billion a year) fueled investment in Somalia and the surrounding region.[60] By taking advantage of trade liberalization and weak government controls in Somalia, refugees in Nairobi were able to monopolize the retail trade once cornered by the Asian population. Over the course of the 1980s and 1990s, they developed an extensive trade network with cities as dispersed as Dubai, Mogadishu, and London. The growth of Eastleigh also brought new economic opportunities to the north and promoted a lively transit trade between towns in northern Kenya and wider international markets.[61]

While government officials, international policy makers, and ordinary citizens tend to think of European businessmen as part of the normal traffic of global commerce, Somali entrepreneurs are often seen as intruders who do not fully belong within the Kenyan nation-state.[62] Nevertheless, Somali migrants, as Joselyne Chebichi argues, are "socially and economically integrated [even] in the absence of legal status."[63] In spite of its inflated reputation as a marginal space infamous for harboring terrorists and funneling profits from piracy, Eastleigh is deeply incorporated into the Kenyan economy. Though often referred to as "Little Mogadishu," the neighborhood is, in reality, cosmopolitan in its makeup and comprises many communities, including Meru khat traders, Kikuyu hawkers, and Ethiopian migrants.[64] The state is also embedded in many of the legal, quasi-legal, and illegal dealings that occur in the neighborhood. In 1997, George Saitoti, then Kenya's finance minister, famously remarked that the "Central Bank fixes its currency exchange rates after checking with the money-dealers in Garissa Lodge."[65] Eastleigh speaks to the importance of the so-called informal economy, which in many cases surpasses official business transactions in Africa.[66]

After World War II, political theorist Hannah Arendt argued that being rendered stateless was a threatening and precarious political condition marked by the absence of political rights and protections. Arendt's concern for statelessness and her insistence on one's "right to have rights" advanced the public's understanding of the implicit dangers refugees faced. Her insights were also highly germane to the immediate post–World War II era (and remain so to this day).[67] However, her arguments need to be revisited in light of neoliberal restructuring. In the 1980s and 1990s, trade liberalization eroded the ability of African states to deliver basic services and welfare to their people, reduced the scope of national sovereignty, and lessened the entitlements of citizenship. Most African countries saw their terms of trade worsen as their citizens' living standards deteriorated.[68] Somali refugees, on the other hand, could frequently skirt labor controls and access global markets blocked to most African citizens.[69] For a small class of Somali entrepreneurs, becoming "stateless" provided them with a unique edge in the global retail trade. While no less politically vulnerable, their economic successes have underscored the stark limitations of national membership.

SECURITIZATION

Some analysts have seen the prosperity of the Somali diaspora as testament to the viability of stateless capitalism, while others have viewed the large refugee population as the threatening outcome of a "failed state." Few, however, have acknowledged the historical roots of this diasporic community. What emerged in the wake of the Cold War was not the liberal democratic civil society that many Western policy makers imagined, but (in many cases) "the renaissance of the indigenous political system."[70] Somali refugees have relied on what Cindy Horst describes as a "nomadic heritage," which she defines as "a strategy of coping with life by looking for greener pastures elsewhere, and of minimizing risks by investing in different activities and people in different places."[71] One must be wary of drawing too linear or crude a connection between the nomadic past and the transnational present. However, it is clear that many Somalis have been reenvisioning what it means to be a "nomad" in the context of war and displacement.

Security analysts often lay blame on the Kenyan government for failing to implement proper registration methods, regulate illegal immigration, or secure its international borders.[72] Yet such normative perspectives assume a level of state surveillance that few governments are capable of achieving.[73] Moreover, efforts to police immigration often rest on an idealized notion of national homogeneity, which naturalizes the categories of "citizen" and "refugee" and disavows older patterns of mobility and circulation.

The Kenyan state has implemented various forms of securitization since the start of the Somali civil war. These include numerous checkpoints that dot the north. One of the most infamous is located on the Tana River between Garissa and what some still refer to as "Kenya," on the main road between the Dadaab refugee camp and Nairobi.[74] It is the site where, as Osman Mohamed Osman notes, Somalis "must prove their 'Kenyanness' to the men in blue staffing the area."[75] In some cases, refugees have been able to acquire national identity cards by paying bribes to underpaid government agents. Kenyans who come from poorer, marginalized communities cannot always obtain these much-coveted documents. Security officers frequently turn to unorthodox (but no less dubious) methods of identification, such as checking for vaccination marks. In other cases, they simply demand bribes to allow entry into and out of the north.[76] The Tana River checkpoint has become notorious for marginalizing citizens, allowing safe passage to unauthorized immigrants, and creating little more than a simulacrum of security.

BECOMING *SIJUI*

The birth of a global Somali refugee community has also had wide-ranging economic and political implications for Kenyan citizens who identify as Somali. Somali immigrants who came to Kenya in the years after the war often labeled their local kin *sijui*, which means "I don't know" in Swahili. Some reject this nickname, which they interpret to be an accusation of cultural and religious loss. For others, it is a playful means of reestablishing kinship ties between Somali- and Swahili-speaking cousins.[77] The term *sijui* embodies, in many respects, the sometimes amicable, sometimes tense relationship between these two sections of the Somali "diaspora."

Kenyan Somalis often spoke about the refugee population in ambivalent and contradictory terms. My interlocutors sometimes described Somali immigrants as fellow brethren and emphasized the underlying unity of all Somali people across the region. At other times, they shared feelings akin to those of the wider Kenyan public. Some expressed concerns that newcomers were interfering with local politics, changing local culture, introducing a polarizing clan rhetoric from Somalia, and driving up the price of bridewealth and real estate.

Many of the long-standing residents of Eastleigh expressed anxieties about losing their rights to the neighborhood.[78] Amina Kinsi, a well-known and respected civic leader, related a parable that encapsulated these concerns. On one particularly hot day in Arabia, she explained, a camel asked a nomad if it could cool off by putting its head inside his tent. After the man invited it in, the camel stood up and lifted the entire tent from over his head. This was an analogy, she explained, for how the Isaaq had been dislocated from Eastleigh.[79]

It is reductive to assume that solidarity is a natural outcome of shared linguistic, ethnic, or religious commonalities. As is often the case with transnational communities whose claim to belong is tenuous, tensions have occasionally emerged between Somalis who possess and those who lack citizenship rights in Kenya.[80] A desire to host their fellow Somali brethren was often undercut by fears of losing economic and political ground within the country and being mistaken for "foreigners." For this reason, it was sometimes difficult for established locals to conceptualize foreigners as guests and immigrants as neighbors. Hospitality, as Derrida argues, is an ethics based on irreconcilable contradictions. There can be no "pure" form of hospitality unencumbered by limits.[81]

BEYOND ELECTORAL POLITICS

The fraught question of Somali citizenship in Kenya became even more contentious in the early 1990s. As the Somali Democratic Republic formally collapsed into civil war, the Kenyan government decriminalized opposition parties at the urging of domestic and international groups. Kenya held its first multiparty elections since independence in 1992. This coincided with the beginning of a drought and an influx of arms from neighboring Somalia, which intensified competition over political constituencies in northern Kenya.[82] As one resident of Garissa lamented, "Multipartyism has just created clan rivalry and clan chauvinism."[83] In 1992, after an Ajuran candidate lost another parliamentary seat in Wajir District, violence was reignited.[84] Ahmed Maalin Abdalle put it succinctly: "In Wajir, we became tribes fighting other tribes."[85] Rather than ushering in a new era, as many Western policymakers predicted, multiparty elections amplified the colonial logic of ethnicity.

The ethnic politics of the state, however, never became so thoroughly institutionalized as to be beyond contestation. Some political elites tried to combat the violence by advocating for more pluralistic political identifications. In Wajir, several leaders promoted the concept of *reer Wajir* (the Wajir family or clan).[86] Their supporters refused to align around the state's ethnic labels and actively drew upon a shared history of migration, interaction, and intermarriage in order to reimagine the meaning of *qabiil*.

Community leaders also looked beyond the limitations of democratic citizenship and juridical politics. The 1992 elections could have easily lapsed into yet another protracted period of communal violence. However, representatives of the various clans were able to institute a remarkable peace settlement, which soon became a model for the rest of the region. Prominent women were at the forefront of the peace process.[87] In 1993, a meeting was convened with women of urban, rural, and various clan backgrounds and a committee known as Wajir Women for Peace (WWP) was formed. This group brought together clan leaders from the majority and minority lineages who, in conjunction with the local administration, signed the al Fatah declaration.[88]

It is an oft-repeated stereotype that women are more peaceful than men and less inclined toward violence. There is little value, however, in attributing the Wajir peace process to such putatively universal feminine characteristics. The structural position of many women within the community provides a better, if only partial, explanation for their mediating role. Competition over political constituencies had intensified, in part, because

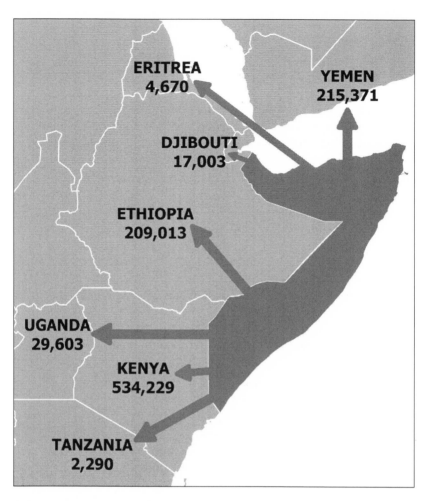

Map 6.2. UNHCR estimates of Somali refugees in Northeast Africa (2012). (Note: Based on UNHCR, "Somali Refugees in the Region as of 22 August 2012," http://www.unhcr .org/en-us/publications/maps/4f6c40de9/somali-refugees-region-map-22-august-2012. html?query=somalia.)

climate change, warfare, and the closure of government parastatals, such as the Kenya Meat Commission (KMC), had eliminated alternative possibilities for survival. Some of the key figures in the WWP were educated professionals, such as teachers. Others were market women. Many sold camel milk or khat, a mildly narcotic but legal plant that is widely chewed in East Africa and the Middle East. Urban women who made their livelihoods from the marketplace or had jobs in the formal sector were not as economically dependent on state-provided ethnic patronage networks and thus were better situated to remain aloof from polarizing electoral contests. Businesswomen also had an interest in keeping trade routes across the region safe and open.[89]

The WWP built upon the discursive techniques of women in the marketplace. By the early 1990s, "Khat is my husband" had become a common expression among market women in Wajir, many of whom were divorced or widowed. Such rhetorical strategies enabled businesswomen to justify their right to sell in the marketplace, highlight the respectability of their professions, and defend their right to leave men who failed to provide for their families.[90] As one successful khat seller in Wajir explained to me, through her business, she was able to pay for her children's school fees, expand her home, construct two wells, and buy two plots of land. The khat trade was her "husband and older brother."[91] Leaders of the WWP drew upon this strategy of shaming men for bad conduct. The late Dekha Ibrahim, one of the movement's main leaders, explained that the WWP first succeeded in securing peace over the marketplace by ensuring that female traders did not engage in clan-based xenophobia. The "market women's theme," Dekha Ibrahim noted, "was that 'the men start the violence, but it is we and our children who suffer.'"[92] She and the other peace builders highlighted female suffering and encouraged women to make demands on male behavior.

Peace was negotiated through a strategic alignment between these female peacemakers and elder male representatives of the minority "corner" clans — groups who had fewer stakes in perpetuating the conflict over political constituencies. Initially, the female activists met with some resistance from elder men, many of whom were apprehensive about the intrusion of relatively young, educated women into what they perceived as their domain. However, as Dekha Ibrahim explained: "Once we had established that trust, we would allow the group that was in the minority to take the lead in the dialogue."[93] By aligning around gender and allying with the leaders of minority groups, the WWP was able to assist clan leaders in negotiating around the fears many had about losing demographic ground to other groups.

The peace agreement that was ultimately put in place challenged a number of normative principles of governance. In collaboration with the district commissioner, various clan representatives signed the al Fatah declaration, which empowered residents of Wajir to resolve disputes according to the stipulations of *xeer* law. One of its provisions stated: "The traditional law pertaining to blood feud will apply to those who commit murder, namely the payment of a hundred camels for a man and fifty camels for a woman."[94] Inhabitants of Wajir were thus able to settle theft, assault, and murder cases through reconciliation processes and communal compensation (*diya*) agreements, rather than the formal court system. By allowing criminal acts to be tried under so-called "traditional" law, the declaration ran in direct contravention to Kenyan law, which allowed customary law to be applied only to civil cases.[95] Ken Menkhaus argues that the peace accord gave birth to a "mediated state," which expanded the jurisdiction of customary law and partially relinquished sovereignty to precolonial institutions.[96] Although the al Fatah declaration broke with ideas of gender equality, individual responsibility, and other notions implicit to secular state law, it also proved remarkably effective.[97] After its implementation, violence subsided dramatically.[98]

The fact that female leaders helped to put in place a settlement that did not favor gender equality also runs counter to many liberal assumptions about the trajectory of female empowerment. The feminist movement in the West has long been entangled in the idea of agency. Many liberal and feminist projects are aimed at shedding atavistic "traditions" deemed to be oppressive to the individual subject whose natural sovereignty is taken to be self-evident. The goals of many of Wajir's women, however, were simply less enmeshed with such a teleological understanding of the human subject. According to some northerners, the discrepancy between punishments for male and female deaths (100 versus 50 camels or the monetary equivalent) resulted from the added obligations placed on men as providers for their families.[99] Hina Azam refers to this way of thinking as "proprietary sexual ethics," in which marriage is based on "an exchange of values, whereby a woman received a dower (and ongoing financial support) in return for her husband's right to sexual enjoyment."[100] Somali women were often divided over whether to support more equitable laws or make demands on men through this "proprietary" conception of marriage.[101] Many of the strategies used during the peace process were predicated on women's ability to appeal to men's prescribed obligations as providers and protectors. While patriarchal power relations remain a significant problem in northern Kenya, there is reason to be skeptical that the abstract equality guaranteed by state law is always a prerequisite for progressive change.[102]

The Wajir Peace Accord is just one of many examples of the ways in which Kenyan Somali leaders had began to renegotiate their relationship with the government in the early 1990s. As Letitia Lawson and Donald Rothchild argue, Africans "have begun moving away from colonially designed juridical statehood to fashion empirical formulas that respond to the messiness of their current realities."[103] The idea of statehood that had captured the imaginations of many Somalis and northerners in the early 1960s had, by the end of the twentieth century, lost a great deal of its credibility. As the next chapter will show, various nonstate actors have competed for control over Somalia in recent decades and, in so doing, have shattered conventional notions of secular and territorial sovereignty. Many Kenyan Somali political thinkers have also abandoned the goal of unifying with Somalia. Upending the territorial imaginary that defined political consciousness after World War II, Somalis living in Kenya have ushered in new models of citizenship and deterritorialized belonging.

7 ↩ "People Will One Day Say Our Children Aren't Kenyan"

And you could clearly see here people telling you when they are traveling to Nairobi and board a bus "Tunaenda Kenya" [We are going to Kenya]. But now that perception has been clearly rubbed off the minds of people. We want to be part and parcel of the development of this country.

—Jumale Abdirahim, a young resident of Garissa, expressing the changing sentiments of northern inhabitants during a 2010 interview for a Kenya Citizen TV report[1]

IN 2013, THE MILITANT GROUP al-Shabaab launched a devastating attack on an upscale shopping mall on the outskirts of Nairobi in retaliation for Kenya's invasion of Somalia. For many, the Westgate attack was especially shocking and transgressive, as it occurred in a wealthy suburb frequented by expatriates, seemingly far removed from the battlefields of Somalia. Journalists, commentators, and pundits rightly condemned this brutal attack on a civilian target. However, the narratives that circulated in the popular media not only elided the political events precipitating the rise of al-Shabaab (and thus abstracted the attack from its political context), but also masked the violence committed by other actors in the ongoing war in southern Somalia. The reporting surrounding the incident reflected an anxiety, not about violence per se, but about violence conducted by a nonstate actor operating outside the boundaries of the nation-state and the international norms of secularism.[2] After al-Shabaab continued its attacks within the country, the

Kenyan government—working in close collaboration with Western security agencies—began to displace blame onto the Somali population at large. In the years after Westgate, the government engaged in various discriminatory practices, including ethnic profiling, indiscriminate arrests, unlawful deportations of Somali refugees, and extrajudicial killings of Muslim clerics.[3]

This chapter reflects on the events that preceded and followed the attacks launched by al-Shabaab and challenges the notion of a "clash of cultures and civilizations."[4] Prior to Kenya's invasion of its northern neighbor, many people were becoming invested in the nation in new ways, as the above quote by Jumale Abdirahim indicates. These bids for greater national inclusion did not preclude a desire for membership in collectivities that extended beyond national borders. The actions taken by Western states, the Kenyan government, and militant organizations like al-Shabaab have, nevertheless, undermined these prospects for integration. Local and foreign state officials have once again painted Somalis as representatives of a foreign nation within Kenya (though this "nation" is now portrayed as a decentralized entity that has broken with conventional understandings of territory, sovereignty, and secularism). Signs of Somalis' cultural or religious difference are often deemed evidence of their disloyalty and refusal to integrate. In spite of this polarizing political climate, many Kenyan Somalis are still invested in the hope of cultivating more flexible, overlapping models of citizenship.[5] Drawing upon Kenya's long-standing commitment to pluralism (as distinct from Western notions of multiculturalism), many people are searching for a means to be both "Kenyan" and "Somali."[6]

A CHANGING POLITICAL CLIMATE

Talal Asad writes: "The old might be remembered in unexpected ways because the future looked forward to is not experienced as such when it arrives."[7] The future that most Kenyan Somalis had imagined in the early 1960s—namely territorial union with Somalia—gradually lost both its political solvency and its appeal over the course of the 1980s and 1990s. The suppression of the Northern Frontier District (NFD) separatist movement, followed by the outbreak of the Somali civil war, led to a profound reconfiguration of the idea of "Greater Somalia."

Rarely is remembering a purely individual activity. Through various public events and ceremonies in recent years, Kenyan Somalis had come together and collectively composed new communal histories. These narratives were also part of the public face presented to outsiders such as myself. People had various overt and covert reasons for their willingness to talk to me. Some were initially suspicious of my intentions, others sought to control my representations of their community, and still others saw me as a potential mouthpiece for publicizing their struggles as marginalized minorities. Stories of victimization enabled individuals to connect diverse memories of oppression, make claims upon the state, and weave themselves into the narrative of Kenyan nationalism. Telling these histories, as Atieno Odhiambo argues, was also a means for individuals and groups to claim a share in the *matunda ya uhuru* (the fruits of independence).[8]

When I began my fieldwork in 2010, Somalis in Kenya were approaching their past and imagining their future in light of the new political order that had emerged over the previous decade. In 2002, a coalition of multiethnic opposition parties under Mwai Kibaki had won the presidential election and pushed the Kenyan African National Union (KANU), the ruling party since independence, out of power. For Somalis in Kenya, life began to look significantly more promising after his election. In the same year, Mohamud Saleh became the first Somali provincial commissioner of the North Eastern Province (NEP). By addressing abuses by security forces and chiefs, Saleh was instrumental in dramatically reducing crime and insecurity in the region.[9] People I spoke to often described Kibaki's and Saleh's rise to power as marking the true end of their "colonialism."[10]

Kibaki's regime, however, did little to depoliticize ethnicity or reform the electoral process. In the wake of highly contested elections in 2007, which were marred by accusations of vote rigging, leaders of the main opposition and ruling parties actively instigated nativist violence.[11] In the wake of the postelection violence, a coalition government rolled out a new and long-awaited constitution, which called for a devolved system. Many scholars have wrongly assumed that "globalization" leads inexorably toward an erosion of state sovereignty.[12] However, in many cases, the changes ushered in by the post–Cold War era led to a reconfiguration of sovereignty and a reterritorialization of the state. Devolution in Kenya mirrored similar constitutional changes in Ethiopia and Somalia. While not without its critics, decentralization has been welcomed by some as a potential arrangement capable of engendering national unity and bringing together disparate regions of a country.[13]

Many Kenyans hoped that under a devolved system, resources would be more evenly distributed and different groups would become minorities among other minorities, rather than minorities facing a dominant majority. By decentralizing power and resources and institutionalizing new forms of identity politics, the 2010 constitution opened up promising political spaces for Kenyan citizens who identified as Somali. It also created a new legal category: the "marginalized community," defined as those who had "been unable to participate in public life in Kenya; an indigenous community that has retained and maintained a traditional livelihood . . . nomadic or sedentary pastoralists; and groups which are geographically isolated."[14] In addition, the new constitution made provision for "community land" to be held by groups "identified on the basis of ethnicity, culture or similar" interests.[15] While the idea of the "community" relocalized problems of poverty, it also offered the possibility for greater recognition on the basis of historical marginalization.[16] Many of the people I spoke to believed that the newly ratified constitution could lessen the economic and political marginalization of regions like the North Eastern Province.

RECOGNITION AND MISRECOGNITION

Claiming a territorial and metaphorical place in the Kenyan nation was particularly important during the time I conducted my fieldwork. The Kenyan constitution had recently been ratified, and many Somalis hoped that under the devolved system, they might be able to secure greater legal entitlements and recognition as citizens. Amina Kinsi, for example, was among several leaders who campaigned to provide the Isaaq with a special code for the 2009 census—"Otherwise, people will one day say our children aren't Kenyan."[17] Isaaq representatives had also revived the Ishakia Association in an effort to make claims on the new constitution. Since the boundary between citizen and alien was blurry and contested, many Somalis feared being branded as foreigners on their own soil and saw the new constitution as an opportunity to position themselves as a "local community."

The Isaaq and Harti populations in Nairobi and other towns, such as Isiolo, had developed a number of communal histories. Maintained and reenacted through regular prayer and community meetings, these narratives allowed them to emphasize their long-standing roots in Kenya and their contributions to the history of both the country and the world. Many people highlighted the important role that Somali soldiers played during World War II. Abdirisaq Egal Mohamed, for instance, recounted how Somali soldiers had "captured Burma at night, with no chain of command," after tying up a general who refused to let them conduct an ambush. He also maintained that Churchill had declared the Isaaq to be "the best fighters."[18] Through celebratory narratives about their forefathers, Somalis could counter widespread perceptions that they were "alien" to the country and emphasize the sacrifices previous generations had made.

Representing themselves as an "ever-elusive local community" also required that certain aspects of the past be submerged.[19] Fearful of being cast as "non-natives," few Somalis highlighted the fact that their forefathers had once demanded the rights of Asians. Many people sought to distance themselves from such comparisons, since Indians were often perceived by other Kenyans to be outsiders.[20] As Thomas B. Hansen explains of the Indian community in South Africa, they had "to tread carefully, remaining sensitive to the dominant discursive formations in the country," which "remain firmly nested within the larger narrative of the predicament of colonialism that long celebrated the autochthony of Africans and their right to rule their own country."[21] While some people argued that Somalis were of Arab descent, many were emphatic that Somalis were Africans and the community was wrong to have once demanded a separate racial status. Others simply elided the racial politics underlying their colonial-era privileges by arguing that in demanding Asiatic status, the Isaaq were merely "fighting for their rights."[22] Many also expressed regret or highlighted their community's lack of support for the separatist cause. Viewed as the cause of their scattering, displacement, and absence of an ethnic "homeland," the Shifta War had become part and parcel of the argument invoked by Isaaq and Harti citizens for their right to minority status and community land.

Several leaders strove to mark out some kind of territorial homeland for the Isaaq population within Kenya. Without land, they recognized, the community lacked both a political constituency and a definitive anchor within the country. Fatuma Ayub, who had served as the deputy coordinator for the Democratic Party, described Isaaq Somalis as Kenya's first internally displaced people (IDPs) and emphasized their need to be resettled within the country.[23] Another such leader was Ahmed Ali Farah, who had campaigned tirelessly for the return of land in Naivasha, which Somalis once occupied with the permission of Lord Delamere.[24] In an article in the *Star* describing their campaign, Isaaq spokesmen portrayed the land as their "ancestral home having settled on it in the 1880s after their forefathers accompanied Lord Delamere from Somaliland to the Rift Valley."[25] "The community alleges," the article states, "that they built settlements and a school on the land before they were driven out by the colonial government for supporting the Mau Mau movement."[26] This chronology is not quite right, as the Kenyatta regime had driven Somalis from Naivasha in 1972.[27] However, the rhetorical force is unmistakable. By equating the loss of their "ancestral" land with their contributions to Mau Mau (baptized as the quintessential anticolonial resistance movement), these Somali leaders positioned themselves within the narrative of Kenyan nationalism and the politics of autochthony. This is not to deny the community's justifiable right to the reinstatement of their lost land, but simply to point to the logic underpinning the claim.

Although securing citizenship rights within Kenya was an important political goal, some people possessed lingering fears that their status in the country was insecure. As Robin Cohen explains, immigrant groups often worry that "the path of assimilation" will "turn out to be an illusion, a trap, ultimately a hoax."[28] In that case, they "would become a liminal people, no longer able to express their distinctive ethnic identity or recover a sense of 'home.'"[29] For this reason, people continued to cultivate a diasporic consciousness and preserve memories of their historical roots in Somaliland. Some also viewed Somaliland as a kind of secondary homeland.[30]

As a revived native land, Somaliland had become an axis around which the Isaaq community in Nairobi gathered to celebrate and re-create a shared past. When the Somali civil war began in 1991, the former territory of British Somaliland seized the opportunity to declare independence from the rest of the country. Although not officially recognized by the international community, the self-proclaimed Republic of Somaliland has remained comparatively stable and relatively prosperous throughout the ongoing war. Even in the absence of direct travel, many Isaaq Somalis in Kenya cultivated imagined links to the land. On numerous occasions during my fieldwork, I was invited to prayer meetings and celebrations held in honor of the independence of the country. The rebirth of Somaliland has enabled members of the Isaaq diaspora living in Nairobi to see themselves in a radically new light: as dispersed citizens of a newly liberated nation-state, rather than a persecuted minority divided between two countries.

Mark Bradbury describes Somaliland as "one of several polities that have emerged since the end of the Cold War that do not fit the normative world of juridical states" and whose "large diasporas are altering notions of citizenship."[31] In the absence of any official foreign assistance, the government of Somaliland has relied on remittances from people in the diaspora. Appropriating the colonial penchant for "inventing" traditional rulers, Somaliland encouraged wealthy members of the diaspora to return and take up positions as "traditional" leaders. Mustafa (Mohamed) Osman Hirsi described traveling back to Somaliland to take up a *suldaan* (ruler) position. A Kenyan Somali who had lived abroad for many years, Hirsi was dubbed "Moses," he said, for "taking people back to the promised land."[32] He thus equated the return to the land of his grandfather's birth with a biblical homecoming.

Hirsi also drew explicit comparisons between the Jewish and the Isaaq diasporas. While this allusion may have been peculiar to our interview, it is also likely that he (as well as other proponents of Somaliland) drew lessons from the history of modern Zionism. After World War II, the Zionist establishment secularized a "traditionally messianic theme," garnered legitimacy for a Jewish state, and built connections between the Jewish diaspora and Israel.[33] Like American Jews, Isaaq Somalis in Kenya were reimagining the nation from outside its borders and trying to promote its legitimacy to the international community.

Many Isaaq and Harti Somalis had to grapple with being a minority in several senses. Hirsi described this predicament. The Isaaq, he explained, had imagined that they would one day "go back to their country" and thus "never unpacked." Avoiding complete assimilation helped maintain a sense of being in an "exclusive club," but also meant that they were "not integrated politically" and remained "an urban community with no land." The new wave of refugees looked down on them, Hirsi complained, but still used them as a "connection into the system."[34] Many Isaaq leaders feared political exclusion not only in Kenya, but also within Somali society more broadly. For this reason, representatives often sought separate political recognition as "Isaaq."

Many people were also wary of being judged as either inadequately "Kenyan" or incompletely "Somali." Misrecognition was possible on both ends, making assimilation a fraught topic of conversation. While it is true that ideas of purity are everywhere a fiction, cultural signs provide identifiable markers of belonging. To some extent, being recognized as "Kenyan" was a performance that required mastery of certain linguistic and cultural signs and symbols. Their ability to speak local languages and their diverse connections to other ethnic groups had given many Isaaq and Harti (as well as other Somalis living outside the north) the cultural capital to be, as one woman in Naivasha explained, "more flexible."[35] On several occasions, people recounted incidents in which they were harassed by police officers who mistook them for unauthorized refugees. They relished the opportunity to counter in fluent Swahili, Kikuyu, or some other local vernacular.[36] At the same time, opportunities for "passing" as a refugee and resettling abroad made possessing the cultural capital to shed one's "Kenyanness" a valuable and viable option. Kenyan Somalis who had grown up in predominantly non-Somali regions were also faced with accusations that they had "lost" their culture. Other members of the Somali population often frowned upon evidence of cultural assimilation, which for some connoted a loss of purity and a sign of religious laxity.[37]

One possible strategy for populations considered liminal, Liisa Malkki explains, is to dissolve "national categories in the course of everyday life" altogether and produce "more cosmopolitan forms of identity instead."[38] Hirsi described the Isaaq as "true global citizens" who "blended in" everywhere. They watched Indian, Chinese, and Western films, knew the lyrics to popular songs from the Middle East and Africa, and followed American, British, and German sports teams.[39] A worldly orientation enabled Somalis to position themselves within multiple worlds and among diverse people, and to remain agnostic in the face of polarizing identity politics.

Many also saw lineage as an important tool for tempering the threat of linguistic and cultural change. As one person explained to me, knowing one's genealogy ensures that "we never get lost." In Nakuru, Halima and Sara Warsame Abdalle described the importance of being able to trace one's descent to the clan and subclan levels:

> It's important because, me, now I come from here [Nakuru, Kenya].
> I go to Somalia. If I reach Somalia people will have forgotten me.
> Me, I know. And me, I am a foreigner. And I don't know anyone

there. What do I ask? Who are you? You are the child of whom? What tribe? I follow the tribe, follow it, follow it, follow it, follow it. . . . You are my brother. And him: his [relative] is mine. Now we meet each other here.[40]

The last few decades have shown that kinship ties can provide a viable alternative to the conventional restrictions of membership in an exclusive nation-state.

One anecdote, which is popular among Isaaq Somalis, highlights the importance attributed to these genealogical bonds. It tells a story of a Somali man nicknamed "German West."[41] According to most popular accounts, West had traveled the world, living for a time in Germany (where he earned his nickname) and later moving to South Africa. There, he married a local woman and fathered two children, who grew up speaking Afrikaans. At age eighteen, the children were given a note from their then-deceased father that detailed their Isaaq genealogy. Having never before known their origins, the siblings published a story in *Drum* magazine in the hope of reaching out to the wider Somali community. Inspired by the article, an Isaaq man from Kenya traveled down to South Africa, married West's daughter, and brought her to Nairobi.[42] This evocative tale suggests that one's "roots" can be maintained and rediscovered. Cultural assimilation did not necessarily spell permanent disconnection from the Somali community.

Most of the people I spoke to articulated a desire to find a place for themselves as Kenyan citizens, as members of the wider Somali diaspora, and as distant members of Somaliland.[43] This was a complex political gamble. While attaining full citizenship rights in Kenya was difficult in a climate of pervasive anti-Somali sentiment, many people nevertheless expressed hope about their future in the country.

REFRAMING THE SEPARATIST WAR

Like Somalis in Nairobi and neighboring towns, northerners also grappled with the prospect of greater political integration into Kenya. The fratricidal war in Somalia and the coerced exodus of people from their homeland had led to profound shifts in people's thinking. The war had not only physically dislocated many people; it had also forced them to confront traces and memories of a nationalist project that had once advocated for the unity of all Somalis across the region.[44] The devastation of the Shifta War and the outbreak of war in Somalia forced many people to rethink their commitment to irredentism. Although an abstract Pan-Somali sentiment was still popular in northern Kenya, the goal of achieving territorial union with the country had been abandoned by many people.

Most northerners I spoke to believed that the only practical future lay within the Kenyan nation-state. Many people also engaged in a retrospective rereading of events in order to reconcile their former support for the separatist movement with modern-day desires to be counted as Kenyans. It would be simplistic to consider such memories "false," since memory itself is a deeply complex process whose very definition is the subject of much scholarly debate.[45] Tales about the Shifta War years were continually invoked by present generations, reworked, encoded into social memory, and memorialized as history.

At least publicly, many northerners expressed regret for the irredentist movement. One resident of Wajir described the Northern Province People's Progressive Party (NPPPP) as a misguided movement run by the Somali government, which manipulated the fighters. When asked, he refused to recount songs or poetry from that era, saying that doing so would be akin to abusing your parents. Somalia is now eating itself (*wey is cunayaan*), he noted.[46] Another inhabitant of Wajir, who had been part of the core leadership of the NPPPP, expressed similar sentiments. He had remained involved in local politics after the war, and was imprisoned on several occasions during the Kenyatta and Moi regimes. Despite his mistreatment at the hands of the Kenyan government, he said it was a mistake to have sought union with Somalia (an idea, he maintained, that "had come from the outside"). Brushing off his role in the NPPPP, he was far more eager to discuss the awards he had won serving as a local government councillor in the Kibaki regime. His positive portrayal of the Kenyan government may have been tailored for a foreigner like myself. However, several of his children were in attendance at the interview and he seemed to be performing, in part, for their benefit. Pointing to his teenage son, he expressed hope that his children would finish their education in Kenya and that Somalis could achieve greater rights under the new constitution.[47]

In order to reframe a weighty past, some people suggested that their community was less involved in the separatist movement. Ahmed Maalin Abdalle argued that the Ogaden had been forewarned against joining the movement. Having kin on the other side of the border, they were more cognizant of the problems of tribalism and corruption in Somalia, he explained. Ogaden leaders were "sending us messages," warning: "Don't abuse the man upon whom you depend." Maalin Abdalle also mentioned that those who fled to Somalia during the Shifta War quickly returned. They had felt like "refugees," unwelcomed by their brothers and desirous of *ugali*, a Kenyan staple food that is often maligned by non-Kenyan Somalis.[48] Craving *ugali* was an elegant metaphor for the contemporary desire to be counted as Kenyan.

The notion of a unified Cushitic nation, another vestige of the separatist moment, had also lost much of its saliency and was rarely invoked as the basis for a territorial nation. Hussein Roba, a well-respected former government worker from Moyale, explained why many minorities could not support the movement for joining Somalia:

> There is a thing called racism. . . . Like these Sheka, they are called "Corner Tribe."[49] These Borana, they are called "Somali Abbo."[50] . . . They are not completely Somalis. . . . There are people with hard hair; they are called *"jareer."*[51] . . . There is a lot of tribalism. And if you go there you will have problems. . . . It is these tribe[s] that refuse to join Somalia.[52]

During the Somali civil war, factions used racist categories to justify targeting minorities, many of whom were displaced from their land and killed due to fighting and famine.[53] The polarizing effects of the war had disappointed many who had once hoped that Somalia could offer a more inclusive form of nationalism.

Many northerners had also come to publicly identify as "minorities" or "majorities." This was partially a legacy of the postindependence political conflicts described in the previous chapter. It also reflected a desire to gain recognition under the new constitution. In Habasweyn, Yusuf Ibrahim Kulow argued that the Ajuran were, in reality, a "hidden" majority. He explained that after the collapse of the Ajuran Sultanate in the seventeenth century, his people were forced to hide among their neighbors by becoming *sheegat* (clients).[54] Through this version of history, Kulow could argue that his community should be recognized as a historically constituted majority entitled to land and political representation.

A palpable shift in public perceptions had taken place over the last few years. Achieving minority status within Kenya had become central for many people who, only a few decades before, had overwhelmingly supported a Pan-Somali nation-state. Many northerners were also optimistic about the new devolved constitution. Around the idea of being a victimized, underdeveloped, and marginalized region, a new nationalist imaginary was forming.

Some northerners still supported the Pan-Somali cause or were simply unconvinced that Somalis could carve out a future within Kenya. The US-led "war on terror"—which, as Hawa Mire argues, has been "remade on the lands and shores of East Africa"—had exacerbated these concerns.[55] Others—inspired by the independence movement of Southern Sudan and the emergence of regional governance and separatist movements within Somalia—toyed with the notion of gaining independence as a region apart from Kenya and Somalia. Still others were drawn to the rhetoric of Islamic reformers and looked toward a future beyond the secular nation-state. Even those who sought greater inclusion with the country often recognized the limits of a juridical politics based upon constitutional reform.[56] Institutional representation as a minority could only offer them certain rights and safeguards, which depended upon the goodwill of the majority. Moreover, many of the bureaucratic exercises through which the state apportioned rights and conferred legal recognition stood at odds with the mobile life-styles of people in the north.[57] Despite the challenges posed by integration, northerners and Somalis, on the whole, spoke in hopeful terms about the changing political climate in Kenya.

THE WAR ON TERROR AND ITS DISCONTENTS

After the election of Kibaki in 2002, Somalis throughout the country began to make bids for greater national inclusion. By the time I began my field-work in 2010, many people had come to see themselves as both "Somali" and "Kenyan." These hopes of integration, however, were undercut by the polarizing discourse of the "war on terror."

The equation between "terrorism" and "failed states" became the dominant logic within security circles in the years after the Cold War. After the devastating bombing of US embassies in Kenya and Tanzania by affiliates of al-Qaeda in 1998, the United States began to focus "on addressing the perceived relationship between weak states" in Africa "and violent extremism."[58] This mind-set became entrenched after the September 11 attacks. The "failed-state paradigm" enabled many policy makers to make sense of the changing configuration of state power that accompanied the end of the Cold War.[59] Such modes of thought were not confined to policy spheres, but also became part of scholarly discourse. Social scientists such as Robert Rotberg connected the battle against terrorism in Africa with the strengthening of good governance.[60]

The seductively easy abstractions and narratives provided by the global war on terror served as a substitute for a more nuanced analysis of events in Somalia. Roland Marchal argues that constructing the "terrorist" as some kind of spectacular yet elusive criminal obscured the complexity of the civil war in Somalia, which quickly took on regional and international dimensions.[61] These ways of seeing often formed the basis for military and humanitarian interventions. Convinced that Somalia would become the new base for al-Qaeda members fleeing the war in Afghanistan, the United States established a Combined Joint Task Force for the Horn of Africa in 2002. Under its aegis, US officials funded Somali faction leaders to root out "Islamists." These covert operations reflected a profound misreading of the political climate in southern Somalia. According to Ken Menkhaus, a former political adviser to the United Nations in Somalia, the number of Somali nationals in early 2002 with "significant links" to al-Qaeda was probably no more than ten to twelve people, alongside a few foreign fighters.[62] Moreover, Somali faction leaders in southern Somalia largely used the inflow of money to pursue their own agendas.

Under the Alliance for the Restoration of Peace and Counterterrorism, which enjoyed the backing of the CIA, leaders assassinated political rivals, many of whom posed little to no security threat to the United States.[63]

Heavy-handed US interventionism, moreover, lent popular support to a new organization emerging in southern Somalia in the early 2000s. The Islamic Courts Union (ICU) began as a series of decentralized and largely experimental projects, before formally coalescing into a rival administration to the transitional federal government (TFG). To cope with the insecurity and highly charged ethnic politics brought on by the civil war, small groups of armed, autonomous militias began to support the implementation of Islamic law, and to provide social services in the regions under their control. Scholars have put forward many theories to explain why inhabitants of southern Somalia, who had long lived under a secular regime, turned to Islamic forms of authority as the basis for a new kind of governance.[64] Perhaps most obviously, the ICU improved the violent and unstable status quo under which they had been living. It also offered civilians an alternative to the divisive political grammar of clannism. By bringing peace to Mogadishu for the first time in sixteen years, the courts garnered a great deal of popular legitimacy.[65]

The emergence of the ICU was a challenge to both neoconservative and liberal common sense. It ran counter to triumphalist accounts about the spread of free-market liberal democracy and fed into fears about a "clash of civilizations" were Islam to become untethered from the supposedly stabilizing forces of empire and nation-state.[66] The turn toward Islamic forms of justice signified a grassroots experimentation with a new notion of sovereignty and political authority. In the eyes of US counterterrorism agents, however, the ICU was not a legitimate polity or a viable contender for political power. Rather, it signified the spread of "radical Islam." Concerns with the rise of a theocratic form of authority (and with the more militant factions within the ICU) were not wholly unwarranted.[67] Yet the conclusions of many counterterrorism experts were based not on a careful assessment of the group, but on anxiety about the rise of a nonsecular and nonliberal polity in the Islamic world and a belief in the legitimacy of American interventionism.

Unwilling to cede space to any nonsecular political entity, Western security agents quickly honed in on the more militant and doctrinaire elements of the ICU, such as al-Shabaab. The organization was not without its rifts, in part because it comprised a broad coalition with a diverse range of religious and ideological tendencies. Its leaders included figures such as Sheikh Sharif Sheikh Ahmed, a neo-Sufi reformist who would later become president of the TFG (and whom the United States would later "rebrand" as an ally). Although some US intelligence officials called for dialogue and reconciliation, recognizing the group's diversity, they were drowned out by those in the

Bush administration who conflated the ICU with al-Qaeda. This precluded any kind of neutral assessment of the ICU's efforts to provide a viable, alternative form of governance or reassert sovereignty over the nation-state. In 2006, the United States backed an Ethiopian invasion of Somalia to bring down the organization and install the TFG. Several journalists and scholars have linked the mistakes of this invasion to the extension of civil war and the genesis of the very radicalism it was intended to forestall.[68]

By destabilizing the region, US and Ethiopian officials enabled al-Shabaab—once a small faction in the diverse coalition of the ICU—to remake itself into a major player in southern Somalia. From the time that Kibaki took power in 2002 to the 2007 postelection crisis, the ICU had come and gone from power—proving to be yet another phase in a protracted war. When the Kenyan government began deliberations over a draft constitution, al-Shaabab had already taken territorial control over much of southern Somalia. While al-Shabaab is itself a more complex political body than the one-dimensional portrait often painted of it, its repressive, militant, and exclusionary tactics have confirmed many people's worst fears.[69]

Most international media outlets ignored the chain of events leading to al-Shabaab's rise to power, focusing instead on its outward Islamic ideology. Such coverage tends to emphasize "cultural" factors over political and economic issues. This "culture talk" also implicitly casts blame on Islam and on Muslims who subscribe to modernist or "reformist" interpretations of the religion.[70] These reports have made it more difficult to carefully assess the changing nature of power in the region and the many ways in which religious Muslims have chosen to engage with (or disengage from) the state.

INTERNAL DEBATES OVER ISLAMIC MILITANCY AND REFORM

Counterterrorist operatives often divide the Muslim world into strict dichotomies. To avoid persecution, many Somali leaders and journalists have taken great pains to portray their community in those very terms (not only as "loyal" citizens of Kenya, but also as "moderate" Muslims).[71] Within the Somali community itself, however, different kinds of debates also circulate over what constitutes acceptable forms of Islamic practice and who may dictate Islamic orthodoxy. These disputes do not neatly fracture around a divide between "liberals" and "fundamentalists," "moderates" and "radicals," or "local" and "global" forms of Islam. Rather, they reflect multifaceted internal traditions of dissent and reform. Recognizing Islam as a tradition—ever-changing, rife with internal contradictions, and containing multiple, intertwined strands of thought—is essential, as Talal Asad argues, to understanding contemporary debates over Islamic practice.[72]

In many respects, Islamic reformists (including those who identify as Salafi or are labeled Wahhabi) have built upon the institutional vestiges and intellectual legacy of empire. Beginning in the 1970s, oil-rich Gulf states, such as Saudi Arabia, began to provide scholarships to Somali youth.[73] Islamic NGOs also built madrassas and health clinics, provided various forms of charity in Muslim-dominated regions of Kenya, and disseminated new ideas of Islamic reform.[74] Much like colonial states before them, these Islamic institutions were rationalist in orientation and supportive of modernizing social programs (even as they claimed to oppose Western modernity). Via madrassa schooling as well as new social media (including cassette tapes and, more recently, the Internet), Somali youth turned toward what some perceive to be more accessible and democratic ways of attaining Islamic knowledge and others view as vehicles for radicalization.[75] These new technologies for the dissemination of *dawah* (proselytizing) have not only allowed Muslims to reimagine a global community in the absence of travel or direct connection, but have also led to epistemological shifts in people's thinking. As Amitav Ghosh argues: "It is all too easy to forget that these reinvented forms of religion are not a repudiation of, but a means of laying claim to, the modern world."[76] Those who subscribe to a reformist vision, for example, tend to reject many "traditional" religious practices—such as making pilgrimages to gravesites, celebrating the *mawlid* (the birthday of the prophet), and reciting *dhikr*.[77]

In northern Kenya, many people have come to associate "controversial" practices with the older cohort of religious experts.[78] One *shaykh* (leader) living in Kotulo lamented the *caasinimo* (disobedience) of youth, who no longer respected the older generation of religious leaders. He also implied that the recent droughts were directly tied to the declining frequency of prayer for rainfall.[79] To some reformers, such forms of intercession are considered *shirk*, questionable forms of devotional practice, or simply embarrassing forms of superstition.[80]

The Sufi concept of *batin* (the inner or hidden meaning) is a powerful recourse for those who feel marginalized by such accusations. On two separate occasions, I was told a famous hadith that has circulated around the Muslim world. According to this hadith, the prophet predicted that the Muslim *umma* (community) would one day fracture into seventy-three sects, only one of which would correctly follow the Qur'an and *sunna*. This story is very popular among reformists, who often cite it to justify "returning" to the *sunna* as the sole basis for Islamic decision making. One *shaykh* in Wajir, however, explained its meaning differently. He argued that the *umma* had indeed split into seventy-three groups, just as the prophet had foretold. However, the group that had chosen the correct path would not be revealed until the Day of Judgment.[81] By suggesting that God's ultimate judgment was yet to come and beyond human determination, he was able to advocate for pluralism and freedom of religious practice.

Due to these religious controversies, which have become more fraught since the emergence of the ICU, many people were reluctant to openly engage in "Sufi" practices. Some religious leaders explained that they continued to help people who sought their spiritual counsel, but often did so secretly.[82] Conducting oral histories under these conditions was difficult. Many were hesitant to discuss such delicate issues with an outsider like myself. Others simply glossed over these disagreements by highlighting the underlying unity of Islam. What became clear, however, is that there is no neat divide between Sufi and Salafi (two homogenizing terms that collapse innumerable distinctions between Muslims). Opinions often overlap, and many people have found ways to reconcile esoteric practices with reformist ideals. Counterterrorist operatives often seek to root out radical elements within society. In so doing, they frequently conflate religious practices and dissenting political expression with violence and treat Islam as an external "other" to liberalism.

THE WESTGATE ATTACK AND ITS AFTERLIVES

Such unwillingness to seriously engage with Islamic currents of thought has led to a broader erasure of Muslim political participation in the nation-state. Fears of Islamic political discourse, for instance, came to the surface during the Kenyan constitutional debates in 2010. During the deliberations, a coalition of politicians and church officials began to contest the legality of *qadi* (judges') courts, a system that had been in place since the colonial era and had jurisdiction exclusively over civil matters between Muslims. These critics conflated the *qadi* system with "sharia law," thus feeding into public hysteria about the emergence of militant and conservative forms of Islamic politics in neighboring Somalia.

Many activists and commentators argued that efforts to abolish *qadi* courts were, at heart, anti-Islamic measures, which threatened Kenya's long history of successfully accommodating cultural and religious plurality. Nanjala Nyabola wrote that it was "disingenuous to imply that institutions that have been part and parcel of the country for almost 50 years are suddenly a threat to the fundamental freedoms of the broader society or a form of favouritism."[83] Although Kenyan politicians ultimately allowed *qadi* courts to be institutionalized in the new constitution, this debate reflected a growing belief that public forms of Islamic worship conflicted with the logic and political rationality of the secular state. The controversy exposed how easily "liberal norms" could be deployed in an illiberal and "exclusionary fashion," especially toward Muslim minorities.[84]

The debate over *qadi* courts was also fueled by media reports about al-Shabaab's presence in Kenya. In 2010, the *Washington Post* published an article that described Eastleigh as an "incubator for jihad" and maintained that radical terrorist cells were embedded in the community.[85] These fears seemed to be confirmed in 2013, when members of al-Shabaab launched an attack on the upscale Westgate mall in the suburbs of Nairobi, killing dozens of civilians and drawing a media spectacle. Kenya—whose government had invaded Somalia in 2011, ostensibly in an effort to secure its borders—soon became the target of a series of sporadic grenade attacks and shootings (including the 2015 attack on Garissa University).

Many media outlets stressed al-Shabaab's growing ties to al-Qaeda as well as its support from members of the Somali diaspora. Analysts also suggested that Westgate signaled a shift in the organization toward a more militant and "global" agenda.[86] Few, however, recognized that the goals of al-Shabaab remained intimately tied to national independence, repelling what was perceived to be yet another foreign invader seeking to profit from the country's instability. Al-Shabaab did not represent a wholesale rejection of the modern nation-state, but rather an experimentation with new forms of statehood and sovereignty. Moreover, the hysteria caused by the attacks in Kenya foreclosed a deeper political analysis of the conflict. Dismissed as an anarchic symptom of state collapse, there was little attempt to seriously analyze the political imaginations of those who sympathized with or supported al-Shabaab.

Capitalizing on growing concerns with unregulated, transnational networks, Kenyan officials instead pursued acts of ethnic profiling. When attacks in the country continued, Kenyan security forces began to explicitly target Somali neighborhoods. In April 2014, security forces arrested approximately four thousand Somalis on suspicion of terrorist activities. Human rights groups and leaders of the Somali community protested against these measures, accusing the Kenyan government of indiscriminately detaining people on the basis of their ethnic background, abusing detainees, and deporting refugees in violation of international law.[87]

The call for greater securitization and militarization to root out disloyal elements within the nation stirred up anti-Somali and anti-Muslim sentiments. It also allowed the Kenyan government to mask its complicity in the violence and instability in neighboring Somalia and stem potential criticism for its invasion. Human Rights Watch has documented abuses by "both al-Shabaab and the forces arrayed against it," which include "a combination of Somali government armed forces, the African Union Mission in Somalia (AMISOM), Ethiopian government troops, and allied militias" (many of which enjoy US support).[88] However, the violence conducted by non-Muslim and state actors has received far less media attention. Often lost to public debate is the ongoing plight of civilians within Somalia, who have suffered at the hands of various factions within this complex and protracted war.

Like the terrorists they seek to combat, counterterrorism agents frequently operate outside the conventional structures of the nation-state—circumventing territorial borders and orthodox understandings of legality and sovereignty. They inhabit a world of shared tactics and common discourses with those they claim to fight, often making reference to a spectral, borderless war "shorn of political or geographical coordinates."[89] The Anti-Terrorist Police Unit in Kenya, for example, which enjoys US and UK backing, has been accused by human rights groups of the extrajudicial killings of clerics in Mombasa.[90] As a result of this all-embracing security discourse, Jeremy Prestholdt argues, "ordinary Kenyans with no perceptible link to terrorists regularly bear the cost of counterterrorism."[91] There is a serious risk that this new antiterrorism security regime—by operating outside the traditional domain of legal rights—will lead to widespread political disenfranchisement.[92]

Since 2013, attacks on civilian targets in Kenya have become the subject of much gossip and speculation. Many ordinary citizens believe that powerful, unnamed parties are secretly behind these acts of violence, using terrorism as a cover to advance their own commercial and political interests.[93] These "conspiracy theories," though especially prevalent within the Somali community, are widespread within Kenya. Even official channels have alluded to the possibility that forces other than al-Shabaab have been involved in some of the recent attacks. In 2014, Farah Maalim, one of Kenya's most outspoken Somali leaders, publicly accused the newly elected Uhuru Kenyatta government of encouraging terrorist attacks in order to fight ICC charges, curry favor with the West, and obtain US antiterrorist funding.[94] After gunmen struck the coastal town of Mpeketoni, President Kenyatta made waves by blaming local forces for masquerading as al-Shabaab in order to drive certain ethnic groups off historically contested land.[95] These official pronouncements gave further credibility to stories that were already circulating on the streets, in bars, in homes, and over Twitter accounts.

Differing explanations for the attacks in the country indicate that the indiscriminate profiling of Somalis will do little to address the complex, underlying forces fueling violence in the region. Moreover, they point to the complexities of assigning guilt.[96] Popular rumors also suggest that concerns over abuse and corruption in the public and private sectors often outstrip fears about terrorism. Regardless of the veracity of these narratives, they speak to a broader social and political truth: namely, that many parties are responsible for fostering instability within Kenya and contributing, both directly and indirectly, to the deaths of civilians.

My interlocutors in Kenya often described themselves in terms that challenged conventional portrayals of Muslims as inassimilable and "out of place." Most of the people I spoke to sought out minority rights within Kenya, even as they resisted certain pressures to assimilate. The aspiration for greater political inclusion in the nation existed in tandem with a desire to participate in a collective life that stretched across national borders. Few saw a contradiction in wanting to be part of Kenya, Somalia, and the wider Islamic *umma*. To be both "Kenyan" and "Somali" became a thinkable possibility for many people in the years after Moi left power.

By the time I did my fieldwork, Somalis were experiencing a moment of hope and optimism. While northerners and Somalis were, at times, skeptical that the government would usher in national reconciliation or fulfill all the promises of devolution, many were encouraged by recent political trends. However, the entry of Kenya into the war in Somalia, the attacks by al-Shabaab, and the counterterrorist operations that followed in their wake undermined these sentiments. The polarizing discourse of the war on terror has narrowed the field for imagining a more inclusive and flexible model of citizenship.

Despite worrying trends, which suggest that the Kenyan government may further disenfranchise Muslims, hope for integration remains. Many Somalis long to be recognized as citizens, while remaining open to futures beyond a bounded territorial nationalism. Kenya has managed to absorb thousands of refugees from Somalia as well as other countries, many of whom are now indistinguishable from citizens. Kenyan citizens of various backgrounds have also shown a remarkable ability to accommodate cultural and religious diversity. The contemporary political landscape in Kenya refracts multiple futures, which suggest neither the "end of history" nor a "clash of civilizations."[97]

Conclusion

"We Are Not Migrants; We Are Living in Our Ancestral Land"

> The whole carriage was full of Somalis who had also entered
> Egypt illegally, all roamers who had only known porous insub-
> stantial borders and were now confronted with countries caged
> behind bars.
>
> —Excerpt from Nadifa Mohamed's novel, Black Mamba Boy[1]

> It is a question of knowing how to transform and improve the
> law, and of knowing if this improvement is possible within an his-
> torical space which takes place between the Law of an uncondi-
> tional hospitality, offered a priori to every other, to all newcomers,
> whoever they may be, and the conditional laws of a right to
> hospitality, without which the unconditional Law of hospitality
> would be in danger of remaining a pious and irresponsible desire,
> without form and without potency, and of even being perverted
> at any moment.
>
> —Derrida, On Cosmopolitanism[2]

IN JULY 2015, I returned to Kenya for a short visit. One day, I was walking in downtown Nairobi with a Kenyan friend when we were approached by three *askari*. The police officers asked for my friend's ID card and began to inquire into his background. Unable to produce his national ID card, which he had misplaced, he instead gave the officers his university student card.

Deeming this form of identification inadequate, the officers demanded that he accompany them to the nearest police station. Though born and raised in Kenya and fluent in multiple local vernaculars, my friend was deemed suspect because he was identifiable (by his facial features) as Somali. I, on the other hand, a foreigner, was never asked to produce any identification. Being white and speaking in an American accent, I did not have to justify my presence in the country. This incident made visceral the inequality of freedom of movement that characterizes not only life in Nairobi, but also travel across the globe.

While a number of scholars, journalists, and pundits have cast doubt on the assumption that we are moving closer to a borderless world, the language surrounding globalization remains potent.[3] Talk of transnationalism, diaspora, and global flows, as Rogers Brubaker suggests, may reflect less a change in the world than a "change in idiom"—a means of explaining the profound reordering of state sovereignty that has accompanied the end of the Cold War as well as an aspiration for a kind of political membership that transcends the nation-state.[4] Yet a discourse that champions (or, alternatively, decries) the dissolution of territorial boundaries tends to shroud and obscure the experiences of those who do not enjoy unhindered freedom of movement. Kenyan citizens who identify as Somali continue to struggle with the legacy of state borders, which have divided them from their kin and grazing land, consigned them to polities much smaller than their imagined communities, and restricted and stigmatized their mobility. Understanding the uneven nature of globalization requires attentiveness toward forms of sociality that long predated the advent of territorial borders.[5] Nevertheless, journalists, pundits, and social scientists frequently discuss the problems of terrorism, security, and refugee movement in East Africa without understanding these deeper histories or engaging with vernacular discourses about borders.

Nation-states have been notoriously wary of certain groups who participate in collectivities that stretch beyond their territorial confines or challenge conventional notions of sovereignty. In Kenya, many of the anxieties and uncertainties surrounding the changing face of nationalism have been displaced onto the Somali population. To many locals, their presence points to the potential for losing demographic and economic ground to "outsiders."[6] The violent acts of al-Shabaab members and sympathizers remind both local and foreign officials that warfare is no longer so exclusively routed through state institutions. The success and vitality of Somali commercial and spiritual networks reveal that new supranational forms of organization may prove to be more important sites of mobilization than the nation-state. Since many Somalis participate in forms of collective life that circumvent state institutions and national borders, it has become all too easy for Kenyan officials and ordinary citizens—already predisposed to think of Somalis as alien—to see anyone who looks, speaks, or acts in a characteristically "Somali" way as potentially suspect and criminal.

The desire to excise foreign elements from a country is frequently grounded on an erasure of shared histories of interrelation.[7] In a public forum in Nairobi, the journalist Mohammed Adow pointed to the long history of Somali presence in the country: "You know, we are not migrants, we are not from another continent, we are not from another country—we are living in our ancestral land."[8] The predicaments faced by Kenyan Somalis reinforce Sara Ahmed's argument that the stranger is someone who is already known to us, who is *already recognized as not belonging*, as being out of place."[9] The Somali were first constructed as quasi-foreign elements in the colony, later as undesirable members of a postcolonial nation, and more recently as national and international security threats.

The need to differentiate between "insiders" and "outsiders" is not only central to the very idea of nationalist inclusion, it is probably intrinsic to all forms of civility and sociality. If, as Derrida suggests, one can never fully open one's borders to the "other," then there is limited value to utopian notions of a completely borderless world. The future of progressive politics will very likely depend—not on an abstract celebration of cultural hybridity or a cheery notion of a global society—but on a concrete reconfiguration of the scope and contours of political membership.[10]

It is tempting to view older forms of mobility, interregional connection, and cosmopolitanism as the natural basis for a contemporary emancipatory politics. However, the lives of transnational actors reflect a more ambiguous array of possibilities. While the liberal democratic state today typically exercises the most power in determining who does or does not belong to a given polity, xenophobia is not solely the preserve of nation-states. Islamic reformist movements can promote intolerance toward Muslims and non-Muslims alike, just as diasporas can experience problems of racism and religious chauvinism. Scholars can remain critical of the nation-state (and liberal concepts of assimilation and multiculturalism), while still recognizing that "subaltern" models of membership may breed their own kinds of exclusion.[11]

Though often pathologized by scholars, African states can provide a ground upon which to think about more flexible models of sovereignty and new types of nationalist and "postnationalist" futures.[12] While the Kenyan state is hardly a paragon of inclusive democracy, Kenyan political thinkers have, at times, created spaces for the recognition and negotiation of difference. The signing of the al Fatah declaration (described in chapter 7) indicates that Kenyan administrators have, under some circumstances, shown a willingness to cede room to nonsecular and nonstatist forms of justice. Moreover, unlike their counterparts in France, Muslims in Kenya do not have to contend with overarching state legislation that has banned public forms of worship and spiritual embodiment, such as the wearing of head scarves.[13] The newly ratified constitution has also created opportunities for greater political and economic inclusion. Though devolution is not without its critics, the promise of more equitable resource distribution and political decentralization under the 2010 constitution has bolstered the hopes of many marginalized groups, including people in northeastern Kenya.[14] In addition, the 2011 Citizenship and Immigration Act for the first time legalized dual citizenship, thus giving greater recognition to those with transnational loyalties.[15] However temporary and fleeting, there have been moments and spaces when people have been able to live relatively freely as Muslims, Somalis, and Kenyans.

Kenya also provides a model for less restrictive kinds of registration and border controls. A cornerstone of normative theories of statecraft is the notion that governments must carefully monitor and protect their borders. The Kenyan government, however, is frequently unable (and, in some cases, unwilling) to regulate international immigration.[16] It would be all too easy to view this as a state failure, as yet another example of an African administration unable to control its borders, accurately issue identity cards, or collect basic demographic data about its population.[17] Such conditions have undoubtedly caused problems, but they have also created spaces where refugee and citizen can coexist and where distinctions between illegality and legality can blur.[18]

In spite of discriminatory state policy and indiscriminate antiterror operations, Kenya hosts hundreds of thousands of immigrants and refugees from diverse backgrounds, many of whom have come to see the country as their primary or secondary homeland. The Kenyan government simply cannot deport the tens of thousands of asylum seekers who have integrated themselves into the social and economic fabric of the country. Despite crackdowns by police and security forces, Eastleigh remains a space of asylum for many migrants—providing an extralegal model for Derrida's "city of refuge."[19] It is also questionable whether Kenya's porous borders are an inherent security threat, as state officials and foreign observers often assume.[20] Moreover, such permeability is essential to nomads, traders, and asylum seekers, many of whom must cross international frontiers for basic survival.

What might appear to be a government "failure" has, in fact, led many scholars and policy makers to rethink the necessity of refugee encampment and advocate for the urban integration of asylum seekers.[21] Such policy shifts do not portend a complete disregard for nation-state borders. After all, without proper demographic data and registration mechanisms, citizens and refugees alike risk being further politically and economically disenfranchised.

However, they do suggest a need for new systems of inclusion and recognition that deprivilege the distinction between "citizen" and "alien."[22]

Examining how Kenyan Somalis cross borders also allows us to rethink prevailing assumptions about citizenship and asylum.[23] Take, for instance, the Somali concept of *sheegat*, which offers a means of reconceptualizing the relationship between locals and foreigners. Through *sheegat*, newcomers can claim asylum, protection, and limited access to resources by being "adopted' by . . . established residents" and acknowledging "the host clan's authority."[24] Lee Cassanelli compares this system to "the venerable Somali institution of the *abbaan* (host or protector), who offered temporary shelter and security for traders or travelers whose business required them to spend time in another clan's territory."[25] Those adopted as *sheegat* do not fully lose memories of their original lineage and typically must accept a subordinate position in their new homes. Host societies do not fully lose hegemony over the area in which they live or its resources, but must cede space and recognition to their guests, who are often acknowledged as fellow or related kin. Assimilation over generations is possible, as is a rediscovery of one's previous roots.

Nation-states, with their pretense to unitary sovereignty, myths of national homogeneity, and concern with fixed boundaries and demographic considerations, can offer only limited paths toward integration. The concept of *sheegat*, however, is predicated on an understanding that the inside and the outside are constantly shifting and that the copresence of sojourners with alternative geographies and loyalties is a regular feature of life. While certainly subject to abuse and coded with its own forms of exclusion, the *sheegat* system can help us to think beyond the limits of democratic inclusion, which has such undue sway over our political imaginations. Perhaps most importantly, *sheegat* invites us to think of people living together in a polity, not as citizens and aliens, but as hosts and guests.

It is also important to consider how Somalis and other marginalized citizens have conceptualized borderlessness. Toward the end of my fieldwork, I was told a story about a Somali woman's journey from Nairobi to London. Recounted by a friend in Nairobi, this narrative reveals many of the aspirations embodied in the concept of *buufis* (the dream/obsession with resettlement): A young Kenyan Somali woman boarded a plane in Nairobi to the United Kingdom, hoping to resettle abroad by passing as a refugee. Upon arrival at the Heathrow airport, she tore up her Kenyan passport and claimed asylum. When immigration officials detained her for questioning, she pretended not to speak English in an effort to play the part of a refugee. However, when a Somali translator was brought in, she began to panic. Having grown up in Nairobi, she spoke very little Somali. Fearful that her ruse would be uncovered, she started to pray, reciting verses of the Qur'an.

Quickly grasping her situation, the translator began to "interpret" her speech. The immigration officials, unable to differentiate between Qur'anic Arabic and vernacular Somali, did not realize that he was creatively spinning a biography for her as she prayed. Thanks to the Somali translator's compassion and ingenuity, she was given refugee status in the UK.[26]

Some may construe this (quite possibly fanciful) narrative as evidence of the "nefarious" activities of Somali refugees or the lapses in state security apparatuses that enable "undeserving" immigrants to enter Western countries. However, the aspirations underlying this story mirror a kind of freedom of movement that many cosmopolitan travelers, especially those from the Western world, often take for granted. Moreover, this story shows that there are ways of envisioning borderlessness that differ from both the neoliberal model of individual actors operating in a global marketplace and the liberal idea of global citizenship realized through transnational institutions of governance. Unable to gain assistance from state agents, the protagonist instead sought spiritual help and was ultimately aided by a fellow kinsman. Seemingly impenetrable borders were thus crossed through the help of a compassionate individual, esoteric cultural knowledge, and (implicitly) divine intervention.

However elusive, the idea of a borderless world remains a key imaginative reference for people across the world. In envisioning a more just and inclusive future, it is worth considering what is at stake in such a vision. Does it entail a world in which capital and multinational corporations are able to flow freely across state borders, as proponents of market liberalization suggest? Will the idea of belonging to a nation be displaced by a global citizenship, as many liberal humanists argue? Or can such a vision accommodate those who cross (or envision crossing) borders in different ways? Achille Mbembe argues that rather than disavow "long traditions of circulation that [have] always been the dynamic motor of change in the continent," African states should rebuff global trends toward enclosure. In an era that has seen a resurgence of xenophobic, nativist, and Islamophobic politics (as evidenced by the recent US elections and the vitriol aimed at Syrian refugees in Europe), it is imperative that political theorists learn from the long-term struggles of those leading transnational lives under political constraints.[27] Only then can we imagine a political ethics in which jurisdictional and territorial borders, however indispensable, can be habitually rethought, amended, and, at times, transgressed.

Abbreviations

ALMO	African Livestock Marketing Organization
AMISOM	African Union Mission in Somalia
DC	district commissioner
GSL	Greater Somali League
GSU	General Service Unit
HDM	Hizbiya Digil-Mirifle (Digil and Mirifle Party; later known as
HDMS	Hizbiya Dastur Mustaqil al-Sumal, or the Somali Independent Constitutional Party)
IBEAC	Imperial British East Africa Company
ICU	Islamic Courts Union
IMF	International Monetary Fund
KADU	Kenya African Democratic Union
KANU	Kenya African National Union
KAR	King's African Rifles
KLC	Kenya Land Commission
KLFA	Kenya Land and Freedom Army
KMC	Kenya Meat Commission
KNA	Kenya National Archives
KWS	Kenya Wildlife Service
Legco	Legislative Council
NEP	North Eastern Province
NFD	Northern Frontier District
NFDLF	Northern Frontier District Liberation Front
NFDP	Northern Frontier Democratic Party
NFP	Northern Frontier Province

NPPPP	Northern Province People's Progressive Party (often abbreviated as **NPP**)
NPUA	Northern Province United Association
OAU	Organization of African Unity
PC	provincial commissioner
SIU	Somali Independent Union
SNA	Somali National Association
SYL	Somali Youth League
TFG	transitional federal government
TJRC	Truth, Justice, and Reconciliation Commission
TNA	The National Archives (UK)
UN	United Nations
UNHCR	United Nations High Commissioner for Refugees
UOSA	United Ogaden Somali Association
USA	United Somali Association
WWP	Wajir Women for Peace

Notes

1. John L. Jackson Jr., *Thin Description: Ethnography and the African Hebrew Israelites of Jerusalem* (Cambridge, MA: Harvard University Press, 2013).

INTRODUCTION: "WE DON'T UNPACK"

1. Christopher Clapham, "Boundary and Territory in the Horn of Africa," in *African Boundaries: Barriers, Conduits and Opportunities*, ed. Paul Nugent and A. I. Asijawu (London: Pinter, 1996), 240.

2. In 1925, the colonial state placed the Northern Frontier District (NFD) under a provincial commissioner and renamed it the Northern Province (NP). In 1934, the government separated Samburu District from the Northern Province and, in 1947, incorporated Turkana District into the administrative region, renaming it the Northern Frontier Province (NFP). Despite these name changes, colonial officials and northern residents continued to refer to the region as the "NFD" throughout colonial rule and into today. This book follows the same convention. Nene Mburu, *Bandits on the Border: The Last Frontier in the Search for Somali Unity* (Trenton, NJ: Red Sea Press, 2005), 46–47.

3. Interview by author, anonymous, Giriftu, 2 April 2011.

4. Scott Steven Reese, *Renewers of the Age: Holy Men and Social Discourse in Colonial Benaadir* (Leiden: Brill, 2008), 41.

5. Interview by author, Fatima Jellow, Wajir, 9 April 2011. "Clan" should not be understood as a rigid system that provides ready-made explanations for social and political phenomena. I use the terms "lineage" and "clan" interchangeably as a means

of breaking with the older anthropological convention of creating hierarchical clan diagrams.

6. Though technically part of the country internationally recognized as Somalia, Berbera is located in an effectively independent region known to many as the Republic of Somaliland.

7. The spelling of clan names is inconsistent across different sources cited in this book. Colonial officials and Somali leaders, for example, have varyingly spelled the Isaaq clan name as Isaak, Ishaak, and Ishak.

8. Interview by author, Mustafa (Mohamed) Osman Hirsi, Nairobi, 5 November 2010.

9. Nor are such sentiments exclusive to Somalis. Huka Gompe, a leader of the Gabra community, gave the following testimony to a local newspaper in 2009: "Here we don't know about boundaries. I was born in Ethiopia but since 1963, I have been herding my livestock in both Kenya and Ethiopia. Even when I was a chief, I would cross over into Kenya to look for pasture when drought ravaged Ethiopia. . . . I have several relatives in Kenya who also don't know whether they are Kenyan or Ethiopian." Muchemi Wachira, "Neither Ethiopian nor Kenyan, Just Gabra, Garre, or Borana," 31 August 2009, http://www.theeastafrican.co.ke/magazine/434746-647554-ec93oo/index. html.

10. Cawo M. Abdi highlights what she refers to as the contradictions of globalization by showing how recent Somali refugees in the United States, South Africa, and the United Arab Emirates remain subject to stringent border controls. Abdi, *Elusive Jannah: The Somali Diaspora and a Borderless Muslim Identity* (Minneapolis: University of Minnesota Press, 2015), 8.

11. For recent work on the Somali refugee experience, see Abdi, *Elusive Jannah*; and Cindy Horst, *Transnational Nomads: How Somalis Cope with Refugee Life in the Dadaab Camps of Kenya* (New York: Berghahn Books, 2006).

12. As H. A. Ibrahim explains: "The arbitrary colonial partition of Somali frontiers was done without consulting the clansmen concerned and with little or no account of clan distribution or grazing needs." Ibrahim, "Politics and Nationalism in North-East Africa, 1919–35," in *General History of Africa*, vol. 7, *Africa under Colonial Domination, 1880–1935*, ed. A. Adu Boahen (Paris: UNESCO, 1985), 599.

13. Anatole Ayissi, "The Politics of Frozen State Borders in Postcolonial Africa," in *African Studies in Geography from Below*, ed. Michel Ben Arrous and Lazare Ki-Zerbo (Dakar: CODESRIA, 2009), 132–59; Achille Mbembe, "At the Edge of the World: Boundaries, Territoriality, and Sovereignty in Africa," trans. Steven Rendall, *Public Culture* 12, no. 1 (January 2000): 259–84; and Mahmood Mamdani, "Beyond Settler and Native as Political Identities: Overcoming the Political Legacy of Colonialism," *Comparative Studies in Society and History* 43, no. 4 (October 2001): 653.

14. Mahmood Mamdani, *When Victims Become Killers: Colonialism, Nativism, and the Genocide in Rwanda* (Princeton, NJ: Princeton University Press, 2001).

15. Critics such as Jonathon Glassman and Bruce Hall argue that Mamdani overstates the reach and impact of the colonial state. Glassman, *War of Words, War of Stones: Racial Thought and Violence in Colonial Zanzibar* (Bloomington: Indiana University Press, 2011); and Hall, *A History of Race in Muslim West Africa, 1600–1960* (Cambridge: Cambridge University Press, 2011). This issue intersects with a long-standing debate among historians of Africa over the "invention of tradition." Thomas T.

Spear, "Neo-Traditionalism and the Limits of Invention in British Colonial Africa," *Journal of African History* 44, no. 1 (2003): 3–27, doi:10.1017/S0021853702008320.

16. Mamdani, *When Victims Become Killers*; Frederick Cooper, *Africa in the World: Capitalism, Empire, Nation-State* (Cambridge, MA: Harvard University Press, 2014); and Jemima Pierre, *The Predicament of Blackness: Postcolonial Ghana and the Politics of Race* (Chicago: University of Chicago Press, 2013). African studies has been beset by both a nationalist framework and what Pierre refers to as the "colonialist model of ethnicizing African phenomena" (202). Similarly, Mamdani argues that the "area studies enterprise . . . sees state boundaries as boundaries of knowledge, thereby turning political into epistemological boundaries" (xii).

17. These groups are often perceived to be "inauthentically" indigenous. For work that bucks this trend, see Jean Marie Allman, *The Quills of the Porcupine: Asante Nationalism in an Emergent Ghana* (Madison: University of Wisconsin Press, 1993); Christopher Joon-Hai Lee, *Unreasonable Histories: Nativism, Multiracial Lives, and the Genealogical Imagination in British Africa* (Durham, NC: Duke University Press, 2014); and Janet Mcintosh, *Unsettled: Denial and Belonging among White Kenyans* (Oakland: University of California Press, 2016).

18. E. S. Atieno Odhiambo, "Matunda ya Uhuru, Fruits of Independence: Seven Theses on Nationalism in Kenya," in *Mau Mau and Nationhood: Arms, Authority, and Narration*, ed. E. S. Atieno Odhiambo and John Lonsdale (Athens: Ohio University Press, 2003), 37–45.

19. Samuel Moyn, "Fantasies of Federalism," *Dissent* 62, no. 1 (Winter 2015): 145–51, https://www.dissentmagazine.org/article/fantasies-of-federalism; and Charles Piot, "Atlantic Aporias: Africa and Gilroy's Black Atlantic," *South Atlantic Quarterly* 100, no. 1 (2001): 155–70.

20. I use the term "community" in the Andersonian sense of "imagined community," though not necessarily in the sense of a sovereign and limited nation based upon "a deep, horizontal comradeship." My usage is also distinct from the notion of community as a legal and discursive category of governance as described by scholars like Nikolas Rose. Benedict R. O'G. Anderson, *Imagined Communities: Reflections on the Origin and Spread of Nationalism*, rev. ed. (London: Verso, 2006), 7; and Nikolas Rose, *Powers of Freedom: Reframing Political Thought* (Cambridge: Cambridge University Press, 2000), 167–96.

21. While there has been a surge of scholarship on the recent emergence of non-state actors, diasporic networks, and transnational entities, researchers have shown that many of these contemporary phenomena have deep, historical roots. See, for example, Janet L. Abu-Lughod, *Before European Hegemony: The World System, A.D. 1250–1350* (New York: Oxford University Press, 1989). Among journalists and social scientists, however, globalization is still frequently understood as a relatively recent and Western phenomenon.

22. Prita Meier, *Swahili Port Cities: The Architecture of Elsewhere* (Bloomington: Indiana University Press, 2016), 183.

23. John Iliffe, *A Modern History of Tanganyika* (Cambridge: Cambridge University Press, 1979); Terence O. Ranger, *The Invention of Tribalism in Zimbabwe* (Gweru, Zimbabwe: Mambo Press, 1985); and Leroy Vail, ed., *The Creation of Tribalism in Southern Africa* (London: James Currey, 1989).

24. John M. Lonsdale, "Moral Ethnicity and Political Tribalism," in *Inventions and Boundaries: Historical and Anthropological Approaches to the Study of Ethnicity and*

Nationalism, ed. Preben Kaarsholm and Jan Hultin (Roskilde, Denmark: Roskilde University, 1994), 131–50; Spear, "Neo-Traditionalism"; and Thomas T. Spear and Richard D. Waller, eds., *Being Maasai: Ethnicity and Identity in East Africa* (London: James Currey, 1993). See also Terence O. Ranger, "The Invention of Tradition Revisited: The Case of Colonial Africa," in *Legitimacy and the State in Twentieth-Century Africa: Essays in Honour of A. H. M. Kirk-Greene*, ed. Terence O. Ranger and Olufemi Vaughan (London: Macmillan, 1993), 62–111.

25. Laura Fair, *Pastimes and Politics: Culture, Community, and Identity in Post-Abolition Urban Zanzibar, 1890–1945* (Athens: Ohio University Press, 2001); Gabrielle Lynch, *I Say to You: Ethnic Politics and the Kalenjin in Kenya* (Chicago: University of Chicago Press, 2011); and Myles Osborne, *Ethnicity and Empire in Kenya: Loyalty and Martial Race among the Kamba, c. 1800 to the Present* (New York: Cambridge University Press, 2014). Africanist scholars have also spilled much ink trying to explain the rise of the "ethnic state" in Africa, of which Kenya is often considered the paradigmatic example. See Daniel Branch, Nicholas Cheeseman, and Leigh Gardner, *Our Turn to Eat: Politics in Kenya since 1950* (Berlin: Lit Verlag, 2010). Studies of ethnic patronage and competition are often predicated on an idealized and normative view of democracy.

26. Nativist discourses in East Africa have always coexisted with cosmopolitan traditions born out of long histories of intermarriage, exchange, and migrancy. Julie MacArthur, *Cartography and the Political Imagination: Mapping Community in Colonial Kenya* (Athens: Ohio University Press, 2016). Derek Peterson's examination of the East African Revivalist movement also shows that there was more to African political life than the patrimonial system of ethnic patriotism. Peterson, *Ethnic Patriotism and the East African Revival: A History of Dissent, c. 1935–1971* (Cambridge: Cambridge University Press, 2012).

27. For more on the media's double standards regarding violence committed by Muslims and non-Muslims, see Mahmood Mamdani, *Good Muslim, Bad Muslim: America, the Cold War, and the Roots of Terror* (New York: Pantheon Books, 2004).

28. Roland Marchal, "Warlordism and Terrorism: How to Obscure an Already Confusing Crisis? The Case of Somalia," *International Affairs* 83, no. 6 (November 2007): 1091–1106, doi:10.1111/j.1468-2346.2007.00675.x.

29. Jeremy Scahill, "Blowback in Somalia: How US Proxy Wars Helped Create a Militant Islamist Threat," *Nation* 293, no. 13 (7 September 2011), http://www.thenation.com/article/163210/blowback-somalia?page=0,1; and Abdi Ismail Samatar, "The Nairobi Massacre and the Genealogy of the Tragedy," *Al-Jazeera* (26 September 2013), http://www.aljazeera.com/indepth/opinion/2013/09/nairobi-massacre-genealogy-tragedy-2013925121727642903.html.

30. Achille Mbembe, *On the Postcolony* (Berkeley: University of California Press, 2001), 8.

31. Paul Tiyambe Zeleza, "Building Intellectual Bridges: From African Studies and African American Studies to Africana Studies in the United States," *Afrika Focus* 24, no. 2 (2011): 13, http://www.gap.ugent.be/africafocus/pdf/2011vol24nr2_zeleza.pdf.

32. In his seminal text, *The Clash of Civilizations*, Samuel Huntington contests the once-popular assumption that liberal, secular democracy would be the only alternative in the wake of the Cold War. He argues instead that the major conflicts of the twenty-first century would occur between subnational "cultures" and supranational "civilizations." Huntington, *The Clash of Civilizations and the Remaking of World Order* (New York: Simon and Schuster, 1996).

33. Steven Feierman, "Colonizers, Scholars, and the Creation of Invisible Histories," in *Beyond the Cultural Turn: New Directions in the Study of Society and Culture*, ed. Victoria E. Bonnell and Lynn Avery Hunt (Berkeley: University of California Press, 1999), 206. There are notable exceptions to these scholarly trends. Intellectual historians of Africa, such as Sean Hanretta and Rudolph Ware, have advocated for writing African macrohistories grounded in wider geographic regions and longer time scales. Ware, *The Walking Qur'an: Islamic Education, Embodied Knowledge, and History in West Africa* (Chapel Hill: University of North Carolina Press, 2014); and Hanretta, *Islam and Social Change in French West Africa: History of an Emancipatory Community* (Cambridge: Cambridge University Press, 2009).

34. Talal Asad, *Genealogies of Religion: Discipline and Reasons of Power in Christianity and Islam* (Baltimore, MD: Johns Hopkins University Press, 1993), 8–9.

35. My arguments build upon the insights of Indian Ocean scholars who have challenged master narratives of Western expansionism. Critical thinkers such as Amitav Ghosh, Gwyn Campbell, Sugata Bose, and Engseng Ho have shown that the Indian Ocean was a space of intercultural exchange that bred religiously mediated forms of cosmopolitanism and universalism long before Europe's rise to dominance on the world stage. Ghosh, *In an Antique Land: History in the Guise of a Traveler's Tale* (New York: Vintage Books, 1994); Campbell, ed., *The Indian Ocean Rim: Southern Africa and Regional Co-Operation* (London: RoutledgeCurzon, 2003); Bose, *A Hundred Horizons: The Indian Ocean in the Age of Global Empire* (Cambridge, MA: Harvard University Press, 2006); and Ho, *The Graves of Tarim: Genealogy and Mobility across the Indian Ocean* (Berkeley: University of California Press, 2006). Much of this scholarship, however, has been beset by a certain romanticism and nostalgia for a more "tolerant" time (thus obscuring the history of slavery, exclusion, and chauvinism that also underpinned relations within the Indian Ocean world). In addition, this literature has tended to adopt an urban and elitist focus. See Hanley's critique of the use of cosmopolitanism in Middle East studies. Hanley, "Grieving Cosmopolitanism in Middle East Studies," *History Compass* 6, no. 5 (September 2008): 1346–67, doi:10.1111/j.1478-0542.2008.00545.x; and Jonathon Glassman, "Creole Nationalists and the Search for Nativist Authenticity in Twentieth-Century Zanzibar: The Limits of Cosmopolitanism," *Journal of African History* 55, no. 2 (July 2014): 229–47, doi:10.1017/S0021853714000024. Moreover, specialists on the Indian Ocean have often wrongly assumed that decolonization led to "the ossification of formerly flexible political allegiances." Felicitas Becker and Joel Cabrita, "Introduction: Performing Citizenship and Enacting Exclusion on Africa's Indian Ocean Littoral," *Journal of African History* 55, no. 2 (July 2014): 168, doi:10.1017/S0021853714000139. Far less attention has been paid to the ways in which these earlier configurations of sociality and polity survived at the margins after independence only to be revived in new ways in the post–Cold War era.

36. "Has the Dergue Had Its Day?" *Guardian*, 15 August 1977, 11.

37. Ali Jimale Ahmed, *Daybreak Is Near: Literature, Clans, and the Nation-State in Somalia* (Lawrenceville, NJ: Red Sea Press, 1996), 113. Similarly, Günther Schlee and Abdullahi A. Shongolo argue that modern nationalist accounts obscure the historical "impression that 'Somali' for many central and southern groups is a fairly recent label." Schlee and Shongolo, *Islam and Ethnicity in Northern Kenya and Southern Ethiopia* (London: James Currey, 2012), 27. My intention is not to dismiss the political and historical importance of Somali nationalism or devalue its relevance to contemporary debates over Somalia's future. Its mythico-history offers an important basis for unity,

especially at this historical juncture. Nevertheless, dominant definitions of *Somalinimo* have excluded certain minority groups and, like all forms of nationalism, are worthy of deconstruction.

38. Ioan M. Lewis, *A Pastoral Democracy: A Study of Pastoralism and Politics among the Northern Somali of the Horn of Africa* (London: Oxford University Press for the International African Institute, 1961); and Lewis, *Blood and Bone: The Call of Kinship in Somali Society* (Lawrenceville, NJ: Red Sea Press, 1994).

39. Catherine L. Besteman, *Unraveling Somalia: Race, Violence, and the Legacy of Slavery* (Philadelphia: University of Pennsylvania Press, 1999), 4.

40. Lidwien Kapteijns, "I. M. Lewis and Somali Clanship: A Critique," *Northeast African Studies* 11, no. 1 (2004): 1–23, http://www.jstor.org/stable/41960543; and Abdi Ismail Samatar, "Destruction of State and Society in Somalia: Beyond the Tribal Convention," *Journal of Modern African Studies* 30, no. 4 (December 1992): 625–41, doi:10.1017/S0022278X00011083. They are among several scholars who have questioned the assumption that the Somali civil war is attributable to ancient clan hatreds.

41. Jean-Loup Amselle, *Mestizo Logics: Anthropology of Identity in Africa and Elsewhere*, trans. Claudia Royal (Stanford, CA: Stanford University Press, 1998).

42. Lidwien Kapteijns, *Clan Cleansing in Somalia: The Ruinous Legacy of 1991* (Philadelphia: University of Pennsylvania Press, 2012), 75.

43. Kapteijns, "I. M. Lewis and Somali Clanship"; and Said S. Samatar, "Poetry in Somali Politics: The Case of Sayyid Mahammad 'Abdille Hasan" (PhD diss., Northwestern University, 1979), 191.

44. Abdi M. Kusow, "The Somali Origin: Myth or Reality," in *The Invention of Somalia*, ed. Ali Jimale Ahmed (Lawrenceville, NJ: Red Sea Press, 1995), 82.

45. Dominant definitions of Somaliness have tended to exclude certain populations. Occupational groups such as the Madhiban, who practice hunting and tanning; and the Tomal, whose hereditary profession is blacksmithing, have been marginalized by narratives that privilege ostensibly "noble" pastoral lineages. This is also true of members of the largely agricultural Rahanweyn, who typically trace their descent to the patriarch Sab. Focusing on patrilineal descent also obscures the importance of matrilineal genealogies. See Kusow, "Somali Origin," 81–106; Virginia Luling, *Somali Sultanate: The Geledi City-State over 150 Years* (London: Haan, 2002), 77–85; and Besteman, *Unraveling Somalia*.

46. One must fight against the tendency to reify clan, which should be understood as a relational and ongoing process rather than a fixed identity. Moreover, it is important to recognize the difficulty of assigning clear "ethnic" labels to large groups of people. Most of the Somalis recruited from Aden and British Somaliland identified as Isaaq, although a minority were members of the Dhulbahante and Warsangeli subclans of the Harti. It is likely that members of other clans and lineages came to identify as Isaaq (and/or Harti) as they journeyed alongside their fellow recruits and/or intermarried with their families. In addition, Harti Somalis from Kismayo also migrated into Kenya, where many settled in townships and took up the role of stockbrokers. Colonial officials also considered them to be "alien Somali." For more on the history of Somali migrants from Kismayo, see Lee V. Cassanelli, "The Opportunistic Economies of the Kenya-Somali Borderland in Historical Perspective," in *Borders and Borderlands as Resources in the Horn of Africa*, ed. Dereje Feyissa and Markus Virgil Hoehne (London: James Currey, 2010), 133–50; and Peter D. Little, *Somalia: Economy without State* (Oxford: James Currey, 2003), 26.

47. Technically the East Africa Protectorate until 1920.

48. For the purposes of the 2009 decennial national census, the Kenyan government used the term "Kenyan Somali," but did not assign a dual identity to the Luo, Maasai, or other communities that also stretch across national borders. Some Somalis rejected the appellation, which they argued set them apart from their fellow Kenyan citizens and made their nationality appear uniquely suspect.

49. Toni Morrison, *Playing in the Dark: Whiteness and the Literary Imagination* (Cambridge, MA: Harvard University Press, 1992), 47.

50. Virtually every community in Kenya is the product of migrations that took place over the past centuries, which to a certain extent casts the very idea of indigeneity into doubt. While first-comer status is at times an important political claim (especially in the context of settler colonialism), it can also become the basis of an exclusionary nativism. Thus, indigeneity is best understood as a political stance, rather than a natural or historical category.

51. See Mamdani, "Beyond Settler and Native."

52. Josue David Cisneros, *The Border Crossed Us: Rhetorics of Borders, Citizenship, and Latina/o Identity* (Tuscaloosa: University of Alabama Press, 2013).

53. Denise Natali, *The Kurds and the State: Evolving National Identity in Iraq, Turkey, and Iran* (Syracuse, NY: Syracuse University Press, 2005).

54. Godfrey Mwakikagile, *Relations between Africans and African Americans: Misconceptions, Myths and Realities* (Dar es Salaam: New Africa Press, 2007); and Emily Alice Katz, *Bringing Zion Home: Israel in American Jewish Culture, 1948–1967* (New York: State University of New York Press, 2015).

55. Comparisons can also be drawn between the northeastern and the coastal regions of Kenya. Coastal politics has also reflected the pull of separatist aspirations and wider regional and Islamic affiliations. See Justin Willis and George Gona, "Pwani C Kenya? Memory, Documents and Secessionist Politics in Coastal Kenya," *African Affairs* 112, no. 446 (2012): 48–71, doi: 10.1093/afraf/ads064.

56. Spear and Waller, *Being Maasai*; and Dawn Chatty, ed., *Nomadic Societies in the Middle East and North Africa: Entering the 21st Century* (Leiden: Brill, 2006).

57. Daniel D. C. Don Nanjira, *The Status of Aliens in East Africa: Asians and Europeans in Tanzania, Uganda, and Kenya* (New York: Praeger, 1976); Timothy H. Parsons, "'Kibra Is Our Blood': The Sudanese Military Legacy in Nairobi's Kibera Location, 1902–1968," *International Journal of African Historical Studies* 30, no. 1 (1997): 87–122, doi: 10.2307/221547; Samantha Balaton-Chrimes, "Counting as Citizens: Recognition of the Nubians in the 2009 Kenyan Census," *Ethnopolitics* 10, no. 2 (2011): 205–18, doi: 10.1080/17449057.2011.570983; and Thomas B. Hansen, *Melancholia of Freedom: Social Life in an Indian Township in South Africa* (Princeton, NJ: Princeton University Press, 2012).

58. Walter Benjamin, "Theses on the Philosophy of History," in *Illuminations*, trans. Harry Zohn, ed. Hannah Arendt (New York: Harcourt, Brace, 1968), 255.

59. Reinhart Koselleck, *Futures Past: On the Semantics of Historical Time*, trans. Keith Tribe (New York: Columbia University Press, 2004).

60. E. J. A. Musa, President of the British Shariff Ishak Community of Kenya Colony, to Colonial Secretary, AG/39/120, KNA.

61. My language is borrowed from Glassman, "Creole Nationalists," 246.

62. Thomas R. Metcalf, *Imperial Connections: India in the Indian Ocean Arena, 1860–1920* (Berkeley: University of California Press, 2007), 2.

63. Frederick Cooper, *Decolonization and African Society: The Labor Question in French and British Africa* (Cambridge: Cambridge University Press, 1996).

64. Glassman, *War of Words*; and Lee, *Unreasonable Histories*.

65. Partha Chatterjee, *The Nation and Its Fragments: Colonial and Postcolonial Histories* (Princeton, NJ: Princeton University Press, 1993).

66. John D. Kelly and Martha Kaplan, *Represented Communities: Fiji and World Decolonization* (Chicago: University of Chicago Press, 2001).

67. Douglas Howland and Luise White, eds., *The State of Sovereignty: Territories, Laws, Populations* (Bloomington: Indiana University Press, 2009).

68. Mburu, *Bandits on the Border*; and Hannah A. Whittaker, "The Socioeconomic Dynamics of the *Shifta* Conflict in Kenya, c. 1963–8," *Journal of African History* 53, no. 3 (2012): 391–408.

69. Gary Wilder, *Freedom Time: Negritude, Decolonization, and the Future of the World* (Durham, NC: Duke University Press, 2015), 16.

70. Peter D. Little, *Somalia: Economy without State* (Oxford: James Currey, 2003); and Nancy Fraser, *Scales of Justice: Reimagining Political Space in a Globalizing World* (New York: Columbia University Press, 2009), 135. Despite his questionable interpretations, Samuel Huntington recognized a significant trend in writing about the post–Cold War era. In recent decades, many communities have been thinking and mobilizing outside the bounds of the international state system, making conflicts over who "belongs" to the nation more pronounced. Huntington, *Clash of Civilizations*.

71. In many ways, the poststructuralist debunking of the nation-state and the celebration of cultural mobility have reproduced many dominant myths about globalization. Scholars such as Michael T. Taussig have depicted a world of cultural hybridity and border crossing. Michael Hardt and Antonio Negri, neo-Marxist scholars influenced by postmodern theory, argue that the next stage of capitalism is an amorphous phase known as "empire" of free-flowing labor and capital. The assumption that "local" cultures have recently been swept up in "global" forces emanating from the Western world continues to seduce many thinkers. Taussig, *Mimesis and Alterity: A Particular History of the Senses* (New York: Routledge, 1993); and Hardt and Negri, *Empire* (Cambridge, MA: Harvard University Press, 2000). As Akhil Gupta and James Ferguson note, these views "can wind up bearing a disturbing resemblance to a sort of recycled modernization theory" in which globalization simply becomes the next rung within the familiar progressive narrative. Gupta and Ferguson, *Culture, Power, Place*, 28. See also J. K. Gibson-Graham, "Beyond Global vs. Local: Economic Politics outside the Binary Frame," in *Geographies of Power: Placing Scale*, ed. Andrew Herod and Melissa W. Wright (Malden, MA: Blackwell, 2002), 25–60; Marwan M. Kraidy, *Hybridity, or the Cultural Logic of Globalization* (Philadelphia: Temple University Press, 2005); and Paul Tiyambe Zeleza, "Rewriting the African Diaspora: Beyond the Black Atlantic," *African Affairs* 104, no. 414 (January 2005): 35–68, http://www.jstor.org/stable/3518632.

72. In *Remotely Global*, Charles Piot argues that the Kabre, a group of cereal farmers in the West African savanna, are "as cosmopolitan as the metropole itself, if by cosmopolitanism we mean that people partake in a social life characterized by flux, uncertainty, encounters with difference, and the experience of processes of transculturation." Piot, *Remotely Global: Village Modernity in West Africa* (Chicago: University of Chicago Press, 1999), 23. While Piot is undoubtedly correct to challenge assumptions about African traditionalism and localism, he overlooks the fact that not all people experience the world as equally "borderless."

73. New patterns of migration and cultural flow and new technologies that allow for rapid, transcontinental exchange have upended older certainties that the world can be mapped into bounded and territorialized "cultures," nations, and ethnicities. Recognizing these trends, scholars such as Arjun Appadurai, Johannes Fabian, Liisa H. Malkki, Akhil Gupta, and James Ferguson have critiqued anthropology's older commitments to "ethnic" studies. They have also contributed to a growing body of literature that seeks to rethink commonplace assumptions that what is "African" (and what is distant from the metropolitan West more broadly) is inherently rooted, limited, and "local." Fabian, *Time and the Other: How Anthropology Makes Its Object* (New York: Columbia University Press, 1983); Appadurai, "Putting Hierarchy in Its Place," *Cultural Anthropology* 3, no. 1 (1988): 36–49, doi: 10.1525/can.1988.3.1.02a00040; Malkki, *Purity and Exile: Violence, Memory, and National Cosmology among Hutu Refugees in Tanzania* (Chicago: University of Chicago Press, 1995); and Gupta and Ferguson, eds., *Culture, Power, Place: Explorations in Critical Anthropology* (Durham, NC: Duke University Press, 1997). Increasingly, African historians are also focusing on the flow of commodities, people, and ideas across areas once thought of as bounded geographic and cultural zones. See Ghislaine Lydon, *On Trans-Saharan Trails: Islamic Law, Trade Networks, and Cross-Cultural Exchange in Nineteenth-Century Western Africa* (Cambridge: Cambridge University Press, 2009); Ralph A. Austen, *Trans-Saharan Africa in World History* (New York: Oxford University Press, 2010); and Peterson, *Ethnic Patriotism*.

74. Historians and political scientists are now more likely to express disillusionment with the African nation-state, which never enjoyed full sovereignty or equality within the international system and rarely lived up to the hopes and expectations of independence. See Michael Crowder, "Whose Dream Was It Anyway? Twenty-Five Years of African Independence," *African Affairs* 86, no. 342 (1987): 7–24, http://www.jstor.org/stable/722863; and Siba N'Zatioula Grovogui, *Sovereigns, Quasi Sovereigns, and Africans: Race and Self-Determination in International Law* (Minneapolis: University of Minnesota Press, 1996).

75. Scholars have long acknowledged that borders continue to remain relevant even in a putatively globalized era. However, as Adam M. McKeown argues, there is a tendency to view border controls as a vestige of a traditional past, rather than as a feature intrinsic to the modern era that developed in tandem with the rise of global mobility. McKeown, *Melancholy Order: Asian Migration and the Globalization of Borders* (New York: Columbia University Press, 2008). See also M. Anne Pitcher, *Transforming Mozambique: The Politics of Privatization, 1975–2000* (Cambridge: Cambridge University Press, 2002); and Brenda Chalfin, *Neoliberal Frontiers: An Ethnography of Sovereignty in West Africa* (Chicago: University of Chicago Press, 2010).

76. Malkki, *Purity and Exile*. Also see Mary Douglas, *Purity and Danger: An Analysis of Concepts of Pollution and Taboo* (New York: Praeger, 1966).

77. Asad, *Genealogies of Religion*, 8.

78. Quoted in Tristan McConnell, "Kenya: Where All Somalis Are Suspects?" *Global Post*, 4 November 2011, http://www.globalpost.com/dispatch/news/regions/africa/kenya/111102/kenya-somalia-al-shabaab-terrorism-discrimination.

79. Arjun Appadurai, *Fear of Small Numbers: An Essay on the Geography of Anger* (Durham, NC: Duke University Press, 2006); Peter Geschiere and Francis B. Nyamnjoh, "Capitalism and Autochthony: The Seesaw of Mobility and Belonging," *Public Culture* 12, no. 2 (2000): 423–52; and Jean Comaroff and John L. Comaroff,

"Alien-Nation: Zombies, Immigrants, and Millennial Capitalism," *South Atlantic Quarterly* 101, no. 4 (2002): 779–805.

80. George E. Marcus, *Ethnography through Thick and Thin* (Princeton, NJ: Princeton University Press, 1998). Scholarship on Kenya, however, has tended to remain wedded to the idea of ethnicity as central to African life. By focusing on the strategic, situational, and socially constructed nature of ethnicity, historians and anthropologists have challenged older scholarly assumptions that saw African societies as timeless and primordial. However, much of this work remains embedded within the traditional model of fieldwork. Bill Bravman, *Making Ethnic Ways: Communities and Their Transformations in Taita, Kenya, 1800–1950* (Portsmouth, NH: Heinemann, 1998); Lee Cronk, *From Mukogodo to Maasai: Ethnicity and Cultural Change in Kenya* (Boulder, CO: Westview Press, 2004); and Lynch, *I Say to You*.

81. Nancy Rose Hunt, *A Colonial Lexicon: Of Birth Ritual, Medicalization, and Mobility in the Congo* (Durham, NC: Duke University Press, 1999), 160.

82. Michel-Rolph Trouillot, *Silencing the Past: Power and the Production of History* (Boston: Beacon Press, 1995), 16.

83. Akhil Gupta and James Ferguson, "Discipline and Practice: 'The Field' as Site, Method, and Location in Anthropology," in *Anthropological Locations: Boundaries and Grounds of a Field Science*, ed. Akhil Gupta and James Ferguson (Berkeley: University of California Press, 1997), 1–46.

84. As Rena Lederman argues: "'The field' is not so much a place as it is a particular relation between oneself and others, involving a difficult combination of commitment and disengagement, relationship and separation." Lederman, "Pretexts for Ethnography: On Reading Fieldnotes," in *Fieldnotes: The Makings of Anthropology*, ed. Roger Sanjek (Ithaca, NY: Cornell University Press, 1990), 88.

85. Trouillot, *Silencing the Past*, 47.

86. See Susan Geiger, "What's So Feminist about Women's Oral History?" *Journal of Women's History* 2, no 1 (Spring 1990): 169–82; and Joan Sangster, "Telling Our Stories: Feminist Debates and the Use of Oral History," *Women's History Review* 3, no. 1 (1994): 5–28.

87. Carolyn Hamilton, *Terrific Majesty: The Powers of Shaka Zulu and the Limits of Historical Invention* (Cambridge, MA: Harvard University Press, 1998).

88. Hanretta, *Islam and Social Change*, 13.

89. According to Megan Vaughan, scholars often deny their authorial power and strategies of authentication through the trope of giving space to African "voices." Vaughan, "Reported Speech and Other Kinds of Testimony," in *African Words, African Voices: Critical Practices in Oral History*, eds. Luise White, Stephan F. Miescher, and David W. Cohen (Bloomington: Indiana University Press, 2001), 65–66.

90. White, Miescher, and Cohen, *African Words, African Voices*.

91. Erin Jessee, "The Limits of Oral History: Ethics and Methodology amid Highly Politicized Research Settings," *Oral History Review* 38, no. 2 (Summer–Fall 2011): 287–307, doi: 10.1093/ohr/ohr098.

92. Eve M. Troutt Powell, *A Different Shade of Colonialism: Egypt, Great Britain, and the Mastery of the Sudan* (Berkeley: University of California Press, 2003). See also Awet Tewelde Weldemichael, *Third World Colonialism and Strategies of Liberation: Eritrea and East Timor Compared* (Cambridge: Cambridge University Press, 2013).

93. See Hall, *History of Race*; Chouki El Hamel, *Black Morocco: A History of Slavery, Race, and Islam* (Cambridge: Cambridge University Press, 2013); and Glassman, *War of Words*.

94. Bethwell A. Ogot, "Britain's Gulag: Review of *Histories of the Hanged*, by David Anderson, and *Britain's Gulag*, by Caroline Elkins," *Journal of African History* 46, no. 3 (2005): 495, http://www.jstor.org/stable/4100642.

CHAPTER 1: "CARRYING THE HISTORY OF THE PROPHETS"

1. L. Aylmer, "The Country between the Juba River and Lake Rudolf," *Geographical Journal* 38, no. 3 (September 1911): 296, doi: 10.2307/1779043.

2. David Northrup, *Africa's Discovery of Europe: 1450–1850* (New York: Oxford University Press, 2002).

3. Richard Francis Burton, *First Footsteps in East Africa; or, An Exploration of Harar*, ed. Isabel Burton (New York: Dover Publications, 1987), 5–6.

4. Ibid., 72.

5. Jonathon Glassman, *War of Words, War of Stones: Racial Thought and Violence in Colonial Zanzibar* (Bloomington: Indiana University Press, 2011), 26; Derek Nurse and Thomas T. Spear, *The Swahili: Reconstructing the History and Language of an African Society, 800–1500* (Philadelphia: University of Pennsylvania Press, 1985), 70–79; and Scott Steven Reese, *Renewers of the Age: Holy Men and Social Discourse in Colonial Benaadir* (Leiden: Brill, 2008), 65–69.

6. Interview by author, Mukhtar Shaiye, Nanyuki, 23 October 2010.

7. "Long-term continuities in political language" can be the "outcome of radical social change." Steven Feierman, *Peasant Intellectuals: Anthropology and History in Tanzania* (Madison: University of Wisconsin Press, 1990), 3.

8. Nurse and Spear, *Swahili*, 4.

9. Mahmood Mamdani, *When Victims Become Killers: Colonialism, Nativism, and the Genocide in Rwanda* (Princeton, NJ: Princeton University Press, 2001), 16.

10. Talal Asad, *Formations of the Secular: Christianity, Islam, Modernity* (Stanford, CA: Stanford University Press, 2003), 197. According to Asad, the theological concept of the *umma* is not equivalent to a "society" capable of being mapped onto a territory, state, or delimited population.

11. Glassman, *War of Words*, 300.

12. Anthony Appiah, *Cosmopolitanism: Ethics in a World of Strangers* (New York: Norton, 2006), 2.

13. Marshall G. S. Hodgson, *The Venture of Islam*, vol. 3, *The Gunpowder Empires and Modern Times* (Chicago: University of Chicago Press, 1974).

14. Engseng Ho, *The Graves of Tarim: Genealogy and Mobility across the Indian Ocean* (Berkeley: University of California Press, 2006), xxi.

15. Appiah, *Cosmopolitanism*, xiv.

16. Abdul Sheriff, *Dhow Cultures of the Indian Ocean: Cosmopolitanism, Commerce and Islam* (New York: Columbia University Press, 2010); Ioan M. Lewis, *Blood and Bone: The Call of Kinship in Somali Society* (Lawrenceville, NJ: Red Sea Press, 1994); Marshall G. S Hodgson, *The Venture of Islam*, vol. 2, *The Expansion of Islam in the*

Middle Periods (Chicago: University of Chicago Press, 1974); Lee V. Cassanelli, *The Shaping of Somali Society: Reconstructing the History of a Pastoral People, 1600–1900* (Philadelphia: University of Pennsylvania Press, 1982); and Reese, *Renewers of the Age.*

17. Mohamed A. Eno and Abdi M. Kusow, "Racial and Caste Prejudice in Somalia," *Journal of Somali Studies* 1, no. 2 (2014): 91–118; and Rasheed Y. Farrah, "A Study of the Indigenous Minorities of Somaliland: Focus on Barriers to Education" (PhD diss., Alliant International University, 2013). The term "caste" should be used cautiously. The role and importance of marginalized occupational groups in Africa has been undertheorized, as has the applicability of the term "caste" to the continent.

18. Catherine L. Besteman, *Unraveling Somalia: Race, Violence, and the Legacy of Slavery* (Philadelphia: University of Pennsylvania Press, 1999).

19. In large swaths of East Africa, livestock owning was a marker of belonging and an important material and conceptual category against which dependency and exclusion were defined. See Jan Bender Shetler, *Imagining Serengeti: A History of Landscape Memory in Tanzania from Earliest Times to the Present* (Athens: Ohio University Press, 2007), 154; and David M. Anderson and Vigdis Broch-Due, eds., *The Poor Are Not Us: Poverty and Pastoralism in Eastern Africa* (Oxford: James Currey, 1999).

20. Faisal Devji, *Landscapes of the Jihad: Militancy, Morality, Modernity* (Ithaca, NY: Cornell University Press, 2005), 72.

21. E. R. Turton, "The Isaq Somali Diaspora and Poll-Tax Agitation in Kenya, 1936–41," *African Affairs* 73, no. 292 (July 1974): 325–46, http://www.jstor.org/stable/720811; The Secretariat, "The Position of Alien Somalis in Kenya Colony, Circulated to All Members of Executive Council," 25 April 1945, VQ/1/21, Kenya National Archives (KNA); interview by author, Hussein Nur, Nairobi, 14 October 2010; and interview by author, Farah Mohamed Awad, Nairobi, 12 October 2010.

22. Peter D. Little, *Somalia: Economy without State* (Oxford: James Currey, 2003), 26; Edmond J. Keller, *Revolutionary Ethiopia: From Empire to People's Republic* (Bloomington: Indiana University Press, 1988), 36–37; and R. G. Turnbull, "Some Notes on the History of the Degodia Up to 1912," September 1953, PC NFD/4/1/1, KNA.

23. Michel-Rolph Trouillot, *Silencing the Past: Power and the Production of History* (Boston: Beacon Press, 1995), 16.

24. As Jonathon Glassman points out, recent conflicts inform how "narratives of events understood to have befallen the ancestors of the ethnic group—are reinscribed as part of the personal experiences of significant numbers of ordinary people." Glassman, *War of Words,* 20.

25. Widespread continuities across different people's narratives and memories do not, however, always equate to facticity. See Alessandro Portelli, *The Order Has Been Carried Out: History, Memory, and Meaning of a Nazi Massacre in Rome* (New York: Palgrave Macmillan, 2003).

26. Rogers Brubaker, *Ethnicity without Groups* (Cambridge, MA: Harvard University Press, 2004), 172.

27. By stressing the fluidity and overlapping nature of clan and ethnic affiliations in northern Kenya, Schlee broke with anthropological convention. See Günther Schlee, *Identities on the Move: Clanship and Pastoralism in Northern Kenya* (Manchester: Manchester University Press, 1989); and Günther Schlee and Abdullahi A. Shongolo, *Pastoralism and Politics in Northern Kenya and Southern Ethiopia* (London: James Currey, 2012).

28. Günther Schlee, "Changing Alliances among the Boran, Garre and Gabra in Northern Kenya and Southern Ethiopia," in *Changing Identifications and Alliances in North-East Africa*, vol. 1, *Ethiopia and Kenya*, ed. Günther Schlee and Elizabeth E. Watson (New York: Berghahn Books, 2009), 203–23; "The Invasion of Jubaland," DC WAJ/3/2, KNA; interview by author, Mohammed Osman Urune, Wajir, 18 December 2010; and interview by author, Hussein Osman Khalid, Wajir, 21 April 2011.

29. Günther Schlee and Abdullahi A. Shongolo, *Islam and Ethnicity in Northern Kenya and Southern Ethiopia* (London: James Currey, 2012), 15, 19. The use of the Gramscian notion of hegemony is indicative of the influence of neo-Marxist thought on Kenyan scholarship.

30. Aylmer, "Country between the Juba River and Lake Rudolf"; Little, *Somalia*, 27–29; Besteman, *Unraveling Somalia*, 65–66; W. Keir, "Note on the Traditional History of Wajir Tribes," 25 January 1939, DC WAJ/3/2, KNA; M. R. Mahony, District Commissioner (DC) Bura, "District Record, Somalis: General Characteristic and Policy," 9 May 1929, DC/GRSSA/3/4 KNA; and H. B. Sharpe, "Additional Notes on Capt. Mahony's Memoranda," 1932, DC/GRSSA/3/4 KNA.

31. F. Elliott, "Jubaland and Its Inhabitants," *Geographical Journal* 41, no. 6 (June 1913): 559–60, doi: 10.2307/1778081.

32. Schlee, *Identities on the Move*, 42–43; and "Land Enquiry Commission: Memorandum Relating to Wajir District," PC NFD/4/2/3, KNA.

33. Bruno Latour, "Why Has Critique Run out of Steam? From Matters of Fact to Matters of Concern," *Critical Inquiry* 30, no. 2 (January 2004): 233–35, doi: 10.1086/421123.

34. Ibid., 246.

35. Interview by author, Ahmed Maalin Abdalle, Habasweyn, 17 July 2011.

36. Charles Eliot, *The East Africa Protectorate* (London: Arnold, 1905), 118, 233.

37. Interview by author, anonymous, Habasweyn, 16 July 2011.

38. Interview by author, Adan Ibrahim Ali, Wajir, 16 April 2011.

39. Though one could argue that he also reaffirmed Somali hegemony by subsuming various people within a Somali genealogical order.

40. See Luise White's discussion about historical "truth" and vernacular rumor. White, *Speaking with Vampires: Rumor and History in Colonial Africa* (Berkeley: University of California Press, 2000).

41. John L. Jackson Jr., *Thin Description: Ethnography and the African Hebrew Israelites of Jerusalem* (Cambridge, MA: Harvard University Press, 2013), 153.

42. Mamdani, *When Victims Become Killers*, 8.

43. Carolyn Hamilton, *Terrific Majesty: The Powers of Shaka Zulu and the Limits of Historical Invention* (Cambridge, MA: Harvard University Press, 1998), 28–30; and Sean Hanretta, *Islam and Social Change in French West Africa: History of an Emancipatory Community* (Cambridge: Cambridge University Press, 2009), 18–19.

44. Virginia Luling, *Somali Sultanate: The Geledi City-State over 150 Years* (London: Haan, 2002), 85.

45. Somali port cities provided Arab and European traders with access to cotton, sesame, and crops grown along the Juba and Shebelle. Somali caravans also brought aromatic woods, livestock, ivory, and slaves from the interior to the coast. By the 1870s, to protect these growing trade routes and ward off European encroachment, the Omani Sultanate began to increase its symbolic and military presence along the Benadir coast.

Cassanelli, *Shaping of Somali Society*, 150–54; and Roman Loimeier, *Muslim Societies in Africa: A Historical Anthropology* (Bloomington: Indiana University Press, 2013), 234.

46. Various forces hastened the spread of an Islamic and Somali identification. According to Catherine Besteman, many of the newly escaped slaves who arrived on the Juba in the 1890s, unlike previous ex-slave populations, had fewer connections to their East African roots, spoke the Af-maay dialect of Somali, adhered to Islam, and often used the Somali clan system as a template for their settlements. She argues that they furthered the spread of Islam in the region and encouraged agrarian groups to adopt dominant cultural features associated with Somali-speaking populations and Somali-identifying lineages. Besteman, *Unraveling Somalia*, 67. The Salahiyya, Ahmadiyya, and Qadiriyya brotherhoods also gained followers along the coast and interior during this era. Scott Reese argues that the "rise of the Sufi Orders in southern Somalia clearly provided merchants with new opportunities for contacts with the interior" and "lessened the social distance between rural and urban inhabitants by emphasizing the unity of *all* Somalis." Reese, "Patricians of the Benaadir: Islamic Learning, Commerce and Somali Urban Identity in the Nineteenth Century" (PhD diss., University of Pennsylvania, 1996), 343, 350. In addition, Sayyid Mohamed Abdullah Hassan and his followers, who waged a twenty-year war against Ethiopian, British, and Italian invaders, deployed Pan-Islamic idioms to incorporate Somalis from wide-ranging clans into their movement. The extent to which Muslim anticolonial resistance leaders, such as the Sayyid, can be considered proto-nationalist heroes is the subject of much scholarly debate. See Alexander De Waal, introduction to *Islamism and Its Enemies in the Horn of Africa* (Bloomington: Indiana University Press, 2004), 4; Devji, *Landscapes of the Jihad*, 34–35; and Hassan Mahaddala, "Pithless Nationalism: The Somali Case," in *Putting the Cart before the Horse: Contested Nationalism and the Crisis of the Nation-State in Somalia*, ed. Abdi Kusow (Trenton, NJ: Red Sea Press, 2004), 68–69.

47. Cassanelli, *Shaping of Somali Society*, 129.

48. Paul T. W. Baxter, "Social Organisation of the Boran of Northern Kenya," shortened version (PhD diss., Lincoln College, Oxford, 1954), 6, PC/NFD/4/1/1, KNA; H. B. Sharpe, "The Somali General History," January 1932, DC/GRSSA/3/4 KNA; M. R. Mahony, DC Bura, "District Record, Somalis: General Characteristic and Policy," 9 May 1929, DC/GRSSA/3/4 KNA; interview by author, Abdi Hassan, Nairobi, 25 January 2011; interview by author, Hussein Osman Khalid, Wajir, 21 April 2011; interview by author, Adan Hassan Baraki and Dekhow Abdi Ogle, Habasweyn, 16 July 2011.

49. "Land Enquiry Commission: Memorandum Relating to Wajir District," PC NFD/4/2/3, KNA.

50. Schlee notes that "this might have corresponded to genealogical truth only for a minority," although he does not address how "truth" itself is constituted in such a setting. Schlee, *Identities on the Move*, 39.

51. Richard D. Waller, "Ecology, Migration, and Expansion in East Africa," *African Affairs* 84, no. 336 (July 1985): 350, http://www.jstor.org/stable/723071.

52. Lidwien Kapteijns, "I. M. Lewis and Somali Clanship: A Critique," *Northeast African Studies* 11, no. 1 (2004): 3–4, http://www.jstor.org/stable/41960543.

53. Ali Jimale Ahmed, ed., *The Invention of Somalia* (Lawrenceville, NJ: Red Sea Press, 1995).

54. T. S. Thomas, *Jubaland and the Northern Frontier District* (Nairobi: Uganda Railway Press, 1917), 22, NFD 7/1/1, KNA.

55. Ibid., 22–24; and Ministry of Defence, "Raids and Border Incidents on the Borders of Kenya," July 1958, DC/ISO/2/5/4, KNA.

56. As Foucault notes, "sovereignty is basically inscribed and functions within a territory." Michel Foucault, *Security, Territory, Population: Lectures at the Collège de France 1977–1978*, ed. Michel Senellart, trans. Graham Burchell (Basingstoke: Palgrave Macmillan, 2007), 11.

57. Nene Mburu, *Bandits on the Border: The Last Frontier in the Search for Somali Unity* (Trenton, NJ: Red Sea Press, 2005), 26–37.

58. See Achille Mbembe, "At the Edge of the World: Boundaries, Territoriality, and Sovereignty in Africa," trans. Steven Rendall, *Public Culture* 12, no. 1 (Winter 2000): 259–84.

59. The Colonial Office hoped to establish an export-oriented economy that would bring raw materials, cash crops, and other commodities from the interior to the port of Mombasa on the Swahili coast, where British officials had already established lines of authority via the Omani Sultanate.

60. Later, the colonial government replaced this legislation with the Closed District and Special Districts Ordinances, which also restricted movement in and out of the NFD.

61. See Thomas, *Jubaland and the Northern Frontier District*, 23–24; Ministry of Defence, "Raids and Border Incidents on the Borders of Kenya," July 1958, DC/ISO/2/5/4, KNA; and Ahmed Issack Hassan, "Legal Impediments to Development in Northern Kenya," *Pambazuka News*, 22 October 2008, http://www.pambazuka.org/governance/legal-impediments-development-northern-kenya.

62. Ignatius N. Dracopoli, *Through Jubaland to the Lorian Swamp: An Adventurous Journey of Exploration* (London: Seeley, Service, 1914), 279.

63. 15 Parl Deb., H. L. (5th series) (30 April 1914): 1180–93.

64. Paul Carter, *The Road to Botany Bay: An Exploration of Landscape and History* (Minneapolis: University of Minnesota Press, 1987), 158.

65. George L. Simpson, "British Perspectives on Aulihan Somali Unrest in the East Africa Protectorate, 1915–18," *Northeast African Studies* 6, nos. 1–2 (1999): 9, doi: 10.1353/nas.2002.0005.

66. Thomas, *Jubaland and the Northern Frontier District*, 53, NFD 7/1/1, KNA.

67. Recognizing oral and written sources as "equal but distinct forms of recording the past" enables richer and more subversive analyses. White, *Speaking with Vampires*, 52.

68. Interview by author, Ahmed Maalin Abdalle, Habasweyn, 16 July 2011.

69. Reese, *Renewers of the Age*, 51.

70. Interview by author, Ladan Mohamed, Wajir, 25 May 2011.

71. Ho, *Graves of Tarim*; and Christine Choi Ahmed, "Finely Etched Chattel: The Invention of Somali Women," in Ahmed, *Invention of Somalia*, 157–89.

72. David W. Cohen, "Doing Social History from Pim's Doorway," in *Reliving the Past: The Worlds of Social History*, ed. Olivier Zunz (Chapel Hill: University of North Carolina Press, 1985), 194.

73. Ibid.

74. Interview by author, Ahmed Maalin Abdalle, Habasweyn, 16 July 2011; and Besteman, *Unraveling Somalia*, 570.

75. Interview by author, anonymous, Garissa, 26 November 2010. See reference to the "Tellemugger Ogaden Somali" in Great Britain and Kenya Land Commission, *Evidence and Memoranda* (London: Her Majesty's Stationary Office, 1934), 1558–61.

76. Abdi M. Kusow, "The Somali Origin: Myth or Reality," in Ahmed, *Invention of Somalia*, 82, 84–85; and PC JUB/1/10/7, KNA.

77. R. G. Turnbull, "The Impact on East Africa of the Galla and the Somali," September 1963, 6, PC NFD/4/1/1, KNA.

CHAPTER 2: "KENYA IS REGARDED BY THE
SOMALI AS AN EL DORADO"

1. Attorney General to Colonial Secretary, 31 May 1934, AG/39/120, KNA.

2. Sections of this chapter have appeared in: Keren Weitzberg, "Producing History from Elisions, Fragments, and Silences: Public Testimony, the Asiatic Poll-Tax Campaign, and the Isaaq Somali Population of Kenya," *Journal of Northeast African Studies* 13, no. 2 (2013): 177–205, doi: 10.14321/nortafristud.13.2.0177; and Weitzberg, "The Unaccountable Census: Colonial Enumeration and Its Implications for the Somali People of Kenya," *Journal of African History* 56, no. 3 (November 2015): 409–28, doi:10.1017/S002185371500033X.

3. Studies of other "liminal" populations, such as the Swahili, have tended to focus on reaffirming their indigenousness, rather than exploring their unique position within the colonial order. Derek Nurse and Thomas T. Spear, *The Swahili: Reconstructing the History and Language of an African Society, 800–1500* (Philadelphia: University of Pennsylvania Press, 1985).

4. For an example of Kenyan labor history, see Anthony Clayton and Donald C. Savage, *Government and Labour in Kenya, 1895–1963* (London: Cass, 1974).

5. Stephanie Jones, "Merchant-Kings and Everymen: Narratives of the South Asian Diaspora of East Africa," *Journal of Eastern African Studies* 1, no. 1 (2007): 16–33.

6. Thomas R. Metcalf, *Imperial Connections: India in the Indian Ocean Arena, 1860–1920* (Berkeley: University of California Press, 2007), 165–66.

7. E. R. Turton, "The Isaq Somali Diaspora and Poll-Tax Agitation in Kenya, 1936–41," *African Affairs* 73, no. 292 (July 1974): 325–46, http://www.jstor.org/stable/720811; The Secretariat, "The Position of Alien Somalis in Kenya Colony, Circulated to All Members of Executive Council," 25 April 1945, VQ/1/21, KNA; Peter D. Little, *Somalia: Economy without State* (Oxford: James Currey, 2003), 26; Lee V. Cassanelli, "The Opportunistic Economies of the Kenya-Somali Borderland in Historical Perspective," in *Borders and Borderlands as Resources in the Horn of Africa*, ed. Dereje Feyissa and Markus Virgil Hoehne (London: James Currey, 2010), 133–50; interview by author, anonymous, Wajir, 10 December 2010; interview by author, Omar Issa and Jama Warsame, Nairobi, 7 October 2010; interview by author, Ali Kabati, Thika, 31 October 2010; interview by author, Halima Warsame Abdalle and Sara Warsame Abdalle, Nakuru, 7 November 2010; and interview by author, Hassan Ahmed Warsame, Nairobi, 4 November 2010.

8. Interview by author, Mukhtar Shaiye (Shaaciye), Nanyuki, 23 October 2010; and Lord Delamere to Acting Colonial Secretary, "Somali Traders: Removal of from Laikipia," 19 August 1925, AG/19/122, KNA.

9. Isak Dinesen [Karen Blixen], *Out of Africa* (New York: Random House, 1938), 184–85.

10. Interview by author, Mohamed Jama Nur, Nairobi, 25 October 2010.

11. Godwin Rapando Murunga, "The Cosmopolitan Tradition and Fissures in

Segregationist Town Planning in Nairobi, 1915–23," *Journal of Eastern African Studies* 6, no. 3 (2012): 463–86.

12. Gavin N. Kitching, *Class and Economic Change in Kenya: The Making of an African Petite Bourgeoisie, 1905–1970* (New Haven, CT: Yale University Press, 1980), 212–13; and interview by author, Yusuf Yasin, Isiolo, 12 February 2011.

13. Interview by author, Hussein Nur and Abdullahi Ahmed, Nairobi, 18 October 2010; and interview by author, Hussein Nur, Nairobi, 14 October 2010.

14. Interview by author, Mukhtar Shaiye (Shaaciye), Nanyuki, 23 October 2010.

15. Janet McIntosh, *The Edge of Islam: Power, Personhood, and Ethnoreligious Boundaries on the Kenya Coast* (Durham, NC: Duke University Press, 2009), 57; and Laura Fair, *Pastimes and Politics: Culture, Community, and Identity in Post-Abolition Urban Zanzibar, 1890–1945* (Athens: Ohio University Press, 2001), 39.

16. Shapley and Schwartze to Chief Secretary of State for the Colonies, 10 October 1916, CO 533/171, TNA; "Report prepared for and on behalf of the Somalis resident in Nairobi relative to the Local Administration's projected removal of such villages," CO 533/171, TNA; Hannah A. Whittaker, "A New Model Village? Nairobi Development and the Somali Question in Kenya, c. 1915–17," *Northeast African Studies* 15, no. 2 (2015): 117–40; Luise White, *The Comforts of Home: Prostitution in Colonial Nairobi* (Chicago: University of Chicago Press, 1990), 47–48; Mahassin A. G. H. El-Safi, "The Position of 'Alien' Somalis in the East Africa Protectorate and Kenya Colony, 1916–1963," *Journal of African Studies* 8, no. 1 (1981): 39–45; and S. M. Kimani, "The Structure of Land Ownership in Nairobi," *Canadian Journal of African Studies* 6, no. 3 (1972): 395–96.

17. E. R. Turton, "Somali Resistance to Colonial Rule and the Development of Somali Political Activity in Kenya, 1893–1960," *Journal of African History* 13, no. 1 (1972): 129, http://www.jstor.org/stable/180970.

18. J. G. Hamilton Ross to Chief Native Commissioner, "Re: Status of Somalis," 11 March 1920, PC/NFD/4/1/6, KNA; and Chief Native Commissioner to all Provincial Commissioners, "Somali Exemption Ordinance 1919 and Liability of Non-Exempted Somalis for Payment of Native Poll Tax," 18 February 1920, PC/NFD/4/1/6, KNA.

19. Note B, 21 November 1930, CO 533/402/6, TNA.

20. Interview by author, Mohamed Ege Musa, 21 November 2010, Nairobi.

21. Interview by author, Abdirisaq Egal Mohamed, Nairobi, 11 October 2010. Unlike their Indian counterparts, however, they never acquired a representative in the Legislative Council until this right was made accessible to all Africans in the 1950s. Chief Native Commissioner to all Provincial Commissioners, "Somali Exemption Ordinance 1919 and the Somali exemption rules 1919," 2 February 1920, PC NFD 4/1/6, KNA; interview by author, Zeinab Sharif, Nairobi, 13 January 2011; and interview by author, Hassan Ahmed Warsame, Nairobi, 11 October 2010.

22. Carina E. Ray, *Crossing the Color Line: Race, Sex, and the Contested Politics of Colonialism in Ghana* (Athens: Ohio University Press, 2015), 10.

23. Mahmood Mamdani, *Citizen and Subject: Contemporary Africa and the Legacy of Late Colonialism* (Princeton, NJ: Princeton University Press, 1996), 18–19.

24. Mahmood Mamdani, *Define and Rule: Native as Political Identity* (Cambridge, MA: Harvard University Press, 2012).

25. James R. Brennan, *Taifa: Making Nation and Race in Urban Tanzania* (Athens: Ohio University Press, 2012), 24–25; and Christopher Joon-Hai Lee, "The 'Native' Undefined: Colonial Categories, Anglo-African Status and the Politics of Kinship in

British Central Africa, 1929–38," *Journal of African History* 46, no. 3 (November 2005): 464, doi:10.1017/S0021853705000861.

26. Turton, "Somali Resistance," 131.

27. H. W. B. Blackall, Ag. Crown Counsel to Chief Native Commissioner, "Re: Status of Somalis," 3 April 1920, PC/Coast/1/3/162, KNA.

28. Ibid.

29. Ibid.

30. PC Nyeri to Chief Native Commissioner, "Tax due by Somalis," 17 March 1920, PC NFD/4/1/6, KNA.

31. Benedict R. O'G. Anderson, *Imagined Communities: Reflections on the Origin and Spread of Nationalism*, rev. ed. (London: Verso, 2006), 170.

32. Homi K. Bhabha, *The Location of Culture* (London: Routledge, 1994).

33. Talal Asad, *Genealogies of Religion: Discipline and Reasons of Power in Christianity and Islam* (Baltimore, MD: Johns Hopkins University Press, 1993), 17.

34. James Brennan argues that colonial officials were aware of the inadequacy of the term "native," especially for "manifestly ambiguous cases like the Swahili, Somali, and Arabs." Brennan, *Taifa*, 24.

35. Jonathon Glassman, *War of Words, War of Stones: Racial Thought and Violence in Colonial Zanzibar* (Bloomington: Indiana University Press, 2011), 8. See also Bruce S. Hall, *A History of Race in Muslim West Africa, 1600–1960* (Cambridge: Cambridge University Press, 2011).

36. See Ann Laura Stoler's argument that cultural racism is a colonial, rather than a postmodern, phenomenon. Stoler, *Carnal Knowledge and Imperial Power: Race and the Intimate in Colonial Rule* (Berkeley: University of California Press, 2002), 17.

37. Dinesen, *Out of Africa*, 175.

38. Interview by author, Farah Mohamed Awad, Nairobi, 12 October 2010; and interview by author, Amina Kinsi, Nairobi, 21 October 2010.

39. Ngũgĩ wa Thiong'o once described *Out of Africa* as "one of the most dangerous books ever written about Africa. . . . The racism in the book is catching, because it is persuasively put forward as love. But it is the love of a man for a horse or for a pet." Thiong'o, *Moving the Centre: The Struggle for Cultural Freedoms* (London: James Currey, 1993), 133.

40. Carolyn Hamilton, *Terrific Majesty: The Powers of Shaka Zulu and the Limits of Historical Invention* (Cambridge, MA: Harvard University Press, 1998), 27–28.

41. Dinesen, *Out of Africa*, 178.

42. Ibid.

43. Blixen described Somali marriage in terms that naturalized racial hierarchies: "A man may marry beneath him . . . and young Somalis have been known to take Masai wives. But while a Somali girl may marry into Arabia, an Arab girl cannot marry into Somaliland, for the Arabs are the superior race on account of their nearer relationship with the Prophet and, amongst the Arabs themselves, a maiden belonging to the Prophet's family cannot marry a husband outside it." Dinesen, *Out of Africa*, 178. Blixen reified Somali custom and glossed over the patriarchal aspects of these marital practices, which she interpreted through a Western racial lens.

44. Engseng Ho, *The Graves of Tarim: Genealogy and Mobility across the Indian Ocean* (Berkeley: University of California Press, 2006), 153.

45. Most scholars agree that marital practices among Muslims in Africa tended to reinforce patriarchy and Arab hegemony. However, to what extent these

genealogical practices were fairly assimilative and inclusive of black populations and to what extent they were exclusive and racialized is a matter of ongoing debate. See Chouki El Hamel's disagreement with Ali Mazrui. El Hamel, *Black Morocco: A History of Slavery, Race, and Islam* (Cambridge: Cambridge University Press, 2013), 94–97.

46. Dinesen, *Out of Africa*, 12.

47. Jonathan M. Marks, *What It Means to Be 98% Chimpanzee: Apes, People, and Their Genes* (Berkeley: University of California Press, 2002), 67.

48. Interview by author, anonymous, Isiolo, 3 February 2011.

49. Sir Charles Dundas, Governor of Uganda, to Oliver Stanley, Secretary of State for Colonies, 13 April 1943, CO/536/209/8, TNA.

50. Stoler, *Carnal Knowledge*.

51. Interview by author, Farah Mohamed Awad, Nairobi, 12 October 2010.

52. Robin Cohen, *Global Diasporas: An Introduction* (London: Routledge, 2008), 166.

53. Interview by author, Zeinab Sharif, Nairobi, 13 January 2011.

54. E-mail Correspondence, Abdi Adan Suleiman, "Fw: How Do Isaaq Community Benefit from the New Constitutional Dispensation?" 7 December 2010.

55. Interview by author, Duthi Jama, Isiolo, 3 February 2011.

56. Interview by author, Mohamed Ege Musa, Nairobi, 21 November 2010.

57. Interview by author, anonymous, Nairobi, 14 October 2010.

58. Interview by author, Amina Kinsi, Nairobi, 21 October 2010.

59. James Clifford, *The Predicament of Culture: Twentieth-Century Ethnography, Literature, and Art* (Cambridge, MA: Harvard University Press, 1988), 12; emphasis in original.

60. Ninna Nyberg Sørensen, "Migration, Development and Conflict," in *Globalizing Migration Regimes: New Challenges to Transnational Cooperation*, ed. Kristof Tamas and Joakim Palme (Aldershot: Ashgate, 2006), 87; and Turton, "Isaq Somali Diaspora," 325–26.

61. The Queen's Proclamation of 1858, which announced British sovereignty over India, declared that "all shall alike enjoy the equal and impartial protection of the Law." Though rarely observed in practice, this declaration of equality among subjects of the British Crown became an important rallying cry for Indian and later African political thinkers. Sukanya Banerjee, *Becoming Imperial Citizens: Indians in the Late-Victorian Empire* (Durham, NC: Duke University Press, 2010), 22.

62. Kathleen Paul, *Whitewashing Britain: Race and Citizenship in the Postwar Era* (Ithaca, NY: Cornell University Press, 1997), 113. See also Ann Dummett and Andrew G. L. Nicol, *Subjects, Citizens, Aliens and Others: Nationality and Immigration Law* (London: Weidenfeld and Nicolson, 1990), 167–69; and Laura Tabili, *"We Ask for British Justice": Workers and Racial Difference in Late Imperial Britain* (Ithaca, NY: Cornell University Press, 1994).

63. Hannah Arendt, *Essays in Understanding, 1930–1954: Formation, Exile, and Totalitarianism*, ed. Jerome Kohn (New York: Harcourt, Brace, 1994).

64. Edward W. Said, *Orientalism* (New York: Vintage Books, 1979).

65. Mae M. Ngai, *Impossible Subjects: Illegal Aliens and the Making of Modern America* (Princeton, NJ: Princeton University Press, 2004), 5, 2. Ngai uses the expression to describe immigrants in modern America, but I have reappropriated it for use in this obviously different context.

66. Racialized citizen-strangers were thus not an anomalous feature of British life, but rather a product of the imperial nation-state. Colonialism was not incidental to European nationalism; rather, fundamental aspects of Western political life were developed in and through overseas empire. See Gary Wilder, *The French Imperial Nation-State: Negritude and Colonial Humanism between the Two World Wars* (Chicago: University of Chicago Press, 2005).

67. Edward Grigg, Governor of Kenya, to Lord Passfield, Secretary of State for the Colonies, 15 September 1930, CO 533/402/6, TNA.

68. Harold Kittermaster to Lord Passfield, Secretary of State for the Colonies, 10 September 1930, CO 533/402/6, TNA.

69. Jeremy Prestholdt, "Kenya, the United States, and Counterterrorism," *Africa Today* 57, no. 4 (Summer 2011): 6.

70. "Population of Colony and Protectorate of Kenya: Machakos, North Nyeri, and Meru," PC/CP/8/3/11, KNA.

71. Michael E. Bonine, Abbas Amanat, and Michael Ezekiel Gasper, eds., *Is There a Middle East? The Evolution of a Geopolitical Concept* (Stanford, CA: Stanford University Press, 2012).

72. Brennan, *Taifa*, 20.

73. Turton, "Isaq Somali Diaspora," 327.

74. Attorney General to Colonial Secretary, 31 May 1934, AG/39/120, KNA.

75. Lee, "Native Undefined," 464.

76. "Return of Jubaland to Kenya: Brief Statement of the Problem," CO 822/2011, TNA; and Jennifer Hyndman, *Managing Displacement: Refugees and the Politics of Humanitarianism* (Minneapolis: University of Minnesota Press, 2000), 44–45.

77. For another look at settler colonial constructions of the "frontier," see Amy Kaplan, *The Anarchy of Empire in the Making of U.S. Culture* (Cambridge, MA: Harvard University Press, 2002).

78. Achille Mbembe, "The Power of the Archive and Its Limits," in *Refiguring the Archive*, ed. Carolyn Hamilton et al. (Cape Town: David Philip, 2002), 19–26; and Steven Feierman, "Colonizers, Scholars, and the Creation of Invisible Histories," in *Beyond the Cultural Turn: New Directions in the Study of Society and Culture*, ed. Victoria E. Bonnell and Lynn Avery Hunt (Berkeley: University of California Press, 1999), 192–93. According to Sean Hanretta, Walter Benjamin's injunction to read documents "against the grain" is more than a matter of "reading between the lines." Hanretta, *Islam and Social Change in French West Africa: History of an Emancipatory Community* (Cambridge: Cambridge University Press, 2009), 15. Historians, he argues, must be attentive to the multiple forms of authorship that shape the production of written records and the ways in which the archives themselves construct certain objects of knowledge (23, 123).

79. Talal Asad, *Formations of the Secular: Christianity, Islam, Modernity* (Stanford, CA: Stanford University Press, 2003).

80. Feierman, "Colonizers, Scholars, and the Creation of Invisible Histories," 182–216.

81. M. R. Mahony, DC of Bura, "District Record, Somalis: General Characteristic and Policy," 9 May 1929, DC/GRSSA/3/4 KNA.

82. Ibid.

83. For example, local officials kept a close eye on Sheikh Abdurrahman bin Sayyid Muhammad Abdullah, the son of the late Sayyid Muhammad Abdullah Hassan

(pejoratively known as the "Mad Mullah"), when he arrived in Wajir in the early 1920s. The officer in charge also relied on him to help resolve a dispute by promoting religious orthodoxy. NFD Annual Report, 1923, PC NFD/1/5/1, KNA; and Wajir District Annual Report, 1923, PC NFD/1/5/1, KNA.

84. Silences can indicate many things: a comparative lack of power; active repression; strategic disengagement; disregard; or an inability to grasp alternative lifeworlds. The much-fetishized injunction to "listen to silences" requires a humility toward what can be known and an awareness of the dangers of bolstering one's own authorial power. Luise White, *Speaking with Vampires: Rumor and History in Colonial Africa* (Berkeley: University of California Press, 2000), 75.

85. Lieut.-Colonel R. H. Smith, *The Tribes of British Somaliland* (Aden: Caxton Press, 1941), DC/ISO/2/4/3, KNA.

86. M. R. Mahony, DC Bura, "District Record, Somalis: General Characteristic and Policy," 9 May 1929, DC/GRSSA/3/4 KNA.

87. Conversation with author, Hassan Kochore, Nairobi, 20 October 2010.

88. F. G. Jennings, Wajir District Annual Report, 1932, 2, PC NFD/1/5/2, KNA; and Saadia Touval, *Somali Nationalism: International Politics and the Drive for Unity in the Horn of Africa* (Cambridge, MA: Harvard University Press, 1963), 68.

89. See Timothy H. Parsons, "Being Kikuyu in Meru: Challenging the Tribal Geography of Colonial Kenya," *Journal of African History* 53, no. 1 (March 2012): 65–86, doi:10.1017/S0021853712000023.

90. Liisa H. Malkki, "National Geographic: The Rooting of Peoples and the Territorialization of National Identity among Scholars and Refugees," *Cultural Anthropology* 7, no. 1 (February 1992): 31, doi: 10.1525/can.1992.7.1.02a00030.

91. Interview by author, Ali Hassan, Nairobi, 3 November 2010; and F. G. Jennings, Wajir District Annual Report, 1932, PC NFD/1/5/2, KNA.

92. Interview by author, anonymous, Wajir, 18 May 2011.

93. Cassanelli, "Opportunistic Economies."

94. F. G. Jennings, Wajir District Annual Report, 1930, 4, PC NFD/1/5/2, KNA.

95. James C. Scott, *Seeing like a State: How Certain Schemes to Improve the Human Condition Have Failed* (New Haven, CT: Yale University Press, 1998), 2–3.

96. F. G. Jennings, Wajir District Annual Report, 1930, 2, PC NFD 1/5/2, KNA; and Günther Schlee, "Territorializing Ethnicity: The Imposition of a Model of Statehood on Pastoralists in Northern Kenya and Southern Ethiopia," *Ethnic and Racial Studies* 36, no. 5 (2013): 860, doi:10.1080/01419870.2011.626058.

97. For another example of "hybrid" forms of governance and layered sovereignties on the borderlands of African states, see Anne Walraet, "State-Making and Emerging Complexes of Power and Accumulation in the Southern Sudan-Kenyan Border Area: The Rise of a Thriving Cross-Border Business Network," in *The Borderlands of South Sudan: Authority and Identity in Contemporary and Historical Perspectives*, ed. Christopher Vaughan, Mareike Schomerus, and Lotje de Vries (New York: Palgrave Macmillan, 2013), 173–92.

98. Jeffrey Herbst, *States and Power in Africa: Comparative Lessons in Authority and Control* (Princeton, NJ: Princeton University Press, 2000), 3.

99. Darshan Vigneswaran and Joel Quirk, eds., *Mobility Makes States: Migration and Power in Africa* (Philadelphia: University of Pennsylvania Press, 2015).

100. The neo-Marxist critique of the colonial migrant labor system remains as relevant as ever. In the 1970s and 1980s, scholars called into question the dual society

model that viewed the "tribal" and "modern" as distinct spheres. They argued instead that the urban colonial economy was predicated upon the exploitation of African rural migrants and that migration between urban and rural areas was an intrinsic feature of the colonial capitalist mode of production. See, for example, Ian R. Phimister and Charles van Onselen, eds., *Studies in the History of African Mine Labour in Colonial Zimbabwe* (Gwelo: Mambo Press, 1978).

101. C. F. G. Doran, Crown Counsel for Attorney General, to Superintendent, Suburban areas, "Re: Eastleigh Rates," 21 February 1927, AG/43/9, KNA; Godwin R. Murunga, "Refugees at Home? Coping with Somalia Conflict in Nairobi, Kenya," in *African Studies in Geography from Below*, ed. Michel Ben Arrous and Lazare Ki-Zerbo (Dakar: CODESRIA, 2009), 213–14; and interview by author, Mohamed Ege Musa, Nairobi, 21 November 2010.

102. This system allowed the colonial state to shift the burden of labor reproduction onto rural areas and onto the backs of African women. Jane L. Parpart and Kathleen A. Staudt, eds., *Women and the State in Africa* (Boulder, CO: Rienner, 1989).

103. White, *Comforts of Home*, 97.

104. Interview by author, Hussein Mohamed Jama, Isiolo, 11 February 2011.

105. Colonial officials believed, as one PC explained, that "nomads should remain nomads." Peter T. Dalleo, "Trade and Pastoralism: Economic Factors in the History of the Somali of Northeastern Kenya, 1892–1948" (PhD diss., Syracuse University, 1975): 128, http://surface.syr.edu/hst_etd/52. Dalleo is quoting from "Minutes of DC's Meetings," 29/31 December 1941, PC NFD/8/1/2, KNA.

106. One colonial official wrote: "It is difficult to resist the feeling that this stock is kept within bounds which favour, under cover of quarantine regulations, the European stock owner as against the native stock owner." Northern Frontier Province Annual Report, 1931, 26–27, PC NFD/1/1/4, KNA.

107. Richard D. Waller, "'Clean' and 'Dirty': Cattle Disease and Control Policy in Colonial Kenya, 1900–40," *Journal of African History* 45, no. 1 (2004): 54. See also Attorney General to Chief Secretary, 1 February 1913, AG/19/128, KNA.

108. Interview by author, Mukhtar Shaiye (Shaaciye), Nanyuki, 23 October 2010; conversation with author, Mohamed Ibrahim, Nanyuki, 23 October 2010; and Peter T. Dalleo, "The Somali Role in Organized Poaching in Northeastern Kenya, c. 1909–1939," *International Journal of African Historical Studies* 12, no. 3 (1 January 1979): 472–82.

109. The Secretariat, "The Position of Alien Somalis in Kenya Colony, Circulated to All Members of Executive Council," 25 April 1945, VQ/1/21, KNA.

110. Kitching, *Class and Economic Change in Kenya*, 213–14.

111. Resident Commissioner, J. A. G. Elliott, to Colonial Secretary, "Removal of Somalis from Laikipia," 5 July 1924, AG/19/122, KNA.

112. The Secretariat, "The Position of Alien Somalis in Kenya Colony, Circulated to All Members of Executive Council," 25 April 1945, VQ/1/21, KNA.

113. Interview by author, Abdullahi Elmi and Hassan Good (with Hassan Guled), Isiolo, 11 February 2011; and Great Britain, *Report of the Kenya Land Commission, September 1933* (London: Her Majesty's Stationery Office, 1934), 239. Administrators also briefly considered allowing other "detribalized" populations, such as the Nubians, Arabs, and Swahili, to relocate to the area. PC NFP to Ag. Chief Native Commissioner, "Sale of Land to Somalis, Nubians, and Detribalised Natives," 14 May 1929, PC/NFD/4/1/6, KNA.

114. Hon. P. Rurumban on behalf of the Samburu tribe to the Northern Province Commission, 1962, CO 896/1 TNA.

115. DC Isiolo to Ag. PC NFP, 6 July 1930, DC ISO 3/6/26, KNA.

116. Great Britain, *Report of the Kenya Land Commission*, 224.

117. Gerald Reece to Chief Secretary, 9 November 1939, AG/39/120, KNA.

118. Interview by author, Abdullahi Elmi and Hassan Good, Isiolo, 11 February 2011.

119. Saafo Roba Boye and Randi Kaarhus, "Competing Claims and Contested Boundaries: Legitimating Land Rights in Isiolo District, Northern Kenya," *Africa Spectrum* 46, no. 2 (2011): 99, http://www.jstor.org/stable/41336256.

120. Interview by author, Hassan Ahmed Warsame, Nairobi, 11 October 2010; and interview by author, Abdi Adan Suleiman, Nairobi, 22 October 2010.

121. Stephanie Chasin, "Citizens of Empire: Jews in the Service of the British Empire, 1906–1940" (PhD diss., University of California, Los Angeles, 2008), 31.

122. Lee, "Native Undefined."

123. Humayun Ansari, *"The Infidel Within": Muslims in Britain since 1800* (London: Hurst, 2004), 110–11.

124. Lt. Abdullah Cardell-Ryan to Principal Secretary of State for the Colonies, 27 August 1930, CO 535/91/10, TNA.

125. Ibid.

126. Many of my interviewees self-identified as "British Somalis." See also Henry Muoria, *Writing for Kenya: The Life and Works of Henry Muoria*, ed. Wangari Muoria-Sal, Bodil Folke Frederiksen, John Lonsdale, and Derek Peterson (Leiden: Brill, 2009), 343; and Tabili, "We Ask for British Justice," 11–12.

127. A. Majid to Under-Secretary of State for the Colonies, 14 September 1934, CO 535/105, TNA. See also The British Somali Society to the Secretary of State for the Colonies, 1934, CO/535/105, TNA.

128. Ansari, "Infidel Within," 97, 136.

129. For more on the political mobilization of coastal Arab and Swahili populations, see A. I. Salim, "Native or Non-Native? The Problem of Identity and Social Stratification of the Arab-Swahili of Kenya," in *History and Social Change in East Africa*, ed. Bethwell A. Ogot (Nairobi: East African Literature Bureau, 1976), 65–85.

130. Members of the Ishaak Shariff Community, "Petition: His Most Gracious and Imperial Majesty King George the Fifth," 14 July 1930, National Archives (UK), CO 533/402/6.

131. Representatives of the "Issak Sheriff Community, Arabs," to Governor of Kenya, "RE: Hospital Accommodation-Native Civil Hospital," 4 May 1932, CO 533/425/7, TNA.

132. Kenya, *Official Gazette of the Colony and Protectorate of Kenya (Special Issue)* 38, no. 49 (Nairobi: Government Printer, 3 October 1936), 949.

133. Abdi Ahmed, Secretary of British Ishak Community, to the Secretary of State for the Colonies, 10 April 1937, CO 533/180/5, TNA.

134. A. de V. Wade, Colonial Secretary, to Secretariat, 26 April 1938, PC/SP 6/1/2, KNA.

135. Gerald Reece, Officer-in-Charge Northern Frontier, to Commissioner of Police, 9 November 1939, AG/39/120, KNA.

136. R. G. Turnbull, DC Isiolo, to Officer-in-Charge, Northern Frontier, 1 November 1939, AG/39/120, KNA.

137. Hall, *History of Race*, 9.

138. Sir Charles Dundas, Governor of Uganda, to Oliver Stanley, Secretary of State for Colonies, 13 April 1943, CO/536/209/8, TNA.

139. The Asiatic campaign sparked tensions between the Isaaq and the Harti populations. Only a year into the campaign, the Darot Somali Welfare Association in Nairobi wrote to the colonial government declaring their intention to pay the twenty-shilling tax. One can surmise why the leaders of this organization abandoned thoughts of joining the poll-tax campaign. The adoption of the term "Darod"—a much wider lineage to which both Harti and other clans in the NFD belonged—hints at the fact that definitions of lineage were being hotly contested during this period. The Darot Somali Welfare Association to the Colonial Secretary, 27 April 1938, AG/39/120, KNA.

140. E. J. A. Musa, President of the British Shariff Ishak Community of Kenya Colony, to Colonial Secretary, AG/39/120, KNA.

141. Christopher Joon-Hai Lee, *Unreasonable Histories: Nativism, Multiracial Lives, and the Genealogical Imagination in British Africa* (Durham, NC: Duke University Press, 2014), 4.

142. For a review of this vast literature, see Thomas T. Spear, "Neo-Traditionalism and the Limits of Invention in British Colonial Africa," *Journal of African History* 44, no. 1 (2003): 3–27, doi:10.1017/S0021853702008320. Some scholars argue that colonial rule reified and hardened previously fluid and permeable ethnic identities.

143. Mary Louise Pratt, *Imperial Eyes: Travel Writing and Transculturation*, 2nd ed. (New York: Routledge, 2008), 9.

144. Hall, *History of Race*, 20; and Rogers Brubaker, *Ethnicity without Groups* (Cambridge, MA: Harvard University Press, 2004).

145. Gerald Reece, Officer-in-Charge, NFD, to Chief Secretary, 14 September 1943, PC/SP 6/1/2, KNA.

146. Anthony Appiah, *In My Father's House: Africa in the Philosophy of Culture* (New York: Oxford University Press, 1993), 175. See also McIntosh, *Edge of Islam*, 57.

147. Asad, *Formations of the Secular*, 223.

148. Clifford, *Predicament of Culture*, 340.

149. James Brennan and Jonathon Glassman are critical of scholarly tendencies to frame ethnic formation solely in terms of rational choice and straightforward material gain. Brennan, *Taifa*, 12; and Glassman, *War of Words*, 14.

150. Jane Burbank and Frederick Cooper, *Empires in World History: Power and the Politics of Difference* (Princeton, NJ: Princeton University Press, 2010).

151. James G. Ferguson, *Global Shadows: Africa in the Neoliberal World Order* (Durham, NC: Duke University Press, 2006), 167.

152. Mamdani, *Citizen and Subject*, 19.

153. Shapley, Schwartze, and Barret to the Colonial Secretary, 5 March 1938, AG/39/120, KNA; and Ege Musa, President of the Ishakia Association, to High Commissioner and Commander-in-Chief of British Somaliland, 16 November 1938, CO 533/506/3, TNA.

154. Jama Mohamed, "The 1944 Somaliland Camel Corps Mutiny and Popular Politics," *History Workshop Journal*, no. 50 (Autumn 2000): 104.

155. Ibid., 104–5; and Ege Musa, President of the Ishakia Association, to High Commissioner and Commander-in-Chief of British Somaliland, 16 November 1938, CO 533/506/3 TNA.

156. Turton, "Isaq Somali Diaspora," 330.

157. Ibid., 331; CO 535/129/4, TNA; and Anthony Olden, "Somali Opposition to Government Education: R. E. Ellison and the Berbera School Affair, 1938–1940," *History of Education* 37, no. 1 (2007): 71–90, doi: 10.1080/00467600701352331.

158. The debate over a Somali script has a long and complex history in Somalia. See David D. Laitin, *Politics, Language, and Thought: The Somali Experience* (Chicago: University of Chicago Press, 1977).

159. Interview by author, anonymous, Isiolo, 11 February 2011.

160. Interview by author, Ali Bule, Garissa, 25 November 2010.

161. For more on Islamic schooling, see Rudolph T. Ware III, *The Walking Qur'an: Islamic Education, Embodied Knowledge, and History in West Africa* (Chapel Hill: University of North Carolina Press, 2014); Louis Brenner, *Controlling Knowledge: Religion, Power, and Schooling in a West African Muslim Society* (Bloomington: Indiana University Press, 2001); and Roman Loimeier, *Between Social Skills and Marketable Skills: The Politics of Islamic Education in 20th Century Zanzibar* (Leiden: Brill, 2009).

162. Haji Farah Omar to Governor and Commander-in-Chief, Somaliland Protectorate, 9 June 1938, CO 535/129/4, TNA; and Abdi Ismail Samatar, *The State and Rural Transformation in Northern Somalia, 1884–1986* (Madison: University of Wisconsin Press, 1989), 49.

163. R. E. Ellison, Superintendent of Education, to Secretary of Government, 14 July 1938, CO 535/129/4, TNA.

164. Haji Farah Omar to Governor and Commander-in-Chief, Somaliland Protectorate, 9 June 1938.

165. Governor's Office of Somaliland Protectorate to Malcolm J. MacDonald, Secretary of State for the Colonies, 2 August 1938, CO 535/129/4, TNA; and "Extract from a Newspaper Entitled 'Al Shabab,'" CO 535/129/4, TNA.

166. Asad, *Formations of the Secular*, 197.

167. A. de V. Wade, Colonial Secretary, to Secretariat, 26 April 1938, PC/SP 6/1/2, KNA.

168. "Objects of the Somali Registration Bill," AG/39/120, KNA.

169. Ibid.

170. Gerald Reece, Office-in-Charge, NFD, to Chief Secretary, 6 February 1941, AG/39/120, KNA.

171. Ibid. See also P. Wyn Harris, Officer-in-Charge of Native Intelligence, "Note on the Status and Control of Somalis in Kenya Colony in Time of War," 24 October 1940, AG/39/120, KNA.

172. Attorney General to the Chief Secretary, 27 January 1940, AG/39/120, KNA; and "The Defence (Northern Frontier District) Regulations (1941)," in Kenya, *The Official Gazette of the Colony and Protectorate of Kenya* 43, no. 24 (Nairobi: Government Printer, 3 June 1941), 169, AG/39/120, KNA.

173. Gerald Reece to G. M. Rennie, Chief Secretary, 16 January 1940, AG/39/120, KNA.

174. Turton, "Isaq Somali Diaspora," 345.

1. Gerald Reece, Officer-in-Charge, NFD, to DCs NFD, "Control of Grazing Areas," 23 July 1945, 1–2, DC/MDA/5/1, KNA.

2. Frederick Cooper, "Modernizing Bureaucrats, Backward Africans, and the Development Concept," in *International Development and the Social Sciences: Essays on the History and Politics of Knowledge,* ed. Frederick Cooper and Randall Packard (Berkeley: University of California Press, 1997), 70.

3. Sections of this chapter have appeared in Keren Weitzberg, "Producing History from Elisions, Fragments, and Silences: Public Testimony, the Asiatic Poll-Tax Campaign, and the Isaaq Somali Population of Kenya," *Journal of Northeast African Studies* 13, no. 2 (2013): 177–205, doi: 10.14321/nortafristud.13.2.0177; and Weitzberg, "The Unaccountable Census: Colonial Enumeration and Its Implications for the Somali People of Kenya," *Journal of African History* 56, no. 3 (November 2015): 409–28, doi:10.1017/S002185371500033X.

4. Frederick Cooper, *Decolonization and African Society: The Labor Question in French and British Africa* (Cambridge: Cambridge University Press, 1996), 65–73.

5. This new outlook, which glorified the role of the "expert," reflected an emerging techno-optimistic view of government intervention. Joseph Morgan Hodge, *Triumph of the Expert: Agrarian Doctrines of Development and the Legacies of British Colonialism* (Athens: Ohio University Press, 2007); and Peter J. Taylor, *Technocratic Optimism, H. T. Odum, and the Partial Transformation of Ecological Metaphor after World War II* (Dordrecht: Reidel, 1988).

6. William M. Hailey, *An African Survey: A Study of Problems Arising in Africa South of the Sahara* (London: Oxford University Press, 1957), 721.

7. Gerald Reece, Officer-in-Charge, NFD, to Attorney General, "Crown Lands Ordinance," 11 May 1939, DC ISO 3/6/26, KNA.

8. Gerald Reece, Office-in-Charge, NFD, to Asst. Superintendent-in-Charge of the Northern Frontier Police, 3 May 1939, DC ISO/2/3/9 KNA; and S. E. Ellis, DC, Isiolo, to PC NP, 8 October 1948, DC ISO/2/3/9 KNA.

9. Interview by author, anonymous, Wajir, 19 December 2010; and interview by author, anonymous, Wajir, 8 December 2010.

10. Teresa Barnes, "Virgin Territory? Travel and Migration by African Women in Twentieth-Century Southern Africa," in *Women in African Colonial Histories,* ed. Jean Allman, Susan Geiger, and Nakanyike Musisi (Bloomington: Indiana University Press, 2002), 164–90.

11. S. I. Ellis, DC, Isiolo, to PC, NP, "Native Leasehold Area," 8 October 1948, DC ISO/3/6/26.

12. Hodge, *Triumph of the Expert,* 178.

13. Gerald Reece, Officer-in-Charge, NFD, to Chief Secretary, "Alien Somali Settlement Scheme," 12 March 1940, 6, DC ISO 3/6/26, KNA.

14. DC Isiolo to Officer-in-Charge, NFD, "Settlement of Alien Somalis," 19 August 1940, DC ISO/3/6/26, KNA; R. J. C. Howes, DC, Isiolo, to Officer-in-Charge, NFP, "Somali Settlement Scheme—Isiolo," 15 August 1941, DC ISO/3/6/26, KNA; and DC Meru to DC Isiolo, "RE: Isiolo Trade Centre and Somali Settlement at Isiolo," 27 April 1943, VQ 1/21, KNA.

15. T. G. Askwith, DC Isiolo, to Officer-in-Charge, NFD, "Alien Somalis," 17 June 1942, DC ISO 3/6/26, KNA.

16. T. G. Askwith, DC Isiolo, to Officer-in-Charge, NFD, "Somali Settlement," 16 April 1943, DC ISO 3/6/26, KNA.

17. D. C. Edwards, Senior Agricultural Officer (Pasture Research), "Report on the Grazing Areas of the Northern Frontier District of Kenya," 20 November 1943, PC NFD 5/5/1, KNA.

18. Gerald Reece, Officer-in-Charge, NFD, to DCs, NFD, "Control of Grazing Areas," 23 July 1945, 1–2, DC/MDA/5/1, KNA.

19. James E. Ellis and David M. Swift, "Stability of African Pastoral Ecosystems: Alternate Paradigms and Implications for Development," *Journal of Range Management* 41, no. 6 (November 1988): 451, https://journals.uair.arizona.edu/index.php/jrm/article/viewFile/8307/7919.

20. Ibid., 453. See also Elliot M. Fratkin and Eric A. Roth, eds., *As Pastoralists Settle: Social, Health, and Economic Consequences of Pastoral Sedentarization in Marsabit District, Kenya* (New York: Kluwer, 2005).

21. R. Frank Dixey, "Hydrographical Survey of the Northern Frontier District, Kenya," 1944, PC NFD/5/2/8, KNA.

22. Colony and Protectorate of Kenya, "Unlawful Occupation of Crown Land Sections 133 and 144 Chapter 140 Laws of Kenya," *Circular to Magistrates* no. 13 (1939), DC ISO 3/6/26, KNA; and The Secretariat to all members of the Executive Council, "The Position of Alien Somalis in Kenya Colony," 25 April 1945, 5, AG 39/120, KNA.

23. Timothy H. Parsons, "'Kibra Is Our Blood': The Sudanese Military Legacy in Nairobi's Kibera Location, 1902–1968," *International Journal of African Historical Studies* 30, no. 1 (1997): 87–122, doi: 10.2307/221547.

24. Mohamed Farah et al. to the Chief Secretary, 20 December 1943, AG 39/120, KNA. See also DC, Isiolo, to Officer-in-Charge, NFD, 19 April 1943, DC ISO/3/6/26, KNA.

25. Gregory Mann, *Native Sons: West African Veterans and France in the Twentieth Century* (Durham, NC: Duke University Press, 2006), 6.

26. Interview by author, Amina Kinsi, Nairobi, 21 October 2010.

27. Interview by author, Hussein Nur and Abdullahi Ahmed, Nairobi, 18 October 2010.

28. Interview by author, Adan Ibrahim Ali, Wajir, 16 April 2011.

29. Gerald Reece to Chief Secretary, 9 November 1939, AG/39/120, KNA.

30. R. J. C. Howes, DC, Isiolo, to Officer-in-Charge, NFD, "Somali Settlement Scheme-Isiolo," 15 August 1941, 3, DC ISO 3/6/26, KNA.

31. Letter to the DC, Kericho, 21 August 1939, PC/NYZ/3/15/105.

32. The Secretariat, "The Position of Alien Somalis in Kenya Colony, Circulated to All Members of Executive Council," 25 April 1945, VQ/1/21, KNA.

33. Mohamed I. Farah, *From Ethnic Response to Clan Identity: A Study of State Penetration among the Somali Nomadic Pastoral Society of Northeastern Kenya* (Uppsala: Academiae Ubsaliensis, 1993), 49. See also D. C. Edwards, Senior Agricultural Officer (Pasture Research), Report on the Grazing Areas of the Northern Frontier District of Kenya, 20 November 1943, PC NFD/5/5/1, KNA.

34. Gavin N. Kitching, *Class and Economic Change in Kenya: The Making of an African Petite Bourgeoisie, 1905–1970* (New Haven, CT: Yale University Press, 1980), 233.

35. Ibid., 234–35; and Hailey, *African Survey*, 883.

36. Secretariat, "The Position of Alien Somalis in Kenya Colony, Circulated to All Members of Executive Council," 25 April 1945, VQ/1/21, KNA.

37. Ibid.

38. Interview by author, anonymous, Nairobi, 21 November 2010.

39. Leif Manger, *The Hadrami Diaspora: Community-Building on the Indian Ocean Rim* (New York: Berghahn Books, 2010), 88–90.

40. Peter T. Dalleo, "Trade and Pastoralism: Economic Factors in the History of the Somali of Northeastern Kenya, 1892–1948" (PhD diss., Syracuse University, 1975), 183, http://surface.syr.edu/hst_etd/52.

41. Kitching, *Class and Economic Change in Kenya*, 234–35.

42. For more on the colonial state's impact on pastoral marketing systems, see Peter D. Little, *The Elusive Granary: Herder, Farmer, and State in Northern Kenya* (Cambridge: Cambridge University Press, 1992).

43. "Northern Frontier District Policy," July 1945, AG 39/120, KNA.

44. E. S. Atieno Odhiambo, "The Formative Years, 1945–55," in *Decolonization and Independence in Kenya, 1940–93*, ed. Bethwell A. Ogot and William R. Ochieng' (Athens: Ohio University Press, 1995), 27–29, 34–37.

45. Frederick Cooper, *Africa since 1940: The Past of the Present* (Cambridge: Cambridge University Press, 2006), 91.

46. Akhil Gupta, "The Song of the Nonaligned World: Transnational Identities and the Reinscription of Space in Late Capitalism," *Cultural Anthropology* 7, no. 1 (February 1992): 71.

47. Samuel Weber, *Benjamin's-abilities* (Cambridge, MA: Harvard University Press, 2008), 133; and Walter Benjamin, *The Origin of German Tragic Drama*, trans. John Osborne (London: Verso, 1998).

48. Abdi M. Kusow, preface to *Putting the Cart before the Horse: Contested Nationalism and the Crisis of the Nation-State in Somalia* (Trenton, NJ: Red Sea Press, 2004), xiv; italics in original. The notion of Somalia as a natural and homogeneous nation pervades much of the scholarly literature prior to the 1990s. See, for example, David D. Laitin and Said S. Samatar, *Somalia: Nation in Search of a State* (Boulder, CO: Westview Press, 1987).

49. See Ali Jimale Ahmed, ed., *The Invention of Somalia* (Lawrenceville, NJ: Red Sea Press, 1995); and Hussein Mohamed Adam and Richard Ford, eds., *Mending Rips in the Sky: Options for Somali Communities in the 21st Century* (Lawrenceville, NJ: Red Sea Press, 1997).

50. Ahmed Ismail Samatar, *Socialist Somalia: Rhetoric and Reality* (London: Zed Books, 1988), 44. See also H. A. Ibrahim, "Politics and Nationalism in North-East Africa, 1919–35," in *General History of Africa*, vol. 7, *Africa under Colonial Domination, 1880–1935*, ed. A. Adu Boahen (Paris: UNESCO, 1985), 600.

51. Timothy Mitchell, *Carbon Democracy: Political Power in the Age of Oil* (London: Verso, 2011), 67–72.

52. In many respects, we can speak about a precolonial Somali "nationalism" that long predated the imposition of the nation-state model. One must be conscientious, however, of that which defies translation (in this case, that which resists the particular Eurocentric histories modifying the concept of nationalism). Dipesh Chakrabarty, *Provincializing Europe: Postcolonial Thought and Historical Difference* (Princeton, NJ: Princeton University Press: 2000), xiv.

53. The agreement with the Ethiopian regime negated the terms of an earlier set of treaties, in which the British government had promised Somaliland elders "never to cede, sell, mortgage, or otherwise give for occupation . . . any portion of the territory

presently inhabited by them, or being under their control." H. A. Ibrahim, "African Initiatives and Resistance in North-East Africa," in Boahen, *General History of Africa*, vol. 7, *Africa under Colonial Domination*, 83; and Jama Mohamed, "Imperial Policies and Nationalism in the Decolonization of Somaliland, 1954–1960," *English Historical Review* 117, no. 474 (November 2002): 1177–1203.

54. As Awet Tewelde Weldemichael argues, African liberation movements were aligned not only against European rule, but also against internal forms of "secondary colonialism." Weldemichael, *Third World Colonialism and Strategies of Liberation: Eritrea and East Timor Compared* (Cambridge: Cambridge University Press, 2013), 8.

55. Abdullah A. Mohamoud, *State Collapse and Post-Conflict Development in Africa: The Case of Somalia (1960–2001)* (West Lafayette, IN: Purdue University Press, 2006), 75–76. See also Saadia Touval, *Somali Nationalism: International Politics and the Drive for Unity in the Horn of Africa* (Cambridge, MA: Harvard University Press, 1963); and John G. S. Drysdale, *The Somali Dispute* (London: Pall Mall, 1964).

56. Yarimar Bonilla, *Non-Sovereign Futures: French Caribbean Politics in the Wake of Disenchantment* (Chicago: University of Chicago Press, 2015), 10.

57. Ali Sheikhdon et. al. to Chief Secretary, 3 May 1943, PC EST 2/1/57, KNA.

58. Ibid.

59. Gerald Reece, Officer-in-Charge, NFD, to Chief Secretary, "Ege Musa and the Isaak Somalis," 17 May 1943, PC EST 2/1/57, KNA.

60. Chakrabarty, *Provincializing Europe*, 51.

61. Interview by author, anonymous, Nairobi, 14 October 2010.

62. Hussein Ali Dualeh, *From Barre to Aideed: Somalia; The Agony of a Nation* (Nairobi: Stellagraphics, 1994), 68; and John Kamau, "Hassan, the Mysterious Somali Trader Who Funded Mau Mau Fighters," *Daily Nation*, 9 April 2017.

63. Henry Muoria, *Writing for Kenya: The Life and Works of Henry Muoria*, ed. Wangari Muoria-Sal, Bodil Folke Frederiksen, John Lonsdale, and Derek Peterson (Leiden: Brill, 2009), 343.

64. Ibid., 343.

65. Ibid., 386.

66. Anthony Appiah, *In My Father's House: Africa in the Philosophy of Culture* (New York: Oxford University Press, 1993), 180.

67. Pan-Africanism in West Africa has received comparatively more attention than in East Africa. See J. Ayodele Langley, *Pan-Africanism and Nationalism in West Africa, 1900–1945: A Study in Ideology and Social Classes* (Oxford: Clarendon Press, 1973); Michael C. Lambert, "From Citizenship to Négritude: 'Making a Difference' in Elite Ideologies of Colonized Francophone West Africa," *Comparative Studies in Society and History* 35, no. 2 (1993): 239–62, http://www.jstor.org/stable/179399; and Toyin Falola, *Nationalism and African Intellectuals* (Rochester, NY: University of Rochester Press, 2001).

68. For more on the variants of Pan-Africanism, see Sabelo J. Ndlovu-Gatsheni, *Empire, Global Coloniality and African Subjectivity* (New York: Berghahn Books, 2013), 60–62, 123.

69. Timothy Parsons notes that Kibera's Sudanese soldiers, who had "called themselves Sudanese to emphasize their claims to non-native status and military patronage," then "switched to the label Nubi after independence in order to portray themselves as an indigenous Kenyan ethnic group." Parsons, "Kibra Is Our Blood," 88. As I have mentioned earlier, we must be wary not to see such shifts in identification through a purely instrumentalist framework.

70. Jama Mohamed, "The 1944 Somaliland Camel Corps Mutiny and Popular Politics," *History Workshop Journal*, no. 50 (Autumn 2000): 94–95.

71. Conversation with author, Mohamed Ibrahim, Nanyuki, 23 October 2010.

72. Gabrielle Lynch, "The Fruits of Perception: 'Ethnic Politics' and the Case of Kenya's Constitutional Referendum," *African Studies* 65, no. 2 (2006): 238.

73. Michel Foucault, *Security, Territory, Population: Lectures at the Collège de France 1977–1978*, ed. Michel Senellart, trans. Graham Burchell (Basingstoke: Palgrave Macmillan, 2009).

74. "Chief's Meeting," 4 January 1949, DC WAJ 2/1/4, KNA; "Meeting of Chiefs," 24 December 1949, DC WAJ 2/1/4, KNA; interview by author, Abdisalat Abdille, Kotulo, 1 June 2011; interview by author, Saman Ali Adan and Abbas Adan Amin Osman, Wajir, 6 April 2011; and Günther Schlee, "Territorializing Ethnicity: The Imposition of a Model of Statehood on Pastoralists in Northern Kenya and Southern Ethiopia," *Ethnic and Racial Studies* 36, no. 5 (2013): 859, doi:10.1080/01419870.201 1.626058.

75. Interview by author, Abbas Adan Amin Osman and Saman Ali Adan, Wajir, 6 April, 2011.

76. Interview by author, Mohammed Sheikh Abdullahi, Wajir, 10 April 2010.

77. Cedric Barnes, "U dhashay—Ku dhashay: Genealogical and Territorial Discourse in Somali History," *Social Identities* 12, no. 4 (2006): 487–98.

78. Interview by author, Abdisalat Abdille, Kotulo, 1 June 2011.

79. "Minutes of Chiefs' and Headmen's Meeting Held at Wajir," 25 January 1948, DC WAJ 2/1/4, KNA.

80. For a reappraisal of James C. Scott's concept of legibility, see Andrew S. Mathews, *Instituting Nature: Authority, Expertise, and Power in Mexican Forests* (Cambridge, MA: MIT Press, 2011), 15.

81. Northern Frontier Province Annual Report, 1951, 2, PC NFD 1/1/10, KNA.

82. Interview by author, anonymous, Wajir, 2 April 2011.

83. Interview by author, Birik Mohamed, Kotulo, 4 June 2011.

84. Interview by author, Mohammed Sheikh Abdullahi, Wajir, 10 April 2010.

85. Godwin Rapando Murunga, "Conflict in Somalia and Crime in Kenya: Understanding the Trans-Territoriality of Crime," *African and Asian Studies* 4, nos. 1–2 (March 2005): 150, doi:10.1163/1569209054547319.

86. See also R. G. Turnbull to J. W. Cusack, Northern Province Handing Over Report, March 1953, PC NFD 2/1/4, KNA.

87. These are names of places in Wajir District.

88. Interview by author, anonymous, Wajir, 8 April 2010.

89. Peter D. Little, *Somalia: Economy without State* (Oxford: James Currey, 2003), 171.

90. NP Annual Report, 1947, 4–5, PC NFD/1/1/9, KNA.

91. W. B. G. Raynor to G. W. Smyth-Osbourne, Wajir Handing Over Report, June 1951, DC/WAJ/20, KNA; and S. I. Ellis to R. G. Brayne-Nicholls, Handing Over Report: Isiolo District, August 1952, DC ISO/2/2, KNA.

92. Interview by author, Ali Hassan, Nairobi, 5 November 2010; and interview by author, anonymous, Kotulo, 5 June 2011.

93. Gerald Reece, PC, NFD, to Chief Secretary, 10 March 1948, PC/GRSSA/2/14/11, KNA; and Ag. PC, NP, to the Member for Law and Order, "Special District Ordinance," 10 July 1948, PC/GRSSA/2/14/11.

94. Interview by author, anonymous, Kotulo, 5 June 2011; and interview by author, Mohamed Hujale Jilaow, Nairobi, 1 November 2010.

95. As Gavin N. Kitching notes, there is even some evidence that "the attempts by the Meat Marketing Board to operate a cattle purchasing monopoly" increased "the growth in support for the Somali Youth League." Kitching, *Class and Economic Change in Kenya*, 235. For an analysis of the growth in popularity of Somali nationalism among predominantly nomadic populations in Ethiopia, see John Markakis, *Ethiopia: The Last Two Frontiers* (London: James Currey, 2011), 143–46.

96. Christopher Clapham, "Boundary and Territory in the Horn of Africa," in *African Boundaries: Barriers, Conduits and Opportunities*, ed. Paul Nugent and A. I. Asijawu (London: Pinter, 1996), 240.

97. Mr. Desmond O'Hagan to Mr. R. G. Turnbull, Northern Province Handing Over Report, June 1951, 3, PC NFD/2/1/4, KNA.

98. Ibid.

99. W. B. G. Raynor to G. W. Smyth-Osbourne, Wajir Handing Over Report, June 1951, DC WAJ/20, KNA.

100. NFP Annual Report, 1951, PC/NFD/1/1/10, KNA.

101. G. O. Krhoda, "The Hydrology and Function of Wetlands," in *Wetlands of Kenya: Proceedings of the KWWG Seminar on Wetlands of Kenya, 3–5 July 1991*, ed. S. A. Crafter, S. G. Njuguna, and G. W. Howard (Gland, Switzerland: IUCN, 1992), 21.

102. Farah, *From Ethnic Response to Clan Identity*, 133.

103. Ibid.

104. Interview by author, Ali Hassan, Nairobi, 3 November 2010.

105. Nancy Rose Hunt, *A Colonial Lexicon: Of Birth Ritual, Medicalization, and Mobility in the Congo* (Durham, NC: Duke University Press, 1999).

106. First built in the 1930s, the canning factory was a means for the colonial government to funnel African livestock through a specially segregated market, which prevented them from competing with white ranchers. Philip L. Raikes, *Livestock Development and Policy in East Africa* (Uppsala: Scandinavian Institute of African Studies, 1981), 119; and Robert L. Tignor, "Kamba Political Protest: The Destocking Controversy of 1938," *African Historical Studies* 4, no. 2 (1971): 24142, doi: 10.2307/216416.

107. PC, NP, to DC, Isiolo, "Petition from Isaak and Herti Somalis," 27 October 1950, DC ISO/3/6/26, KNA; DC, Isiolo, to Isaak and Herti Somalis, 1 November 1950, DC ISO/3/6/26, KNA; DC, Isiolo, to PC, NP, "Petition from Isaak and Herti Somalis," 17 November 1950, DC ISO/3/6/26, KNA; and DC, Isiolo, to PC, NP, "Petition from the United Somali Association," 27 February 1951, DC ISO/3/6/26, KNA.

108. "Report of the Committee Set Up to Consider the Problems of the Somali Settlements at Gilgil and Naivasha," CO/822/819, TNA (appended to: The All Muslim Association of Naivasha and Gilgil to the Secretary of State for the Colonies, 27 October 1955).

109. Jan Bender Shetler, *Imagining Serengeti: A History of Landscape Memory in Tanzania from Earliest Times to the Present* (Athens: Ohio University Press, 2007); and Kevin C. Dunn, "Environmental Security, Spatial Preservation, and State Sovereignty in Central Africa," in *The State of Sovereignty: Territories, Laws, Populations*, ed. Douglas Howland and Luise White (Bloomington: Indiana University Press, 2009), 222–42.

110. Interview by author, Mohamed Ege Musa, Nairobi, 21 November 2010. Some Somalis in Eastleigh served as mechanics. Interview by author, Amina Kinsi, Nairobi, 21 October 2010.

111. Sana Aiyar, *Indians in Kenya: The Politics of Diaspora* (Cambridge, MA: Harvard University Press, 2015), 9.

112. H.E. Mr. Turnbull's Speech at Opening of Nairobi Somali Primary School, 11 January 1958, GH/1/54, KNA; "African Muslim School, Nairobi" (appended to: Director of Education to Private Secretary, Government House, Nairobi, 7 January 1958) GH/1/54, KNA; "Report of the Committee Set Up to Consider the Problems of the Somali Settlements at Gilgil and Naivasha" (appended to: The All Muslim Association of Naivasha and Gilgil to the Secretary of State for the Colonies, 27 October 1955) CO/822/819, TNA; and Mohamed Farah, Secretary of United Somali Association, to Director of Education, "Proposed Intermediate Somali School in Naivasha," AV/12/380 KNA.

113. Speech by Mr. Bille Issa, 11 January 1958, GH/1/54, KNA.

114. Interview by author, anonymous, Wajir, 19 December 2010.

115. "New Somali School at Naivasha," *Kenya News* no. 841 (21 August 1957), CO 822/1855 TNA.

116. Sean Hanretta, *Islam and Social Change in French West Africa: History of an Emancipatory Community* (Cambridge: Cambridge University Press, 2009), 273.

117. Waruhiu Itote, *"Mau Mau" General* (Nairobi: East African Publishing House, 1967), 48.

118. Salah Abdi Sheikh, *Blood on the Runway: The Wagalla Massacre of 1984* (Nairobi: Northern Publishing House, 2007), 95.

119. Interview by author, Ahmed Ali Farah and Jon Bøhmer, Nairobi, 1 November 2010.

120. Interview by author, Ali Kabati and Jon Bøhmer, Thika, 31 October 2010.

121. Bethwell A. Ogot, "Britain's Gulag: Review of *Histories of the Hanged*, by David Anderson, and *Britain's Gulag*, by Caroline Elkins," *Journal of African History* 46, no. 3 (2005): 493–505, http://www.jstor.org/stable/4100642.

122. Michel-Rolph Trouillot, *Silencing the Past: Power and the Production of History* (Boston: Beacon Press, 1995), 13.

123. Interview by author, Ahmed Ali Farah and Jon Bøhmer, Nairobi, 1 November 2010.

124. Interview by author, Yusuf Yasin, Isiolo, 12 February 2011.

125. Interview by author, Mohamed Ibrahim, Nairobi, 20 October 2010.

126. Andrew Arsan, *Interlopers of Empire: The Lebanese Diaspora in Colonial French West Africa* (New York: Oxford University Press, 2014), 255.

CHAPTER 4: "THE FATTENED SHE-CAMEL HAS BEEN SNATCHED BY THE HYENA"

1. Somalia Ministry of Information, *British Public Opinion on the Northern Frontier District* (Mogadishu: Ministry of Information, May 1963), 12.

2. Sections of this chapter have appeared in: Keren Weitzberg, "Rethinking the *Shifta* War Fifty Years after Independence: Myth, Memory, and Marginalization," in *Kenya after Fifty: Reconfiguring Historical, Political, and Policy Milestones*, ed. Michael Mwenda Kithinji, Mickie Mwanzia Koster, and Jerono P. Rotich (New York: Palgrave Macmillan, 2016), 65–81.

3. Samuel Moyn, "Fantasies of Federalism," *Dissent* 62, no. 1 (Winter 2015): 145–51, https://www.dissentmagazine.org/article/fantasies-of-federalism.

4. As Jonathon Glassman argues, colonial subjects did not make claims exclusively in "the language of territorial nation-states"; their efforts "also reflected the pull of extra-territorial and universalist allegiances." Glassman, "Creole Nationalists and the Search for Nativist Authenticity in Twentieth-Century Zanzibar: The Limits of Cosmopolitanism," *Journal of African History* 55, no. 2 (July 2014): 246, doi:10.1017/S0021853714000024.

5. Engseng Ho, *The Graves of Tarim: Genealogy and Mobility across the Indian Ocean* (Berkeley: University of California Press, 2006), 306. Disillusionment with the nation-state is indicative of today's zeitgeist. Such sentiments should not, however, blind scholars to the appeal or liberatory potential of nationalism, particularly during the era of decolonization.

6. Anthony Appiah, *Cosmopolitanism: Ethics in a World of Strangers* (New York: Norton, 2006), 78–80.

7. Liisa H. Malkki, *Purity and Exile: Violence, Memory, and National Cosmology among Hutu Refugees in Tanzania* (Chicago: University of Chicago Press, 1995), 2.

8. Talal Asad, *Formations of the Secular: Christianity, Islam, Modernity* (Stanford, CA: Stanford University Press, 2003), 193; emphasis in original.

9. Cooper's recent work is indicative of this sentiment. See Frederick Cooper, *Africa in the World: Capitalism, Empire, Nation-State* (Cambridge, MA: Harvard University Press, 2014); and Cooper, *Citizenship between Empire and Nation: Remaking France and French Africa, 1945–1960* (Princeton, NJ: Princeton University Press, 2014).

10. As Samuel Moyn points out, many Africans ultimately gravitated toward the principle of postcolonial sovereignty and national citizenship, through which they "hoped to win more serious equality on the ruins of imperial hierarchy." Moyn, "Fantasies of Federalism."

11. Anthony Low, "The End of the British Empire in Africa," in *Decolonization and African Independence: The Transfers of Power, 1960–1980*, ed. Prosser Gifford and William R. Louis (New Haven, CT: Yale University Press, 1988), 33–72; and Charles Hornsby, *Kenya: A History since Independence* (London: Tauris, 2012), 53–55.

12. For more on the decolonization process, see Bruce Berman and John Lonsdale, *Unhappy Valley: Conflict in Kenya and Africa*, bk. 2, *Violence and Ethnicity* (London: James Currey, 1992); Bethwell A. Ogot and William R. Ochieng', *Decolonization and Independence in Kenya, 1940–93* (Athens: Ohio University Press, 1995); Timothy H. Parsons, *The 1964 Army Mutinies and the Making of Modern East Africa* (Westport, CT: Praeger, 2003); and David M. Anderson, *Histories of the Hanged: The Dirty War in Kenya and the End of Empire* (New York: Norton, 2005).

13. Siba N'Zatioula Grovogui, *Sovereigns, Quasi-Sovereigns, and Africans: Race and Self-Determination in International Law* (Minneapolis: University of Minnesota Press, 1996).

14. The legal fiction of formal equality between nation-states obscured the inequalities not only between colonizer and colonized, but also between different people and regions of the colonized world.

15. Partha Chatterjee, *The Nation and Its Fragments: Colonial and Postcolonial Histories* (Princeton, NJ: Princeton University Press, 1993).

16. Mahmood Mamdani, *Citizen and Subject: Contemporary Africa and the Legacy of Late Colonialism* (Princeton, NJ: Princeton University Press, 1996).

17. Parsons, *1964 Army Mutinies*, 77.

18. Kenya Constitutional Conference, Record of the Ninth Meeting in Lancaster House, 21 February 1962; and Kenya Constitutional Conference, Record of the Eleventh

Meeting in Lancaster House, 22 February 1962, GO/1/1/26, KNA; and Statement by the Secretary of State, Lancaster House, 21 March 1962, GO/1/1/13, KNA.

19. Central Office of Information, "Kenya Constitutional Conference," 17 January 1962, CO 822/2367, TNA.

20. E. S. Atieno Odhiambo and John Lonsdale, eds., *Mau Mau and Nationhood: Arms, Authority, and Narration* (Athens: Ohio University Press, 2003).

21. For a recent piece that rethinks KADU's majimboism, see David M. Anderson, "'Yours in Struggle for Majimbo': Nationalism and the Party Politics of Decolonization in Kenya, 1955–64," *Journal of Contemporary History* 40, no. 3 (July 2005): 547–64.

22. A. A. Castagno, "The Somali-Kenyan Controversy: Implications for the Future," *Journal of Modern African Studies* 2, no. 2 (1964): 171; and "A People in Isolation: A Call by Political Parties of the Northern Frontier District of Kenya for Union with the Somali Republic," (March 1962), CO 896/1 TNA.

23. Nene Mburu, *Bandits on the Border: The Last Frontier in the Search for Somali Unity* (Trenton, NJ: Red Sea Press, 2005), 87.

24. Ali Jimale Ahmed, "'Daybreak Is Near, Won't You Become Sour?' Going beyond the Current Rhetoric in Somali Studies," in *The Invention of Somalia*, ed. Ali Jimale Ahmed (Lawrenceville, NJ: Red Sea Press), 141–43.

25. Priya Lal, *African Socialism in Postcolonial Tanzania: Between the Village and the World* (New York: Cambridge University Press, 2015), 36.

26. Rogers Brubaker, "The Manichean Myth: Rethinking the Distinction between 'Civic' and 'Ethnic' Nationalism," in *Nation and National Identity: The European Experience in Perspective*, ed. Hanspeter Kriesi, Klaus Armingeon, Hannes Siegrist, and Andreas Wimmer (West Lafayette, IN: Purdue University Press, 2004), 55–71.

27. David D. Laitin, *Identity in Formation: The Russian-Speaking Populations in the Near Abroad* (Ithaca, NY: Cornell University Press, 1998), 334–35.

28. Inyani K. Simala and Michel Ben Arrous, "Whose Self-Determination? Conflicting Nationalisms and the Collapse of Somalia," in *African Studies in Geography from Below*, ed. Michel Ben Arrous and Lazare Ki-Zerbo (Dakar: CODESRIA, 2009), 173; and Saadia Touval, *Somali Nationalism: International Politics and the Drive for Unity in the Horn of Africa* (Cambridge, MA: Harvard University Press, 1963), 92, 96. To circumvent antitribal legislation, the party changed its name to Hizbiya Dastur Mustaqil al-Sumal (HDMS), or the Somali Independent Constitutional Party.

29. Jean Marie Allman, *The Quills of the Porcupine: Asante Nationalism in an Emergent Ghana* (Madison: University of Wisconsin Press, 1993), 8–13.

30. John D. Kelly and Martha Kaplan, *Represented Communities: Fiji and World Decolonization* (Chicago: University of Chicago Press, 2001), 5.

31. Amitav Ghosh, "The Fundamentalist Challenge," in *The Writer and Religion*, ed. William H. Gass and Lorin Cuoco (Carbondale: Southern Illinois University Press, 2000), 88.

32. Walter Johnson, "On Agency," *Journal of Social History* 37, no. 1 (2003): 113–24, doi: 10.1353/jsh.2003.0143.

33. James Clifford, *The Predicament of Culture: Twentieth-Century Ethnography, Literature, and Art* (Cambridge, MA: Harvard University Press, 1988), 340.

34. PC/GRSSA/2/14/11, KNA; and Kenya, *Report of the Northern Frontier District Commission*, 9–11.

35. John G. S. Drysdale, *The Somali Dispute* (London: Pall Mall, 1964), 103.

36. Interview by author, Deghow Maalim Stamboul, Garissa, 25 November 2010; interview by author, Mohamed Nur Ali, Wajir, 10 April 2010; and interview by author, Abbas Mohamed Omar, Wajir, 12 December 2010. Deghow Maalim Stamboul, Alex Kholkholle, and Wako Hapi's names were spelled inconsistently across different sources.

37. Interview by author, Abbas Adan Amin Osman and Saman Ali Adan, Wajir, 6 April 2011. The NPPPP was often abbreviated to NPP or NPPP.

38. Hassan Sheikh Nur, vice president of the Galla Political Union, explained that his party chose to join the Somali Republic "because we Galla people are of the same origin as the Somali people and have the same way of life." Nur, "Memorandum by the Galla Political Union to the N.F.D. Commission," 13 October 1962, CO 896/1, TNA. Virtually identical wording can be found in other petitions to the commission. See, for example, Chief Abdi Laga et al., "Memorandum by Moyale Sakuye to the N.F.D. Commission," CO 896/1, TNA. See the related issue of the "Somali Abo/Abbo": Fekadu Adugna, "Overlapping Nationalist Projects and Contested Spaces: the Oromo–Somali Borderlands in Southern Ethiopia," Journal of Eastern African Studies 5, no. 4 (2011): 775, doi: 10.1080/17531055.2011.642540; and Günther Schlee and Abdullahi A. Shongolo, Islam and Ethnicity in Northern Kenya and Southern Ethiopia (London: James Currey, 2012), 160.

39. Interview by author, Gadudow Garad Alasow, Eastleigh, 9 November 2010.

40. Günther Schlee argues that such "identity games" are commonplace in the north. Groups that possess the appropriate cultural capital can produce genealogies that enable them to affiliate "into the Somali fold." Schlee, "Brothers of the Boran Once Again: On the Fading Popularity of Certain Somali Identities in Northern Kenya," Journal of Eastern African Studies 1, no. 3 (2007): 417, doi: 10.1080/17531050701625524; and interview by author, Hassan Ahmed Warsame, Nairobi, 11 October 2010.

41. Interview by author, Fatima Jellow, Wajir, 9 April 2011.

42. "Cushite" is a linguistic term derived from the Bible, which was given racial connotations by European ethnographers, who employed the concept to describe various groups in the Horn of Africa who spoke related Afro-Asiatic languages. For more on the genealogy and etymology of Cushite, see Rodney S. Sadler Jr., Can a Cushite Change His Skin? an Examination of Race, Ethnicity, and Othering in the Hebrew Bible (New York: T & T Clark, 2005).

43. This idea was repeated across many interviews.

44. Kenya, Report of the Northern Frontier District Commission, 18.

45. Interview by author, Fatima Jellow, Wajir, 9 April 2011. Karinkow derives from the Arabic word karim.

46. Interview by author, Hassan Kochore, Nairobi, 11 November 2010.

47. Adan Goha, Vice-Chairman of the Northern Province United Association, Moyale Branch, et al., "Memorandum For Presentation to the Northern Frontier Province Commission," 2 October 1962, CO 896/1, TNA; interview by author, Hussein Roba, Nairobi, 12 January 2011; and "Constitutional Talks: Northern Province's Demand," Africa Digest (14–20 October 1961): 137.

48. For example: Abdi Ali et al., "Memorandum to the N.F.P. Commission on Behalf of the Burji Community of Marsabit," CO 896/1, TNA.

49. Ali Abdi, President of United Ogaden Somali Association, to Iain Macleod, Secretary of State for the Colonies, 18 February 1961, GH/1/54, KNA.

50. Ibid.

51. Wako Happi, President of the NPPPP, and D. M. Stanbul, General Secretary, to Governor of Kenya, 23 July 1961, CS/8/22/5, KNA.

52. Christopher Clapham, "Boundary and Territory in the Horn of Africa," in *African Boundaries: Barriers, Conduits and Opportunities*, ed. Paul Nugent and A. I. Asijawu (London: Pinter, 1996), 240.

53. Colin Legum, "Somali Liberation Songs," *Journal of Modern African Studies* 1, no. 4 (December 1963): 503–19.

54. Interview by author, Idhoy Ibrahim, Wajir, 16 December 2010.

55. Said S. Samatar, *Oral Poetry and Somali Nationalism: The Case of Sayyid Mahammad 'Abdille Hasan* (Cambridge: Cambridge University Press, 1982), 20.

56. Interview by author, Idhoy Ibrahim, Wajir, 16 December 2010.

57. Yusuf's latest book addresses the lives of Somalis in Minnesota. Ahmed Ismail Yusuf, *Somalis in Minnesota* (St. Paul: Minnesota Historical Society, 2012).

58. E-mail correspondence, Ahmed Ismail Yusuf, 28 August 2016.

59. Chantal Logan, "The Enduring Power of Somali 'Oral Political Poetry': Songs and Poems of Peace in the Midst of Chaos," in *Songs and Politics in Eastern Africa*, ed. Kimani Njogu and Hervé Maupeu (Dar es Salaam: Mkuki na Nyota, 2007), 362–65. For a point of comparison, see James R. Brennan's work on Radio Cairo. Brennan, "Radio Cairo and the Decolonization of East Africa, 1953–64," in *Making a World after Empire: The Bandung Moment and Its Political Afterlives*, ed. Christopher J. Lee (Athens: Ohio University Press, 2010), 173–95.

60. Interview by author, Abbas Adan Amin Osman and Saman Ali Adan, Wajir, 6 April 2010.

61. Esther Mwangi, *Socioeconomic Change and Land Use in Africa: The Transformation of Property Rights in Maasailand* (New York: Palgrave Macmillan, 2007), 68; and Richard D. Waller, "Acceptees and Aliens; Kikuyu Settlement in Maasailand," in *Being Maasai: Ethnicity and Idenity in East Africa*, ed. Thomas T. Spear and Richard D. Waller (London: James Currey, 1993), 240, 261–62.

62. Kenya, *Legislative Council Debates: Official Report*, vol. 87, pt. 2 (22 June 1961), 1581.

63. See Vincent Bakpetu Thompson, *Conflict in the Horn of Africa: The Kenya-Somalia Border Problem, 1941–2014* (Lanham, MD: University Press of America, 2015).

64. Shahid Amin and Christine Piot, "Un saint guerrier: Sur la conquête de l'Inde du Nord par les Turcs au XIe siècle," *Annales* 60, no. 2 (March–April 2005): 269–70, http://www.jstor.org/stable/27587609.

65. Interview by author, Ahmed Maalin Abdalle, Habasweyn, 23 April 2011.

66. See, for example, Abdul Adan's brilliant and biting short story. Adan, "The Somalification of James Karangi," in *Gambit: Newer African Writing*, ed. Emmanuel Iduma and Shaun Randol (New York: Mantle, 2014).

67. Interview by author, anonymous, Garissa, 25 November 2010.

68. Interview by author, anonymous, Garissa, 24 November 2010.

69. Northern Frontier Province Annual Report, 1931, PC NFD/1/1/4, KNA; Catherine L. Besteman, "Public History and Private Knowledge: On Disputed History in Southern Somalia," *Ethnohistory* 40, no. 4 (Autumn 1993): 563–86, doi: 10.2307/482588; and Besteman, *Unraveling Somalia: Race, Violence, and the Legacy of Slavery* (Philadelphia: University of Pennsylvania Press, 1999).

70. Bruce S. Hall, *A History of Race in Muslim West Africa, 1600–1960* (Cambridge: Cambridge University Press, 2011); and Chouki El Hamel, *Black Morocco: A History*

of Slavery, Race, and Islam (Cambridge: Cambridge University Press, 2013). See also Jonathon Glassman, *War of Words, War of Stones: Racial Thought and Violence in Colonial Zanzibar* (Bloomington: Indiana University Press, 2011).

71. Rasul Miller, "Is Islam an Anti-Black Religion?" Sapelo Square (25 April 2017), https://sapelosquare.com/2017/04/25/is-islam-an-anti-black-religion/.

72. See Sana Aiyar, *Indians in Kenya: The Politics of Diaspora* (Cambridge, MA: Harvard University Press, 2015).

73. This was Ahmed Farah, who was eventually succeeded by Ali Aden Lord, another Somali. Mburu, *Bandits on the Border,* 87; and NP Annual Report, 1958, PC/NFD/1/1/12, KNA. Eventually, locals elected Abdirashid Khalif, who served as the special representative for the NFD prior to independence.

74. In 1948, several Arabs were killed and injured in anti-Arab riots in Mogadishu. Leif Manger, *The Hadrami Diaspora: Community-Building on the Indian Ocean Rim* (New York: Berghahn Books, 2010), 95. Although vetoed by the president, the Somali parliament almost passed legislation that would give retail licenses exclusively to Somali citizens, which was widely perceived as an attack on Arab business interests. D. J. McCarthy, High Commissioner's Office, Aden, to Ronnie Scrivener, North and East Africa Department, Foreign Office, "Arabs in Somalia and East Africa," 26 June 1965, FO 371/179/742, TNA. Such xenophobia is particularly ironic given that in 1974, the Somali Democratic Republic joined the Arab League. David D. Laitin, *Politics, Language, and Thought: The Somali Experience* (Chicago: University of Chicago Press, 1977), 52.

75. In Wajir, supporters of the separatism sang a poem whose title was explicitly anti-Arab ("The short Arabs with the bad hair; Tomorrow you will be moving"). It is possible that the author of this song was intentionally playing on the term *jareer*—a derogatory label typically used to refer to "Africans." Interview by author, anonymous, Wajir, 9 April 2011; and interview by author, anonymous, Giriftu, 2 April 2011.

76. Manger, *Hadrami Diaspora,* 95.

77. James McDougall, *History and the Culture of Nationalism in Algeria* (Cambridge: Cambridge University Press, 2006), 2.

78. Interview by author, Mustafa (Mohamed) Osman Hirsi, Nairobi, 5 November 2010; and interview by author, Hassan Ahmed Warsame, Nairobi, 11 October 2010.

79. Interview by author, Deghow Maalim Stamboul, Garissa, 25 November 2010; and Kenya, *Report of the Northern Frontier District Commission, Presented to Parliament by the Secretary of State for the Colonies by Command of Her Majesty* (London: Her Majesty's Stationery Office, 1962), 10.

80. G. H. Webb, Permanent Secretary for Defence, "Somali Independent Union," September 1961, FCO 141/6643, British National Archives (TNA). In January 1962, Deghow Maalim Stamboul (Deqo Mohamed Stanbul), general secretary of the NPPPP, publicly attacked the president of the Somali Independent Union (SIU), a Nairobi-based party that also supported secession, in the *Daily Nation.* He accused the leader of being "an alien Somali who has no say in Northern Frontier District affairs" and who was not entitled to represent Somalis in the constitutional talks in London. "Opportunist' Somali Leaders Condemned," *Daily Nation,* 22 January 1962.

81. Hornsby, *Kenya,* 54.

82. Somali National Association to Chief Secretary, 24 February 1959, CS 28/2/2, KNA.

83. Interview by author, Abdi Haji Abdulla, Nairobi, 30 October 2010.

84. Director of Intelligence and Security to Permanent Secretary, Ministry of Defence, and Permanent Secretary, Ministry of African Affairs, "Somali Affairs-Somali National Association," 9 January 1959, FCO 141/6717, TNA.

85. Ibid.

86. Ibid.

87. Ibid.

88. Karuti Kanyinga, "Contestation over Political Space: The State and the Demobilisation of Opposition Politics in Kenya," in *The Politics of Opposition in Contemporary Africa*, ed. Adebayo O. Olukoshi (Stockholm: Nordic Africa Institute, 1998), 47.

89. Mburu, *Bandits on the Border*, 85.

90. President of the United Ogaden Somali Association to Governor of Kenya, 14 June 1960, CS 8/22/3, KNA; and Kenya, *Report of the Northern Frontier District Commission*, 11. Certain parties in northern Kenya and Somalia had greater followings among members of specific lineages, who sometimes preferred to identify on the basis of their clan for the sake of political representation. Ahmed, *Invention of Somalia*.

91. UOSA to British Parliament through Colonial Secretary, "The Claims of the Ogaden Tribe," 11 December 1961, CS/8/22/3, KNA.

92. Kenya, *Report of the Northern Frontier District Commission*, 9.

93. James Clifford, *The Predicament of Culture: Twentieth-Century Ethnography, Literature, and Art* (Cambridge, MA: Harvard University Press, 1988), 343.

94. Interview by author, Abdisalat Ahmed, Garissa, 25 November 2010.

95. Interview by author, Fatima Jellow, Wajir, 9 April 2011.

96. Interview by author, Ahmed Maalin Abdalle, Habasweyn, 16 July 2011.

97. Interview by author, Yusuf Yasin, Isiolo, 12 February 2011.

98. Interview by author, Deghow Maalim Stamboul, Garissa, 23 November 2010.

99. Lotte Hughes, "Malice in Maasailand: The Historical Roots of Current Political Struggles," *African Affairs* 104, no. 415 (April 2005): 217.

100. Somalia Ministry of Information, *British Public Opinion on the Northern Frontier District* (Mogadishu: Ministry of Information, May 1963), 14.

101. Akhil Gupta and James Ferguson, eds., *Culture, Power, Place: Explorations in Critical Anthropology* (Durham, NC: Duke University Press, 1997); and Malkki, *Purity and Exile*.

102. Anatole Ayissi, "The Politics of Frozen State Borders in Postcolonial Africa," in Arrous and Ki-Zerbo, *African Studies in Geography from Below*, 135.

103. Allaine Cerwonka, *Native to the Nation: Disciplining Landscapes and Bodies in Australia* (Minneapolis: University of Minnesota Press, 2004), 30.

CHAPTER 5: "IF WE WERE BROTHERS, WE WOULD HAVE MET LONG AGO"

1. Abdinoor Ali Khansoy, "All for Lost Glory" (unpublished manuscript, Mandera, Kenya, 2002–2003).

2. Michel-Rolph Trouillot, *Silencing the Past: Power and the Production of History* (Boston: Beacon Press, 1995), 27.

3. Sections of this chapter have appeared in Keren Weitzberg, "Rethinking the *Shifta* War Fifty Years after Independence: Myth, Memory, and Marginalization,"

in *Kenya after Fifty: Reconfiguring Historical, Political, and Policy Milestones*, ed. Michael Mwenda Kithinji, Mickie Mwanzia Koster, and Jerono P. Rotich (New York: Palgrave Macmillan, 2016), 65–81.

4. The word is thus crossed out, but remains legible. Michael Crotty, *The Foundations of Social Research: Meaning and Perspective in the Research Process* (London: SAGE, 1998), 205–6.

5. Etienne Balibar, "Racism and Nationalism," in *Race, Nation, Class: Ambiguous Identities*, ed. Etienne Balibar and Immanuel Wallerstein (London: Verso, 1991), 37.

6. See Jonathon Glassman, *War of Words, War of Stones: Racial Thought and Violence in Colonial Zanzibar* (Bloomington: Indiana University Press, 2011); and Christopher Joon-Hai Lee, *Unreasonable Histories: Nativism, Multiracial Lives, and the Genealogical Imagination in British Africa* (Durham, NC: Duke University Press, 2014).

7. Minutes of the Seventh Meeting on the Discussions on Constitutional Advance and Related Matters Held in the Government House, Nairobi, at 2:30 p.m. on 12 September 1961, FO 371/158906, TNA.

8. Ibid.

9. Ibid.

10. James G. Ferguson, "Of Mimicry and Membership: Africans and the 'New World Society,'" *Cultural Anthropology* 17, no. 4 (2002): 559, http://www.jstor.org /stable/3651618.

11. Minutes of the Seventh Meeting on the Discussions on Constitutional Advance and Related Matters Held in the Government House, Nairobi, at 2:30 p.m. on 12 September 1961, FO 371/158906, TNA.

12. Ibid.

13. Ibid.

14. As Talal Asad argues, the concern of minorities is not "merely a matter of 'recognition'"—it is also "a matter of embodied memories and practices that are articulated by traditions, and of political institutions through which these traditions can be fully represented." Asad, *Formations of the Secular: Christianity, Islam, Modernity* (Stanford, CA: Stanford University Press, 2003), 178.

15. For the need to historicize race and racism, see Thomas C. Holt, *The Problem of Race in the Twenty-First Century* (Cambridge, MA: Harvard University Press, 2002), 18–20.

16. Joseph R. Barndt, *Dismantling Racism: The Continuing Challenge to White America* (Minneapolis, MN: Augsburg Fortress, 1991), 28.

17. Within Somalia, many non-Somali minority groups have suffered due to government discrimination and pervasive racism. See Catherine L. Besteman, *Unraveling Somalia: Race, Violence, and the Legacy of Slavery* (Philadelphia: University of Pennsylvania Press, 1999).

18. Balibar, "Racism and Nationalism," 46, 45.

19. Colonial Office, *Report of the Kenya Constitutional Conference, 1962* (London: Her Majesty's Stationery Office, 1962), 11.

20. John D. Kelly and Martha Kaplan, "Legal Fictions after Empire," in *The State of Sovereignty: Territories, Laws, Populations*, ed. Douglas Howland and Luise White (Bloomington: Indiana University Press, 2009), 170.

21. Statement by the Secretary of State, 21 March 1962, 4, GO/1/13, KNA; Kenya Constitutional Conference, Record of the Ninth Meeting, Lancaster House, 21 February 1962, GO/1/1/26, KNA; Kenya Constitutional Conference, Record of the

Seventh Meeting, Lancaster House, 20 February 1962, GO/1/1/26, KNA; and Bethwell A. Ogot, "The Decisive Years," in *Decolonization and Independence in Kenya, 1940–93*, ed. Bethwell A. Ogot and William R. Ochieng' (Athens: Ohio University Press, 1995), 69–77.

22. Kenya Constitutional Conference, Record of the Third Meeting, 16 February 1962, GO/1/1/26, KNA.

23. Hurst Hannum, *Autonomy, Sovereignty, and Self-Determination: The Accommodation of Conflicting Rights* (Philadelphia: University of Pennsylvania Press, 1996), 27.

24. Howland and White, "Introduction: Sovereignty and the Study of States," in *State of Sovereignty*, 10.

25. Foreign Office to Addis Ababa, 11 April 1962, FO 371/165454, TNA.

26. Colonial Office, *Report of the Kenya Constitutional Conference*, 11.

27. Ibid.

28. "Kenyatta Visits Somalia," *Africa Digest*, 11–17 August 1962, 699. Kenya's final constitution was an outcome of a power-sharing agreement between the KADU, the KANU, and the British government, who agreed upon an adapted federalist system. Most scholars argue that Kenyatta accepted this arrangement out of a desire to speed up the transition to independence.

29. The Cabinet Office, Seventy-Third Meeting (Council of Ministers), 5 September 1961, WC/CM/1/6, KNA; A. J. Williams, "Somalis in Northern Kenya," 23 November 1961, CO 822/2003 TNA. Secretary of State for the Colonies to Governor of Kenya, 14 August 1963, OD 8/91 TNA; and Foreign Office to Political Office, Middle East Command (Aden) 30 July 1963, FO 371/172977 TNA.

30. Northerners often referred to the commission as a referendum. According to Amos Kareithi, an estimated 40,000 attended the various *baraza*, and the commissioners received 134 delegations and 106 written submissions. Kareithi, "Tracing the Roots of Insecurity in Northern Kenya," *Standard Digital*, 5 May 2013, http://www.standardmedia .co.ke/lifestyle/article/2000082950/tracing-the-roots-of-insecurity-in-northern-kenya.

31. Liisa H. Malkki, *Purity and Exile: Violence, Memory, and National Cosmology among Hutu Refugees in Tanzania* (Chicago: University of Chicago Press, 1995), 2.

32. Kenya, *Report of the Northern Frontier District Commission, Presented to Parliament by the Secretary of State for the Colonies by Command of Her Majesty* (London: Her Majesty's Stationery Office, 1962), 18.

33. Ibid., 7, 18–19.

34. Ibid., 19. For an example of colonial-era ethnography, see Eric J. Webster, *The Boran, Rendille, and Samburu: The Nomadic Tribes of the Northern Frontier District* (Nairobi: Ndia Kuu Press, 1944).

35. James Ferguson, *Expectations of Modernity Myths and Meanings of Urban Life on the Zambian Copperbelt* (Berkeley: University of California Press, 1999), 97.

36. For a critique of the "culture of poverty" argument, see Stephen Steinberg, "Poor Reason" *Boston Review*, 13 January 2011, http://bostonreview.net/steinberg.php.

37. The Ajuran Dynasty ruled parts of southern Somalia until the seventeenth century. Interview by author, Hassan Ahmed Warsame, Nairobi, 11 October 2010.

38. Unfortunately, the deadly effects of the civil war proved these fears warranted. Besteman, *Unraveling Somalia*.

39. Boran, Sakuye, and Watta tribesmen of Isiolo District to the Chairman, NFD Commission, 1962, CO 896/1, PRO.

40. Galgalo Wario, Secretary of Northern Province United Association, Moyale Branch, et al., to Commissions of Inquiry for the North Province (Kenya), "Memorandum: The Position of the Borana Community in the Isiolo District," 19 November 1962, CO 896/1, TNA.

41. Duba Gindole, "Memorandum for Presentation to the Northern Frontier Province Commission, on Behalf of the Boran Community (Marsabit District)," 9 November 1962, CO 896/1, TNA.

42. Kenya, *Report of the Northern Frontier District Commission*, 18.

43. Those who dissented were primarily located in Marsabit and Moyale Districts (regions that were predominantly non-Muslim and non-Somali).

44. Press Communiqué Issued by the Somali Delegation to the Rome Conference on the Future of the Northern Frontier District, 29 August 1963, FO 371/172982, TNA.

45. Benedict R. O'G. Anderson, *Imagined Communities: Reflections on the Origin and Spread of Nationalism*, rev. ed. (London: Verso, 2006), 4; and Sabelo J. Ndlovu-Gatsheni, *Do "Zimbabweans" Exist? Trajectories of Nationalism, National Identity Formation and Crisis in a Postcolonial State* (New York: Peter Lang, 2009), 48–51.

46. See Frederick Cooper, *Citizenship between Empire and Nation: Remaking France and French Africa, 1945–1960* (Princeton, NJ: Princeton University Press, 2014); and Gary Wilder, *Freedom Time: Negritude, Decolonization, and the Future of the World* (Durham, NC: Duke University Press, 2015).

47. Korwa G. Adar, *Kenyan Foreign Policy Behavior towards Somalia, 1963–1983* (Lanham, MD: University Press of America, 1994), 91.

48. David D. Laitin, *Identity in Formation: The Russian-Speaking Populations in the Near Abroad* (Ithaca, NY: Cornell University Press, 1998), 336.

49. 253 Parl. Deb., H.L. Deb (5th ser.) (2 December 1963): 872–92; and Outward Telegram, Secretary of State for the Colonies to Office of Attorney General, Kenya, 17 February 1962, CO 822/2003, TNA.

50. J. R. V. Prescott, "The Geographical Basis of Kenya's Political Problems," *Australian Outlook* 16, no. 3 (1962): 270–82.

51. Janet McIntosh, *The Edge of Islam: Power, Personhood, and Ethnoreligious Boundaries on the Kenya Coast* (Durham, NC: Duke University Press, 2009), 58; and Lotte Hughes, "Malice in Maasailand: The Historical Roots of Current Political Struggles," *African Affairs* 104, no. 415 (April 2005): 212.

52. Kenya, *The National Assembly Debates, House of Representatives: Official Report* (23 July–29 November 1963), 1370; and "Ethiopia and the Somalis" (From: Wolde Mariam Mesfin, *The Ethiopia-Somalia Boundary Dispute* [1964], 27–29; and Margery Perham, *The Government of Ethiopia* [1948], 434–36"), in *Case Studies in African Diplomacy*, vol. 2, *The Ethiopia-Somali-Kenya Dispute, 1960–67*, ed. Catherine Hoskyns (Dar Es Salaam: Oxford University Press, 1969), 4–6. For more on the controversy and political maneuvering that attended the debate over the future of the NFD, see A. A. Castagno, "The Somali-Kenyan Controversy: Implications for the Future," *Journal of Modern African Studies* 2, no. 2 (1964): 165–88; and Ioan M. Lewis, "The Problem of the Northern Frontier District of Kenya," *Race and Class* 5, no. 1 (April 1963): 48–60.

53. Inyani K. Simala and Michel Ben Arrous, "Whose Self-Determination? Conflicting Nationalisms and the Collapse of Somalia," in *African Studies in Geography from Below*, ed. Michel Ben Arrous and Lazare Ki-Zerbo (Dakar: CODESRIA, 2009), 173.

54. Jonathan M. Markakis, *Ethiopia: The Last Two Frontiers* (London: James Currey, 2011), 180–82.

55. Arjun Appadurai, *Fear of Small Numbers: An Essay on the Geography of Anger* (Durham, NC: Duke University Press, 2006).

56. Interview by author, anonymous, Habasweyn, 24 April 2011. Many fighters complained that the Somali government supplied them with old Italian rifles, which they scornfully nicknamed the *lixle* because they held only six bullets.

57. Hannah Arendt, *The Origins of Totalitarianism* (San Diego: Harcourt, 1966).

58. "Commissions Will Visit N. Province," *East Africa Standard*, 30 August 1962, CO 822/2536, TNA; and "Party Warns: Keep Commissions Away," *East Africa Standard*, 29 August 1962, CO 822/2536, TNA.

59. 253 Parl. Deb., H.L. Deb (5th ser.) (2 December 1963): 872–92; and Timothy H. Parsons, *The 1964 Army Mutinies and the Making of Modern East Africa* (Westport, CT: Praeger, 2003), 78.

60. Telegram, F. D. Webber, Colonial Office, to E. N. Griffith-Jones, 7 November 1962, FCO 141/7126, TNA.

61. Ibid.; and telegram, E. N. Griffith-Jones, Acting Governor, to F. D. Webber, Colonial Office, 9 November 1962, FCO 141/7126, TNA.

62. Kenya, *Report of the Regional Boundaries Commission* (London: Her Majesty's Stationery Office, December 1962), 44.

63. Ibid., 95.

64. Kenya, *Report of the Northern Frontier District Commission*, 18.

65. A Joint Memorandum Addressed to the Independence Commission for the Northern Frontier District of Kenya by Political Parties and Elders Acting on Behalf of the People of that District, 2, CO 896/1, TNA.

66. Kenya, *Report of the Northern Frontier District Commission*, 18.

67. Archives are what Walter Benjamin refers to as documents of "barbarism." Benjamin, "Theses on the Philosophy of History," in *Illuminations*, trans. Harry Zohn, ed. Hannah Arendt (New York: Harcourt, Brace, 1968), 256.

68. Interview by author, anonymous, Wajir, 15 December 2010.

69. Interview by author, Gadudow Garad Alasow, Eastleigh, 9 November 2010; and Minutes of the First Meeting of Northeastern Provincial Advisory Council, PR/1/5, KNA.

70. Somalia, *The Issue of the Northern Frontier District: A Report on Events Leading to the Severance of Diplomatic Relations Between the Somali Republic and the United Kingdom* (Mogadishu: Government of the Somali Republic, May 1963); interview by author, Haithar Sheikh Abdi and Dora Hassan, Nairobi, 26 October 2010; Somalia, *NFD: Frontier Problem, Planted by Britain between Kenya and Somalia* (Mogadishu: Somali Ministry of Information, 1963), 29; Clyde Sanger and John Nottingham, "The Kenya General Election of 1963," *Journal of Modern African Studies* 2, no. 1 (March 1964): 1, 17; and Nene Mburu, *Bandits on the Border: The Last Frontier in the Search for Somali Unity* (Trenton, NJ: Red Sea Press, 2005), 107–30.

71. Shahid Amin, *Event, Metaphor, Memory: Chauri Chaura, 1922–1992* (Delhi: Oxford University Press, 1996), 3.

72. Joe Ombuor, "First African DC's Name Stands out in Bustling Metropolitan Street," *Standard*, 18 September 2008, 3; courtesy of Abdi Haji Abdulla; interview by author, Abdi Haji Abdulla, Nairobi, 30 October 2010; and "Today in History," *Daily Nation*, 1 July 2008.

73. Interview by author, Hassan Kochore, Nairobi, 11 November 2010; interview by author, Abdi Haji Abdulla, Nairobi, 30 October 2010; and interview by author, Hussein Roba, Nairobi, 12 January 2011.

74. Interview by author, Ali Hassan, Nairobi, 3 November 2010.

75. Interview by author, Abdi Haji Abdulla, Nairobi, 30 October 2010.

76. That Haile Selassie of Ethiopia was the OAU's first chairman also did not help the Somali cause. With the 1964 Cairo Resolution, the OAU formally upheld the territorial integrity of colonial boundaries. See Paul Nugent and A. I. Asiwaju, "Introduction: The Paradox of African Boundaries," in *African Boundaries: Barriers, Conduits and Opportunities*, ed. Paul Nugent and A. I. Asiwaju (London: Pinter, 1996), 5–6; Christopher Clapham, "Boundary and Territory in the Horn of Africa," in Nugent and Asiwaju, *African Boundaries*, 240; and P. Mweti Munya, "The Organization of African Unity and Its Role in Regional Conflict Resolution and Dispute Settlement: A Critical Evaluation," *Boston College Third World Law Journal* 19, no. 2 (1 May 1999): 558–61.

77. "Memorandum submitted to the Conference by the Kenya Delegation and entitled 'Pan African Unity and the NFD Question in Kenya,'" in Hoskyns, *Case Studies in African Diplomacy*, 36–37.

78. Ibid., 37.

79. Telegram from Malcolm MacDonald, Governor of Kenya, to Secretary of State for the Colonies, 25 July 1963, FO 371/172977, TNA; telegram from Malcolm MacDonald, Governor of Kenya, to Secretary of State for the Colonies, 19 August 1963, OD 8/91, TNA; Press Communiqué Issued by Somali Delegation to Rome Conference on Future for NFD, 29 August 1963, FCO 141/7133, TNA; and Adar, *Kenyan Foreign Policy Behavior*, 100.

80. Adar, *Kenyan Foreign Policy Behavior*, 99, 100.

81. Secretary of State for the Colonies to Malcolm Macdonald, 14 August 1963, OD 8/91, TNA; and FO 371/172982, TNA.

82. Interview by author, Gadudow Garad Alasow, Eastleigh, 9 November 2010; and interview by author, Deghow Maalim Stamboul, Garissa, 23 November 2010.

83. Interview by author, Gadudow Garad Alasow, Eastleigh, 9 November 2010. Some British and colonial officials supported the Pan-Somali cause and saw the handover of the NFD to Kenya as an abdication of imperial responsibility. See, for example, Peter Fullerton's account in *Colony to Nation*. Fullerton, "An Incident at Isiolo," in *Colony to Nation: British Administrators in Kenya, 1940–1963*, ed. John Johnson (Banham: Erskine Press, 2002), 249–53.

84. "Emergency in North Eastern Region of Kenya: Kenya Government, *Kenya Calling*, 28 December 1963," in *Case Studies in African Diplomacy*, 43.

85. Schlee notes that "this guerilla war was part of an international conflict which shifted in the seventies from northern Kenyan into the Ogaden." Günther Schlee, *Identities on the Move: Clanship and Pastoralism in Northern Kenya* (Manchester: Manchester University Press, 1989), 52.

86. Telegram from Malcolm MacDonald, Governor of Kenya, to Secretary of State for the Colonies, 25 July 1963, FO 371/172977, TNA; and L. B. Walsh Atkins to Secretary of State, "Kenya: Military Aid," FO 371/178534, TNA. The secret memo written by Walsh Atkins indicates that the British government had knowledge of serious human rights abuses that the Kenyan government was about to carry out, including the "forced removal of villages and livestock to 'controlled areas' and the poisoning of

water supplies." See also Daniel Branch, "Violence, Decolonisation and the Cold War in Kenya's North-Eastern Province, 1963–1978," *Journal of Eastern African Studies* 8, no. 4 (2014): 642–57.

87. Interview by author, anonymous, Nairobi, 1 November 2010; interview by author, anonymous, Habasweyn, 24 April 2011; and Governor of Kenya to Secretary of State for the Colonies, "Press Statement: Somalia Complicity and Interference in Kenya's Affairs in Former NFD," December 1963, CO 822/3055, TNA.

88. Markakis, *Ethiopia*, 147–48; Charles Hornsby, *Kenya: A History since Independence* (London: Tauris, 2012), 179; and Saadia Touval, "The Organization of African Unity and African Borders," *International Organization* 21, no. 1 (Winter 1967): 116, 122, 126, doi:10.1017/S0020818300013151.

89. Interview by author, anonymous, Habasweyn, 24 April 2011; and interview by author, anonymous, Habasweyn, 23 April 2011.

90. Giorgio Agamben, *State of Exception*, trans. Kevin Attell (Chicago: University of Chicago Press, 2005).

91. Parsons, *1964 Army Mutinies*, 175.

92. Alexander De Waal, *Famine Crimes: Politics and the Disaster Relief Industry in Africa* (Bloomington: Indiana University Press, 1997), 40; Minute of the Fifth Meeting of the Regional Assembly of the North Eastern Region held on 2–3 July 1964 at the County Council Hall, Garissa, AHC 9/38, KNA; Ben Rawlence, *"Bring the Gun or You'll Die": Torture, Rape and Other Serious Human Rights Violations by Kenyan Security Forces in the Mandera Triangle* (New York: Human Rights Watch, 2009); Salah Abdi Sheikh, *Blood on the Runway: The Wagalla Massacre of 1984* (Nairobi: Northern Publishing House, 2007); Rose Odengo, "We Were Herded into Camps Like Animals and Raped at Gunpoint," *Daily Nation*, 29 June 2011, DN2; and interview by author, anonymous, Wajir, 9 April 2011.

93. Kenya, National Assembly, *Official Record (Hansard)*, 1 June–30 July 1965, 229.

94. De Waal, *Famine Crimes*, 40.

95. Interview by author, Maalim (Mo'alim) Ahmed and Deghow Maalim Stamboul, Garissa, 24 November 2010; and interview by author, Haithar Sheikh Abdi and Dora Hassan, Nairobi, 26 October 2010.

96. Richard Hogg, "Development in Kenya: Drought, Desertification and Food Scarcity," *African Affairs* 86, no. 342 (January 1987): 53.

97. Schlee, *Identities on the Move*, 51–52.

98. Hassan Wario Arero, "Coming to Kenya: Imagining and Perceiving a Nation among the Borana of Kenya," *Journal of Eastern African Studies* 1, no. 2 (2007): 297, doi: 10.1080/17531050701452598. See also Zeinabu Kabale Khalif and Gufu Oba, "*Gaafa Dhaabaa*—The Period of Stop: Narrating Impacts of *Shifta* Insurgency on Pastoral Economy in Northern Kenya, c. 1963 to 2007," *Pastoralism* 3, no. 14 (2013): 1–20.

99. Paul T. W. Baxter, "The 'New' East African Pastoralist: An Overview," in *Conflict and the Decline of Pastoralism in the Horn of Africa*, ed. John Markakis (Basingstoke: Macmillan, 1995), 145–46.

100. For more about the violence of the "Shifta War," see Hannah A. Whittaker, *Insurgency and Counterinsurgency in Kenya: A Social History of the Shifta Conflict, c. 1963–1968* (Boston: Brill, 2014), 89–106.

101. "Strong Denial on 'Nazi Tactics' in Garissa," *Daily Nation*, 29 October 1966, 17.

102. Timiro Ahmed Sofa to DC Isiolo, 25 October 1971, DC/ISO/4/7/4, KNA.

103. AHC/9/38; AHC/1/23; and AHC/18/62, KNA.

104. Kenya, National Assembly, *Official Record (Hansard)*, 7 May 1965, 2083.

105. Hannah A. Whittaker, "Pursuing Pastoralists: The Stigma of Shifta during the 'Shifta War' in Kenya, 1963–68," *Eras* 10 (2008), http://bura.brunel.ac.uk /handle/2438/8018.

106. Senator J. K. Kebaso to Ex-Chief Mallin Stampul and Ex-Chief Maalin Aden, 15 January 1965, AHC/18/62, KNA.

107. Interview by author, Ahmed Maalin Abdalle, Habasweyn, 23 April 2011; and interview by author, Maulid Keynan Ahmed, Habasweyn, 24 April 2011.

108. Interview by author, anonymous, Kotulo, 5 June 2011.

109. Linda Åhäll, *Sexing War/Policing Gender: Motherhood, Myth and Women's Political Violence* (London: Routledge, 2015), 50–53.

110. Somalis at the time sometimes referred to Jomo Kenyatta as "John."

111. *Karrarid* are cloth bags used for carrying goods.

112. Addo and Liban are regions in Ethiopia where Degodia from Kotulo and other areas of Kenya migrate to graze their animals.

113. Interview by author, Birik Mohamed and Bishar Omar, Kotulo, 2 June 2011.

114. PC E. M. Mahihu, Eastern Province Annual Report, 1965; and interview by author, Gadudow Garad Alasow, Eastleigh, 9 November 2010; and DC/ISO/4/7/14.

115. Sandra E. Greene, "Whispers and Silences: Explorations in African Oral History," *Africa Today* 50, no. 2 (Fall–Winter 2003): 41–53, doi: 10.1353/at.2004.0011; and Martin A. Klein, "Studying the History of Those Who Would Rather Forget: Oral History and the Experience of Slavery," *History in Africa* 16 (1989): 209–17, doi: 10.2307/3171785.

116. Richard Kearney, "On the Hermeneutics of Evil," in *Reading Ricoeur*, ed. David M. Kaplan (Albany: State University of New York Press, 2008), 82–83; emphasis in original.

117. Allesandro Portelli, *The Order Has Been Carried Out: History, Memory, and Meaning of a Nazi Massacre in Rome* (New York: Palgrave Macmillan, 2003), 233.

118. Jeffrey A. Lefebvre, *Arms for the Horn: U.S. Security Policy in Ethiopia and Somalia, 1953–1991* (Pittsburgh: University of Pittsburgh Press, 1992), 138.

119. Somalia's economic isolation was exacerbated by the 1967 Israeli-Arab war and the closure of the Suez Canal.

120. Saadia Touval, "Somalia and Its Neighbors," in *Conflict in World Politics*, ed. Steven L. Spiegel and Kenneth Neal Waltz (Cambridge, MA: Winthrop, 1971), 337–38.

121. Isobel Birch and Halima A. O. Shuria, *Perspectives on Pastoral Development: A Casebook from Kenya* (Oxford: Oxfam, 2001), 19.

122. The Indemnity Act was eventually repealed in 2010. "The Indemnity (Repeal) Bill," *Kenya National Assembly Official Report (Hansard)*, 8 April 2010, 23–30.

123. Wajir District Monthly Report, September 1963, PC GRSSA/3/1/63, KNA.

124. "Kidnap 'Denied,'" *Daily Nation*, 20 November 1963, 1.

125. Interview by author, anonymous, Wajir, 16 April 2011.

126. Interview by author, anonymous, Eastleigh, 23 January 2011.

127. Interview by author, Zeinab Abdi Ali, Wajir, 19 December 2010.

128. Interview by author, Duale Khalif, Mukhtar Khalif, Hussein Garad, Mohamed Nur, Abdi Gani, and Ahmed Khalif, Wajir, 14 December 2010.

129. James McDougall, "Martyrdom and Destiny: The Inscription and Imagination of Algerian History," in *Memory and Violence in the Middle East and North Africa*,

ed. Ussama Makdisi and Paul A. Silverstein (Bloomington: Indiana University Press, 2006), 60.

130. Luise White, *Speaking with Vampires: Rumor and History in Colonial Africa* (Berkeley: University of California Press, 2000), 30, 43.

131. Portelli, *Order Has Been Carried Out*, 289.

132. Interview by author, anonymous, Wajir, 19 December 2010.

CHAPTER 6: "THEIR PEOPLE CAME HERE TO SEEK ASYLUM"

1. A. Mirimo Wandati, "Screening: No Laughing Matter," *Daily Nation*, 29 November 1989, 7.

2. Wendy Brown, *Walled States, Waning Sovereignty* (New York: Zone Books, 2010).

3. Richard Hogg, "The New Pastoralism: Poverty and Dependency in Northern Kenya," *Africa* 56, no. 3 (1986): 319–33, http://www.jstor.org/stable/1160687.

4. Elliot Fratkin, "East African Pastoralism in Transition: Maasai, Boran, and Rendille Cases," *African Studies Review* 44, no. 3 (December 2001): 16, doi: 10.2307/525591.

5. Interview by author, Osman Abdisalat, Kotulo, 30 May 2011.

6. Interview by author, Abdullahi Sheikh, Habasweyn, 16 July 2011.

7. Frank Toboa Curaruku, "I Meet One of the Shifta in Our Midst," *Standard*, 24 October 1977; "'Keep Away from Shifta'—PC," *Standard*, 4 August 1977, 3; and Albert A. Musasia, Annual Report for 1980, 10 March 1981, SA 15/3, KNA.

8. Hussein A. Mahmoud, "Conflict and Constraints to Peace among Pastoralists in Northern Kenya," in *Understanding Obstacles to Peace: Actors, Interests, and Strategies in Africa's Great Lakes Region*, ed. Mwesiga Baregu (Kampala: Fountain Publishers, 2011), 150.

9. Günther Schlee, "Territorializing Ethnicity Ethnicity: The Imposition of a Model of Statehood on Pastoralists in Northern Kenya and Southern Ethiopia," *Ethnic and Racial Studies* 36, no. 5 (2013): 857–74, doi:10.1080/01419870.2011.626058.

10. *Kenya Population Census*, vol. 1, *1969* (Statistical Division, Ministry of Finance and Economic Planning, November 1970).

11. Sheikh, *Blood on the Runway*, 24.

12. John O. Oucho, *Undercurrents of Ethnic Conflict in Kenya* (Leiden: Brill, 2002); Mamdani, *Citizen*; and Peter Geschiere, *The Perils of Belonging: Autochthony, Citizenship, and Exclusion in Africa and Europe* (Chicago: University of Chicago Press, 2009). As Geschiere shows, nativist politics and anti-immigrant sentiments are also problems within Europe and thus can hardly be considered exclusive to Africa.

13. Interview by author, anonymous, Wajir, 3 June 2011.

14. Cedric Barnes, "*U dhashay—Ku dhashay*: Genealogical and Territorial Discourse in Somali History," *Social Identities* 12, no. 4 (2006): 487–98; and Ken Menkhaus, "Kenya-Somalia Border Conflict Analysis," Report Commissioned by USAID, 31 August 2005, http://pdf.usaid.gov/pdf_docs/Pnadt520.pdf.

15. Menkhaus, "Kenya-Somalia Border Conflict Analysis," 8.

16. Ahmed Ismail Samatar warns that scholars must resist the "seductive simplicity" of assuming that to "decipher any Somali context, a stranger need only ask the clan affiliations of the protagonists." Samatar, "Review of Lewis, I. M., A *Modern History of the Somali: Nation and State in the Horn of Africa*," *H-Africa, H-Net Reviews* (December 2003), http://www.h-net.org/reviews/showrev.php?id=8552.

17. William Easterly and Ross Levine, "Africa's Growth Tragedy: Policies and Ethnic Divisions," *Quarterly Journal of Economics* 112, no. 4 (November 1997): 1203–50, http://www .jstor.org/stable/2951270; and Robert Kaplan, "The Coming Anarchy," *Atlantic*, February 1994, http://www.theatlantic.com/magazine/archive/1994/02/the-coming-anarchy/304670/.

18. Jean-François Bayart, *The State in Africa: The Politics of the Belly* (London: Longman, 1993).

19. James Ferguson, *Give a Man a Fish: Reflections on the* New *Politics of Distribution* (Durham, NC: Duke University Press, 2015), 162.

20. Moradewun Adejunmobi notes that the politics of autochthony appeals to citizens who lack a sense of security over their home and "seek . . . a place where they can live, work, and realize their public and private aspirations in relative safety." While denouncing xenophobia, Moradewun Adejunmobi proposes an "ethics of locality" that could productively engage with people's desire for security of tenure and rights to citizenship. Adejunmobi, "Urgent Tasks for African Scholars in the Humanities," *Transition* 101 (2009): 86, 91, doi: 10.2979/trs.2009.-.101.80.

21. Koigi wa Wamwere, *Negative Ethnicity: From Bias to Genocide* (New York: Seven Stories Press, 2003); and Manfred Berg and Simon Wendt, eds., *Racism in the Modern World: Historical Perspectives on Cultural Transfer and Adaptation* (New York: Berghahn Books, 2011). The twentieth century is rife with examples of political leaders perpetuating exclusionary and ethnonationalist ideologies.

22. Mohamed Haji Ingiriis, *The Suicidal State in Somalia: The Rise and Fall of the Siad Barre Regime, 1969–1991* (Lanham, MD: University Press of America, 2016), 36.

23. Lidwien Kapteijns, *Clan Cleansing in Somalia: The Ruinous Legacy of 1991* (Philadelphia: University of Pennsylvania Press, 2012), 203–8.

24. Marleen Renders, *Consider Somaliland: State-Building with Traditional Leaders and Institutions* (Leiden: Brill, 2012), 59, 85.

25. Interview by author, Maalim (Mo'alim) Ahmed and Deghow Maalim Stamboul, Garissa, 24 November 2010.

26. The Kenyan national news often described these clashes as conflicts between "warring clans" or incidents of "cattle rustling." Such accounts obscure the politically instigated nature of the violence and the complicity of political elites. See, for example, articles in the *Daily Nation*: "Warring Clans Get Warning," 10 December 1982; and "Warring Clans in Peace Pledge," 7 December 1983.

27. Mahmoud, "Conflict and Constraints to Peace," 156–58.

28. Interview by author, Yusuf Ibrahim Kulow, Habasweyn, 17 July 2011.

29. Kapteijns, *Clan Cleansing*, 72.

30. Ibid., 71–75.

31. Sheikh, *Blood on the Runway*.

32. David Njagi, "Wagalla Massacre: In Search of Elusive Justice 25 Years On," *Daily Nation*, 20 October 2009, 28.

33. Interview by author, Maalim (Mo'alim) Ahmed and Deghow Maalim Stamboul, Garissa, 24 November 2010; interview by author, Maulid Keynan Ahmed, Habasweyn, 24 April 2011; interview by author, Osman Abdi Ibrahim, Garissa, 24 November 2010; interview by author, Duale Khalif, Mukhtar Khalif, Hussein Garad, Mohamed Nur, Abdi Gani, and Ahmed Khalif, Wajir, 14 December 2010; and Emma Lochery, "Rendering Difference Visible: The Kenyan State and Its Somali Citizens," *African Affairs* 111, no. 445 (2012): 624–25, doi: 10.1093/afraf/ads059.

34. Interview by author, anonymous, Wajir, 14 December 2010.

35. Sheikh, *Blood on the Runway*; and David M. Anderson, "Remembering Wagalla: State Violence in Northern Kenya, 1962–1991," *Journal of Eastern African Studies* 8, no. 4 (October 2014): 658–76, doi: 10.1080/17531055.2014.946237.

36. As the late Dekha Ibrahim, a community leader and peace builder in Wajir, explained, "We became keenly aware of the international dimensions of conflicts, including the Cold War. We could see signs everywhere around us. National and international politics played out in our community." "A Discussion with Dekha Ibrahim, Founder, Wajir Peace and Development Committee, Kenya," Berkley Center for Religion, Peace and World Affairs, 29 May 2010, http://berkleycenter.georgetown.edu/interviews/a-discussion-with-dekha-ibrahim-founder-wajir-peace-and-development-committee-kenya.

37. One of the legacies of the Shifta War was the normalization of the use of communal punishment. Although the conflict formally ended in 1967, the Kenyan government continued to respond to insecurity in the north by collectively punishing citizens. Residents recounted various atrocities, such as the burning of Garissa (Garissa *Gubay*) in 1980 and the Malka Mari Massacre in Mandera in 1981, among others. See Al Jazeera Correspondent, "Not Yet Kenyan," *Al Jazeera*, 15 December 2013, http://www.aljazeera.com/programmes/aljazeeracorrespondent/2013/10/not-yet-kenyan-20131028581844121218.html.

38. David W. Cohen and E. S. Atieno Odhiambo, *The Risks of Knowledge: Investigations into the Death of the Hon. Minister John Robert Ouko in Kenya, 1990* (Athens: Ohio University Press, 2004), 17–18.

39. Interview by author, anonymous, Kotulo, 3 June 2011.

40. Patricia A. Turner, *I Heard It through the Grapevine: Rumor in African-American Culture* (Berkeley: University of California Press, 1993).

41. Luise White, *Speaking with Vampires: Rumor and History in Colonial Africa* (Berkeley: University of California Press, 2000), 42.

42. Lee V. Cassanelli, "The Partition of Knowledge in Somali Studies: Reflections on Somalia's Fragmented Intellectual Heritage," *Bildhaan* 9, no. 1 (May 2011): 9, http://digitalcommons.macalester.edu/bildhaan/vol9/iss1/7.

43. Arjun Appadurai, *Fear of Small Numbers: An Essay on the Geography of Anger* (Durham, NC: Duke University Press, 2006), 5.

44. Giovanni Arrighi, "The African Crisis." *New Left Review* 15 (May–June 2002), http://newleftreview.org/A2387.

45. Clark C. Gibson, *Politicians and Poachers: The Political Economy of Wildlife Policy in Africa* (Cambridge: Cambridge University Press, 1999), 73–74. Environmentalism and militarization are not mutually exclusive. See Roderick P. Neumann, *Imposing Wilderness: Struggles over Livelihood and Nature Preservation in Africa* (Berkeley: University of California Press, 1998), 6.

46. Interview by author, Abdullahi Sheikh, Habasweyn, 16 July 2011; and Jonathan S. Adams and Thomas O. McShane, *The Myth of Wild Africa: Conservation without Illusion* (Berkeley: University of California Press, 1992), 68.

47. Peter Geschiere and Francis B. Nyamnjoh, "Capitalism and Autochthony: The Seesaw of Mobility and Belonging," *Public Culture* 12, no. 2 (2000): 423. Electoral politics tends to breed anxieties among majorities about the growth and political rise of minority groups. See Appadurai, *Fear of Small Numbers*.

48. "Screening Backed," *Daily Nation*, 24 November 1989, 26; "Leaders Back Screening," *Daily Nation*, 20 November 1989, 3; and "10 Somalis Must Go Back to Mogadishu," *Daily Nation*, 19 December 1989, 1, 13.

49. Wandati, "Screening: No Laughing Matter," *Daily Nation*, 29 November 1989, 7.

50. Interview by author, anonymous, Garissa, 26 November 2010.

51. Lochery, "Rendering Difference Visible," 627.

52. Serena Parekh, *Hannah Arendt and the Challenge of Modernity: A Phenomenology of Human Rights* (New York: Routledge, 2008), 20.

53. Ibid.

54. Wandati, "Screening: No Laughing Matter," 7.

55. Horst, *Transnational Nomads*, 109.

56. Francesca Declich, "Can Boundaries Not Border on One Another? The Zigula (Somali Bantu) between Somalia and Tanzania," in *Borders and Borderlands as Resources in the Horn of Africa*, ed. Dereje Feyissa and Markus Virgil Hoehne (London: James Currey, 2010), 169–86.

57. UNHCR, "Somali Refugees in the Region as of 20 September 2012," http://reliefweb .int/sites/reliefweb.int/files/resources/20_Sep_Somalia_IDPS%26Refugees_A3PC_ v2.pdf.

58. Ioan M. Lewis, *Understanding Somalia and Somaliland: Culture, History, Society* (New York: Columbia University Press, 2008), 65.

59. Gordon Mathews, Gustavo Lins Ribeiro, and Carlos Alba Vega, eds., *Globalization from Below: The World's Other Economy* (London: Routledge, 2012).

60. Parseleleo Kantai, "Eastleigh and the Rise of Somali Diaspora Capital," *PesaTalk*, 12 June 2012, http://pesatalk.com/eastleigh-and-the-rise-of-somali-diaspora-capital/.

61. David M. Anderson et al., "Camel Herders, Middlewomen, and Urban Milk Bars: The Commodification of Camel Milk in Kenya," *Journal of Eastern African Studies* 6, no. 3 (2012): 383–404, doi: 10.1080/17531055.2012.696886. After the outbreak of the Somali civil war, for example, livestock traders in Somalia started marketing their animals through Kenya, which created "a booming unofficial export trade" that "partially compensated for the loss of overseas markets in the 1990s." Peter D. Little, *Somalia: Economy without State* (Oxford: James Currey, 2003), 18. Garissa, which is situated between the Dadaab refugee camp and Eastleigh, also experienced considerable growth in the years after the war, becoming far more economically integrated with the rest of the country. These new opportunities have been particularly important for people from North Eastern and Eastern Provinces, who are less able to rely on historical methods of rearing livestock for basic survival. Interview by author, Osman Abdisalat and another resident, Kotulo, 30 May 2011.

62. Aihwa Ong, *Neoliberalism as Exception: Mutations in Citizenship and Sovereignty* (Durham, NC: Duke University Press, 2006), 16. As in many parts of the world, real (or perceived) increases in immigration during periods of economic downturn often lead "to an intensification of the politics of belonging." Geschiere and Nyamnjoh, "Capitalism and Autochthony," 423. These nativist sentiments are frequently directed against refugees. Liisa H. Malkki, *Purity and Exile: Violence, Memory, and National Cosmology among Hutu Refugees in Tanzania* (Chicago: University of Chicago Press, 1995), 7.

63. Joselyne Chebichi, "The 'Legality' of Illegal Somali Migrants in Eastleigh Estate in Nairobi, Kenya" (MA thesis, University of Witwatersrand, 2010), v, http:// wiredspace.wits.ac.za//handle/10539/8194.

64. Neil Carrier, *Little Mogadishu: Eastleigh, Nairobi's Global Somali Hub* (London: Hurst, 2016).

65. Paul Goldsmith, "Eastleigh Goes Global," *East African*, 17 August 2008, http:// www.theeastafrican.co.ke/magazine/-/434746/457396/-/view/printVersion/-/1susaz/-/ index.html.

66. Jane I. Guyer, *Marginal Gains: Monetary Transactions in Atlantic Africa* (Chicago: University of Chicago Press, 2004); and Morten Jerven, *Poor Numbers: How We Are Misled by African Development Statistics and What to Do about It* (Ithaca, NY: Cornell University Press, 2013).

67. Arendt's arguments remain relevant today, when many European countries continue to institute policies that undermine the long-standing Western tradition of the right to asylum. Hannah Arendt, *Origins of Totalitarianism* (San Diego: Harcourt, 1966), 296.

68. Godwin R. Murunga, "Governance and the Politics of Structural Adjustment in Kenya," in *Kenya: The Struggle for Democracy*, ed. Godwin R. Murunga and Shadrack W. Nasong'o (Dakar: CODESRIA, 2007), 263–300.

69. Elizabeth H. Campbell, "Economic Globalization from Below: Transnational Refugee Trade Networks in Nairobi," in *Cities in Contemporary Africa*, ed. Martin J. Murray and Garth A. Myers (New York: Palgrave Macmillan, 2006), 134.

70. Little, *Somalia*, 14.

71. Horst, *Transnational Nomads*, 47.

72. Manase Otsialo, "Experts Urge Kenya to Secure Border in Al Shabaab Fight," *East African*, 6 December 2014, http://www.www.theeastafrican.co.ke/news/Experts-urge-Kenya-to-secure-border-in-Al-Shabaab-fight-/-/2558/2547096/-/paewrgz/-/index .html.

73. As Mai Ngai argues, the "illegal alien" is "a problem that cannot be solved." Mae M. Ngai, *Impossible Subjects: Illegal Aliens and the Making of Modern America* (Princeton, NJ: Princeton University Press, 2004), 5.

74. Cindy Horst, *Transnational Nomads: How Somalis Cope with Refugee Life in the Dadaab Camps of Kenya* (New York: Berghahn Books, 2006), 23.

75. Osman Mohamed Osman, "For Kenyan-Somalis, One Bridge Defines Their Belonging," *Sahan Journal*, 14 November 2014, http://sahanjournal.com/kenyan-somalis-garissa-bridge-defines-belonging/#.VoQlRsArK2w.

76. Ibid.; and conversation with author, anonymous, Wajir, 20 May 2011.

77. The *"sijui"* appellation came up frequently during many interviews and conversations.

78. Interview by author, Hassan Yusuf, Nairobi, 31 January 2011; interview by author, Amina Kinsi, Nairobi, 21 October 2010; interview by author, Omar Issa and Jama Warsame, Nairobi, 7 October 2010; and interview by author, Mohamed Jama Nur, Nairobi, 25 October 2010.

79. Interview by author, Amina Kinsi, Nairobi, 22 December 2010. Several of my interviewees emphasized that they were the "original" inhabitants of the neighborhood. Some also expressed nostalgia for a time when Eastleigh was clean, orderly, and had regular bus routes. Archival evidence, however, suggests that the infrastructural neglect of Eastleigh can be traced to the colonial era. Property Holders of Eastleigh Township to Sir Edward Denham, Acting Governor and Commander in Chief, 5 August 1927, BN/9/14, KNA; and "Eastleigh," *East African Standard*, 14 July 1958.

80. Similar tensions have shaped the relationship between Mexicans and Mexican-Americans/Chicanos living in the United States as well as Palestinians divided between Israel and the West Bank.

81. Jacques Derrida, *Of Hospitality: Anne Dufourmantelle Invites Jacques Derrida to Respond*, trans. Rachel Bowlby (Stanford, CA: Stanford University Press, 2000).

82. Ken Opala, "Kenyan Refugees Stranded at Border," *Daily Nation*, 4 November 1999, 19.

83. Interview by author, anonymous, Garissa, 26 November 2010.

84. A. M. Akiwumi and Kenya, *Report of the Judicial Commission Appointed to Inquiry into Tribal Clashes in Kenya* (Nairobi: Government Printer, 1999), 515–22.

85. Interview by author, Ahmed Maalin Abdalle, Habasweyn, 16 July 2011.

86. Ibid.

87. Conversation with author, Abdi Billow Ibrahim, Wajir, 17 December 2010; and interview by author, Ahmed Maalin Abdalle, Habasweyn, 23 April 2011.

88. Ken Menkhaus, "The Rise of a Mediated State in Northern Kenya: The Wajir Story and Its Implications for State-Building," *Afrika Focus* 21, no. 2 (2008): 23–38.

89. Interview by author, Abdi Billow Ibrahim, Nairobi, 12 December 2013; interview by author, Fican Gayle Nuur, Wajir, 21 May 2011; and interview by author, Fatima Musa, Wajir, 26 July 2011.

90. Several businesswomen who sold khat (or *miraa*, as it is known locally) used this expression during interviews. See also Anders Hjort, "Trading Miraa: From School-Leaver to Shop-Owner in Kenya," *Ethnos* 39 (January 1974): 27–43; and Hjort, *Savanna Town: Rural Ties and Urban Opportunities in Northern Kenya* (Stockholm: University of Stockholm, 1979).

91. Interview by author, anonymous, Wajir, 25 May 2011.

92. Dekha Ibrahim, "Women's Roles in Peace-Making in the Somali Community in North Eastern Kenya," in *Somalia—The Untold Story: The War through the Eyes of Somali Women*, ed. Judith Gardner and Judy El Bushra (London: Pluto Press, 2004), 169.

93. "Discussion with Dekha Ibrahim."

94. Stephen Ndegwa, "Greater Horn of Africa Peace Building Project, Case Study Five: Peace Building Among Northeastern Pastoralists in Kenya: The Wajir Peace and Development Committee," appendix from the report titled *The Effectiveness of Civil Society Initiatives in Controlling Violent Conflicts and Building Peace: A Study of Three Approaches in the Greater Horn of Africa* (Washington, DC: Management Systems International, March 2001), 25.

95. George Otieno Ochich, "The Withering Province of Customary Law in Kenya: A Case of Design or Indifference?" in *The Future of African Customary Law*, ed. Jeanmarie Fenrich, Paolo Galizzi, and Tracy E. Higgins (Cambridge: Cambridge University Press, 2011), 109.

96. Menkhaus, "Rise of a Mediated State in Northern Kenya."

97. For a less optimistic perspective on the role of *xeer* in mediation processes, see Günther Schlee, "Customary Law and the Joys of Statelessness: Idealised Traditions versus Somali Realities," *Journal of Eastern African Studies* 7, no. 2 (2013): 258–71, doi: 10.1080/17531055.2013.776276.

98. In 1997, the government created a new constituency for the Ajuran, which formally put an end to the clashes (although it ignited new conflicts between the Garre and the Ajuran).

99. While married women can typically claim exclusive control over their personal property, men must make payments to their wives and future in-laws before marriage (exchanges that outsiders have often glossed as "bridewealth"). Men are also, at least normatively, expected to provide for their families.

100. Hina Azam, "Competing Approaches to Rape in Islamic Law," in *Feminism, Law, and Religion*, ed. Marie A. Failinger, Elizabeth R. Schiltz, and Susan J. Stabile (Farnham, Surrey, UK: Ashgate, 2013), 330, 333. Somali khat traders, for example, often noted that men had certain monetary responsibilities to their families. Referring to khat as their "husbands" was a means for women to highlight the notable absence of male caregivers, who were unable to meet the obligations contingent to their roles as heads of households.

101. Formal equality, as a number of feminist thinkers have argued, can be a hollow promise that can easily obscure the sexual differences and modes of inequality that shape actual gender relations. See Joan Wallach Scott's description of the tensions between abstract political equality and sexual difference in French republican theory. Scott, *The Politics of the Veil* (Princeton, NJ: Princeton University Press, 2007), 169–74.

102. For many Somali women, marriage was understood as a partnership between men and women, who were conceptualized as having different, rather than identical rights. Thus, marriage was predicated on a set of (largely financial) responsibilities to which they could expect and demand certain entitlements. This is not to suggest that marriage was purely instrumental for Somali women or that issues of love and affection were irrelevant, but rather that love and money were morally and conceptually intermeshed. See Jennifer Cole, "Love, Money, and Economies of Intimacy in Tamatave, Madagascar," in *Love in Africa*, ed. Jennifer Cole and Lynn M. Thomas (Chicago: University of Chicago Press: 2009), 109–34.

103. Letitia Lawson and Donald Rothchild, "Sovereignty Reconsidered," *Current History* 104, no. 682 (2005): 228.

CHAPTER 7: "PEOPLE WILL ONE DAY SAY OUR CHILDREN AREN'T KENYAN"

1. "NFD Frontier," Kenya Citizen TV, 6 August 2010, http://www.youtube.com/watch?v=zYxgpfuO7AQ&feature=youtube_gdata_player.

2. Talal Asad, *On Suicide Bombing* (New York: Columbia University Press, 2007).

3. Monica Kathina Juma and Peter Mwangi Kagwanja, "Securing Refuge from Terror: Refugee Protection in East Africa after September 11," in *Problems of Protection: The UNHCR, Refugees, and Human Rights*, ed. Niklaus Steiner, Mark Gibney, and Gil Loescher (New York: Routledge: 2012), 225–36.

4. Samuel P. Huntington, *The Clash of Civilizations and the Remaking of World Order* (New York: Simon and Schuster, 1996).

5. Aihwa Ong, *Flexible Citizenship: The Cultural Logics of Transnationality* (Durham, NC: Duke University Press, 1999).

6. Multicultural systems of inclusion in the United States and Europe grant political representation on the basis of communal identities, but are not always capable of accommodating diverse ways of life. Though Muslims, pastoralists, and other minorities experience marginalization within Kenya, they also frequently face fewer pressures to assimilate. Moreover, Kenya is, in some ways, more accepting of populations with multiple, overlapping affiliations and loyalties. I expand upon this point in the conclusion.

7. Talal Asad, *Formations of the Secular: Christianity, Islam, Modernity* (Stanford, CA: Stanford University Press, 2003), 223.

8. E. S. Atieno Odhiambo, "Matunda ya Uhuru, Fruits of Independence: Seven Theses on Nationalism in Kenya," in *Mau Mau and Nationhood: Arms, Authority, and Narration*, ed. E. S. Atieno Odhiambo and John Lonsdale (Athens: Ohio University Press, 2003).

9. Interview by author, Ali Abdi Ogle, Habasweyn, 25 April 2011.

10. Interview by author, Adan Ibrahim Ali, Wajir, 16 April 2011.

11. See Philip N. Waki, Kenya, and Commission of Inquiry into Post Election Violence, *Report of the Commission of Inquiry into Post-Election Violence* (Nairobi: Government Printer, 2008). The North Eastern Province was one of the few regions that remained peaceful—overturning decades of popular perceptions of the area.

12. See Wendy Brown for a counterargument to this position: Brown, *Walled States, Waning Sovereignty* (New York: Zone Books, 2010).

13. Alemante G. Selassie, "Ethnic Federalism: Its Promise and Pitfalls for Africa," *Yale Journal of International Law* 28 (2003): 51–107.

14. Korir Sing'Oei Abraham, *Kenya at Fifty: Unrealized Rights of Minorities and Indigenous Peoples* (London: Minority Rights Group International, 2012), 7, http://responsibilitytoprotect.org/Kenya%20report%20Jan12%202011.pdf.

15. Republic of Kenya, *The Constitution of Kenya* (National Council for Law Reporting with the Authority of the Attorney General, 2010), 44, www.kenyalaw.org/klr/fileadmin/pdfdownloads/Constitution_of_Kenya__2010.pdf.

16. Tania Murray Li, who discusses the rise of the "community" as a site of development intervention in Indonesia, suggests that the concept provided a "containerized, local" way of framing poverty. Li, *The Will to Improve: Governmentality, Development, and the Practice of Politics* (Durham, NC: Duke University Press, 2007), 234.

17. Interview by author, Amina Kinsi, Nairobi, 22 December 2010.

18. Interview by author, Abdirisaq Egal Mohamed, Nairobi, 11 October 2010.

19. Cori Hayden, *When Nature Goes Public: The Making and Unmaking of Bioprospecting in Mexico* (Princeton, NJ: Princeton University Press, 2003), 187.

20. In 1984, during the attempted coup of Moi, Asians became the target of mob violence. For more on anti-Asian sentiment in Kenya, see Frank Furedi, "The Development of Anti-Asian Opinion among Africans in Nakuru District, Kenya," *African Affairs* 73, no. 292 (July 1974): 347–58, http://www.jstor.org/stable/720812.

21. Thomas B. Hansen, "Between Autochthony and Diaspora: Indians in the 'New' South Africa," in *Dislocating Nation-States: Globalization in Asia And Africa*, ed. Patricio N. Abinales, Noboru Ishikawa, and Akio Tanabe (Kyoto: Trans Pacific Press, 2005), 165.

22. Interview by author, Hussein Mohammed Jama, Isiolo, 11 February 2011.

23. Interview by author, Fatuma Ayub, Nairobi, 29 October 2010. The political climate following the 2007 postelection violence, which produced hundreds of thousands of IDPs, no doubt shaped Fatuma Ayub's rhetorical appeals.

24. Interview by author, Ahmed Ali Farah, Nairobi, 1 November 2010.

25. Irene Wairimu, "Isahakia Ordered to Allow Survey of Naivasha Plot," *Star*, 10 June 2011, http://allafrica.com/stories/201106101038.html.

26. Ibid.

27. Interview by author, Ahmed Ali Farah, Nairobi, 1 November 2010.

28. Robin Cohen, *Global Diasporas: An Introduction* (London: Routledge, 2008), 129.

29. Ibid.

30. Members of the Harti Dhulbahante and Warsangeli in Kenya sometimes had a more ambivalent relationship to Somaliland. The semi-autonomous region of Puntland and the self-declared Republic of Somaliland have been engaged in territorial conflicts over regions some deem to be "Harti" land. In Kenya, where Harti and Isaaq Somalis have lived together and intermarried extensively, such disputes were often irrelevant, but did occasionally come to the surface.

31. Mark Bradbury, *Becoming Somaliland* (Oxford: James Currey, 2008), 6.

32. Interview by author, Mustafa (Mohamed) Osman Hirsi, Nairobi, 5 November 2010.

33. Henry Munson, "Fundamentalism," in *The Blackwell Companion to the Study of Religion*, ed. Robert A. Segal (Malden, MA: Blackwell, 2006), 261.

34. Interview by author, Mustafa (Mohamed) Osman Hirsi, Nairobi, 5 November 2010.

35. Interview by author, Rahimo Aden Abdi, Ahmed Ali Farah, Zeinab Ali, and others, Naivasha, 6 November 2010.

36. Conversation with author, anonymous, Nanyuki, 23 October 2010.

37. Liisa H. Malkki, *Purity and Exile: Violence, Memory, and National Cosmology among Hutu Refugees in Tanzania* (Chicago: University of Chicago Press, 1995).

38. Ibid., 4.

39. Interview by author, Mustafa (Mohamed) Osman Hirsi, Nairobi, 5 November 2010.

40. Interview by author, Halima Warsame Abdalle and Sara Warsame Abdalle, Nakuru, 7 November 2010.

41. Anecdotes about the life and death of German West, a notorious gangster in South Africa, would occasionally appear on the pages of *Drum* magazine. See "My Life in the Underworld—by 'Old Man Kajee,'" *Drum* (May 1953): 8; "The Power of Old Man Y," *Drum* (June 1971): 20.

42. Interview by author, Hussein Nur, Nairobi, 14 October 2010.

43. Interview by author, anonymous, Nanyuki, 24 October 2010.

44. Nuruddin Farah, one of Somalia's greatest literary figures, has tackled this issue in his novels.

45. David C. Berliner, "The Abuses of Memory: Reflections on the Memory Boom in Anthropology," *Anthropological Quarterly* 78, no.1 (2005): 197–211.

46. Interview by author, anonymous, Wajir, 16 April 2011.

47. Interview by author, anonymous, Wajir, 10 April 2010.

48. Interviews by author, Ahmed Maalin Abdalle, Habasweyn, 16 and 17 July 2011.

49. Small groups in the north who do not belong to any of the larger ethnic constituencies often join together under the name "Corner Tribe" to make political claims.

50. *Abbo* is a way of greeting in the Oromo language.

51. *Jareer* is a term with derogatory connotations used to describe people with Afro-textured hair.

52. Interview by author, Hussein Roba, Nairobi, 12 January 2011.

53. Catherine Besteman, "Representing Violence and 'Othering' Somalia," *Cultural Anthropology* 11, no. 1 (February 1996): 120–33, http://www.jstor.org/stable/656211.

54. Interview by author, Yusuf Ibrahim Kulow, Habasweyn, 16 July 2011. The Ajuran were the ruling elites of a powerful sultanate that controlled much of mainland Somalia between the sixteenth and seventeenth centuries.

55. Hawa Y. Mire, "The Politics of Being Somali in Kenya," 30 August 2015, http://themaandeeq.com/the-politics-of-being-somali-in-east-africa/.

56. Some were skeptical that the changes promised by proponents of devolution could reverse decades of economic marginalization in the north. In addition, it was not always easy for Somalis or inhabitants of the north to conceptualize themselves as "Kenyan" after decades of government abuse and marginalization. The Truth, Justice, and Reconciliation Commission (TJRC), organized after of the postelection violence of 2007, was intended to enable those affected by state-sponsored violence to achieve some closure. While the TJRC provided Somalis with an important vehicle for drawing public attention to their treatment at the hands of government forces and connecting their stories of trauma to a broader narrative of national suffering, it was also marred by accusations that its chairman was a coconspirator in the Wagalla Massacre. Many saw this as a symbol of their ongoing marginalization within the country and the hollowness of the coalition government's promise of national integration.

57. Gaining access to education, food aid, and political entitlements, for example, required that people register and reside in defined territorial jurisdictions. The state's enumerative and classificatory projects often ran counter to citizens' transnational loyalties. See Keren Weitzberg, "The Unaccountable Census: Colonial Enumeration and Its Implications for the Somali People of Kenya." *Journal of African History* 56, no. 3 (November 2015): 409–28, doi:10.1017/S002185371500033X.

58. Jeremy Prestholdt, "Kenya, the United States, and Counterterrorism," *Africa Today* 57, no. 4 (Summer 2011): 3; George W. Bush's 2002 National Security Strategy stated that America is "threatened less by conquering states than we are by failing ones." US National Security Council, *The National Security Strategy of the United States of America* (Washington, DC: Government Printing Office, September 2002), http://georgewbush-whitehouse.archives.gov/nsc/nss/2002/.

59. Michael J. Mazarr, "The Rise and Fall of the Failed-State Paradigm: Requiem for a Decade of Distraction," *Foreign Affairs* (January–February 2014), https://www.foreignaffairs.com/articles/2013-12-06/rise-and-fall-failed-state-paradigm.

60. Robert I. Rotberg, ed., *Battling Terrorism in the Horn of Africa* (Washington, DC: Brookings Institution Press, 2005). See also John Davis, ed., *Terrorism in Africa: The Evolving Front in the War on Terror* (Lanham, MD: Lexington Books, 2010); and Christopher L. Daniels, *Somali Piracy and Terrorism in the Horn of Africa* (Lanham, MD: Scarecrow Press, 2012).

61. Roland Marchal, "A Tentative Assessment of the Somali *Harakat Al-Shabaab*," *Journal of Eastern African Studies* 3, no. 3 (2009): 399.

62. Ken Menkhaus, "Somalia: Next Up in the War on Terrorism?" *Africa Notes* 6 (January 2002): 3.

63. Jeremy Scahill, *Dirty Wars: The World Is a Battlefield* (New York: Nation Books, 2013).

64. Much like Nasser and other Muslim and Arab leaders of his era, Barre advocated for a secular socialist regime and tried to keep Islamic authorities out of matters he believed to be under the purview of the state.

65. Xan Rice, "Mogadishu's Miracle: Peace in the World's Most Lawless City," *Guardian*, 26 June 2006, http://www.theguardian.com/world/2006/jun/26/mainsection.international11.

66. Francis Fukuyama, *The End of History and the Last Man* (New York: Free Press, 1992); and Huntington, *Clash of Civilizations*.

67. It is important to avoid either an overly denunciatory or an overly romantic portrayal of the ICU. See the nuanced account of the ICU put forward by Cedric Barnes and Harun Hassan. Barnes and Hassan, "The Rise and Fall of Mogadishu's Islamic Courts," *Journal of Eastern African Studies* 1, no. 2 (July 2007): 151–60, doi: 10.1080/17531050701452382.

68. Abdi Ismail Samatar, "The Nairobi Massacre and the Genealogy of the Tragedy," *Al-Jazeera* (26 September 2013), http://www.aljazeera.com/indepth/opinion/2013/09 /nairobi-massacre-genealogy-tragedy-201392512172764290.html; Roland Marchal, "Warlordism and Terrorism: How to Obscure an Already Confusing Crisis? The Case of Somalia," *International Affairs* 83, no. 6 (November 2007): 1091–1106, doi:10.1111 /j.1468-2346.2007.00675.x; and Jeremy Scahill, "Blowback in Somalia: How US Proxy Wars Helped Create a Militant Islamist Threat," *Nation* 293, no. 13 (7 September 2011), http://www.thenation.com/article/163210/blowback-somalia?page=0,1.

69. International Crisis Group, "Somalia: Al-Shabaab—It Will Be a Long War," *Africa Briefing* no. 99 (Nairobi/Brussels, 26 June 2014): 1–23, https://www.crisisgroup .org/africa/horn-africa/somalia/somalia-al-shabaab-it-will-be-long-war; Stig Jarle Hansen, *Al-Shabaab in Somalia: The History and Ideology of a Militant Islamist Group, 2005–2012* (Oxford, NY: Oxford University Press, 2013); and Lorenzo Vidino, Raffaello Pantucci, and Evan Kohlmann, "Bringing Global Jihad to the Horn of Africa: Al Shabaab, Western Fighters, and the Sacralization of the Somali Conflict," *African Security* 3, no. 4 (November 2010): 216–38.

70. Mahmood Mamdani, *Good Muslim, Bad Muslim: America, the Cold War, and the Roots of Terror* (New York: Pantheon Books, 2004), 17–62.

71. "Not Yet Kenyan," *Al Jazeera*, 15 December 2013, http://www.aljazeera.com /programmes/aljazeeracorrespondent/2013/10/not-yet-kenyan-20131028858184211218.html.

72. Anjum Ovamir, "Islam as a Discursive Tradition: Talal Asad and His Interlocutors," *Comparative Studies of South Asia, Africa and the Middle East* 27, no. 3 (2007): 656–72.

73. As Mark Bradbury and Michel Kleinman note, until recently, "as many as two hundred students from madrassas in Garissa, with no secondary education, were annually given scholarships to universities in Saudi Arabia; more than the number who went to Kenyan universities from the whole of North Eastern province." Bradbury and Kleinman, *Winning Hearts and Minds? Examining the Relationship between Aid and Security in Kenya* (Boston: Feinstein International Center, Tufts University, 2010), 31.

74. International Crisis Group, "Kenyan Somali Islamist Radicalisation," *Africa Policy Briefing* no. 85 (Nairobi/Brussels: 25 January 2012), 5, https://www.crisisgroup. org/africa/horn-africa/kenya/kenyan-somali-islamist-radicalisation.

75. Louis Brenner argues that the modern madrassa school changed the nature of Islamic education by appropriating aspects of secular schooling and interpreting Islamic texts through a "rationalist episteme." Brenner, *Controlling Knowledge: Religion, Power, and Schooling in a West African Muslim Society* (Bloomington: Indiana University Press, 2001), 8–9, 306.

76. This explains why, according to Ghosh, the "advance-guard" of these movements "are never traditional religious specialists but rather young college graduates or engineering students—products, in other words, of secularly oriented, modernist institutions." Amitav Ghosh, *The Imam and the Indian: Prose Pieces* (New Delhi: Ravi Dayal, 2002), 270. See also Brenner, *Controlling Knowledge*; and Rudolph T. Ware III,

The Walking Qur'an: Islamic Education, Embodied Knowledge, and History in West Africa (Chapel Hill: University of North Carolina Press, 2014), 15–16.

77. Interview by author, anonymous, Kotulo, 5 June 2011; and interview by author, anonymous, Nairobi, 3 November 2010.

78. Conversation with author, anonymous, Wajir, 18 May 2011; and interview by author, anonymous, Nairobi, 3 November 2010. It is not uncommon for detractors to paint Islamic reformism (which may have support among various age-groups) as a "youth problem." See Simon Turner, "'These Young Men Show No Respect for Local Customs'—Globalisation and Revival in Zanzibar," *Journal of Religion in Africa* 39, no. 3 (2009): 237–61, http://www.jstor.org/stable/20696816.

79. Interview by author, anonymous, Kotulo, 5 June 2011. The people I interviewed sometimes gave moral and spiritual explanations for drought. For example, the lack of rain was seen by some to be a punishment for moral laxity and corruption. Nevertheless, northerners also subsumed material and political explanations within a general religious and "moral" framework. See Alexander De Waal, *The Famine That Kills: Darfur, Sudan, 1984–1985*. (Oxford: Oxford University Press, 1989), 78.

80. Miracles are socially composed ways of understanding the world that "work" when reinforced by a population of followers.

81. Interview by author, anonymous, Wajir, 18 May 2011.

82. Ibid.

83. Nanjala Nyabola, "Kenya's Constitutional Reform Requires Diversity," *Guardian*, 27 May 2010, http://www.guardian.co.uk/commentisfree/2010/may/27/kenya-constitutional-reform-diversity.

84. Fiona B. Adamson, Triadafilos Triadafilopoulos, and Aristide R. Zolberg, "The Limits of the Liberal State: Migration, Identity and Belonging in Europe," *Journal of Ethnic and Migration Studies* 37, no. 6 (July 2011): 845.

85. Sudarsan Raghavan, "In Kenya's Capital, Somali Immigrant Neighborhood Is Incubator for Jihad," *Washington Post*, 22 August 2010, http://www.washingtonpost.com/wp-dyn/content/article/2010/08/21/AR2010082102682.html.

86. Bruce Riedel, "Kenya Terror Strike Al-Qaeda's Latest Global Jihad," *Al-Monitor*, 27 September 2013, http://www.al-monitor.com/pulse/originals/2013/09/global-jihad-kenya-shabab-al-qaeda.html#; and Daniel E. Agiboa, "Al-Shabab, the Global Jihad, and Terrorism without Borders," *Al Jazeera*, 24 September 2013, http://www.aljazeera.com/indepth/opinion/2013/09/al-shabab-global-jihad-terroris-201392484238627603.html.

87. "Kenyan sends back 'illegal' Somalis after Nairobi raids," *BBC News*, 9 April 2014, http://www.bbc.com/news/world-africa-26955803.

88. Human Rights Watch, "Somalia: A Country Study," January 2014, 1, https://www.hrw.org/world-report/2014/country-chapters/somalia.

89. Jeremy Prestholdt, "Fighting Phantoms: The United States and Counterterrorism in Eastern Africa," in *Lessons and Legacies of the War on Terror: From Moral Panic to Permanent War*, ed. Gershon Shafir, Everard Meade, and William J. Aceve (London: Routledge, 2013), 131.

90. Jonathan Horowitz, Open Society Justice Initiative, and Muslims for Human Rights, *We're Tired of Taking You to the Court: Human Rights Abuses by Kenya's Anti-Terrorism Police Unit* (New York: Open Society Foundations, 2013), http://www.opensocietyfoundations.org/reports/were-tired-taking-you-court-human-rights-abuses-kenyas-anti-terrorism-police-unit.

91. Prestholdt, "Kenya, the United States, and Counterterrorism," 20.

92. New forms of transnational authority and patronage have also enabled states and state-like entities to expand their power into new domains. The war in Somalia, for example, led to the dramatic collapse of a centralized state based out of Mogadishu. However, it also gave birth to new military and security regimes made up of alliances between East African and Western nations. The United Nations supported the establishment of the African Union Mission in Somalia (AMISOM), which Kenya formally joined in 2012. A joint military task force, AMISOM has effectively taken on much of the role of governance in southern Somalia. See Samar Al-Bulushi, "'Peacekeeping' as Occupation: Managing the Market for Violent Labor in Somalia," *Transforming Anthropology* 22, no. 1 (2014): 31–37, doi: 10.1111/traa.12026; and Paul D. Williams, "AMISOM in Transition: The Future of the African Union Mission in Somalia," *Rift Valley Institute Briefing Paper* (13 February 2013), http://riftvalley.net/download/file/fid/1488.

93. For more on the cultural production of truth and rumor in Kenya, see Grace A. Musila, *A Death Retold in Truth and Rumour: Kenya, Britain and the Julie Ward Murder* (London: James Currey, 2015).

94. Geoffrey Mosoku, "Former National Assembly Deputy Speaker Farah Maalim Summoned by Anti-Terrorism Police Unit," *Standard Digital*, 16 April 2014, http://www.standardmedia.co.ke/?articleID=2000109563.

95. "Kenya Attacks: Al-Shabab Not Involved—Kenyatta," *BBC News*, 18 June 2014, http://www.bbc.com/news/world-africa-27882084; and Murithi Mutiga, "Al Shabab Lays a Trap for Kenya," *New York Times*, 29 June 2014, http://www.nytimes.com/2014/06/30/opinion/al-shabab-lays-a-trap-for-kenya.html?_r=0.

96. David W. Cohen and E. S. Atieno Odhiambo, *The Risks of Knowledge: Investigations into the Death of the Hon. Minister John Robert Ouko in Kenya, 1990* (Athens: Ohio University Press, 2004).

97. Fukuyama, *End of History*; and Huntington, *Clash of Civilizations*.

CONCLUSION: "WE ARE NOT MIGRANTS; WE ARE LIVING IN OUR ANCESTRAL LAND"

1. Nadifa Mohamed, *Black Mamba Boy: A Novel* (New York: Farrar, Straus and Giroux, 2010), 223.

2. Jacques Derrida, "On Cosmopolitanism," in *The Cosmopolitanism Reader*, ed. Garrett Wallace Brown and David Held (Cambridge: Polity, 2010), 421.

3. Scholars such as James Ferguson, Cindi Katz, and Wendy Brown have challenged popular conceptions about globalization by calling attention to populations that have experienced disconnection and restrictions on their mobility. They have pointed to the ongoing relevancy of border controls, which have excluded certain regions from contemporary circuits of economic exchange and prevented particular groups, such as refugees, from traveling across countries and continents. Ferguson, *Global Shadows: Africa in the Neoliberal World Order* (Durham, NC: Duke University Press, 2006); Katz, *Growing Up Global: Economic Restructuring and Children's Everyday Lives* (Minneapolis: University of Minnesota Press, 2004); and Brown, *Walled States, Waning Sovereignty* (New York: Zone Books, 2010).

4. Rogers Brubaker, "The 'Diaspora' Diaspora," *Ethic and Racial Studies* 28, no. 1 (2005): 7.

5. David Ludden, "Presidential Address: Maps in the Mind and the Mobility of Asia," *Journal of Asian Studies* 62, no. 4 (November 2003): 1057–78, doi: 10.2307/3591759.

6. Peter Geschiere and Francis B. Nyamnjoh, "Capitalism and Autochthony: The Seesaw of Mobility and Belonging," *Public Culture* 12, no. 2 (2000): 423–52.

7. Michel-Rolph Trouillot, *Global Transformations: Anthropology and the Modern World* (New York: Palgrave Macmillan, 2003), 34.

8. Anne Weru, "The 'Other' Kenya: A Conversation with Mohammed Adow of *Al Jazeera*," *Rift Valley Forum*, 18 December 2013, http://riftvalley.net/event/other-kenya-conversation-mohammed-adow-al-jazeera#.VBr3k-dwW2w.

9. Sara Ahmed, *Strange Encounters: Embodied Others in Post-Coloniality* (London: Routledge, 2000), 21; emphasis in original.

10. While activists have successfully mobilized around the radical call to eliminate all borders, translating principles into practice demands a pragmatic appreciation of the struggles and strategies of migrants, refugees, and others "on the move." Recognizing the fact that Kenyan Somalis have historically engaged in mobile, deterritorialized networks is especially important at this historical juncture. Although the nation-state has not withered away, it has proved to be a limited and, at times, inadequate site of redress. In many parts of Africa, citizenship is no longer (if it ever was) the primary or exclusive site of allegiance. Individuals and groups have been relying upon and making political demands through a variety of extraterritorial networks and allegiances. See Achille Mbembe, "Ways of Seeing: Beyond the New Nativism: Introduction," *African Studies Review* 44, no. 2 (2001): 1–14, http://www.jstor.org/stable/525572.

11. Over the past decade, some left-leaning scholars, such as Susan Buck-Morss, have celebrated the emergence of global Islamist movements in the postcolonial world. Buck-Morss argues that political Islam points toward a future beyond a hegemonic global capitalism, an idea that Arya Zahedi calls into question. Zahedi, "Review of Susan Buck-Morss, *Thinking Past Terror: Islamism and Critical Theory on the Left* (Verso, 2003)," *Insurgent Notes* (5 October 2013), http://insurgentnotes.com/2013/10/review-susan-buck-morss/. See also Jonathon Glassman, "Creole Nationalists and the Search for Nativist Authenticity in Twentieth-Century Zanzibar: The Limits of Cosmopolitanism," *Journal of African History* 55, no. 2 (July 2014): 246, doi:10.1017/S0021853714000024.

12. What would it mean to develop a political theory from the Global South? This question is somewhat distinct from the Comaroffs' (intentionally provocative) injunction to view the "North" as "evolving" toward Africa. Jean Comaroff and John L. Comaroff, "Theory from the South: Or, How Euro-America Is Evolving toward Africa" *Anthropological Forum* 22, no. 2 (2012): 113–31.

13. Talal Asad and Joan Wallach Scott have critiqued the idea that Muslim minorities must assimilate or face exclusion—a belief that is widespread within both liberal and conservative circles in Europe and the United States. They also point to the possibility of imagining a form of political sovereignty that could accommodate nonstatist, nonsecular, and nonterritorial models of belonging. Asad, *Formations of the Secular: Christianity, Islam, Modernity* (Stanford, CA: Stanford University Press, 2003); and Scott, *The Politics of the Veil* (Princeton, NJ: Princeton University Press, 2007). A Kenyan appellate court recently ruled that Christian-run schools cannot ban students from wearing head scarves to class.

14. Agnes Cornell and Michelle D'Arcy, "*Plus ça Change?* County-Level Politics in Kenya after Devolution," *Journal of Eastern African Studies* 8, no. 1 (2014): 173–91.

15. Beth Elise Whitaker, "The Politics of Home: Dual Citizenship and the African Diaspora," *International Migration Review* 45, no. 4 (Winter 2011): 755–83, doi: 10.1111/j.1747-7379.2011.00867.x.

16. See Keren Weitzberg, "The Unaccountable Census: Colonial Enumeration and Its Implications for the Somali People of Kenya," *Journal of African History* 56, no. 3 (November 2015): 409–28, doi:10.1017/S002185371500033X. Sections of this chapter have appeared in Keren Weitzberg, "Can African States Offer New Approaches to Refugee Asylum?" *Africa Is a Country* (23 December 2016), http://africasacountry.com/2016/12/can-african-states-offer-new-approaches-to-refugee-asylum/.

17. Debates over the African state have often revolved around too diametric an understanding of power. The popular distinction between "weak" and "strong" states, for example, not only reinforces normative understandings of statecraft, but also greatly simplifies the operation of colonial power. Jeffrey Herbst argues that colonial states were weak due to their inability to project power over their territories. Herbst, *States and Power in Africa: Comparative Lessons in Authority and Control* (Princeton, NJ: Princeton University Press, 2000).

18. For discussions of "illegal but licit" migration, see Barak Kalir, "Illegality Rules: Chinese Migrant Workers Caught Up in the Illegal but Licit Operations of Labour Migration Regimes," in *Transnational Flows and Permissive Polities: Ethnographies of Human Mobilities in Asia*, ed. Barak Kalir and Malini Sur (Amsterdam: Amsterdam University Press, 2012), 27–54.

19. Derrida, "On Cosmopolitanism," 415. According to Amnesty International, Kenya was among the world's top ten refugee host countries, all of which lay outside the Western world, in 2015. "Global Refugee Crisis—by the numbers," 12 October 2015, https://www.amnesty.org/en/latest/news/2015/10/global-refugee-crisis-by-the-numbers/.

20. There is little evidence that an upsurge in poorly regulated immigration poses an inherent security threat. Over two decades of mass migration from Somalia brought about no substantial terrorist attacks. Only when the Kenyan government decided to invade southern Somalia in 2011 did al-Shabaab begin conducting retaliatory attacks within the country.

21. Elizabeth H. Campbell, "Urban Refugees in Nairobi: Problems of Protection, Mechanisms of Survival, and Possibilities for Integration," *Journal of Refugee Studies* 19, no. 3 (2006): 396–413, doi: 10.1093/jrs/fel011.

22. Joseph H. Carens, *The Ethics of Immigration* (New York: Oxford University Press, 2013).

23. Françoise Lionnet and Shu-Mei Shih, eds., *Minor Transnationalism* (Durham, NC: Duke University Press, 2005).

24. Lee Cassanelli, "Hosts and Guests: A Historical Interpretation of Land Conflicts in Southern and Central Somalia," *Rift Valley Institute Research Paper 2* (London: Rift Valley Institute, 2015), 16.

25. Ibid.

26. Conversation with author, anonymous, Nairobi, 20 August 2011.

27. According to Achille Mbembe, "The capacity to decide who can move and who can settle, where and under what conditions" will be one of the key factors shaping global politics in the twenty-first century. Mbembe, "Scrap the Borders That Divide Africans," *Mail and Guardian* (17 March 2017), https://mg.co.za/article/2017-03-17-00-scrap-the-borders-that-divide-africans.

Selected Bibliography

INTERVIEWS AND CONVERSATIONS

The names of some people interviewed for this book have been kept confidential either upon the request of the interviewee or upon my own judgment of the politically sensitive nature of the content quoted or referenced. In other cases, in an effort to be transparent about my sources and to give recognition to my interlocutors, I have included names, especially in the case of well-known public figures or those who insisted on having their names used.

Abdalle, Ahmed Maalin: Habasweyn, 23 April 2011; 16 and 17 July 2011
Abdalle, Halima Warsame: Nakuru, 7 November 2010
Abdalle, Sara Warsame: Nakuru, 7 November 2010
Abdi, Haithar Sheikh: Nairobi, 26 October 2010
Abdi, Rahimo Aden: Naivasha, 6 November 2010
Abdille, Abdisalat: Kotulo, 1 June 2011
Abdisalat, Osman: Kotulo, 30 May 2011
Abdulla, Abdi Haji: Nairobi, 30 October 2010
Abdullahi, Mohammed Sheikh: Wajir, 10 April 2010
Adan, Saman Ali: Wajir, 6 April 2011
Ahmed, Abdisalat: Garissa, 25 November 2010
Ahmed, Abdullahi: Nairobi, 18 October 2010
Ahmed, Maalim (Mo'alim): Garissa, 24 November 2010
Ahmed, Maulid Keynan: Habasweyn, 24 April 2011
Alasow, Gadudow Garad: Eastleigh, 9 November 2010

Ali, Adan Ibrahim: Wajir, 16 April 2011
Ali, Mohamed Nur: Wajir, 10 April 2010
Ali, Zeinab: Naivasha, 6 November 2010
Ali, Zeinab Abdi: Wajir, 19 December 2010
Anonymous: Eastleigh, 23 January 2011
Anonymous: Garissa, 24, 25, and 26 November 2010
Anonymous: Giriftu, 2 April 2011
Anonymous: Habasweyn, 23 and 24 April 2011; 16 July 2011
Anonymous: Isiolo, 3 and 11 February 2011
Anonymous: Kotulo, 30 May 2011; 3 and 5 June 2011
Anonymous: Nairobi, 14 October 2010; 1, 3, and 21 November 2010; 20 August 2011
Anonymous: Nanyuki, 23 and 24 October 2010
Anonymous: Wajir, 8 and 10 April 2010; 8, 10, 14, 15, and 19 December 2010; 2, 9, and
    16 April 2011; 18, 20, and 25 May 2011; 3 June 2011
Awad, Farah Mohamed: Nairobi, 12 October 2010
Ayub, Fatuma: Nairobi, 29 October 2010
Baraki, Adan Hassan: Habasweyn, 16 July 2011
Bøhmer, Jon: Nairobi, 1 November 2010; Thika, 31 October 2010
Bule, Ali: Garissa, 25 November 2010
Elmi, Abdullahi: Isiolo, 11 February 2011
Farah, Ahmed Ali: Nairobi, 1 November 2010; Naivasha, 6 November 2010
Gani, Abdi: Wajir, 14 December 2010
Garad, Hussein: Wajir, 14 December 2010
Good, Hassan: Isiolo, 11 February 2011
Guled, Hassan: Isiolo, 11 February 2011
Hassan, Abdi: Nairobi, 25 January 2011
Hassan, Ali: Nairobi, 3 and 5 November 2010
Hassan, Dora: Nairobi, 26 October 2010
Hirsi, Mustafa (Mohamed) Osman: Nairobi, 5 November 2010
Ibrahim, Abdi Billow: Wajir, 17 December 2010; Nairobi, 12 December 2013
Ibrahim, Osman Abdi: Garissa, 24 November 2010
Ibrahim, Idhoy: Wajir, 16 December 2010
Ibrahim, Mohamed: Nairobi, 20 October 2010; Nanyuki, 23 October 2010
Issa, Omar: Nairobi, 7 October 2010
Jama, Duthi: Isiolo, 3 February 2011
Jama, Hussein Mohamed: Isiolo, 11 February 2011
Jellow, Fatima: Wajir, 9 April 2011
Jilaow, Mohamed Hujale: Nairobi, 1 November 2010
Kabati, Ali: Thika, 31 October 2010
Khalid, Hussein Osman: Wajir, 21 April 2011
Khalif, Ahmed: Wajir, 14 December 2010
Khalif, Duale: Wajir, 14 December 2010
Khalif, Mukhtar: Wajir, 14 December 2010
Kinsi, Amina: Nairobi, 21 October 2010; 22 December 2010
Kochore, Hassan: Nairobi, 20 October, 2010; 11 November 2010
Kulow, Yusuf Ibrahim: Habasweyn, 16 and 17 July 2011
Mohamed, Abdirisaq Egal: Nairobi, 11 October 2010
Mohamed, Birik: Kotulo, 2 and 4 June 2011

Mohamed, Ladan: Wajir, 25 May 2011
Musa, Fatima: Wajir, 26 July 2011
Musa, Mohamed Ege: Nairobi, 21 November 2010
Nur, Hussein: Nairobi, 14 and 18 October 2010
Nur, Mohamed: Wajir, 14 December 2010
Nur, Mohamed Jama: Nairobi, 25 October 2010
Nuur, Fican Gayle: Wajir, 21 May 2011
Ogle, Ali Abdi: Habasweyn, 25 April 2011
Ogle, Dekhow Abdi: Habasweyn, 16 July 2011
Omar, Abbas Mohamed: Wajir, 12 December 2010
Omar, Bishar: Kotulo, 2 June 2011
Osman, Abbas Adan Amin: Wajir, 6 April 2011
Roba, Hussein; Nairobi, 12 January 2011
Shaiye (Shaaciye), Mukhtar: Nanyuki, 23 October 2010
Sharif, Zeinab: Nairobi, 13 January 2011
Sheikh, Abdullahi: Habasweyn, 16 July 2011
Stamboul, Deghow Maalim: Garissa, 23, 24, and 25 November 2010
Suleiman, Abdi Adan: Nairobi, 22 October 2010
Urune, Mohammed Osman: Wajir, 18 December 2010
Warsame, Hassan Ahmed: Nairobi, 11 October 2010; 4 November 2010
Warsame, Jama: Nairobi, 7 October 2010
Yasin, Yusuf: Isiolo, 12 February 2011
Yusuf, Hassan: Nairobi, 31 January 2011

BOOKS AND ARTICLES

Abdi, Cawo M. *Elusive Jannah: The Somali Diaspora and a Borderless Muslim Identity*. Minneapolis: University of Minnesota Press, 2015.

Abraham, Korir Sing'Oei. *Kenya at Fifty: Unrealized Rights of Minorities and Indigenous Peoples*. London: Minority Rights Group International, 2012.

Abu-Lughod, Janet L. *Before European Hegemony: The World System, A.D. 1250–1350*. New York: Oxford University Press, 1989.

Adam, Hussein Mohamed, and Richard Ford, eds. *Mending Rips in the Sky: Options for Somali Communities in the 21st Century*. Lawrenceville, NJ: Red Sea Press, 1997.

Adams, Jonathan S., and Thomas O. McShane. *The Myth of Wild Africa: Conservation without Illusion*. Berkeley: University of California Press, 1992.

Adamson, Fiona B., Triadafilos Triadafilopoulos, and Aristide R. Zolberg. "The Limits of the Liberal State: Migration, Identity and Belonging in Europe." *Journal of Ethnic and Migration Studies* 37, no. 6 (July 2011): 843–59.

Adan, Abdul. "The Somalification of James Karangi." In *Gambit: Newer African Writing*, edited by Emmanuel Iduma and Shaun Randol. New York: Mantle, 2014.

Adar, Korwa G. *Kenyan Foreign Policy Behavior towards Somalia, 1963–1983*. Lanham, MD: University Press of America, 1994.

Adejunmobi, Moradewun. "Urgent Tasks for African Scholars in the Humanities." *Transition* 101 (2009): 80–93. doi: 10.2979/trs.2009.-.101.80.

Adugna, Fekadu. "Overlapping Nationalist Projects and Contested Spaces: The Oromo–Somali Borderlands in Southern Ethiopia." *Journal of Eastern African Studies* 5, no. 4 (2011): 773-87. doi: 10.1080/17531055.2011.642540.

Agamben, Giorgio. *State of Exception*. Translated by Kevin Attell. Chicago: University of Chicago Press, 2005.

Åhäll, Linda. *Sexing War/Policing Gender: Motherhood, Myth and Women's Political Violence*. London: Routledge, 2015.

Ahmed, Ali Jimale. *Daybreak Is Near: Literature, Clans, and the Nation-State in Somalia*. Lawrenceville, NJ: Red Sea Press, 1996.

———. "'Daybreak Is Near, Won't You Become Sour?' Going beyond the Current Rhetoric in Somali Studies." In Ahmed, *Invention of Somalia*, 135–55.

———, ed. *The Invention of Somalia*. Lawrenceville, NJ: Red Sea Press, 1995.

Ahmed, Christine Choi. "Finely Etched Chattel: The Invention of a Somali Woman." In Ahmed, *Invention of Somalia*, 157–89.

Ahmed, Sara. *Strange Encounters: Embodied Others in Post-Coloniality*. London: Routledge, 2000.

Aiyar, Sana. *Indians in Kenya: The Politics of Diaspora*. Cambridge, MA: Harvard University Press, 2015.

Allman, Jean Marie. *The Quills of the Porcupine: Asante Nationalism in an Emergent Ghana*. Madison: University of Wisconsin Press, 1993.

Amin, Shahid. *Event, Metaphor, Memory: Chauri Chaura, 1922–1992*. Delhi: Oxford University Press, 1996.

Amin, Shahid, and Christine Piot. "Un saint guerrier: Sur la conquête de l'Inde du Nord par les Turcs au XIe siècle." *Annales* 60, no. 2 (March–April 2005): 265–92. http://www.jstor.org/stable/27587609.

Amselle, Jean-Loup. *Mestizo Logics: Anthropology of Identity in Africa and Elsewhere*. Translated by Claudia Royal. Stanford, CA: Stanford University Press, 1998.

Anderson, Benedict R. O'G. *Imagined Communities: Reflections on the Origin and Spread of Nationalism*. Rev. ed. London: Verso, 2006.

Anderson, David M. *Histories of the Hanged: The Dirty War in Kenya and the End of Empire*. New York: Norton, 2005.

———. "Remembering Wagalla: State Violence in Northern Kenya, 1962–1991." *Journal of Eastern African Studies* 8, no. 4 (October 2014): 658–76. doi: 10.1080/17531055.2014.946237.

———. "'Yours in Struggle for Majimbo': Nationalism and the Party Politics of Decolonization in Kenya, 1955–64." *Journal of Contemporary History* 40, no. 3 (July 2005): 547–64.

Anderson, David M., and Vigdis Broch-Due, eds. *The Poor Are Not Us: Poverty and Pastoralism in Eastern Africa*. Oxford: James Currey, 1999.

Anderson, David M., Hannah Elliott, Hassan Hussein Kochore, and Emma Lochery. "Camel Herders, Middlewomen, and Urban Milk Bars: The Commodification of Camel Milk in Kenya." *Journal of Eastern African Studies* 6, no. 3 (2012): 383–404. doi: 10.1080/17531055.2012.696886.

Ansari, Humayun. *"The Infidel Within": Muslims in Britain since 1800*. London: Hurst, 2004.

Appadurai, Arjun. *Fear of Small Numbers: An Essay on the Geography of Anger*. Durham, NC: Duke University Press, 2006.

———. "Putting Hierarchy in Its Place." *Cultural Anthropology* 3, no. 1 (1988): 36–49. doi: 10.1525/can.1988.3.1.02a00040.

Appiah, Anthony. *Cosmopolitanism: Ethics in a World of Strangers*. New York: Norton, 2006.

————. *In My Father's House: Africa in the Philosophy of Culture.* New York: Oxford University Press, 1993.

Arendt, Hannah. *Essays in Understanding, 1930–1954: Formation, Exile, and Totalitarianism.* Edited by Jerome Kohn. New York: Harcourt, Brace, 1994.

————. *The Origins of Totalitarianism.* San Diego: Harcourt, 1966.

Arero, Hassan Wario. "Coming to Kenya: Imagining and Perceiving a Nation among the Borana of Kenya." *Journal of Eastern African Studies* 1, no. 2 (2007): 292–304. doi: 10.1080/17531050701452598.

Arrighi, Giovanni. "The African Crisis." *New Left Review* 15 (May–June 2002): 5. http://newleftreview.org/A2387.

Arrous, Michel Ben, and Lazare Ki-Zerbo, eds. *African Studies in Geography from Below.* Dakar: CODESRIA, 2009.

Arsan, Andrew. *Interlopers of Empire: The Lebanese Diaspora in Colonial French West Africa.* New York: Oxford University Press, 2014.

Asad, Talal. *Formations of the Secular: Christianity, Islam, Modernity.* Stanford, CA: Stanford University Press, 2003.

————. *Genealogies of Religion: Discipline and Reasons of Power in Christianity and Islam.* Baltimore, MD: Johns Hopkins University Press, 1993.

————. *On Suicide Bombing.* New York: Columbia University Press, 2007.

Atieno Odhiambo, E. S. "The Formative Years, 1945–55." In Ogot and Ochieng', *Decolonization and Independence in Kenya,* 25–47.

————. "Matunda ya Uhuru, Fruits of Independence: Seven Theses on Nationalism in Kenya." In Atieno Odhiambo and Lonsdale, *Mau Mau and Nationhood,* 37–45.

Atieno Odhiambo, E. S., and John Lonsdale, eds. *Mau Mau and Nationhood: Arms, Authority, and Narration.* Athens: Ohio University Press, 2003.

Austen, Ralph A. *Trans-Saharan Africa in World History.* New York: Oxford University Press, 2010.

Ayissi, Anatole. "The Politics of Frozen State Borders in Postcolonial Africa." In Arrous and Ki-Zerbo, *African Studies in Geography from Below,* 132–59.

Aylmer, L. "The Country between the Juba River and Lake Rudolf." *Geographical Journal* 38, no. 3 (September 1911): 289–96. doi: 10.2307/1779043.

Azam, Hina. "Competing Approaches to Rape in Islamic Law." In *Feminism, Law, and Religion,* edited by Marie A. Failinger, Elizabeth R. Schiltz, and Susan J. Stabile, 327–41. Farnham, Surrey, UK: Ashgate, 2013.

Balaton-Chrimes, Samantha. "Counting as Citizens: Recognition of the Nubians in the 2009 Kenyan Census." *Ethnopolitics* 10, no. 2 (2011): 205–18. doi: 10.1080/17449057.2011.570983.

Balibar, Etienne. "Racism and Nationalism." In *Race, Nation, Class: Ambiguous Identities,* edited by Etienne Balibar and Immanuel Wallerstein, 37–85. London: Verso, 1991.

Banerjee, Sukanya. *Becoming Imperial Citizens: Indians in the Late-Victorian Empire.* Durham, NC: Duke University Press, 2010.

Barndt, Joseph R. *Dismantling Racism: The Continuing Challenge to White America.* Minneapolis, MN: Augsburg Fortress, 1991.

Barnes, Cedric. "*U dhashay—Ku dhashay*: Genealogical and Territorial Discourse in Somali History." *Social Identities* 12, no. 4 (2006): 487–98.

Barnes, Cedric, and Harun Hassan. "The Rise and Fall of Mogadishu's Islamic Courts." *Journal of Eastern African Studies* 1, no. 2 (24 July 2007): 151–60.

Barnes, Teresa. "Virgin Territory? Travel and Migration by African Women in Twentieth-Century Southern Africa." In *Women in African Colonial Histories,* edited by Jean Allman, Susan Geiger, and Nakanyike Musisi, 164–90. Bloomington: Indiana University Press, 2002.

Baxter, Paul T. W. "The 'New' East African Pastoralist: An Overview." In *Conflict and the Decline of Pastoralism in the Horn of Africa,* edited by John Markakis, 143–62. Basingstoke: Macmillan, 1995.

Baxter, Paul T. W., Jan Hultin, and Alessandro Triulzi, eds. *Being and Becoming Oromo: Historical and Anthropological Enquiries.* Uppsala: Nordic Africa Institute, 1996.

Bayart, Jean-François. *The State in Africa: The Politics of the Belly.* London: Longman, 1993.

Becker, Felicitas, and Joel Cabrita. "Introduction: Performing Citizenship and Enacting Exclusion on Africa's Indian Ocean Littoral." *Journal of African History* 55, no. 2 (July 2014): 161–71. doi:10.1017/S0021853714000139.

Benjamin, Walter. *Illuminations.* Translated by Harry Zohn. Edited by Hannah Arendt. New York: Harcourt, Brace, 1968.

———. *The Origin of German Tragic Drama.* Translated by John Osborne. London: Verso, 1998.

Berg, Manfred, and Simon Wendt, eds. *Racism in the Modern World: Historical Perspectives on Cultural Transfer and Adaptation.* New York: Berghahn Books, 2011.

Berliner, David C. "The Abuses of Memory: Reflections on the Memory Boom in Anthropology." *Anthropological Quarterly* 78, no. 1 (2005): 197–211.

Berman, Bruce, and John Lonsdale. *Unhappy Valley: Conflict in Kenya and Africa.* Bk. 2, *Violence and Ethnicity.* London: James Currey, 1992.

Besteman, Catherine L. "Public History and Private Knowledge: On Disputed History in Southern Somalia." *Ethnohistory* 40, no. 4 (Autumn 1993): 563–86. doi: 10.2307/482588.

———. "Representing Violence and 'Othering' Somalia." *Cultural Anthropology* 11, no. 1 (February 1996): 120–33. http://www.jstor.org/stable/656211.

———. *Unraveling Somalia: Race, Violence, and the Legacy of Slavery.* Philadelphia: University of Pennsylvania Press, 1999.

Bhabha, Homi K. *The Location of Culture.* London: Routledge, 1994.

Birch, Isobel, and Halima A. O. Shuria. *Perspectives on Pastoral Development: A Casebook from Kenya.* Oxford: Oxfam, 2001.

Boahen, A. Adu, ed. *General History of Africa.* Vol. 7, *Africa under Colonial Domination, 1880–1935.* Paris: UNESCO, 1985.

Bonilla, Yarimar. *Non-Sovereign Futures: French Caribbean Politics in the Wake of Disenchantment.* Chicago: University of Chicago Press, 2015.

Bonine, Michael E., Abbas Amanat, and Michael Ezekiel Gasper, eds. *Is There a Middle East? The Evolution of a Geopolitical Concept.* Stanford, CA: Stanford University Press, 2012.

Bose, Sugata. *A Hundred Horizons: The Indian Ocean in the Age of Global Empire.* Cambridge, MA: Harvard University Press, 2006.

Boye, Saafo Roba, and Randi Kaarhus. "Competing Claims and Contested Boundaries: Legitimating Land Rights in Isiolo District, Northern Kenya." *Africa Spectrum* 46, no. 2 (2011): 99–124. http://www.jstor.org/stable/41336256.

Bradbury, Mark. *Becoming Somaliland.* Oxford: James Currey, 2008.

Bradbury, Mark, and Michael Kleinman. *Winning Hearts and Minds? Examining the Relationship between Aid and Security in Kenya.* Boston: Feinstein International Center, Tufts University, 2010.

Branch, Daniel. "Violence, Decolonisation and the Cold War in Kenya's North-Eastern Province, 1963–1978." *Journal of Eastern African Studies* 8, no. 4 (2014): 642–57.

Branch, Daniel, Nicholas Cheeseman, and Leigh Gardner. *Our Turn to Eat: Politics in Kenya since 1950.* Berlin: Lit Verlag, 2010.

Bravman, Bill. *Making Ethnic Ways: Communities and Their Transformations in Taita, Kenya, 1800–1950.* Portsmouth, NH: Heinemann, 1998.

Brennan, James R. "Radio Cairo and the Decolonization of East Africa, 1953–64." In *Making a World after Empire: The Bandung Moment and Its Political Afterlives,* edited by Christopher J. Lee, 173–95. Athens: Ohio University Press, 2010.

———. *Taifa: Making Nation and Race in Urban Tanzania.* Athens: Ohio University Press, 2012.

Brenner, Louis. *Controlling Knowledge: Religion, Power, and Schooling in a West African Muslim Society.* Bloomington: Indiana University Press, 2001.

Brown, Wendy. *Walled States, Waning Sovereignty.* New York: Zone Books, 2010.

Brubaker, Rogers. "The 'Diaspora' Diaspora." *Ethnic and Racial Studies* 28, no. 1 (2005): 1–19.

———. *Ethnicity without Groups.* Cambridge, MA: Harvard University Press, 2004.

———. "The Manichean Myth: Rethinking the Distinction between 'Civic' and 'Ethnic' Nationalism." In *Nation and National Identity: The European Experience in Perspective,* edited by Hanspeter Kriesi, Klaus Armingeon, Hannes Siegrist, and Andreas Wimmer, 55–71. West Lafayette, IN: Purdue University Press, 2004.

Bruder, Edith. *The Black Jews of Africa: History, Religion, Identity.* Oxford: Oxford University Press, 2008.

Bulushi, Samar Al-. "'Peacekeeping' as Occupation: Managing the Market for Violent Labor in Somalia." *Transforming Anthropology* 22, no. 1 (2014): 31–37. doi: 10.1111/traa.12026.

Burbank, Jane, and Frederick Cooper. *Empires in World History: Power and the Politics of Difference.* Princeton, NJ: Princeton University Press, 2010.

Burton, Richard Francis. *First Footsteps in East Africa; or, An Exploration of Harar.* Edited by Isabel Burton. New York: Dover Publications, 1987.

Campbell, Elizabeth H. "Economic Globalization from Below: Transnational Refugee Trade Networks in Nairobi." In *Cities in Contemporary Africa,* edited by Martin J. Murray and Garth A. Myers, 125–47. New York: Palgrave Macmillan, 2006.

———. "Urban Refugees in Nairobi: Problems of Protection, Mechanisms of Survival, and Possibilities for Integration." *Journal of Refugee Studies* 19, no. 3 (2006): 396–413. doi: 10.1093/jrs/fel011.

Campbell, Gwyn, ed. *The Indian Ocean Rim: Southern Africa and Regional Co-Operation.* London: RoutledgeCurzon, 2003.

Carens, Joseph H. *The Ethics of Immigration.* New York: Oxford University Press, 2013.

Carrier, Neil. *Little Mogadishu: Eastleigh, Nairobi's Global Somali Hub.* London: Hurst, 2016.

Carter, Paul. *The Road to Botany Bay: An Exploration of Landscape and History.* Minneapolis: University of Minnesota Press, 1987.

Cassanelli, Lee V. "Hosts and Guests: A Historical Interpretation of Land Conflicts in Southern and Central Somalia." *Rift Valley Institute Research Paper* 2. London: Rift Valley Institute, 2015.

——. "The Opportunistic Economies of the Kenya-Somali Borderland in Historical Perspective." In Feyissa and Hoehne, *Borders and Borderlands*, 133–50.

——. "The Partition of Knowledge in Somali Studies: Reflections on Somalia's Fragmented Intellectual Heritage." *Bildhaan* 9, no. 1 (May 2011): 4–17. http://digitalcommons.macalester.edu/bildhaan/vol9/iss1/7.

——. *The Shaping of Somali Society: Reconstructing the History of a Pastoral People, 1600–1900.* Philadelphia: University of Pennsylvania Press, 1982.

Castagno, A. A. "The Somali-Kenyan Controversy: Implications for the Future." *Journal of Modern African Studies* 2, no. 2 (1964): 165–88.

Cerwonka, Allaine. *Native to the Nation: Disciplining Landscapes and Bodies in Australia.* Minneapolis: University of Minnesota Press, 2004.

Chakrabarty, Dipesh. *Provincializing Europe: Postcolonial Thought and Historical Difference.* Princeton, NJ: Princeton University Press, 2000.

Chalfin, Brenda. *Neoliberal Frontiers: An Ethnography of Sovereignty in West Africa.* Chicago: University of Chicago Press, 2010.

Chasin, Stephanie. "Citizens of Empire: Jews in the Service of the British Empire, 1906–1940." PhD diss., University of California, Los Angeles, 2008.

Chatterjee, Partha. *The Nation and Its Fragments: Colonial and Postcolonial Histories.* Princeton, NJ: Princeton University Press, 1993.

Chatty, Dawn, ed. *Nomadic Societies in the Middle East and North Africa: Entering the 21st Century.* Leiden: Brill, 2006.

Chebichi, Joselyne. "The 'Legality' of Illegal Somali Migrants in Eastleigh Estate in Nairobi, Kenya." MA thesis, University of Witwatersrand, 2010. http://wiredspace.wits.ac.za//handle/10539/8194.

Cisneros, Josue David. *The Border Crossed Us: Rhetorics of Borders, Citizenship, and Latina/o Identity.* Tuscaloosa: University of Alabama Press, 2013.

Clapham, Christopher. "Boundary and Territory in the Horn of Africa." In Nugent and Asiwaju, *African Boundaries*, 237–50.

Clayton, Anthony, and Donald C. Savage. *Government and Labour in Kenya, 1895–1963.* London: Cass, 1974.

Clifford, James. "Diasporas." *Cultural Anthropology* 9, no. 3 (August 1994): 302–38.

——. *The Predicament of Culture: Twentieth-Century Ethnography, Literature, and Art.* Cambridge, MA: Harvard University Press, 1988.

Cohen, David W. "Doing Social History from Pim's Doorway." In *Reliving the Past: The Worlds of Social History,* edited by Olivier Zunz, 191–235. Chapel Hill: University of North Carolina Press, 1985.

Cohen, David W., and E. S. Atieno Odhiambo. *The Risks of Knowledge: Investigations into the Death of the Hon. Minister John Robert Ouko in Kenya, 1990.* Athens: Ohio University Press, 2004.

Cohen, Robin. *Global Diasporas: An Introduction.* London: Routledge, 2008.

Cole, Jennifer. "Love, Money, and Economies of Intimacy in Tamatave, Madagascar." In *Love in Africa,* edited by Jennifer Cole and Lynn M. Thomas, 109–34. Chicago: University of Chicago Press: 2009.

Comaroff, Jean, and John L. Comaroff. "Alien-Nation: Zombies, Immigrants, and Millennial Capitalism." *South Atlantic Quarterly* 101, no. 4 (2002): 779–805.

———. "Theory from the South: Or, How Euro-America Is Evolving toward Africa." *Anthropological Forum* 22, no. 2 (2012): 113–31.

Cooper, Frederick. *Africa in the World: Capitalism, Empire, Nation-State*. Cambridge, MA: Harvard University Press, 2014.

———. *Africa since 1940: The Past of the Present*. Cambridge: Cambridge University Press, 2002.

———. *Citizenship between Empire and Nation: Remaking France and French Africa, 1945–1960*. Princeton, NJ: Princeton University Press, 2014.

———. *Decolonization and African Society: The Labor Question in French and British Africa*. Cambridge: Cambridge University Press, 1996.

———. "Modernizing Bureaucrats, Backward Africans, and the Development Concept." In Cooper and Packard, *International Development and the Social Sciences*, 64–92.

Cooper, Frederick, and Randall Packard, eds. *International Development and the Social Sciences: Essays on the History and Politics of Knowledge*. Berkeley: University of California Press, 1997.

Cooper, Frederick, and Ann Laura Stoler, eds. *Tensions of Empire: Colonial Cultures in a Bourgeois World*. Berkeley: University of California Press, 1997.

Cornell, Agnes, and Michelle D'Arcy. "*Plus ça Change?* County-Level Politics in Kenya after Devolution." *Journal of Eastern African Studies* 8, no. 1 (2014): 173–91.

Cronk, Lee. *From Mukogodo to Maasai: Ethnicity and Cultural Change in Kenya*. Boulder, CO: Westview Press, 2004.

Crotty, Michael. *The Foundations of Social Research: Meaning and Perspective in the Research Process*. London: SAGE, 1998.

Crowder, Michael. "Whose Dream Was It Anyway? Twenty-Five Years of African Independence." *African Affairs* 86, no. 342 (1987): 7–24. http://www.jstor.org/stable /722863.

Dalleo, Peter T. "The Somali Role in Organized Poaching in Northeastern Kenya, c. 1909–1939." *International Journal of African Historical Studies* 12, no. 3 (1979): 472–82.

———. "Trade and Pastoralism: Economic Factors in the History of the Somali of Northeastern Kenya, 1892–1948." PhD diss., Syracuse University, 1975. http://surface .syr.edu/hst_etd/52.

Daniels, Christopher L. *Somali Piracy and Terrorism in the Horn of Africa*. Lanham, MD: Scarecrow Press, 2012.

Davis, John, ed. *Terrorism in Africa: The Evolving Front in the War on Terror*. Lanham, MD: Lexington Books, 2010.

Declich, Francesca. "Can Boundaries Not Border on One Another? The Zigula (Somali Bantu) between Somalia and Tanzania." In Feyissa and Hoehne, *Borders and Borderlands*, 169–86.

Derrida, Jacques. *Of Hospitality: Anne Dufourmantelle Invites Jacques Derrida to Respond*. Translated by Rachel Bowlby. Stanford, CA: Stanford University Press, 2000.

———. "On Cosmopolitanism." In *The Cosmopolitanism Reader*, edited by Garrett Wallace Brown and David Held, 413–22. Cambridge: Polity, 2010.

Devji, Faisal. *Landscapes of the Jihad: Militancy, Morality, Modernity*. Ithaca, NY: Cornell University Press, 2005.

De Waal, Alexander. *Famine Crimes: Politics and the Disaster Relief Industry in Africa.* Bloomington: Indiana University Press, 1997.

———. *Famine That Kills: Darfur, Sudan, 1984–1985.* Oxford: Oxford University Press, 1989.

———, ed. *Islamism and Its Enemies in the Horn of Africa.* Bloomington: Indiana University Press, 2004.

Dinesen, Isak [Karen Blixen]. *Out of Africa.* New York: Random House, 1938.

Douglas, Mary. *Purity and Danger; An Analysis of Concepts of Pollution and Taboo.* New York: Praeger, 1966.

Dracopoli, Ignatius N. *Through Jubaland to the Lorian Swamp: An Adventurous Journey of Exploration.* London: Seeley, Service, 1914.

Drysdale, John G. S. *The Somali Dispute.* London: Pall Mall, 1964.

Dualeh, Hussein Ali. *From Barre to Aideed: Somalia; The Agony of a Nation.* Nairobi: Stellagraphics, 1994.

Dummett, Ann, and Andrew G. L. Nicol. *Subjects, Citizens, Aliens and Others: Nationality and Immigration Law.* London: Weidenfeld and Nicolson, 1990.

Dunn, Kevin C. "Environmental Security, Spatial Preservation, and State Sovereignty in Central Africa." In Howland and White, *State of Sovereignty,* 222–42.

Easterly, William, and Ross Levine. "Africa's Growth Tragedy: Policies and Ethnic Divisions." *Quarterly Journal of Economics* 112, no. 4 (November 1997): 1203–50. http://www.jstor.org/stable/2951270.

El Hamel, Chouki. *Black Morocco: A History of Slavery, Race, and Islam.* Cambridge: Cambridge University Press, 2013.

Eliot, Charles. *The East Africa Protectorate.* London: Arnold, 1905.

Elliott, F. "Jubaland and Its Inhabitants." *Geographical Journal* 41, no. 6 (June 1913): 554–61. doi: 10.2307/1778081.

Ellis, James E., and David M. Swift. "Stability of African Pastoral Ecosystems: Alternate Paradigms and Implications for Development." *Journal of Range Management* 41, no. 6 (November 1988): 450–59. https://journals.uair.arizona.edu/index.php/jrm /article/viewFile/8307/7919.

El-Safi, Mahassin A. G. H. "The Position of 'Alien' Somalis in the East Africa Protectorate and Kenya Colony, 1916–1963." *Journal of African Studies* 8, no. 1 (1981): 39–45.

Eno, Mohamed A., and Abdi M. Kusow. "Racial and Caste Prejudice in Somalia." *Journal of Somali Studies* 1, no. 2 (2014): 91–118.

Fabian, Johannes. *Time and the Other: How Anthropology Makes Its Object.* New York: Columbia University Press, 1983.

Fair, Laura. *Pastimes and Politics: Culture, Community, and Identity in Post-Abolition Urban Zanzibar, 1890–1945.* Athens: Ohio University Press, 2001.

Falola, Toyin. *Nationalism and African Intellectuals.* Rochester, NY: University of Rochester Press, 2001.

Farah, Mohamed I. *From Ethnic Response to Clan Identity: A Study of State Penetration among the Somali Nomadic Pastoral Society of Northeastern Kenya.* Uppsala: Academiae Ubsaliensis, 1993.

Farrah, Rasheed Y. "A Study of the Indigenous Minorities of Somaliland: Focus on Barriers to Education." PhD diss., Alliant International University, 2013.

Feierman, Steven. "Colonizers, Scholars, and the Creation of Invisible Histories." In *Beyond the Cultural Turn: New Directions in the Study of Society and Culture,* edited by Victoria E. Bonnell and Lynn Avery Hunt, 182–216. Berkeley: University of California Press, 1999.

———. *Peasant Intellectuals: Anthropology and History in Tanzania*. Madison: University of Wisconsin Press, 1990.

Ferguson, James G. *The Anti-Politics Machine: "Development," Depoliticization, and Bureaucratic Power in Lesotho*. Cambridge: Cambridge University Press, 1990.

———. *Expectations of Modernity: Myths and Meanings of Urban Life on the Zambian Copperbelt*. Berkeley: University of California Press, 1999.

———. *Give a Man a Fish: Reflections on the New Politics of Distribution*. Durham, NC: Duke University Press, 2015.

———. *Global Shadows: Africa in the Neoliberal World Order*. Durham, NC: Duke University Press, 2006.

———. "Of Mimicry and Membership: Africans and the 'New World Society.'" *Cultural Anthropology* 17, no. 4 (2002): 551–69. http://www.jstor.org/stable/3651618.

Feyissa, Dereje, and Markus Virgil Hoehne, eds. *Borders and Borderlands as Resources in the Horn of Africa*. London: James Currey, 2010.

Foucault, Michel. *Security, Territory, Population: Lectures at the Collège de France 1977–1978*. Edited by Michel Senellart. Translated by Graham Burchell. Basingstoke: Palgrave Macmillan, 2009.

Fraser, Nancy. *Scales of Justice: Reimagining Political Space in a Globalizing World*. New York: Columbia University Press, 2009.

Fratkin, Elliot. "East African Pastoralism in Transition: Maasai, Boran, and Rendille Cases." *African Studies Review* 44, no. 3 (December 2001): 1–25. doi: 10.2307/525591.

Fratkin, Elliot M., and Eric A. Roth, eds. *As Pastoralists Settle: Social, Health, and Economic Consequences of Pastoral Sedentarization in Marsabit District, Kenya*. New York: Kluwer, 2005.

Fukuyama, Francis. *The End of History and the Last Man*. New York: Free Press, 1992.

Fullerton, Peter. "An Incident at Isiolo." In *Colony to Nation: British Administrators in Kenya, 1940–1963*, edited by John Johnson, 249–53. Banham: Erskine Press, 2002.

Furedi, Frank. "The Development of Anti-Asian Opinion among Africans in Nakuru District, Kenya." *African Affairs* 73, no. 292 (July 1974): 347–58. http://www.jstor.org /stable/720812.

Geiger, Susan. "What's So Feminist about Women's Oral History?" *Journal of Women's History* 2, no. 1 (Spring 1990): 169–82.

Geschiere, Peter. *The Perils of Belonging: Autochthony, Citizenship, and Exclusion in Africa and Europe*. Chicago: University of Chicago Press, 2009.

Geschiere, Peter, and Francis B. Nyamnjoh. "Capitalism and Autochthony: The Seesaw of Mobility and Belonging." *Public Culture* 12, no. 2 (2000): 423–52.

Ghosh, Amitav. "The Fundamentalist Challenge." In *The Writer and Religion*, edited by William H. Gass and Lorin Cuoco, 86–97. Carbondale: Southern Illinois University Press, 2000.

———. *The Imam and the Indian: Prose Pieces*. New Delhi: Ravi Dayal, 2002.

———. *In an Antique Land: History in the Guise of a Traveler's Tale*. New York: Vintage Books, 1994.

Gibson, Clark C. *Politicians and Poachers: The Political Economy of Wildlife Policy in Africa*. Cambridge: Cambridge University Press, 1999.

Gibson-Graham, J. K. "Beyond Global vs. Local: Economic Politics outside the Binary Frame." In *Geographies of Power: Placing Scale*, edited by Andrew Herod and Melissa W. Wright, 25–60. Malden, MA: Blackwell, 2002.

Glassman, Jonathon. "Creole Nationalists and the Search for Nativist Authenticity in Twentieth-Century Zanzibar: The Limits of Cosmopolitanism." *Journal of African History* 55, no. 2 (July 2014): 229–47. doi:10.1017/S0021853714000024.

———. *War of Words, War of Stones: Racial Thought and Violence in Colonial Zanzibar*. Bloomington: Indiana University Press, 2011.

Greene, Sandra E. "Whispers and Silences: Explorations in African Oral History." *Africa Today* 50, no. 2 (Fall–Winter 2003): 41–53. doi: 10.1353/at.2004.0011.

Grovogui, Siba N'Zatioula. *Sovereigns, Quasi Sovereigns, and Africans: Race and Self-Determination in International Law*. Minneapolis: University of Minnesota Press, 1996.

Gupta, Akhil. "The Song of the Nonaligned World: Transnational Identities and the Reinscription of Space in Late Capitalism." *Cultural Anthropology* 7, no. 1 (February 1992): 63–79.

Gupta, Akhil, and James Ferguson. "Discipline and Practice: 'The Field' as Site, Method, and Location in Anthropology." In *Anthropological Locations: Boundaries and Grounds of a Field Science*, edited by Akhil Gupta and James Ferguson, 1–46. Berkeley: University of California Press, 1997.

———, eds. *Culture, Power, Place: Explorations in Critical Anthropology*. Durham, NC: Duke University Press, 1997.

Guyer, Jane I. *Marginal Gains: Monetary Transactions in Atlantic Africa*. Chicago: University of Chicago Press, 2004.

Hailey, William M. *An African Survey: A Study of Problems Arising in Africa South of the Sahara*. London: Oxford University Press, 1957.

Hall, Bruce S. *A History of Race in Muslim West Africa, 1600–1960*. Cambridge: Cambridge University Press, 2011.

Hamilton, Carolyn. *Terrific Majesty: The Powers of Shaka Zulu and the Limits of Historical Invention*. Cambridge, MA: Harvard University Press, 1998.

Hamilton, Carolyn, Verne Harris, Jane Taylor, Michele Pickover, Graeme Reid, and Razia Saleh, eds. *Refiguring the Archive*. Cape Town: David Philip, 2002.

Hanley, Will. "Grieving Cosmopolitanism in Middle East Studies." *History Compass* 6, no. 5 (September 2008): 1346–67. doi:10.1111/j.1478-0542.2008.00545.x.

Hannum, Hurst. *Autonomy, Sovereignty, and Self-Determination: The Accommodation of Conflicting Rights*. Philadelphia: University of Pennsylvania Press, 1996.

Hanretta, Sean. *Islam and Social Change in French West Africa: History of an Emancipatory Community*. Cambridge: Cambridge University Press, 2009.

Hansen, Stig Jarle. *Al-Shabaab in Somalia: The History and Ideology of a Militant Islamist Group, 2005–2012*. Oxford, NY: Oxford University Press, 2013.

Hansen, Thomas B. "Between Autochthony and Diaspora: Indians in the 'New' South Africa." In *Dislocating Nation-States: Globalization in Asia and Africa*, edited by Patricio N. Abinales, Noboru Ishikawa, and Akio Tanabe, 147–70. Kyoto: Trans Pacific Press, 2005.

———. *Melancholia of Freedom: Social Life in an Indian Township in South Africa*. Princeton, NJ: Princeton University Press, 2012.

Hardt, Michael, and Antonio Negri. *Empire*. Cambridge, MA: Harvard University Press, 2000.

Hassan, Ahmed Issack. "Legal Impediments to Development in Northern Kenya." *Pambazuka News* (22 October 2008). http://www.pambazuka.org/governance/legal-impediments-development-northern-kenya.

Hayden, Cori. *When Nature Goes Public: The Making and Unmaking of Bioprospecting in Mexico.* Princeton, NJ: Princeton University Press, 2003.

Herbst, Jeffrey. *States and Power in Africa: Comparative Lessons in Authority and Control.* Princeton, NJ: Princeton University Press, 2000.

Hjort, Anders *Savanna Town: Rural Ties and Urban Opportunities in Northern Kenya.* Stockholm: University of Stockholm, 1979.

———. "Trading Miraa: From School-Leaver to Shop-Owner in Kenya." *Ethnos* 39 (January 1974): 27–43.

Ho, Engseng. *The Graves of Tarim: Genealogy and Mobility across the Indian Ocean.* Berkeley: University of California Press, 2006.

Hodge, Joseph Morgan. *Triumph of the Expert: Agrarian Doctrines of Development and the Legacies of British Colonialism.* Athens: Ohio University Press, 2007.

Hodgson, Marshall G. S. *The Venture of Islam.* Vol. 2, *The Expansion of Islam in the Middle Periods.* Vol. 3, *The Gunpowder Empires and Modern Times.* Chicago: University of Chicago Press, 1974.

Hogg, Richard. "Development in Kenya: Drought, Desertification and Food Scarcity." *African Affairs* 86, no. 342 (January 1987): 47–58.

———. "The New Pastoralism: Poverty and Dependency in Northern Kenya." *Africa* 56, no. 3 (1986): 319–33. http://www.jstor.org/stable/1160687.

Holt, Thomas C. *The Problem of Race in the Twenty-First Century.* Cambridge, MA: Harvard University Press, 2002.

Hornsby, Charles. *Kenya: A History since Independence.* London: Tauris, 2012.

Horowitz, Jonathan, Open Society Justice Initiative, and Muslims for Human Rights. *We're Tired of Taking You to the Court: Human Rights Abuses by Kenya's Anti-Terrorism Police Unit.* New York: Open Society Foundations, 2013. http://www.opensocietyfoundations.org/reports/were-tired-taking-you-court-human-rights-abuses-kenyas-anti-terrorism-police-unit.

Horst, Cindy. *Transnational Nomads: How Somalis Cope with Refugee Life in the Dadaab Camps of Kenya.* New York: Berghahn Books, 2006.

Hoskyns, Catherine, ed. *Case Studies in African Diplomacy.* Vol. 2, *The Ethiopia-Somali-Kenya Dispute, 1960–67.* Dar es Salaam: Oxford University Press, 1969.

Howland, Douglas, and Luise White. "Introduction: Sovereignty and the Study of States." In Howland and White, *State of Sovereignty,* 1–18.

———, eds. *The State of Sovereignty: Territories, Laws, Populations.* Bloomington: Indiana University Press, 2009.

Hughes, David McDermott. *From Enslavement to Environmentalism: Politics on a Southern African Frontier.* Seattle: University of Washington Press, 2006.

Hughes, Lotte. "Malice in Maasailand: The Historical Roots of Current Political Struggles." *African Affairs* 104, no. 415 (April 2005): 207–24.

Hunt, Nancy Rose. *A Colonial Lexicon: Of Birth Ritual, Medicalization, and Mobility in the Congo.* Durham, NC: Duke University Press, 1999.

Huntington, Samuel P. *The Clash of Civilizations and the Remaking of World Order.* New York: Simon and Schuster, 1996.

Hyndman, Jennifer. *Managing Displacement: Refugees and the Politics of Humanitarianism.* Minneapolis: University of Minnesota Press, 2000.

Ibrahim, Dekha. "Women's Roles in Peace-Making in the Somali Community in North Eastern Kenya." In *Somalia—The Untold Story: The War through the Eyes of Somali Women*, edited by Judith Gardner and Judy El Bushra, 166–74. London: Pluto Press, 2004.

Ibrahim, H. A. "African Initiatives and Resistance in North-East Africa." In Boahen, *General History of Africa*, vol. 7, *Africa under Colonial Domination*, 63–86.

———. "Politics and Nationalism in North-East Africa, 1919–35." In Boahen, *General History of Africa*, vol. 7, *Africa under Colonial Domination*, 580–602.

Iliffe, John. *A Modern History of Tanganyika*. Cambridge: Cambridge University Press, 1979.

Ingiriis, Mohamed Haji. *The Suicidal State in Somalia: The Rise and Fall of the Siad Barre Regime, 1969–1991*. Lanham, MD: University Press of America, 2016.

International Crisis Group. "Kenyan Somali Islamist Radicalisation." *Africa Policy Briefing* no. 85 (Nairobi/Brussels, 25 January 2012): 1–15. http://www.crisisgroup.org /en/regions/africa/horn-of-africa/kenya/b085-kenyan-somali-islamist-radicalisation .aspx.

———. "Somalia: Al-Shabaab—It Will Be a Long War." *Africa Policy Briefing* no. 99 (Nairobi/Brussels, 26 June 2014): 1–23. http://www.crisisgroup.org/en/regions/africa/ horn-of-africa/somalia/b099-somalia-al-shabaab-it-will-be-a-long-war.aspx.

Itote, Waruhiu. *"Mau Mau" General*. Nairobi: East African Publishing House, 1967.

Jackson, Ashley. *The British Empire and the Second World War*. London: Hambledon Continuum, 2006.

Jackson, John L., Jr. *Thin Description: Ethnography and the African Hebrew Israelites of Jerusalem*. Cambridge, MA: Harvard University Press, 2013.

Jerven, Morten. *Poor Numbers: How We Are Misled by African Development Statistics and What to Do about It*. Ithaca, NY: Cornell University Press, 2013.

Jessee, Erin. "The Limits of Oral History: Ethics and Methodology amid Highly Politicized Research Settings." *Oral History Review* 38, no. 2 (Summer–Fall 2011): 287–307. doi: 10.1093/ohr/ohr098.

Johnson, Walter. "On Agency." *Journal of Social History* 37, no. 1 (2003): 113–24. doi: 10.1353/jsh.2003.0143.

Jones, Stephanie. "Merchant-Kings and Everymen: Narratives of the South Asian Diaspora of East Africa." *Journal of Eastern African Studies* 1, no. 1 (2007): 16–33.

Juma, Monica Kathina, and Peter Mwangi Kagwanja. "Securing Refuge from Terror: Refugee Protection in East Africa after September 11." In *Problems of Protection: The UNHCR, Refugees, and Human Rights*, edited by Niklaus Steiner, Mark Gibney, and Gil Loescher, 225–36. New York: Routledge, 2012.

Kalir, Barak. "Illegality Rules: Chinese Migrant Workers Caught Up in the Illegal but Licit Operations of Labour Migration Regimes." In *Transnational Flows and Permissive Polities: Ethnographies of Human Mobilities in Asia*, edited by Barak Kalir and Malini Sur, 27–54. Amsterdam: Amsterdam University Press, 2012.

Kanyinga, Karuti. "Contestation over Political Space: The State and the Demobilisation of Opposition Politics in Kenya." In *The Politics of Opposition in Contemporary Africa*, edited by Adebayo O. Olukoshi, 39–90. Uppsala: Nordic Africa Institute, 1998.

Kaplan, Amy. *The Anarchy of Empire in the Making of U.S. Culture*. Cambridge, MA: Harvard University Press, 2002.

Kapteijns, Lidwien. *Clan Cleansing in Somalia: The Ruinous Legacy of 1991*. Philadelphia: University of Pennsylvania Press, 2012.

——. "I. M. Lewis and Somali Clanship: A Critique." *Northeast African Studies* 11, no. 1 (2004): 1–23. http://www.jstor.org/stable/41960543.

Katz, Emily Alice. *Bringing Zion Home: Israel in American Jewish Culture, 1948–1967.* New York: State University of New York Press, 2015.

Katz, Cindi. *Growing Up Global: Economic Restructuring and Children's Everyday Lives.* Minneapolis: University of Minnesota Press, 2004.

Kearney, Richard. "On the Hermeneutics of Evil." In *Reading Ricoeur,* edited by David M. Kaplan, 71–88. Albany: State University of New York Press, 2008.

Keller, Edmond J. *Revolutionary Ethiopia: From Empire to People's Republic.* Bloomington: Indiana University Press, 1988.

Kelly, John D., and Martha Kaplan. "Legal Fictions after Empire." In Howland and White, *State of Sovereignty,* 169–95.

——. *Represented Communities: Fiji and World Decolonization.* Chicago: University of Chicago Press, 2001.

Khalif, Zeinabu Kabale, and Gufu Oba. "'*Gaafa Dhaabaa*—The Period of Stop': Narrating Impacts of *Shifta* Insurgency on Pastoral Economy in Northern Kenya, c. 1963 to 2007." *Pastoralism* 3, no. 14 (2013): 1–20.

Khansoy, Abdinoor Ali. "All for Lost Glory." Unpublished manuscript, Mandera, Kenya, 2002–2003.

Kimani, S. M. "The Structure of Land Ownership in Nairobi." *Canadian Journal of African Studies* 6, no. 3 (1972): 379–402.

Kitching, Gavin N. *Class and Economic Change in Kenya: The Making of an African Petite Bourgeoisie, 1905–1970.* New Haven, CT: Yale University Press, 1980.

Klein, Martin A. "Studying the History of Those Who Would Rather Forget: Oral History and the Experience of Slavery." *History in Africa* 16 (1989): 209–17. doi: 10.2307/3171785.

Koselleck, Reinhart. *Futures Past: On the Semantics of Historical Time.* Translated by Keith Tribe. New York: Columbia University Press, 2004.

Kraidy, Marwan M. *Hybridity, or the Cultural Logic of Globalization.* Philadelphia: Temple University Press, 2005.

Krhoda, G. O. "The Hydrology and Function of Wetlands." In *Wetlands of Kenya: Proceedings of the KWWG Seminar on Wetlands of Kenya, 3–5 July 1991,* edited by S. A. Crafter, S. G. Njuguna, and G. W. Howard, 13–22. Gland, Switzerland: IUCN, 1992.

Kusow, Abdi M., ed. *Putting the Cart before the Horse: Contested Nationalism and the Crisis of the Nation-State in Somalia.* Trenton, NJ: Red Sea Press, 2004.

——. "The Somali Origin: Myth or Reality." In Ahmed, *Invention of Somalia,* 81–106.

Laitin, David D. *Identity in Formation: The Russian-Speaking Populations in the Near Abroad.* Ithaca, NY: Cornell University Press, 1998.

——. *Politics, Language, and Thought: The Somali Experience.* Chicago: University of Chicago Press, 1977.

Laitin, David D., and Said S. Samatar. *Somalia: Nation in Search of a State.* Boulder, CO: Westview Press, 1987.

Lal, Priya. *African Socialism in Postcolonial Tanzania: Between the Village and the World.* New York: Cambridge University Press, 2015.

Lambert, Michael C. "From Citizenship to Négritude: 'Making a Difference' in Elite Ideologies of Colonized Francophone West Africa." *Comparative Studies in Society and History* 35, no. 2 (1993): 239–62. http://www.jstor.org/stable/179399.

Langley, J. Ayodele. *Pan-Africanism and Nationalism in West Africa, 1900–1945: A Study in Ideology and Social Classes*. Oxford: Clarendon Press, 1973.

Latour, Bruno. "Why Has Critique Run out of Steam? From Matters of Fact to Matters of Concern." *Critical Inquiry* 30, no. 2 (January 2004): 225–48. doi: 10.1086/421123.

Lawson, Letitia, and Donald Rothchild. "Sovereignty Reconsidered." *Current History* 104, no. 682 (2005): 228–35.

Lederman, Rena. "Pretexts for Ethnography: On Reading Fieldnotes." In *Fieldnotes: The Makings of Anthropology*, edited by Roger Sanjek, 71–91. Ithaca, NY: Cornell University Press, 1990.

Lee, Christopher Joon-Hai. "The 'Native' Undefined: Colonial Categories, Anglo-African Status and the Politics of Kinship in British Central Africa, 1929–38." *Journal of African History* 46, no. 3 (November 2005): 455–78. doi:10.1017/S0021853705000861.

———. *Unreasonable Histories: Nativism, Multiracial Lives, and the Genealogical Imagination in British Africa*. Durham, NC: Duke University Press, 2014.

Lefebvre, Jeffrey A. *Arms for the Horn: U.S. Security Policy in Ethiopia and Somalia, 1953–1991*. Pittsburgh, PA: University of Pittsburgh Press, 1992.

Legum, Colin. "Somali Liberation Songs." *Journal of Modern African Studies* 1, no. 4 (December 1963): 503–19.

Lewis, Ioan M. *Blood and Bone: The Call of Kinship in Somali Society*. Lawrenceville, NJ: Red Sea Press, 1994.

———. *A Pastoral Democracy: A Study of Pastoralism and Politics among the Northern Somali of the Horn of Africa*. London: Oxford University Press for the International African Institute, 1961.

———. "The Problem of the Northern Frontier District of Kenya." *Race and Class* 5, no. 1 (April 1963): 48–60.

———. *Understanding Somalia and Somaliland: Culture, History, Society*. New York: Columbia University Press, 2008.

Li, Tania Murray. *The Will to Improve: Governmentality, Development, and the Practice of Politics*. Durham, NC: Duke University Press, 2007.

Lionnet, Françoise, and Shu-Mei Shih, eds. *Minor Transnationalism*. Durham, NC: Duke University Press, 2005.

Little, Peter D. *The Elusive Granary: Herder, Farmer, and State in Northern Kenya*. Cambridge: Cambridge University Press, 1992.

———. *Somalia: Economy without State*. Oxford: James Currey, 2003.

Lochery, Emma. "Rendering Difference Visible: The Kenyan State and Its Somali Citizens." *African Affairs* 111, no. 445 (2012): 615–39. doi: 10.1093/afraf/ads059.

Logan, Chantal. "The Enduring Power of Somali 'Oral Political Poetry': Songs and Poems of Peace in the Midst of Chaos." In *Songs and Politics in Eastern Africa*, edited by Kimani Njogu and Hervé Maupeu, 355–76. Dar es Salaam: Mkuki na Nyota, 2007.

Loimeier, Roman. *Between Social Skills and Marketable Skills: The Politics of Islamic Education in 20th Century Zanzibar*. Leiden: Brill, 2009.

———. *Muslim Societies in Africa: A Historical Anthropology*. Bloomington: Indiana University Press, 2013.

Lonsdale, John M. "Moral Ethnicity and Political Tribalism." In *Inventions and Boundaries: Historical and Anthropological Approaches to the Study of Ethnicity and Nationalism*, edited by Preben Kaarsholm and Jan Hultin, 131–50. Roskilde, Denmark: Roskilde University, 1994.

Low, Anthony. "The End of the British Empire in Africa." In *Decolonization and African Independence: The Transfers of Power, 1960–1980*, edited by Prosser Gifford and William R. Louis, 33–72. New Haven, CT: Yale University Press, 1988.

Ludden, David. "Presidential Address: Maps in the Mind and the Mobility of Asia." *Journal of Asian Studies* 62, no. 4 (November 2003): 1057–78. doi: 10.2307/3591759.

Luling, Virginia. *Somali Sultanate: The Geledi City-State over 150 Years*. London: Haan, 2002.

Lydon, Ghislaine. *On Trans-Saharan Trails: Islamic Law, Trade Networks, and Cross-Cultural Exchange in Nineteenth-Century Western Africa*. Cambridge: Cambridge University Press, 2009.

Lynch, Gabrielle. "The Fruits of Perception: 'Ethnic Politics' and the Case of Kenya's Constitutional Referendum." *African Studies* 65, no. 2 (2006): 233–70.

———. *I Say to You: Ethnic Politics and the Kalenjin in Kenya*. Chicago: University of Chicago Press, 2011.

MacArthur, Julie. *Cartography and the Political Imagination: Mapping Community in Colonial Kenya*. Athens: Ohio University Press, 2016.

Mahaddala, Hassan. "Pithless Nationalism: The Somali Case." In Kusow, *Putting the Cart before the Horse*, 59–74.

Mahmoud, Hussein A. "Conflict and Constraints to Peace among Pastoralists in Northern Kenya." In *Understanding Obstacles to Peace: Actors, Interests, and Strategies in Africa's Great Lakes Region*, edited by Mwesiga Baregu, 146–69. Kampala: Fountain Publishers, 2011.

Malkki, Liisa H. "National Geographic: The Rooting of Peoples and the Territorialization of National Identity among Scholars and Refugees." *Cultural Anthropology* 7, no. 1 (February 1992): 24–44. doi: 10.1525/can.1992.7.1.02a00030.

———. *Purity and Exile: Violence, Memory, and National Cosmology among Hutu Refugees in Tanzania*. Chicago: University of Chicago Press, 1995.

Mamdani, Mahmood. "Beyond Settler and Native as Political Identities: Overcoming the Political Legacy of Colonialism." *Comparative Studies in Society and History* 43, no. 4 (October 2001): 651–64.

———. *Citizen and Subject: Contemporary Africa and the Legacy of Late Colonialism*. Princeton, NJ: Princeton University Press, 1996.

———. *Define and Rule: Native as Political Identity*. Cambridge, MA: Harvard University Press, 2012.

———. *Good Muslim, Bad Muslim: America, the Cold War, and the Roots of Terror*. New York: Pantheon Books, 2004.

———. *When Victims Become Killers: Colonialism, Nativism, and the Genocide in Rwanda*. Princeton, NJ: Princeton University Press, 2001.

Manger, Leif. *The Hadrami Diaspora: Community-Building on the Indian Ocean Rim*. New York: Berghahn Books, 2010.

Mann, Gregory. *Native Sons: West African Veterans and France in the Twentieth Century*. Durham, NC: Duke University Press, 2006.

Marchal, Roland. "A Tentative Assessment of the Somali *Harakat Al-Shabaab*." *Journal of Eastern African Studies* 3, no. 3 (2009): 381–404.

———. "Warlordism and Terrorism: How to Obscure an Already Confusing Crisis? The Case of Somalia." *International Affairs* 83, no. 6 (November 2007): 1091–1106. doi:10.1111/j.1468-2346.2007.00675.x.

Marcus, George E. *Ethnography through Thick and Thin.* Princeton, NJ: Princeton University Press, 1998.

Markakis, John. *Ethiopia: The Last Two Frontiers.* London: James Currey, 2011.

Marks, Jonathan M. *What It Means to Be 98% Chimpanzee: Apes, People, and Their Genes.* Berkeley: University of California Press, 2002.

Mathews, Andrew S. *Instituting Nature: Authority, Expertise, and Power in Mexican Forests.* Cambridge, MA: MIT Press, 2011.

Mathews, Gordon, Gustavo Lins Ribeiro, and Carlos Alba Vega, eds. *Globalization from Below: The World's Other Economy.* London: Routledge, 2012.

Mazarr, Michael J. "The Rise and Fall of the Failed-State Paradigm: Requiem for a Decade of Distraction." *Foreign Affairs* (January–February 2014). https://www.foreignaffairs.com/articles/2013-12-06/rise-and-fall-failed-state-paradigm.

Mbembe, Achille. "At the Edge of the World: Boundaries, Territoriality, and Sovereignty in Africa." Translated by Steven Rendall. *Public Culture* 12, no. 1 (Winter 2000): 259–84.

———. *On the Postcolony.* Berkeley: University of California Press, 2001.

———. "The Power of the Archive and Its Limits." In Hamilton et al., *Refiguring the Archive,* 12–26.

———. "Scrap the Borders That Divide Africans." *Mail and Guardian* (17 March 2017). https://mg.co.za/article/2017-03-17-00-scrap-the-borders-that-divide-africans.

———. "Ways of Seeing: Beyond the New Nativism: Introduction." *African Studies Review* 44, no. 2 (2001): 1–14. http://www.jstor.org/stable/525572.

Mburu, Nene. *Bandits on the Border: The Last Frontier in the Search for Somali Unity.* Trenton, NJ: Red Sea Press, 2005.

McDougall, James. *History and the Culture of Nationalism in Algeria.* Cambridge: Cambridge University Press, 2006.

———. "Martyrdom and Destiny: The Inscription and Imagination of Algerian History." In *Memory and Violence in the Middle East and North Africa,* edited by Ussama Makdisi and Paul A. Silverstein, 50–72. Bloomington: Indiana University Press, 2006.

McIntosh, Janet. *The Edge of Islam: Power, Personhood, and Ethnoreligious Boundaries on the Kenya Coast.* Durham, NC: Duke University Press, 2009.

———. *Unsettled: Denial and Belonging among White Kenyans.* Oakland: University of California Press, 2016.

McKeown, Adam M. *Melancholy Order: Asian Migration and the Globalization of Borders.* New York: Columbia University Press, 2008.

Meier, Prita. *Swahili Port Cities: The Architecture of Elsewhere.* Bloomington: Indiana University Press, 2016.

Menkhaus, Ken. "Kenya-Somalia Border Conflict Analysis." Report Commissioned by USAID, 31 August 2005. http://pdf.usaid.gov/pdf_docs/Pnadt520.pdf.

———. "The Rise of a Mediated State in Northern Kenya: The Wajir Story and Its Implications for State-Building." *Afrika Focus* 21, no. 2 (2008): 23–38.

———. "Somalia: Next Up in the War on Terrorism?" *Africa Notes* 6 (January 2002): 1–9.

Metcalf, Thomas R. *Imperial Connections: India in the Indian Ocean Arena, 1860–1920.* Berkeley: University of California Press, 2007.

Miller, Rasul. "Is Islam an Anti-Black Religion?" *Sapelo Square* (25 April 2017). https://sapelosquare.com/2017/04/25/is-islam-an-anti-black-religion/.

Mitchell, Timothy. *Carbon Democracy: Political Power in the Age of Oil.* London: Verso, 2011.

Mohamed, Jama. "Imperial Policies and Nationalism in the Decolonization of Somaliland, 1954–1960." *English Historical Review* 117, no. 474 (November 2002): 1177–1203.

———. "The 1944 Somaliland Camel Corps Mutiny and Popular Politics." *History Workshop Journal*, no. 50 (Autumn 2000): 93–113.

Mohamed, Nadifa. *Black Mamba Boy: A Novel*. New York: Farrar, Straus and Giroux, 2010.

Mohamoud, Abdullah A. *State Collapse and Post-Conflict Development in Africa: The Case of Somalia (1960–2001)*. West Lafayette, IN: Purdue University Press, 2006.

Morrison, Toni. *Playing in the Dark: Whiteness and the Literary Imagination*. Cambridge, MA: Harvard University Press, 1992.

Moyn, Samuel. "Fantasies of Federalism." *Dissent* 62, no. 1 (Winter 2015): 145–51. https://www.dissentmagazine.org/article/fantasies-of-federalism.

Munson, Henry. "Fundamentalism." In *The Blackwell Companion to the Study of Religion*, edited by Robert A. Segal, 255–69. Malden, MA: Blackwell, 2006.

Munya, P. Mweti. "The Organization of African Unity and Its Role in Regional Conflict Resolution and Dispute Settlement: A Critical Evaluation." *Boston College Third World Law Journal* 19, no. 2 (1 May 1999): 537–92.

Muoria, Henry. *Writing for Kenya: The Life and Works of Henry Muoria*. Edited by Wangari Muoria-Sal, Bodil Folke Frederiksen, John Lonsdale, and Derek Peterson. Leiden: Brill, 2009.

Murunga, Godwin Rapando. "Conflict in Somalia and Crime in Kenya: Understanding the Trans-Territoriality of Crime." *African and Asian Studies* 4, nos. 1–2 (March 2005): 137–62. doi:10.1163/1569209054547319.

———. "The Cosmopolitan Tradition and Fissures in Segregationist Town Planning in Nairobi, 1915–23." *Journal of Eastern African Studies* 6, no. 3 (2012): 463–86.

———. "Governance and the Politics of Structural Adjustment in Kenya." In *Kenya: The Struggle for Democracy*, edited by Godwin Rapando Murunga and Shadrack W. Nasong'o, 263–300. Dakar: CODESRIA, 2007.

———. "Refugees at Home? Coping with Somalia Conflict in Nairobi, Kenya." In Arrous and Ki-Zerbo, *African Studies in Geography from Below*, 198–232.

Musila, Grace A. *A Death Retold in Truth and Rumour: Kenya, Britain and the Julie Ward Murder*. London: James Currey, 2015.

Mwakikagile, Godfrey. *Relations between Africans and African Americans: Misconceptions, Myths and Realities*. Dar es Salaam: New Africa Press, 2007.

Mwangi, Esther. *Socioeconomic Change and Land Use in Africa: The Transformation of Property Rights in Maasailand*. New York: Palgrave Macmillan, 2007.

Nanjira, Daniel D. C. Don. *The Status of Aliens in East Africa: Asians and Europeans in Tanzania, Uganda, and Kenya*. New York: Praeger, 1976.

Natali, Denise. *The Kurds and the State: Evolving National Identity in Iraq, Turkey, and Iran*. Syracuse, NY: Syracuse University Press, 2005.

Ndlovu-Gatsheni, Sabelo J. *Do "Zimbabweans" Exist? Trajectories of Nationalism, National Identity Formation and Crisis in a Postcolonial State*. New York: Peter Lang, 2009.

———. *Empire, Global Coloniality and African Subjectivity*. New York: Berghahn Books, 2013.

Neumann, Roderick P. *Imposing Wilderness: Struggles over Livelihood and Nature Preservation in Africa*. Berkeley: University of California Press, 1998.

Ngai, Mae M. *Impossible Subjects: Illegal Aliens and the Making of Modern America*. Princeton, NJ: Princeton University Press, 2004.

Nimtz, August H., Jr. *Islam and Politics in East Africa: The Sufi Order in Tanzania*. Minneapolis: University of Minnesota Press, 1980.

Northrup, David. *Africa's Discovery of Europe: 1450–1850*. New York: Oxford University Press, 2002.

Nugent, Paul, and A. I. Asiwaju. "Introduction: The Paradox of African Boundaries." In Nugent and Asiwaju, *African Boundaries*, 1–17.

———, eds. *African Boundaries: Barriers, Conduits and Opportunities*. New York: Pinter, 1996.

Nurse, Derek, and Thomas T. Spear. *The Swahili: Reconstructing the History and Language of an African Society, 800–1500*. Philadelphia: University of Pennsylvania Press, 1985.

Ochich, George Otieno. "The Withering Province of Customary Law in Kenya: A Case of Design or Indifference?" In *The Future of African Customary Law*, edited by Jeanmarie Fenrich, Paolo Galizzi, and Tracy E. Higgins, 103–28. Cambridge: Cambridge University Press, 2011.

Ogot, Bethwell A. "Britain's Gulag: Review of *Histories of the Hanged*, by David Anderson, and *Britain's Gulag*, by Caroline Elkins." *Journal of African History* 46, no. 3 (2005): 493–505. http://www.jstor.org/stable/4100642.

———. "The Decisive Years, 1956–63." In Ogot and Ochieng', *Decolonization and Independence in Kenya*, 48–79.

———. "Mau Mau and Nationhood: The Untold Story." In Atieno Odhiambo and Lonsdale, *Mau Mau and Nationhood*, 8–36.

Ogot, Bethwell A., and William R. Ochieng', eds. *Decolonization and Independence in Kenya, 1940–93*. Athens: Ohio University Press, 1995.

Olden, Anthony. "Somali Opposition to Government Education: R. E. Ellison and the Berbera School Affair, 1938–1940." *History of Education* 37, no. 1 (2008): 71–90. doi: 10.1080/00467600701352331.

Ong, Aihwa. *Flexible Citizenship: The Cultural Logics of Transnationality*. Durham, NC: Duke University Press, 1999.

———. *Neoliberalism as Exception: Mutations in Citizenship and Sovereignty*. Durham, NC: Duke University Press, 2006.

Osborne, Myles. *Ethnicity and Empire in Kenya: Loyalty and Martial Race among the Kamba, c. 1800 to the Present*. New York: Cambridge University Press, 2014.

Oucho, John O. *Undercurrents of Ethnic Conflict in Kenya*. Leiden: Brill, 2002.

Ovamir, Anjum. "Islam as a Discursive Tradition: Talal Asad and His Interlocutors." *Comparative Studies of South Asia, Africa and the Middle East* 27, no. 3 (2007): 656–72.

Parekh, Serena. *Hannah Arendt and the Challenge of Modernity: A Phenomenology of Human Rights*. New York: Routledge, 2008.

Parpart, Jane L., and Kathleen A. Staudt, eds. *Women and the State in Africa*. Boulder, CO: Rienner, 1989.

Parsons, Timothy H. "Being Kikuyu in Meru: Challenging the Tribal Geography of Colonial Kenya." *Journal of African History* 53, no. 1 (March 2012): 65–86. doi:10.1017/S0021853712000023.

———. "'Kibra Is Our Blood': The Sudanese Military Legacy in Nairobi's Kibera

Location, 1902–1968." *International Journal of African Historical Studies* 30, no. 1 (1997): 87–122. doi: 10.2307/221547.

———. *The 1964 Army Mutinies and the Making of Modern East Africa*. Westport, CT: Praeger, 2003.

Paul, Kathleen. *Whitewashing Britain: Race and Citizenship in the Postwar Era*. Ithaca, NY: Cornell University Press, 1997.

Peterson, Derek R. *Ethnic Patriotism and the East African Revival: A History of Dissent, c. 1935–1972*. Cambridge: Cambridge University Press, 2012.

Phimister, Ian R., and Charles van Onselen, eds. *Studies in the History of African Mine Labour in Colonial Zimbabwe*. Gwelo: Mambo Press, 1978.

Pierre, Jemima. *The Predicament of Blackness: Postcolonial Ghana and the Politics of Race*. Chicago: University of Chicago Press, 2013.

Piot, Charles. "Atlantic Aporias: Africa and Gilroy's Black Atlantic." *South Atlantic Quarterly* 100, no. 1 (2001): 155–70.

———. *Remotely Global: Village Modernity in West Africa*. Chicago: University of Chicago Press, 1999.

Pitcher, M. Anne. *Transforming Mozambique: The Politics of Privatization, 1975–2000*. Cambridge: Cambridge University Press, 2002.

Portelli, Alessandro. *The Order Has Been Carried Out: History, Memory, and Meaning of a Nazi Massacre in Rome*. New York: Palgrave Macmillan, 2003.

Powell, Eve M. Troutt. *A Different Shade of Colonialism: Egypt, Great Britain, and the Mastery of the Sudan*. Berkeley: University of California Press, 2003.

Pratt, Mary Louise. *Imperial Eyes: Travel Writing and Transculturation*. 2nd ed. London: Routledge, 2008.

Prestholdt, Jeremy. "Fighting Phantoms: The United States and Counterterrorism in Eastern Africa." In *Lessons and Legacies of the War on Terror: From Moral Panic to Permanent War*, edited by Gershon Shafir, Everard Meade, and William J. Aceves, 127–56. London: Routledge, 2013.

———. "Kenya, the United States, and Counterterrorism." *Africa Today* 57, no. 4 (Summer 2011): 2–27.

Raikes, Philip L. *Livestock Development and Policy in East Africa*. Uppsala: Scandinavian Institute of African Studies, 1981.

Ranger, Terence O. "The Invention of Tradition Revisited: The Case of Colonial Africa." In *Legitimacy and the State in Twentieth-Century Africa: Essays in Honour of A. H. M. Kirk-Greene*, edited by Terence O. Ranger and Olufemi Vaughan, 62–111. London: Macmillan, 1993.

———. *The Invention of Tribalism in Zimbabwe*. Gweru: Mambo Press, 1985.

Rawlence, Ben. *"Bring the Gun or You'll Die": Torture, Rape and Other Serious Human Rights Violations by Kenyan Security Forces in the Mandera Triangle*. New York: Human Rights Watch, 2009.

Ray, Carina E. *Crossing the Color Line: Race, Sex, and the Contested Politics of Colonialism in Ghana*. Athens: Ohio University Press, 2015.

Reese, Scott Steven. "Patricians of the Benaadir: Islamic Learning, Commerce and Somali Urban Identity in the Nineteenth Century." PhD diss., University of Pennsylvania, 1996.

———. *Renewers of the Age: Holy Men and Social Discourse in Colonial Benaadir*. Leiden: Brill, 2008.

Renders, Marleen. *Consider Somaliland: State-Building with Traditional Leaders and Institutions*. Leiden: Brill, 2012.

Rose, Nikolas. *Powers of Freedom: Reframing Political Thought*. Cambridge: Cambridge University Press, 2000.

Rotberg, Robert I., ed. *Battling Terrorism in the Horn of Africa*. Washington, DC: Brookings Institution Press, 2005.

Rothermund, Dietmar. *The Routledge Companion to Decolonization*. London: Routledge, 2006.

Sadler, Rodney S., Jr. *Can a Cushite Change His Skin? An Examination of Race, Ethnicity, and Othering in the Hebrew Bible*. New York: T & T Clark, 2005.

Said, Edward W. *Orientalism*. New York: Vintage Books, 1979.

Salim, A. I. "Native or Non-Native? The Problem of Identity and Social Stratification of the Arab-Swahili of Kenya." In *History and Social Change in East Africa*, edited by Bethwell A. Ogot, 65–85. Nairobi: East African Literature Bureau, 1976.

Samatar, Abdi Ismail. "Destruction of State and Society in Somalia: Beyond the Tribal Convention." *Journal of Modern African Studies* 30, no. 4 (December 1992): 625–41. doi:10.1017/S0022278X00011083.

——. *The State and Rural Transformation in Northern Somalia, 1884–1986*. Madison: University of Wisconsin Press, 1989.

Samatar, Ahmed Ismail. "Review of Lewis, I. M., *A Modern History of the Somali: Nation and State in the Horn of Africa*." H-Africa, H-Net Reviews (December 2003). http://www.h-net.org/reviews/showrev.php?id=8552.

——. *Socialist Somalia: Rhetoric and Reality*. London: Zed Books, 1988.

Samatar, Said S. *Oral Poetry and Somali Nationalism: The Case of Sayyid Mahammad 'Abdille Hasan*. Cambridge: Cambridge University Press, 1982.

——. "Poetry in Somali Politics: The Case of Sayyid Mahammad 'Abdille Hasan." PhD diss., Northwestern University, 1979.

Sanger, Clyde, and John Nottingham. "The Kenya General Election of 1963." *Journal of Modern African Studies* 2, no. 1 (March 1964): 1–40.

Sangster, Joan. "Telling Our Stories: Feminist Debates and the Use of Oral History." *Women's History Review* 3, no. 1 (1994): 5–28.

Scahill, Jeremy. *Dirty Wars: The World Is a Battlefield*. New York: Nation Books, 2013.

Schlee, Günther. "Brothers of the Boran Once Again: On the Fading Popularity of Certain Somali Identities in Northern Kenya." *Journal of Eastern African Studies* 1, no. 3 (2007): 417–35. doi: 10.1080/17531050701625524.

——. "Changing Alliances among the Boran, Garre and Gabra in Northern Kenya and Southern Ethiopia." In *Changing Identifications and Alliances in North-East Africa*, vol. 1, *Ethiopia and Kenya*, edited by Günther Schlee and Elizabeth E. Watson, 203–23. New York: Berghahn Books, 2009.

——. "Customary Law and the Joys of Statelessness: Idealised Traditions versus Somali Realities." *Journal of Eastern African Studies* 7, no. 2 (2013): 258–71. doi: 10.1080/17531055.2013.776276.

——. *Identities on the Move: Clanship and Pastoralism in Northern Kenya*. Manchester: Manchester University Press, 1989.

——. "Territorializing Ethnicity: The Imposition of a Model of Statehood on Pastoralists in Northern Kenya and Southern Ethiopia." *Ethnic and Racial Studies* 36, no. 5 (2013): 857–74. doi:10.1080/01419870.2011.626058.

Schlee, Günther, and Abdullahi A. Shongolo. *Islam and Ethnicity in Northern Kenya and Southern Ethiopia.* London: James Currey, 2012.

———. *Pastoralism and Politics in Northern Kenya and Southern Ethiopia.* London: James Currey, 2012.

Scott, James C. *Seeing Like a State: How Certain Schemes to Improve the Human Condition Have Failed.* New Haven, CT: Yale University Press, 1998.

Scott, Joan Wallach. *The Politics of the Veil.* Princeton, NJ: Princeton University Press, 2007.

Selassie, Alemante G. "Ethnic Federalism: Its Promise and Pitfalls for Africa." *Yale Journal of International Law* 28 (2003): 51–107.

Sheikh, Salah Abdi. *Blood on the Runway: The Wagalla Massacre of 1984.* Nairobi: Northern Publishing House, 2007.

Sheriff, Abdul. *Dhow Cultures of the Indian Ocean: Cosmopolitanism, Commerce and Islam.* New York: Columbia University Press, 2010.

Shetler, Jan Bender. *Imagining Serengeti: A History of Landscape Memory in Tanzania from Earliest Times to the Present.* Athens: Ohio University Press, 2007.

Simala, Inyani K., and Michel Ben Arrous. "Whose Self-Determination? Conflicting Nationalisms and the Collapse of Somalia." In Arrous and Ki-Zerbo, *African Studies in Geography from Below,* 161–96.

Simpson, George L. "British Perspectives on Aulihan Somali Unrest in the East Africa Protectorate, 1915–18." *Northeast African Studies* 6, nos. 1–2 (1999): 7–43. doi: 10.1353/nas.2002.0005.

Sørensen, Ninna Nyberg. "Migration, Development and Conflict." In *Globalizing Migration Regimes: New Challenges to Transnational Cooperation,* edited by Kristof Tamas and Joakim Palme, 84–99. Aldershot: Ashgate, 2006.

Spear, Thomas T. "Neo-Traditionalism and the Limits of Invention in British Colonial Africa." *Journal of African History* 44, no. 1 (2003): 3–27. doi:10.1017/S0021853702008320.

Spear, Thomas T., and Richard D. Waller, eds. *Being Maasai: Ethnicity and Identity in East Africa.* London: James Currey, 1993.

Stoler, Ann Laura. *Carnal Knowledge and Imperial Power: Race and the Intimate in Colonial Rule.* Berkeley: University of California Press, 2002.

Tabili, Laura. "We Ask for British Justice": Workers and Racial Difference in Late Imperial Britain.* Ithaca, NY: Cornell University Press, 1994.

Taussig, Michael T. *Mimesis and Alterity: A Particular History of the Senses.* New York: Routledge, 1993.

Taylor, Peter J. *Technocratic Optimism, H. T. Odum, and the Partial Transformation of Ecological Metaphor after World War II.* Dordrecht: Reidel, 1988.

Thiong'o, Ngũgĩ wa. *Moving the Centre: The Struggle for Cultural Freedoms.* London: James Currey, 1993.

Thompson, Vincent Bakpetu. *Conflict in the Horn of Africa: The Kenya-Somalia Border Problem, 1941–2014.* Lanham, MD: University Press of America, 2015.

Tignor, Robert L. "Kamba Political Protest: The Destocking Controversy of 1938." *African Historical Studies* 4, no. 2 (1971): 237–51. doi: 10.2307/216416.

Touval, Saadia. "The Organization of African Unity and African Borders." *International Organization* 21, no. 1 (Winter 1967): 102–27. doi:10.1017/S0020818300013151.

———. *Somali Nationalism: International Politics and the Drive for Unity in the Horn of Africa.* Cambridge, MA: Harvard University Press, 1963.

———. "Somalia and Its Neighbors." In *Conflict in World Politics*, edited by Steven L. Spiegel and Kenneth Neal Waltz, 323–41. Cambridge, MA: Winthrop, 1971.

Trouillot, Michel-Rolph. *Global Transformations: Anthropology and the Modern World*. New York: Palgrave Macmillan, 2003.

———. *Silencing the Past: Power and the Production of History*. Boston: Beacon Press, 1995.

Turner, Patricia A. *I Heard It through the Grapevine: Rumor in African-American Culture*. Berkeley: University of California Press, 1993.

Turner, Simon. "'These Young Men Show No Respect for Local Customs'—Globalisation and Revival in Zanzibar." *Journal of Religion in Africa* 39, no. 3 (2009): 237–61. http://www.jstor.org/stable/20696816.

Turton, E. R. "The Isaq Somali Diaspora and Poll-Tax Agitation in Kenya, 1936–41." *African Affairs* 73, no. 292 (July 1974): 325–46. http://www.jstor.org/stable/720811.

———. "Somali Resistance to Colonial Rule and the Development of Somali Political Activity in Kenya, 1893–1960." *Journal of African History* 13, no. 1 (1972): 119–43. http://www.jstor.org/stable/180970.

Vail, Leroy, ed. *The Creation of Tribalism in Southern Africa*. London: James Currey, 1989.

Vaughan, Megan. "Reported Speech and Other Kinds of Testimony." In White, Miescher, and Cohen, *African Words, African Voices*, 53–77.

Vidino, Lorenzo, Raffaello Pantucci, and Evan Kohlmann. "Bringing Global Jihad to the Horn of Africa: Al Shabaab, Western Fighters, and the Sacralization of the Somali Conflict." *African Security* 3, no. 4 (November 2010): 216–38.

Vigneswaran, Darshan, and Joel Quirk, eds. *Mobility Makes States: Migration and Power in Africa*. Philadelphia: University of Pennsylvania Press, 2015.

Waller, Richard D. "Acceptees and Aliens: Kikuyu Settlement in Maasailand." In Spear and Waller, *Being Maasai*, 226–57.

———. "'Clean' and 'Dirty': Cattle Disease and Control Policy in Colonial Kenya, 1900–40." *Journal of African History* 45, no. 1 (2004): 45–80.

———. "Ecology, Migration, and Expansion in East Africa." *African Affairs* 84, no. 336 (July 1985): 347–70. http://www.jstor.org/stable/723071.

Walraet, Anne. "State-Making and Emerging Complexes of Power and Accumulation in the Southern Sudan–Kenyan Border Area: The Rise of a Thriving Cross-Border Business Network." In *The Borderlands of South Sudan: Authority and Identity in Contemporary and Historical Perspectives*, edited by Christopher Vaughan, Mareike Schomerus, and Lotje de Vries, 173–92. New York: Palgrave Macmillan, 2013.

Wamwere, Koigi wa. *Negative Ethnicity: From Bias to Genocide*. New York: Seven Stories Press, 2003.

Ware, Rudolph T., III. *The Walking Qur'an: Islamic Education, Embodied Knowledge, and History in West Africa*. Chapel Hill: University of North Carolina Press, 2014.

Weber, Samuel. *Benjamin's-abilities*. Cambridge, MA: Harvard University Press, 2008.

Webster, Eric J. *The Boran, Rendille, and Samburu: The Nomadic Tribes of the Northern Frontier District*. Nairobi: Ndia Kuu Press, 1944.

Weitzberg, Keren. "Can African States Offer New Approaches to Refugee Asylum?" *Africa Is a Country* (23 December 2016). http://africasacountry.com/2016/12/can-african-states-offer-new-approaches-to-refugee-asylum/.

———. "Producing History from Elisions, Fragments, and Silences: Public Testimony, the Asiatic Poll-Tax Campaign, and the Isaaq Somali Population of Kenya." *Journal of Northeast African Studies* 13, no. 2 (2013): 177–205. doi: 10.14321/nortafristud.13.2.0177.

——. "Rethinking the *Shifta* War Fifty Years after Independence: Myth, Memory, and Marginalization." In *Kenya after Fifty: Reconfiguring Historical, Political, and Policy Milestones*, edited by Michael Mwenda Kithinji, Mickie Mwanzia Koster, and Jerono P. Rotich, 65–81. New York: Palgrave Macmillan, 2016.

——. "The Unaccountable Census: Colonial Enumeration and Its Implications for the Somali People of Kenya." *Journal of African History* 56, no. 3 (November 2015): 409–28. doi:10.1017/S002185371500033X.

Weldemichael, Awet Tewelde. *Third World Colonialism and Strategies of Liberation: Eritrea and East Timor Compared*. Cambridge: Cambridge University Press, 2013.

Whitaker, Beth Elise. "The Politics of Home: Dual Citizenship and the African Diaspora." *International Migration Review* 45, no. 4 (Winter 2011): 755–83. doi: 10.1111/j.1747-7379.2011.00867.x.

White, Luise. *The Comforts of Home: Prostitution in Colonial Nairobi*. Chicago: University of Chicago Press, 1990.

——. *Speaking with Vampires: Rumor and History in Colonial Africa*. Berkeley: University of California Press, 2000.

White, Luise, Stephan F. Miescher, and David W. Cohen, eds. *African Words, African Voices: Critical Practices in Oral History*. Bloomington: Indiana University Press, 2001.

Whittaker, Hannah A. *Insurgency and Counterinsurgency in Kenya: A Social History of the Shifta Conflict, c. 1963–1968*. Boston: Brill, 2014.

——. "A New Model Village? Nairobi Development and the Somali Question in Kenya, c. 1915–17." *Northeast African Studies* 15, no. 2 (2015): 117–40.

——. "Pursuing Pastoralists: The Stigma of Shifta during the 'Shifta War' in Kenya, 1963–68." *Eras* 10 (2008). http://bura.brunel.ac.uk/handle/2438/8018.

——. "The Socioeconomic Dynamics of the *Shifta* Conflict in Kenya, c. 1963–8." *Journal of African History* 53, no. 3 (2012): 391–408.

Wilder, Gary. *Freedom Time: Negritude, Decolonization, and the Future of the World*. Durham, NC: Duke University Press, 2015.

——. *The French Imperial Nation-State: Negritude and Colonial Humanism between the Two World Wars*. Chicago: University of Chicago Press, 2005.

Williams, Paul D. "AMISOM in Transition: The Future of the African Union Mission in Somalia." *Rift Valley Institute Briefing Paper* (13 February 2013). http://riftvalley.net/download/file/fid/1488.

Willis, Justin, and George Gona. "Pwani C Kenya? Memory, Documents and Secessionist Politics in Coastal Kenya." *African Affairs* 112, no. 446 (2012): 48–71. doi: 10.1093/afraf/ads064.

Yusuf, Ahmed Ismail. *Somalis in Minnesota*. St. Paul: Minnesota Historical Society, 2012.

Zahedi, Arya. "Review of Susan Buck-Morss, *Thinking Past Terror: Islamism and Critical Theory on the Left* (Verso, 2003)." *Insurgent Notes* (5 October 2013). http://insurgentnotes.com/2013/10/review-susan-buck-morss/.

Zeleza, Paul Tiyambe. "Building Intellectual Bridges: From African Studies and African American Studies to Africana Studies in the United States." *Afrika Focus* 24, no. 2 (2011): 9–31. http://www.gap.ugent.be/africafocus/pdf/2011vol24nr2_zeleza.pdf.

——. "Rewriting the African Diaspora: Beyond the Black Atlantic." *African Affairs* 104, no. 414 (January 2005): 35–68. http://www.jstor.org/stable/3518632.

Index

caravan trade, 8, 25–26, 30–31, 72, 147, 195n45
Cassanelli, Lee, 29, 179
census, 53, 63, 68, 98, 140, 160, 189n48, 237n57
Central East African Ishaakia Association, 108
Chatterjee, Partha, 11, 94
Chebichi, Joselyne, 150
"chiefly" authorities, 80
Churchill, Winston, 160
citizenship, 3, 4, 9, 12, 23, 49, 56, 64, 66, 76,
    98, 110; flexible, 110, 158, 174; imperial, 38,
    58, 69–71, 80, 201n61; postindependence
    issues, 138, 140–41, 148–53, 158, 162
Citizenship and Immigration Act, 178
"civilization" concept, 22, 28, 39, 44, 51, 56, 61;
    "clash of civilizations" concept, 158, 168,
    174, 186n32
civil rights, 56–57, 61, 71
clan: clan cleansing campaigns, 138;
    clannism, 7, 25, 29, 52, 140–43, 148;
    clanocracy, 142, 153; defined, 183n5,
    188n46; epistemology of, 14, 52, 138
Clapham, Christopher, 84
Clifford, James, 48, 60, 98, 109
Cohen, David W., 34–35
Cohen, Robin, 47, 161
Cold War, 93, 147, 128, 230n36
collaboration vs. resistance dichotomy, 95, 135
Colonial Development and Welfare Act, 66
Colonial Office, 40–41, 57, 61, 64, 66, 70, 93,
    95, 117, 123–25, 197n59
Comaroff, Jean and John, 241n12
community term, 185n20, 235n16
conquest narratives, 19–20, 30–36
constitutional politics: devolution and, 159,
    174, 178, 237n56; *majimboism* and, 95, 108.
    See also Lancaster House Constitutional
    Conferences
Cooper, Frederick, 3–4, 65
cosmopolitanism, 3, 22–23, 25, 163, 177, 190n72
culturalist explanations, 118–19, 169
Cushitic concept, 4, 19, 96, 165; Pan-Cushitic
    alliances, 99–100; term, 217n42

decentralization, 12, 94, 108, 158, 159
Degodia people, 8, 24–26, 29, 81, 85, 142–46
Delamere, Hugh Chomondeley, Lord, 24,
    39–40, 161
demographic politics, 4–5, 97, 122, 138, 140,
    155, 176, 178–79, 230n47
Derrida, Jacques, 153, 175, 177, 178
descent, 21–24, 28, 29, 34, 44–47, 59–60;
    "casted" lineages, 23–24, 29; matrilineality,
    35, 188n188; patrilineality, 7, 21, 29, 34–35,
    44–45, 188n188; prophetic genealogies,
    21, 23, 29, 45, 81; Western concepts of, 46,
    59–60
developmentalism (developmental
    imperialism), 11, 69–71, 73, 85, 86–90;
    and denigration of pastoralism, 66, 80,
    84, 90; parastatals and, 71–72, 86, 154;
    technocratic expertise, 68–69, 85

De Waal, Alex, 129
diaspora(s), 12, 14, 24, 44, 47, 64, 74, 79,
    149–51, 162, 164
Digo people, 9
Dinesen, Isak. *See* Blixen, Karen
Dixey, R. Frank, 69, 85
Dracopoli, Ignatius N., 32

East Africa Protectorate, 20, 30–32
Eastleigh, 54, 150, 152, 172, 178, 232n79
ecological issues, 66–69, 73, 83, 85–86;
    climate change, 85–86
education, 61–62, 87, 89, 102; epistemological
    shifts in Islamic education, 63, 170,
    238n75; Intermediate Somali Boarding
    School, 89–90; madrassas, 170, 238n73,
    238n75; Qur'anic schooling (*dugsi*), 62,
    100
Edwards, D. C., 68–69
Egal, Ali Sugule, 103
Egal, Mohamed Haji Ibrahim, 133
El Hamel, Chouki, 105
Ellis, James E., 68
Ellis, S. I., 67
Ellison, R. E., 62
ethnicity: ethnic profiling and screening, 143,
    148–50, 158, 172, 175–76; ethnogenesis, 5;
    politics and, 138–43, 153; prejudice and, 17,
    25, 49–50, 60; scholarship on, 192n80. *See
    also* racism

"failed state" paradigm, 5–6, 151, 167; weak/
    strong state dichotomy, 53, 242n17
Fair, Laura, 5
Farah, Abby, 61
Farah, Ahmed Ali, 106, 161, 219n73
Farah, Mohamed, 85
Farah, Nuruddin, 236n44
Ferguson, James, 114, 118
fieldwork, ix–x, 13–5, 45, 159–60, 162, 167, 174,
    179, 192n80, 192n84; concept, 13–15, 45,
    192n80, 192n84; method, ix–x, 13–15
Foucault, Michel, 197n56
Fratkin, Elliot, 139
French Somaliland, 59, 75, 91
frontier concept, 32, 51, 129; closed district, 32,
    51, 197n197

Gabra people, 99, 126
"Galla" term, 19, 28, 36, 52, 217n38
Galma Dido, Haji, 125–26
Garissa, 14, 33, 62, 83, 105, 109–10, 114, 121,
    140, 145, 151, 153, 157, 172, 230n37, 231n61,
    238n73
Garre people, 8, 99
Gelubba people, 118
gender, 15–16, 27, 34–35, 45–46, 67, 156,
    234n102; education and, 87; labor and, 45,
    67, 131, 204n102; masculinity, 27, 35, 135;
    nonliberal ideas of, 156, 234nn100–102;
    patriarchy, 5–16, 27, 34, 39, 45, 133, 156,

200n43; property and, 34, 233n99; women and warfare, 130–33. *See also* marriage; Wajir Women for Peace

genealogies. *See* descent

George V, 58

George VI, 61

Geschiere, Peter, 147–48

Ghosh, Amitav, 97, 170, 238n76

Glassman, Jonathon, 44, 194n24, 215n4

globalization, 13, 150, 159, 176, 184n10, 190n71, 240n3, 241n11

Gloucester, Henry, Duke of, 61

Gompe, Huka, 184n9

grazing issues, 2, 8, 25, 52, 54–55, 66, 80, 81, 83, 85, 101–2, 140; overgrazing, 55, 66, 68–69

Greater Somalia, 11, 12, 74–76, 78, 83–84, 91–92, 96, 106–10, 158

Griffith-Jones, E. N., 123

Grovogui, Siba N'Zatioula, 94

Guleid, Ali, 108

Gupta, Akhil, 73

Gurey, Ahmed [Ahmed Ibrahim Al-Ghazi], 74

Haile Selassie, 75, 128, 225n76

Hall, Bruce, 105

Hamilton, Carolyn, 16, 45

Hamitic mythology, 22, 91

Hansen, Thomas B., 160–61

Hapi, Wako, 99, 115, 134

Hargeisa, 62, 74

Hassan, Muhammad Abdullah, 74, 196n46, 202n83

Herbst, Jeffrey, 53, 242n17

Hinde, Sidney and Hildegarde, 110

historicism, limits of, 16–17, 25, 26–27, 28, 34–35, 88

Hizbiya Digil-Mirifle (HDM), 96

Ho, Engseng, 22, 45, 92

Hogg, Richard, 129

Holt, Thomas, 221n15

Horst, Cindy, 149, 151

hospitality, 1, 27, 81, 132; Derrida on, 153, 175

Howes, R. J. C., 70–71

Howland, Douglas, 116

Hunt, Nancy Rose, 14, 86

Huntington, Samuel, 6, 186n32, 190n70

Huxley, Elspeth, 40

Ibrahim, Dekha, 155, 230n36

Ibrahim, H. A., 184n12

identification/registration systems, 53, 63, 138; *kipande*, 41; national ID cards, 140, 142, 152, 178, 175; passports, 14, 41, 47–48, 179; screening cards, 148

Iliffe, John, 5

immigration, 64, 89, 231n62; to East Africa/Kenya, 24, 26, 39, 44, 48, 56, 164; to England, 49–50, 57–58, 178–79; "illegal," 9, 151

Imperial British East Africa Company (IBEAC), 30–32

Indian Ocean, 4, 10, 19, 20, 22–23, 45, 46, 50; Indian Ocean scholarship, 187n35

Indians, 9, 39, 40–41, 44, 50, 54, 58, 59, 72, 78, 86, 105, 160, 199n21

indigeneity, 12–13, 37, 50–51, 66, 189n50

"informal" economy, 150

Ingiriis, Mohammed Haji, 142

invention term, 60; "invention" of Somalia, 30; invention of tradition debate, 184–85

irredentism term, 97

Ishakia Association, 48, 59, 60, 77, 106, 160

Ishaq ibn Ahmed al-Hashimi, 21

Isiolo, 55–56, 67–68, 69–70, 77, 129–30, 139

Islam: archives and, 51; conversion, 52, 57, 100; cross-religious alliances and, 17, 99, 118–19, 174; *Dar al-Islam* term, 23, 61; Islamic Courts Union (ICU), 168–69, 171, 238n67; Pan-Islamic movements/affiliations, 63, 74, 83–84, 92, 100, 106, 107; "reformist" movements, 168–71, 177, 239n78; spread of, 21, 196n46; *umma* concept, 22, 63, 74, 82, 170, 174, 193n10. *See also* religious polarization

Ismail, Mohamed Hassan, 78

Issa, Bille, 87

Italian Somaliland, 59, 75, 91, 96

Itote, Waruhiu, 88

ivory trade, 33–34, 147

Jackson, John, 28

Jattani, Guyo, 113–14, 115

Jennings, F. G., 53

Jews, xi–xii, 9, 162

Jubaland, 25, 30–31, 32, 51

justice, 40, 57–58, 104–5, 123, 126, 145, 168, 237n56; nonjuridical concepts of, 146, 155–56, 177–78; nonsecular concepts of, 168, 177–78

Kaarhus, Randi, 56

Kabati, Ali (Mohamed Ali), 88

Kalaluud, the, 33–34, 35

Kaplan, Martha, 116

Kapteijns, Lidwien, 7, 143

Kareithi, Amos, 222n30

Kaunda, Kenneth, 133

Kearney, Richard, 133

Kelly, John D., 116

Kenya: decolonization of, 91–97, 100–101, 104, 107–25; postindependence era, 137–56; securitization efforts, 151–52; Somali prejudice against, 104–5, 138

Kenya African Democratic Union (KADU), 94–96, 100, 108, 115–16, 123

Kenya African Union, 73, 78

Kenya African National Union (KANU), 94–96, 115–16, 123, 159

Kenya Land Commission, 55, 67

Kenya Meat Commission, 86

secularism, 6, 62, 92, 156, 158, 162, 171, 186n32, 237n64, 238n76; nonsecular political forms, 4–5, 10, 11, 92, 156–57, 166, 168, 177, 241n13; secular narratives, 136, 146; secular time, 22, 75
self-determination, 73–75, 113, 116–17
separatism term, 97
sexual relations, 45–47; rape, 27, 129, 134, 143
sheegat status, 26, 29, 52, 81, 179
Sheikh, Salah Abdi, 88, 140, 145
Shermarke, Abdirashid Ali, 133
shifta term, 112, 129–30, 139
Shifta War, 12, 112–36, 138–39, 161, 164–65, 230n37
Shongolo, Abdullahi A., 26, 27, 187n37
sijui term, 152, 232n77
Simpson, George, 33
slavery, 8, 9, 20, 23–24, 27, 29, 105
soldiers and veterans, 24, 39, 44, 54, 57, 69–71, 160, 211n69, 224n56; General Service Unit, 129; imperial citizenship and, 57–8, 69–71; Kenya Land and Freedom Army, 88; King's African Rifles, 109, 128–29; Somaliland Camel Corps, 79
Somalia, Western perceptions of, 5–7, 21–22, 59
Somali civil war, 6–7, 8, 74, 138, 142, 153, 158, 162, 164, 167–68, 240n92; racism and, 166; US intervention into, 169
Somali Independent Union, 106–7
Somali Islamic Association, 74
Somali National Association, 108
Somali National League, 74
Somali National Movement, 142
Somaliness, 5–9, 10, 13, 14–15, 20–21, 25, 28–29, 60, 73–74, 90, 107, 111, 188n45; "British Somalis," 57, 78, 205n126; descent and, 45, 47; exclusions from, 96, 1878n37, 188n45; "origins" of, 37, 44, 73–74l postcolonial notions of, 11, 158, 164; Somali and *gaal* distinction, 29, 52. *See also* Pan-Somali nationalism
Somali Republic, creation of, 96
Somali Union, 119, 121, 142
Somali Youth League (SYL), 73, 75, 83–86, 98, 213n95
sous rature term, 113
sovereignty, 11–12, 73–5, 116–17, 197n56
Spear, Thomas, 5
Speke, John Hanning, 20
Stamboul, Deghow Maalim, 110, 219n80
statelessness, 150–51
Stoler, Ann Laura, 47
Swahili people, 9, 21, 40, 44, 50, 58
Swift, David M., 68

taxation, 54, 58–64, 81, 85
terrorism, 5–6, 166–73, 242n20; "war on terror," 13, 166–72, 174, 178
Teso people, 9, 149
Thiong'o, Ngũgĩ wa, 200n39
Thomas, T. S., 30–31
Thuku, Harry, 78
Todd, H. R., 31
transnational turn, 3, 12, 93, 176, 185n21, 215n5
Trouillot, Michel-Rolph, 15, 25, 88, 112
Truth, Justice, and Reconciliation Commission, 145, 237n56
Turkana people, 56, 70, 72
Turnbull, Richard G., 35–36, 59
Turton, E. R., 61

Uganda-Mombasa railway, 32, 39
United Nations, 127, 240n92
United Nations High Commissioner for Refugees (UNHCR), Office of, 149, 154
United Ogaden Somali Association (UOSA), 101–2, 109
United Somali Association (USA), 106, 107, 108
United States/Mexico borderlands, 8–9, 232n80

Vail, Leroy, 5
Vaughan, Megan, 192n89
Vigneswaran, Darshan, 53
violence: dangers of narrating, 133, 143; memory and, 135 ; normalization of, 133–34, 230n37; peaceful resolutions to, 153–56, 168; sexual violence, 27, 129, 131, 134, 143, 147; violence by nonstate actors (and double standards), 6, 157, 186n27

Wabera, Daudi Dabasso, 125–26
Wagalla Massacre, 88, 143–46, 237n56
Wajir, 1–2, 15, 26, 53, 81, 82, 143, 153–56
Wajir Women for Peace (WWP), 153–56
Waller, Richard, 5, 29
Wandati, A. Mirimo, 137, 149
Webber, F. D., 123
Weber, Max, 146
West, German, 164, 236n41
Westgate mall attack, 157–58, 172
White, Luise, 116, 146
white minority rule, 93
Whittaker, Hannah, 130
Wildemichael, Awet Tewelde, 211n54

xeer term, 155–56

Yusuf, Ahmed Ismail, 103

Zeleza, Paul, 6